WRITING MORMON HISTORY
HISTORIANS AND THEIR BOOKS

WRITING MORMON HISTORY

HISTORIANS AND THEIR BOOKS

EDITED BY
**JOSEPH W.
GEISNER**

SIGNATURE BOOKS | 2020 | SALT LAKE CITY

For Susan, Rebeca, Benjamin, and Stephanie.

Cover design by Aaron Fisher.
Interior design and typesetting by Jason Francis.

FIRST EDITION | 2020

LIBRARY OF CONGRESS CATALOGING-IN-PUBLICATION DATA

Names:	Geisner, Joseph W., editor.
Title:	Writing Mormon history : historians and their books / edited by Joseph W. Geisner.
Description:	First edition.	Salt Lake City : Signature Books, 2020.	Summary: "Every great book has a great backstory. Here well-known historians describe their journeys of writing books that have influenced our understanding of the Mormon past, offering an unprecedented glimpse into why they wrote these important works. Writing Mormon History is a must-read for historians, students of history, scholars, and aspiring authors."—Provided by publisher.
Identifiers:	LCCN 2019056110 (print)	LCCN 2019056111 (ebook)	ISBN 9781560852810 (hardback)	ISBN 9781560852827 (paperback)	ISBN 9781560853817 (ebook)
Subjects:	LCSH: Mormons—Historiography.	Religion historians—Biography.	Mormon Church—Study and teaching.	Mormon Church—History.	LCGFT: Autobiographies.
Classification:	LCC BX8611 .W84 2020 (print)	LCC BX8611 (ebook)	DDC 289.3072/2—dc23

LC record available at https://lccn.loc.gov/2019056110
LC ebook record available at https://lccn.loc.gov/2019056111

CONTENTS

INTRODUCTION

In the summer of 1977, my mother, sister, and I drove east from California to Minnesota and Wisconsin to work on family geneal-ogy and to visit relatives whom my mother had visited as a girl or had never previously met. On the return trip, our car broke down, and we struggled to get into Salt Lake City for repairs. This delay resulted in an incredible experience for me and started me on a path that has become a lifetime hobby. I visited various historical sites in the city that I could either walk or take a bus to.

Temple Square was where I spent most of my time, but one day I was in the LDS Church Office Building on North Temple Street standing in front of the sign listing personnel in the Historical Department, with Leonard J. Arrington as Church Historian. I was a teen with a full beard and 1970s long hair in a place where I felt completely out of place. Thirty-seven-year-old PhD grad-uate student Ronald W. Walker saw me, approached, and asked, "Can I help you, young man?" I answered, perhaps a little too arro-gantly as I now think about it, "Yeah, I'd like to meet the Church Historian." Ron replied, "Let's go upstairs and see if you can see Brother Arrington," and then took me up the elevator to the his-torical department's office area on the second floor of the east wing. Leonard's secretary was at her desk. Ron said, "This young man would like to talk with Brother Arrington." She responded, "I think I can make that happen," buzzed Leonard on his telephone, and then invited me into Leonard's office.

I have no idea how long I was in Leonard's office. It could have been five minutes or five hours. But Leonard treated me with courtesy and kindness and answered my questions about some controversial episodes in LDS history I had learned about while on this trip back east. I asked Leonard if I should buy Joseph Fielding Smith's *Essentials in Church History*. He walked over to his bookshelf, pulled down James B. Allen and Glen M. Leonard's

Story of the Latter-day Saints (published the previous year) and told me that this book had replaced *Essentials* and that I should buy and read it instead. Jim and Glen's book became one of my Christmas presents that year and, ultimately, started my book collection and lifetime hobby.

After a few years, I jumped into the New Mormon History with both feet and completely immersed both body and mind, reading everything I could find in scholarly journals and books. (The New Mormon History, while initially defined as a blending of a variety of disciplines to talk about the LDS past—something like "Mormon Studies" today—quickly became associated with greater access to and use of original sources and a commitment to transparency and balance in narrating the Mormon past.) Later, I made the trek from California to Salt Lake City to attend the annual Sunstone symposium, where I was privileged to meet many of the authors whose articles and books I was reading. I was pleasantly surprised by most of these scholars' openness, kindness, and patience with me and my questions. To this day, I still feel this way toward these—now "senior"—scholars as well as the younger scholars who are developing their own paths in the field of Mormon history.

When Signature Books broached the idea of compiling an anthology, I proposed assembling a collection of essays by eminent historians—women and men whose writings had so impacted my life—telling their own stories about writing their books. When Signature gave me the go-ahead, I reached out to writers whom I had met over the years and, in many cases, had developed friendships with. Fifteen of the historians I contacted agreed to write their stories. I believe that their essays enable readers to understand the Mormon past, and especially its construction, better than we did before.

Vickie Cleverley Speek writes about her experience working on a biography of James J. Strang, one of the claimants hoping to succeed Joseph Smith as president of the LDS Church following Smith's death. Will Bagley tackles his study of the 1857 Mountain Meadows Massacre and the horror of writing about the worst mass murder of overland travel during the immigration west. D Michael Quinn provides an intimate decades-long glimpse into

his professional life as a working Mormon historian through revealing excerpts from his personal journals and memoirs. William MacKinnon addresses his "sixty-year hitch" to the Utah War and the resulting two volumes of primary historical sources that forever alter our understanding of this war and its influence on the nation. Polly Aird takes us into her confidence as she chronicles her experience writing about one of her ancestors and how he and his family were branded as "apostates" during the Mormon Reformation of the mid-nineteenth century. John Turner provides a window into how he managed to write what many consider to be the best biography yet written of the complicated, controversial Brigham Young. Gregory Prince writes of his trail-blazing biography of LDS Church President David O. McKay, drawing on both McKay's previously untapped voluminous diaries and the scores of interviews Greg conducted. Brian Hales delves into the fascinating background of his three-volume history of Joseph Smith's practice of plural marriage. Susan Staker is currently writing a study of Joseph Smith's stories and writes as a scholar whose study in still in process. George D. Smith details his work on four seminal books: a scholarly edition of William Clayton's diaries, George's own study of the beginnings of Mormon plural marriage, his support of the publication of B. H. Roberts's analyses of the Book of Mormon, and his work on a fully annotated edition of Brigham Young's diaries and journals. Daniel Stone takes us into the world of an all but forgotten Mormon prophet, William Bickerton. Melvin Johnson offers suggestions to historians based on his experience writing biographies of two interesting but lesser known figures from the Mormon past: Lyman Wight and John Hawley. Linda King Newell narrates in considerable detail her collaboration with Valeen Tippetts Avery (deceased) in writing the first ever scholarly biography of Emma Hale Smith, wife of church founder Joseph Smith, including the controversy that followed the book's publication. Todd Compton recalls the ups and downs of studying Joseph Smith's plural wives during a time when such research predated easy access to the internet. Craig Smith, who has published an edition of the letters of pioneering Mormon historian Juanita Brooks, looks closely at the complicated publication history of Brooks's biography of her grandfather Dudley Leavitt.

As I contemplate a possible second volume, I see an omission in the present volume that I would hope to correct. There are no authors who are persons of color. I would also like to include more women's voices. I am pleased to have authors whose studies of Restoration churches include those groups other than the Church of Jesus Christ of Latter-day Saints. I would try to expand this group too.

I thank all of the authors for their contributions, but especially the many kindnesses they have extended to me as they took time out of their busy schedules to write their essays. Each author was a pleasure to work with—their essays greatly exceeded my expectations. My goal was to showcase their voices and theirs alone. I believe each essay achieves this. I hope readers agree and get a glimpse into the sacrifice and work each author has put into her or his studies.

I thank Signature Books for enabling me to help shepherd this volume from conception to publication. This book is now in the hands of readers because of Signature's incredible team.

Some of the historians included here have asked me why I wanted to do this project. I firmly believe our history allows us to understand our present. I am convinced that capturing the personal stories of these authors helps us to appreciate more fully the work being done by historians and other scholars today. It is now up to the reader to see if we—the authors and I—have succeeded.

LADDER TO THE MOON
POLLY AIRD

The past can be studied, plundered, dramatized, consumed, fought over—it is at once a museum, a theater, a flea market, and a bone of contention. The only thing it cannot be is put to rest.

—Imogen Sara Smith, "Ghosts and Replicas: Bisbee '17 and Museo," Sept. 20, 2018, www.filmcomment.com

I was lured into Mormon history in unlikely ways. I can trace the path back to my grandfather, John W. Aird, when he was about to graduate from the University of Deseret (now the University of Utah). Dr. John R. Park, president of the university, said to him, "I see you spell the same word in two or three ways." Park mentioned that such poor spelling could be cause for not graduating him, but his studies were so good, they did.[1] My grandfather went on to medical school at the University of California in San Francisco and became a skilled surgeon.[2]

Like my grandfather, I too had dyslexia and trouble with spelling. In my elementary school, reading was taught not by learning phonetics, but by a system that I remember as "see and read"—look

---

1. John W. Aird, Letter to Juliaetta Bateman Jensen, Jan. 20, 1949, in Emily McAuslan Aird, "The Family History," 1950, 38, copy in the Polly Aird Papers, Utah State Historical Society, Salt Lake City.

2. With two other doctors, he opened the first general hospital in Provo, Utah, in 1903. The doctors were Fred W. Taylor and George E. Robison. For more on the hospital, see my "Small but Significant: The School of Nursing at Provo General Hospital, 1904–1924," *Utah Historical Quarterly* 86 (Spring 2018): 102–27.

at a word, its shape, and say what it is.[3] The problem is that "adobe" and "abode" look the same to me. I also have to pay close attention to "through," "though," and "thorough." Nevertheless, like my grandfather, I did well in my studies and graduated "with distinction" and Phi Beta Kappa from Stanford University with a bachelor's degree in modern European history. I loved history.

What do historians do? I asked myself. Well, teach. But the idea of getting up in front of a classroom to write something on the board and not knowing how to spell it was intimidating. I was quite shy and unwilling to admit my struggles with spelling. Today I would tell the students that I have a problem and need their help, but I could not have done that then. I also realize now that historians can do things other than teach, though teaching is certainly a major career choice. The result was I decided it was pointless to go on for graduate degrees. History thus became an avocation, not a profession.

In spite of my difficulty with spelling, I could usually recognize when a word was misspelled. My first job was working for the retired assistant director of the National Zoo, Ernest P. Walker, in Washington, DC, on a three-volume work on mammals of the world. It was to be short term as it was near the end of the project. I started by filing and mounting photographs, but then, when the writer suddenly left, Walker asked me to take over his position. Just before the manuscript was to go to the publisher, Johns Hopkins Press, Walker contracted pneumonia. As a result, I ended up working with the editors who taught me how to edit. My next job was as assistant editor for special publications at the National Academy of Sciences, also in Washington, DC, which I got thanks to letters of recommendation from Johns Hopkins Press. I enjoyed scientific editing and was good at it. One paper I edited was by the cultural anthropologist Margaret Mead, who complimented my work.

About a year after marrying a writer from *National Geographic*, we moved to Tucson, Arizona, so that he could get a master's degree in wildlife biology at the University of Arizona. Thanks to my connections at the National Academy of Sciences, I found a job at

---

3. The proper name of this reading method is "Whole Word" or "Look and Say."

the Lunar and Planetary Laboratory, which was connected to the university. There I worked under the director, the Dutch astronomer Gerard P. Kuiper, as editor of their quarterly scientific journal.

Two children, three years living as caretakers on a Nature Conservancy sanctuary near the Mexican border, a move to Seattle, and a divorce with no child support left me needing a job that paid better than the freelance editing I was doing for the University of Arizona Press. A neighbor in Seattle persuaded me to try Boeing as it paid well, had good benefits, and offered flexibility for something like a sick child. I was hired by the director of a communications group in Boeing Aerospace in part because he was an amateur astronomer and impressed with my having worked for Kuiper (for whom the Kuiper Belt is named). I started off working on proposals for the surveillance aircraft, the AWACS, and then a long-range executive 747 plane with gold faucets for the Shah of Iran (Imperial Iranian Air Force 1), but he was deposed in 1979 before the proposal was finished. Although this work had its fascinating aspects, it was not very satisfying as I never saw more than a sliver of the multi-volume proposals.

I moved on to working in Congressional affairs, which involved tracking proposals and programs of interest to Boeing through the Armed Services, Authorization, and Appropriation Committees of the US Congress. I also wrote a newsletter for the company executives to keep them apprised of what was going on in Congress that related to Boeing programs.

My commute was an hour each way south to Kent, Washington, which made for a long day separated from my young daughters. In the mid-1980s, I found a new job fifteen minutes away from home. It was with the computer science division of Boeing. Here I became a manager of communications of a small group of writers and graphic artists. Much of our work was developing presentations for the director of the Advanced Technology Applications Division to give to company executives explaining why the company was spending so much money developing software. When talking to the computer scientists, the executives wanted to hear a business case, but the scientists only talked technology. My role became to talk to the scientists long enough to elicit how their work in such fields as artificial intelligence or natural-language processing would benefit the company. The work was interesting, but I needed something more personally satisfying.

And I found it. In 1986, my father, then retired as chair of the neurology department in the medical school at the University of California in San Francisco and in his eighties, decided to expand the story his mother had written about her family. He wanted to add historical and religious context. As I had been an editor for many years, he asked if I would go over his manuscript.

My grandmother, Emily McAuslan Aird, had written about her parents' background in Scotland, their conversion to Mormonism, their emigration to Utah, the events there that shocked them and led to their disillusionment, and their escape from Utah with the help of the US Army. Emily was a good story teller, and it is a rousing tale.[4] But, I wondered, how much was it like an oral history, with embellishments, subjectivity, and unknown reliability?

4. Aird, "The Family History." What follows is from pp. 4–15.

In Scotland, she wrote, our oldest known ancestor was Peter McAuslan who was born in 1690 in Stookadoo Castle at Luss on the shores of Loch Lomond. He was knighted a baron shortly after the union of Scotland and England and was therefore a member of the British Parliament. Baron McAuslan had three sons "educated to be doctors" at the universities of Edinburgh and London. "The eldest son was knighted a Lord. The second son inherited the title of Baron. The third brother was made a member of the House of Commons." The three went to the East Indies in the diplomatic service of the United Kingdom where "they amassed large fortunes. One after the other died and the last of them left their vast accumulations amounting to 2,500,000 pounds sterling to the descendants of Baron McAuslan," but the money ended up in the Court of Chancery.

Emily continued that her mother was descended from the second son, Baron William McAuslan, and then gave a variation on the story of the fortune made in the East Indies. On the ship returning him to Scotland, the baron was killed and his bags of gold stolen. Two perpetrators were caught, with one being hung and the other sent to Britain's penal colony in Australia. The money was divided among the baron's twelve descendants rather than going into Chancery.

Emily's great grandfather, one of those descendants who was born in 1781, was named Peter McAuslan. He and his wife Jane Marshall had an "overpowering passion for freedom and liberty: Freedom to worship as they wished and freedom to live as they wished." Their burning desire was to "break the shackles and loosen the tyranny of established religion," and they became pioneers in both the Free Kirk and temperance movements, walking "all over Scotland preaching temperance and the curse of whiskey."[5] In their business, the McAuslan Designing and Art House, they offered promotions to those who avoided whisky. Some employees resented their "guardianship over their free-born right to take a sip."

Eventually, according to Emily, her great grandparents, distressed by the condition of workers in factories in this early period

---

5. In Scotland, the word is spelled "whisky," not "whiskey," which is the American term for bourbon.

of the Industrial Revolution, became supporters of Robert Owen. Owen had established humane cotton-spinning mills in New Lanark with a school for the youngest children, housing for the workers, and fewer working hours for all. Peter McAuslan put most of his fortune into this venture, but eventually it failed—people were not ready for such radical changes as Owen promoted, Emily said. The McAuslans lost their Designing and Art House, leaving the sons to seek jobs elsewhere. "That was the first time in the history of the McAuslan family that any member ever asked employment of others." Peter McAuslan then urged his sons to go to America, the Land of Liberty.

Emily told how her grandfather, another Peter McAuslan, born in 1801, became interested in Mormonism from the missionaries who were traveling around Scotland:

> Coming from America which was synonymous with freedom and liberty and whose foundation had been laid on justice and equality for all, Grandfather invited them to his home. They described a Zion which they were building in Utah, where men and women should be free and whose leaders were founding a future empire devoted to the building up of an intelligent and spiritual people.

Emily described how her grandparents with nine of their ten children set sail on the ship *John M. Wood*, from Liverpool, England, on March 10, 1854, bound for New Orleans. She said they lived in New Orleans for about a year and then started up the Mississippi River. They got off at various places to see the country, but they were horrified by slave markets, and in the small towns and camps, they saw adventurers and sharpers, and women and men around the campfires smoking long corn-cob pipes; everywhere there was ignorance, crudeness and superstition, excepting in the plantation mansions where dwelt the aristocracy of the country, which looked down upon the poor whites, terming them "trash."

Although disillusioned with what they had seen, Grandfather Peter "could not be daunted." It was slavery that debased the South, so westward they would go. He and his sons Peter and William (Emily's father) bought the best covered wagons, oxen, cattle, and sheep and all the necessities they would need on the trip and after they arrived. "People stopped to admire the caravan, exclaiming, 'A colony is moving west.'"

On the journey, Emily wrote, the youngest child was killed by an Indian arrow. "They made a grave and buried him on the plains, frightening the buffaloes away while they were burying the dead." Also, the youngest daughter was kicked in the head by one of the animals, "which affected her until she died." Then Grandmother became ill and died:

> The hardships were too much for her frail little body which never weighed over one hundred pounds. She could not get over the death of her youngest child and its burial on the lonely plains. Before she died, she said, "Peter, I want to be buried by the baby." He was not a baby but he was her baby child. Grandfather turned his caravan back in the face of Indians, buffaloes, heat and dust and buried her by her child. They then turned their faces westward again.

Emily described their arrival in Salt Lake City in September 1856 and that Brigham Young invited the senior Peter McAuslan and the two eldest sons, Peter and William, to dine at his home. President Young said he had established a bank "for the safety of all members of the Church," and suggested that the McAuslans place their money and other valuables there. That they did, "as they had considerable money with them in addition to many fine family relics."

Emily wrote that on the ship crossing the ocean, the McAuslans became acquainted with a young Scot named David who was working his way to America. Eventually the family took him "unto their bosom." Davy told them about polygamy, which was the first the family had heard of it. He was strong and helped them prepare for the overland journey. The family bought him a covered wagon, oxen, and an outfit for the trip. Rather than sleep in the wagon, Davy turned it into a hospital for those who were ill or worn out.

Settled in Salt Lake City, Davy helped them build a barn for the animals. They were so busy that they failed to attend meetings, and the church authorities complained they were not working for the common good. The bishop came and said they needed to turn over their grain as part of their tithing and that the barn was needed to shelter some incoming immigrants.

Emily's grandfather was astonished and said that what they had accomplished was the result of their labor and that they had paid the men they had hired to help. The bishop said, "This comes from the Head of the Church whose word comes from God." Davy's strenuous objection to this appropriation had a disastrous result:

> Davy was so enraged, he rose up and told them they were not one of God's children, and that they belonged to the Devil. They took him away. Poor honest Davy. He was one of the many. Grandfather and sons hunted everywhere for him and enquired of everybody if they had seen him. A few shook their heads saying in whispered voices: "Many have disappeared." The majority of them said, "We must obey our Prophet. We all know that God spoke to the Prophet."

The alarmed family needed to prepare for winter and save their animals, which they feared the church would take next. They decided to move south where there was still grass for the oxen. But as there were babies and more expected, the women were left behind with provisions. "With sad hearts the women saw the men depart in the middle of the night and with troubled hearts the men wondered if they would ever see them again."

It wasn't long before the bishop came to visit the women and took their provisions, for "in Zion every one must share and share alike." They were left without food. But the bishop had additional intentions:

> A few days after, the bishop made another visit, bringing with him a basket of food. He became a continual visitor, each time bringing food, and as time went on, his visits became longer and longer. He complimented mother for her bravery, her neat housekeeping, how lovely she kept the baby, and the beauty of her shiny black hair, and then finally he brought her a big ham and proposed to her.

Mother said: "Do you not know that I have a husband?" To which he replied: "Don't worry, dear, we can easily fix that." She threw the ham in his face, saying: "You dirty dog, be gone!" She was not bothered with him again.

The women in the family now needed to find a way to support themselves. The McAuslans had helped a family in crossing the plains, and their daughters had married apostles as plural wives. The parents often visited Brigham Young and his many wives in the Lion House, and they knew that the wives wanted good-looking clothes "so that they could shine in Brigham's eyes." The women wanted a good seamstress. They could sew themselves, "but why should they, when Brigham was rolling in money?" Emily's mother, Mary, applied for the job of seamstress. President Young thanked her and said she could "call for all the provisions and needs in her household."

Mary told the president that the bishop had taken all their provisions, that they were destitute, and that she needed food for the family left in Salt Lake. She reminded him that their money was in his bank. He replied that the money in the bank was now "in the hands of the Lord," but that she could get what she needed in exchange for her work as a seamstress. Mary thus became the provider for the family.

Emily's story continued that one night, when the women were especially discouraged, the men returned. Grandfather said they must bundle what they had and leave that night. "Johnston's army is close by to protect us, if we need protection, but it is better for us to slip quietly out." And before the night was over, they were with the US Army under the command of General Albert S. Johnston. They then remained under the army's protection until they were safely on their way to California. The family eventually reached the Sacramento Valley where they settled.

Here was a story to engage my mind! Beyond editing my father's expanded account, I wanted to know more. But what did I know about Scottish history, Utah history, or Mormonism? When my father's grandparents left the Mormons, they left organized religion. My mother, from near Philadelphia, had been brought up half Quaker and half Episcopalian. Our family lived just north of San Francisco in Marin County, California, and there my mother and we children attended a small, non-denominational community church, the minister of which had been trained in a Congregational seminary.[6]

---

6. My husband and I eventually converted to Catholicism.

Immersing myself in the history of that period was the only way to begin to figure out how accurately Emily had portrayed the family history. I knew Wallace Stegner had written *The Gathering of Zion: The Story of the Mormon Trail*, part of the American Trail series of which I had already read George Stewart's *The California Trail* and Jonathan Daniel's *The Devil's Backbone: The Story of the Natchez Trace*. So that was where I started. It was a good launching spot, with Stegner's beautiful writing and a story that went far beyond a trail narrative. His book had a bibliography, which opened the way to further reading. I ordered books through the library and then through Interlibrary Loan on Scottish, Utah, and Mormon history. I bought books. I read more. I joined the Pacific Northwest Historians Guild, not because I was doing Northwestern history, but to associate with historians. And they suggested books. I wrote to Leonard Arrington with a synopsis of Emily's story. In his kindly way, he wrote back a two-page, single-spaced typed letter with suggestions of books to read and historians to contact. He wished me good luck in my project.[7] I was on my way!

Meanwhile, my father wrote to Wallace Stegner after also reading *The Gathering of Zion* to ask his ideas where he might get his expanded family story published. Stegner, then in Vermont, wrote back a short letter saying that he doubted my father could find a publisher for it. Stegner did not think a story of conversion to Mormonism and then apostasy would appeal to any publisher.[8] In contrast, regarding my proposed book, Arrington wrote, "For publication, I should think your chances would be excellent," followed by recommendations of the university presses of Illinois, Nebraska, Oklahoma, Utah, and Utah State.

When I was working in Congressional affairs at Boeing, I quickly discovered that Congress took a recess for the month of August. My workload thus dropped off. I looked into the company policies about taking unpaid leaves of absence and discovered that if I took less than thirty days, I only needed my immediate boss's permission. More than that, it had to be approved by a vice president. As a single mother and with a long daily commute, I never

---

7. Leonard J. Arrington, Letter to Polly Aird, Apr. 17, 1989, Aird Papers.
8. Wallace Stegner, Letter to Robert B. Aird, Sept. 20, 1986, Aird Papers.

felt I had enough time with my daughters—weekends seemed to be taken up with laundry, grocery shopping, paying bills, and other errands. Summers brought an extra challenge as at that time there were few day camps, I had no relatives living nearby to lean on, and the girls were too young to leave on their own.

I decided a month off in the summer would solve both problems—I could take care of them when they were not in school for a big portion of the summer, and we could have some quality time together. I would add my two weeks of vacation to a month's leave-without-pay, and we would go off exploring the country, car camping along the way, tracing parts of the Mormon trail, and visiting the girls' father and grandparents in Nashville as well as my parents in the Bay Area. We had such a good time that I carried on with six weeks off every summer for about eight years, long after I had left Congressional affairs. I always arranged for how the work would be done in my absence, which, of course, was the concern of my bosses. And I would come back refreshed, ready to dive back into work. Colleagues asked if I wasn't afraid my absence would hurt my career, but it never seemed to, and one summer when I returned, I found I had been promoted to manager over a communications group. For me, leaves were a way to balance work and personal life and to be a better parent.

At the time I belonged to a professional women's association. We met once a month for breakfast and had speakers talk about working women. There were only one or two of us from Boeing, and it was a satisfying reminder that there was life outside of the company, which then employed some 110,000 in the Seattle area. The association started a scholarship to help women advance in their professions. In 1989 I applied as I wanted to attend that year's Pacific Northwest Writer's Conference in September and also the Western History Association conference which was going to be in nearby Tacoma in October. Happily I won the scholarship to attend both conferences. The Pacific Northwest Writer's Conference had a contest for unpublished works in various categories. With great eagerness, I wrote a one-page synopsis plus twenty-seven pages of what would be the beginning of my book and submitted it in the nonfiction category. Each submission would be critiqued by two editors or agents.

My submission won first place! It came with $300 in prize money and a contact from an agent. The latter wanted to see the whole manuscript, which, of course, I did not have. But it was a great boost to my morale.

In October I went off to the Western History Association conference. At the first lunch Leonard Arrington by chance came and sat next to me, though we had not yet met. With him were Chas Peterson and Val Avery, co-author with Linda King Newell of the biography of Joseph Smith's wife, Emma. I knew Linda through the connection between her husband, Jack Newell, and my father, both of whom had attended Deep Springs College in eastern California on the Nevada border. Jack was then on the board of trustees, and my father had been director of the college in the 1960s when Jack was a student. The second day of the conference, I brought a couple of books for Arrington to sign. At the banquet that second night, I happened to sit next to Max Evans, then director of the Utah State Historical Society. Altogether it was a highly profitable chance to meet some of the great Utah and Mormon historians.

By this time I realized that I needed to go to Salt Lake City and look up primary sources—this was long before much was available on the Internet. I began a series of research trips. I started at the Utah State Historical Society, where Gary Topping, then the curator of manuscripts, was helpful. He encouraged me to go to what was then called the LDS Church Archives (now the Church History Library), on the second floor of the Church Office Building. I was hesitant, if not somewhat afraid. Here was I, a Catholic, wanting access to the Mormon Church's innermost historical records so I could write a book about a horrific period in their history which drove my ancestors out of Utah fearing for their lives. It was now the early 1990s, not that many years after Leonard Arrington, then Church Historian, and his cadre of researchers and writers were exiled to Provo to form the Joseph Fielding Smith Institute on the campus of Brigham Young University (BYU). The reason for the banishment was that the group's writings were too scholarly and not faith-promoting enough. I had read Arrington and Davis Bitton's book, *Mormons and Their Historians* (published by the University of Utah Press in 1988) in which they said that many documents in the Archives had become highly restricted (on p. 165). I was sure I would not be allowed in.

Gary Topping, however, said to go and introduce myself to Ron Watt whom he knew through the Historical Society. Ron, he said, was as kind a person as one could hope to meet. Thus, with my heart in my mouth—and no crucifix showing—I found my way to the Archives. There I was confronted with a statement to sign giving the church the right to review anything I wrote that involved material from the Archives. I was afraid to sign—I was sure what I wrote about people leaving the faith would not be accepted—but there was no other way to get in to see what they had. (This form is no longer required.) I signed with trepidation. I asked for Ron Watt and introduced myself. To my enormous relief, he was unreservedly friendly and showed me around. I spent day after day there. Here was what I needed: membership and conference records in Scotland, emigration records of those who sailed from Liverpool to New Orleans and up the Mississippi and Missouri rivers, overland company records, diaries and journals from McAuslan contemporaries, and Salt Lake City ward records, for a start.

It did not take long before I discovered that everyone in the Archives would go out of their way to help. In particular, Ron Barney and Randy Dixon in addition to Ron Watt—as well as many outside the Archives—patiently, even cheerfully, answered my questions, no matter how odd and ignorant they may have seemed.

In 1992 my father and I took a trip to Scotland to see the places where the McAuslans had once lived. My mother had died four years before, which had left my father at a loss. So this trip was both therapeutic and stimulating. We went first to Luss on the western shore of Loch Lomond and found tombstones of McAuslans in the old churchyard, including one of a tenant farmer who died in 1795. We then visited towns where by that time I knew the family had lived: Bonhill in the Vale of Leven, Kirkintilloch, Kilmarnock, and Barrhead. We also visited Robert Owen's New Lanark, now a World Heritage Site, in which Emily said her great grandparents had invested.

The technological changes brought by the Industrial Revolution in the first half of the nineteenth century had forced the McAuslans to move from place to place where their skill in hand-block calico printing was still done. Not much remained after 150 years except for the occasional old building and crooked streets, but it helped to get a feel for the climate, the sky, the distances, and the topography of the land. The local librarians everywhere were helpful in our search for information.

After that trip, I decided it would be useful to become more proficient in genealogy and researching primary sources. The University of Washington offered a nine-month certificate course in genealogy and family history through their Professional and Continuing Education program. It was taught by a genealogist and a social historian. I signed up. We met once a week for two hours, and in the spring term, the course included writing a family history project. When it came to my project, the social historian encouraged me to take Emily's family history—her voice—and alternate it with my own voice. A creative idea, but as I worked along, I realized how many inaccuracies there were in Emily's version, and my voice kept commenting, "Wrong!" So I gave up that idea, took the family history, and went through the Scottish parts to show what research revealed. In the process I discovered that Emily's account was a mix of truth and family myth.

To give my grandmother her due, Emily wrote her account when she was in her mid-eighties. It was based on what her mother had told her (Emily was not born until after the family had settled in California), and her mother had been dead for forty years. Most importantly for me, however, was that if she had not written it, I would never have known the family story and would thus not have had this great adventure which absorbed me for so many years.

How much of Emily's account was true? The historical record shows she was partially right. For instance, there were Baron McAuslans, the earliest having been born about 1375. They continued on until the last baron, Alexander McAuslan, who died sometime after 1696. This last baron got into financial trouble with a neighboring baron, was known as a freebooter, and had mortgaged his estates. As he was a land or minor baron, not knighted by the king, once he lost ownership of the land, he no longer held the title.[9] The land once owned by McAuslans was in Glens Fruin, Mallan, and Douglas not far from the village of Luss. One of the farms in Glen Fruin was called Stuckiedow and is obviously the Stookadoo that Emily gave. But it was a poor, rock strewn land in Glen Fruin, not a castle.[10]

After the McAuslans lost the land, they became tenant farmers in the same area, probably on the land the family had formerly owned. No record has been found of McAuslans being educated in London or Edinburgh or any place else. They were not doctors or members of Parliament. There is a story of a large lost fortune made by one or more McAuslans in India which persisted into the late nineteenth century among McAuslans (also spelled McAusland) in Scotland as well as in Ireland and Australia where McAuslans had migrated. The Public Record Office of Northern Ireland in Belfast has a large file of letters dating from the mid 1850s among Irish McCauslands (those who emigrated from Scotland in the early 1600s adopted the changed spelling) trying to track down this fortune.

A Scottish newspaper, the *Greenock Telegraph*, published a paragraph about the fortune in 1857, which resulted in a meeting in Glasgow and then the hiring of a solicitor from London to track this money down.[11] I have letters written by Australian McAuslands in the 1990s, still trying to find out what happened.

---

9. The main sources for the various barons are William Fraser, *The Chiefs of Colquhoun and Their Country*, 2 vols. (Edinburgh: Privately printed, 1869), 1:100, 187, 2:281, 287, 339; Draft Genealogical Account of the Macauslan Family of Calderoth, Adv. MS. 19.2.17, f. 301, ca. 1824, National Library of Scotland; Particular Register of Sasines for Argyll, Dumbarton and Bute, June 30, 1651 (RS9/3 fol. 114), May 8, 1656 (RS9/3 fol. 171), May 21, 1678 (RS10/1 fol. 256), June 10, 1690 (RS10/2 fol. 273), and Mar. 4, 1692 (RS10/2 fol. 330).

10. The name Stuckiedow is spelled many ways. Alistair McIntyre, "Place Names: Row Parish" and "Place Names: Luss Parish," Dumbarton Library, Dumbarton, Scotland. Donald MacLeod, *Historic Families, Notable People, and Memorabilia, of the Lennox* (Dumbarton: A. Lawrance, 1891), 225; John MacAuslane, letter dated Jan. 4, 1813, Maccausland Family Papers, 1250–1942, Public Records Office of Northern Ireland, Belfast, D669/136; Polly Aird, *Mormon Convert, Mormon Defector: A Scottish Immigrant in the American West, 1848–1861* (Norman: Arthur H. Clark Co./University of Oklahoma Press, 2009), 31–32.

11. Referred to in the *Caledonian Mercury*, Edinburgh, Apr. 20, 1857.

One of the most entertaining accounts tells of Baron John McAusland of Loch Lomond who went to the hill country north of Calcutta, India, in the early nineteenth century where he grew coffee and later indigo. On his way home to retire in Scotland, he drowned or died of illness on the Ganges River. His factor (business agent) was supposed to wind up his affairs and bring the money home, but the money disappeared. The heirs hired a private investigator, and the search led to Canada and the Yukon. With the help of a guide and dog sled, the investigator found the factor's cabin, but it was a smoking ruin and the new fallen snow had obliterated all tracks.[12]

Another Australian account had Baron John McAusland's fortune ending up in chancery. A vital paper pertaining to the baron's will was smuggled out of Great Britain in a woman's corset and taken to America.[13] Nevertheless, hopeful descendants over the years hired solicitors and contacted the Courts of Chancery, India House, the Bank of England, the Courts of Probate, the Secretary of the Treasury in Ceylon, the Comptroller General of Accounts at Calcutta, and the Accountant General in Bengal.

A lesson, perhaps, in how family legends can morph. It is always possible that a McAuslan did go to India in the days of the East India Company and made what would have looked like a fortune to the tenant farmers and working class relatives at home when compared to their subsistence wages. Probably like compound interest in a savings account, the story and the amount of the fortune compounded over time. For certain, there is a large discrepancy between the socio-economic position of the McAuslans of the lost fortune and any McAuslan found in parish, census, or other records of the eighteenth and early nineteenth centuries in Scotland.

The earliest known direct ancestors are Peter McAuslan, born in 1772, and his wife Jane Marshall. They appear to have been the first generation to have left their tenant farm and moved south to the Vale of Leven, the outlet of Loch Lomond where textile works

12. John Harding Chinner (Dean of Melbourne University), Letter to John Matsen Guest, Feb. 27, 1994.

13. Yvonne Constance Roberts, Letter to John Matsen Guest, Apr. 13, 1994, which appears to repeat information from a letter by James Howden of Pike River Road, Quebec, Canada, in 1863.

were being established. Peter became a textile dyer, and his son Peter, born in 1801 (Emily's grandfather), was a hand-block calico printer. The third Peter, born in 1824 (Emily's uncle), became a calico print designer. Their artisan skills carried more status than such textile work as spinning and weaving.

The first Peter and his wife, Jane Marshall, whom Emily described as lovers of freedom of religion and active reformers in the Free Kirk and temperance movements, do not turn up in my research into any of those efforts.[14] They are not listed among the supporters of Robert Owen's New Lanark model factory,[15] and there was no "McAuslan Designing and Art House."[16] Rather the family lived in what was described by a contemporary as "old-world, peat-reeked, thatch houses" under whose blackened roofs many generations had found shelter. "The same must be said of a rather long range of grimy houses of the same character ... , appropriately enough named Blackstick, where at least three families lived." One of these families, at least for a time, was the McAuslans, as their second child was born there.[17] Peter and Jane's son Peter, born in 1801, and his wife, Betsy Adamson McAuslan, appear to have joined the temperance movement, but did not walk "all over Scotland ... preaching temperance and the curse of whiskey." Labor in the textile printing factories and the

---

14. No McAuslan is mentioned in Peter T. Winskill, *The Temperance Movement and Its Workers*, 4 vols. (London: Blackie & Son, 1891–92), or Peter T. Winskill, *Temperance Standard Bearers of the Nineteenth Century*, 2 vols. (Manchester: Darrah Bros. printers, 1897–98).

15. There is no McAuslan or variation of the name listed as an investor in New Lanark, all of whose partners are known. It was a profitable business that did not go bankrupt. Sidney Pollard, Robert Owen, and John Salt, *Robert Owen, Prophet of the Poor: Essays in Honour of the Two Hundredth Anniversary of His Birth* (Lewisburg, Pennsylvania: Bucknell University Press, 1971).

16. There is no mention of a business of this name or any variation of it in the early histories of Bonhill and the Vale of Leven, which cover businesses involved in textile dyeing, bleaching, and calico printing. The Glasgow City directories starting in 1807 also do not list such a business. The 1841 Census lists Peter McAuslan (b. 1801) as a calico printer and his son Peter (fifteen years old) as a pattern drawer.

17. James Barr, *Balloch and Around: Life in Balloch, the Vale of Leven & Loch Lomondside, 1820–45*, articles originally published in *The Lennox Herald* between November 1892 and March 1893, compiled and annotated by Graham Hopner (Dumbarton: Dumbarton Public Libraries, 1992), 29; Old Parish Records, Dunbartonshire (493/2) Births/Baptisms, 1797.

birth of one child after another prevented that.[18] Peter and Betsy also did not join the Free Kirk movement or leave the established Church of Scotland.[19]

I came to realize that Emily's emphasis on the values that the family had held for generations—including their drive for freedom of religion, factory reforms, and temperance—and what she said that the Mormon missionaries taught—could not be supported by the record, but could easily be ascribed to her own ideals. Emily was active in pursing those same goals. She was elected president of many Provo and Utah County organizations: the Utah County Chapter of the Red Cross, the Federation of Women's Clubs, the 19th Century Club, the Women's Prohibition League, and the State Welfare League. Her interest in education led to her being appointed to the University of Utah's Board of Regents (1929–31), and then being elected to two terms to the Utah State Legislature (1935–39). In addition, she was a sought-after speaker in the state.[20] Her ability to attract listeners and tell a compelling story is certainly displayed in her family history. I found myself admiring Emily for her singleness of purpose even in her old age, her passion for helping others, and her desire to pass on these values as a legacy to her descendants.

My class project ended with the family's conversion to Mormonism. The research had taken months, a number of trips to Utah, and one to Scotland. In spite of Emily's many inaccuracies and aggrandizing of the family's history, she got the broad outline right: the area of Scotland where the McAuslans came from including the name of the farm, that there were barons even if not of the knighted type, that the family was involved in art and design, the family's conversion to Mormonism, and that part of the family had sailed on the *John M. Wood*. She had included some of the economic and social turmoil of the Industrial Revolution and the confusion in religious belief with the loss of the old established church's former standing. It does not seem surprising that

18. Emily McAuslan, "Family History," 6; Aird, *Mormon Convert, Mormon Defector*, 50.

19. Aird, *Mormon Convert, Mormon Defector*, 55.

20. Delila M. Abbott and Beverly J. White, comp., *Women Legislators of Utah, 1896–1993* (Tooele, Utah: Governor's Commission for Women and Families, 1993), 98–99.

a family was attracted to a new religion with its promises of truth untainted by politics or status, and a life in a new world with all that that implied.

In the mid-1990s, I met a woman who taught creative writing at Southern Methodist University. She was fascinated by the research I was doing and my grandmother's dramatic story. She suggested that it would make a great fictional book. After discussing the idea with her quite a bit, I decided to go back to the University of Washington's Continuing Education program and take another certificate program, this time in fiction writing. My thought was that no matter whether I wrote the story as fiction or history, I could learn techniques of writing such as character development, scene description, and how to frame the story—where to start it and where to end it, and pinpointing the conflict and how it develops. Nine months later I was quite convinced that I was not cut out to write fiction.

I had discovered that I did not want to imagine what had happened, I wanted to know—as far as one could know—what had happened to this family: Why had they converted to Mormonism in Scotland? What happened in Utah that so disillusioned them? And then what? Was there a spiritual vacuum in their lives that they filled with something else? By this time, I saw my book in terms of a human story, and although the characters were ancestors or relatives, that seemed less important. I did gain confidence in my writing abilities in the fiction writing course. But as the instructors used the creative writing workshop method—the sharing of your writing followed by comments on it by the other students—without reference to literature or composition, I did not learn the elements of telling a story that I had hoped for.

I was more and more distracted from my job at Boeing. The McAuslan family story was becoming an obsession. I had found a poster which featured a painting by Georgia O'Keeffe titled *Ladder to the Moon* (oil on canvas, 1958, at the Whitney Museum of American Art, New York City). It showed a handmade wooden ladder suspended in the azure sky above the New Mexican mountains she loved. I had it framed and hung it in my office. This was me—suspended between my job that kept me and my daughters grounded and fed, and the book I wanted to write represented by the moon. It looked impossible to get there, but the picture was a constant reminder of my aspirations

In the early 1990s I stumbled across an article in the *Wall Street Journal*, a paper I rarely read, about the conditions creative people need to be productive—whether the person is a writer, a painter, a developer of software, or something else that takes time and focus. The article pointed out that the typical business calendar has appointment times for every half hour, but that someone doing creative work needs blocks of time. To have a meeting at 10:30 a.m. ruins the morning. No wonder I felt frustrated. I finally decided to work part time, to have two days a week for history. That worked pretty well, but then due to various circumstances, I decided to take the plunge and retire early. I was free to do history!

In the late 1980s, I had joined the Mormon History Association (MHA) and went to my first conference in 1991, which was held at Claremont College, California. A high school friend, who was then a professor at Pitzer College, one of the Claremont group, lived close to campus, so I stayed with her and her husband. The conference overwhelmed me—so much Mormonism! I remember coming back from an afternoon session to my friend's house and saying, "Susan, I need a glass of wine!" Linda King Newell was at the conference and kindly introduced me to a number of people, but I found the experience mostly exhausting and mind-boggling. I had stepped into a strange foreign country. It was another five years before I went to the next one in Snowbird, Utah. By this time I was much farther along in my research and thus found the conference talks fascinating. At dinner one night in a restaurant in the Snowbird Lodge, a friend who had come with me from Seattle and I sat at a table near a man who turned out to be Will Bagley, whose history of the Mountain Meadows Massacre would be published in 2002, and a conversation soon started.

In 1997 I gave my first paper at an MHA conference, which that year was in Omaha, Nebraska. I was placed in a session with Davis Bitton, a distinguished Mormon historian who was speaking on George Q. Cannon's travels. Fred Buchanan, an educator and a Scot who had lived long in Utah, commented on our papers.

Mine was titled "The Pull of the Gathering, the Push of Social Conditions: Religion and Economics Entwined in Mid-19th Century Scotland." It seemed to be well received.

Before the conference there was a four-day tour through Iowa led by William "Bill" Hartley, an associate professor at BYU, author of many books, and an expert historian of the Mormon trails in Iowa. We went eastward following the 1856 handcart trail in reverse, stayed two nights in Nauvoo, Illinois, and returned to Omaha following the pioneer trail of 1846, visiting sites such as Garden Grove and Mt. Pisgah along the way. We were one busload of people, and it was there I discovered the benefits of MHA tours, for not only do you learn more about Mormon history in the places you visit, but you have a chance to meet and talk with other people. On that trip I met Suzanne Brady, the managing editor of Deseret Book Company. We discovered we were third cousins once removed, our common ancestor being Agnes Baird Adamson. I also met Marie Clegg Jones, then in her seventies from Alaska, who one day asked if I was related to the Airds of Provo. Yes, I said, my grandparents lived there. Dr. Aird? Yes, I answered. She then told me she had gone to high school in Provo and had known my grandfather. Suddenly I felt less of an outsider.

My daughters and I had traced good stretches of the Mormon Trail, but by 1997 they had both graduated from college and were pursuing graduate studies. After the Omaha conference, a friend from Calgary, Alberta, joined me to trace the parts I had not seen—from Fort Laramie, over South Pass, and into the Salt Lake Valley. In 1999 we followed the route the McAuslans had taken in their escape from Utah across Nevada, over the Sierra Nevada, and to Live Oak, California, just north of Yuba City in the Sacramento Valley. Later that year we flew to New Orleans and took a steamboat up the Mississippi River to Memphis. We did not go as far as St. Louis, as the pioneers did, but the trip gave me an idea of what the country must have looked like to those Scottish eyes. The most surprising part was seeing the sun rise in the west—or seemingly so—when our northward direction was temporarily changed by a big southward loop in the river.

Peter McAuslan, born in 1824 and Emily's uncle, had settled

in Live Oak, California, with his family, and I knew some of his descendants still lived in the area. I had the family tree and so started looking up the oddest names in the phone book. Ansel Miller seemed like a good place to start. I called him, he knew who I was and told me that his daughter had the trunk of Peter McAuslan's papers. Papers? I had had no idea such existed. The biggest obstacle to writing a book was that I had no family primary sources beyond Emily's account, which was written some ninety years after the Utah events it detailed. By this time I knew her family history was not accurate except in its broadest outlines. I called Ansel's daughter Donna Forguson, she described what she had, and then started sending me letters from the collection.

Thus I changed the focus of my book to Peter McAuslan, the oldest son of the McAuslan family. In October 1848, he was the first in the immediate family to convert to Mormonism. His grandmother, Agnes Baird Adamson, and his two uncles, Sandy (Alexander) and Dougal Adamson, had already converted in 1843 and sailed to New Orleans in February 1848.[21] The catalyst for Peter's conversion appears to be the arrival of LDS Church Apostle Orson Pratt in Great Britain. His talks were published in the British Mormon newspaper, the *Millennial Star*, and the wording of them is reflected in what Peter later wrote about his motivation for conversion: "The idea of a redeemed World took a strong hold on my mind, for did not God's prophets declare that the time would come when man would beat there [sic] Swords into Ploughshirs and there Speers into proomhooks [pruning hooks] and study war no more?" A month after his joining the church, his parents, two brothers, and one sister were baptized.[22] Economics, however, was also a motivator, as all textile work was being mechanized, and women and teenagers, not the artisans, were being hired to run the new machines. The McAuslans had moved from town to town to find places that still did fine calico hand-block printing.[23]

Peter and his wife, Agnes, had come on the *John M. Wood*,

21. General Conference, Nov. 5, 1843, "Glasgow Branch, Record of Members, 1840–1854," film #0104152, LDS Church Family History Library; Aird, *Mormon Convert, Mormon Defector*, 66.

22. Aird, *Mormon Convert, Mormon Defector*, 72, 75.

23. Ibid., 38, 42–44, 47, 60–61, 80–81, 84, 86, 146.

arriving in New Orleans on May 2, 1854, a year after the bulk of the family had sailed on the ship *International*. It is quite possible that before sailing in 1853, the McAuslans did not know about Mormon polygamy. The LDS elders in Great Britain had denied the rumor for years, and later when asked why they would lie about it, they said it was because the revelation applied only to those in Zion who had proven themselves before the Lord. The announcement was made in Utah in late August 1852, but, this being before the telegraph spanned the Atlantic Ocean, the British *Millennial Star* did not report on it until the January 1, 1853, issue.[24] Few in Scotland had individual subscriptions to the *Star* and thus only read it when it was passed around.[25] What with selling their possessions and packing for a long journey—which began when they left Glasgow and headed for Liverpool on a coastal steamer on February 19, 1853—they may well have set sail on the ship *International* before they learned of this new revelation. Of the ten McAuslan children, nine eventually migrated to Utah. Their daughter Betsy did not go as she was engaged to William Cunningham, an active member of the Free Kirk who was adamantly opposed to Mormonism.[26]

Mormon emigrants paid ahead or borrowed from the Perpetual Emigrating Fund to cover the costs of their journey from Liverpool to Salt Lake City. A Mormon agent in Liverpool procured their bookings on ships. In the 1850s when their ships landed, initially in New Orleans and, in later years when steamships came in, in East Coast cities, the immigrants were met by Mormon agents who then hired transportation to get them to the outfitting camp.

Mormon immigrants never stayed a year in New Orleans because of the threat of disease in the summer season—1853 saw an epidemic of yellow fever in which some 8,000 people died. In

---

24. "Revelation, Given to Joseph Smith, Nauvoo, July 12, 1843," *Millennial Star* 15 (Jan. 1, 1853): 5–8. For the denials of polygamy, see Aird, *Mormon Convert, Mormon Defector*, 88–90.

25. See, for instance, "To the Presiding Elders and General Book Agents of the Conferences of the Church in the United Kingdom," *Millennial Star* 13 (May 15, 1853): 153, which discusses tract societies and book clubs as a means of circulating the church's printed material.

26. Aird, *Mormon Convert, Mormon Defector*, 88, 90, 95–101, 152.

1854 an epidemic of cholera broke out on the Mississippi River, carried by steamboats. No one wanted to linger near swampy areas in the hot months. Thus the McAuslans saw no adventurers and sharpers smoking long corncob pipes around campfires. In 1853 the immigrants were hurried up the Mississippi River to the out-fitting camp in Keokuk, in the southeast corner of Iowa on the Mississippi River. In 1854 Peter and Agnes continued from St. Louis up the Missouri River to Independence, Missouri, where the outfitting camp was that year.

The McAuslans did not outfit themselves with fine wagons and animals. In the outfitting camps, experienced Mormon agents procured wagons, ox teams, food, and all the other things the em-igrants would need. As most British converts were from industrial cities, they had much to learn, such as hitching and driving oxen, cooking over an open fire, and tarring wagon wheels so they did not screech. In the camps the people were formed into companies to travel overland under a Mormon leader. In 1853 when the main McAuslan family emigrated, they were assigned to the Jacob Gates Overland Company. There were 262 emigrants and thirty-three wagons, which meant about eight people per wagon. No hospital wagon is mentioned in any report or journal of the company.[27]

The youngest McAuslan child, David, was not killed by Indians. He died in California in 1927. Grandmother McAuslan also did not die on the plains—she survived the trek to Utah in 1853, the further trek to California in 1859, and died in 1871. The young-est McAuslan daughter, Janet, was not kicked in the head. Aside from her being cross-eyed, there was nothing physically wrong with her. Although four young children in the overland company died, they were not killed by Native Americans.[28] Mormon wagon

---

27. See www.history.lds.org/overlandtravel/companies/124/jacob-gates-company. One of the "Down and Back" church wagon trains in 1861 did have a hospital wagon, according to the autobiography of William John Hill. www.history.lds.org/over-landtravel/sources/20785hill-william-john-autobiography-in-utah-pioneer-biogra-phies-44-vols-32-85.

28. In 1853, thirteen Mormon companies with some 2,580 immigrants, crossed the plains and no one was killed by an Indian. In the Jacob Gates Overland Company, the children who died were William Davies (age two, died June 21), a Thirkell child (no age given, died August 3), Mary Thirkell (age six, died August 11), and Richard Squires (age four, died September 12).

trains were large and closely organized with the result that an occasional stolen cow was the only Native American depredation. In addition, by 1853, Native Americans were well equipped with guns, not arrows. A wagon train would never turn back to bury someone—every day was precious in making their way westward, both in terms of not running out of food and for getting over the Rocky Mountains before the first snows.

The main McAuslan family arrived in Salt Lake City in 1853, not 1856 as Emily gave it. There is no evidence any of the McAuslans ever dined with Brigham Young or put money or anything else into Brigham's "bank" for safekeeping.[29] The McAuslans, though better off than many emigrants, had ten people in their group.[30] They had paid for the trip through a half-price scheme called the Thirteen Pound Company.[31] They were not flush with money or family relics.

What did the McAuslans find when they settled in Utah? The 1850s turned out to be horrendous years: There were locust and cricket plagues, which wiped out crops; harsh winters in which half the livestock in northern Utah froze to death; drought and famine. In 1856 two handcart companies started too late in the season from the Missouri River and encountered winter snows in the Rockies. Although rescuers came from Salt Lake City with food and warm clothes, more than 200 died, and those who survived were frostbitten and emaciated.

Brigham Young felt God was sending these calamities as punishment for Mormon sins and so began a program of purification—questioning people, forcing confessions, and re-baptizing them. This Mormon Reformation included radical preaching about "blood atonement" in which some sins were so egregious that the only way to atone was by having the transgressor's blood spilled

---

29. Brigham Young would invite only church leaders or visiting dignitaries to his house, but then it was a formal meeting, not for a meal. There was no bank in those early days. From a conversation with Leonard Arrington, the church treasury was the only place of safekeeping. Polly Aird, Letter to Robert B. Aird, Oct. 15, 1989, Aird Papers.

30. Those in the McAuslan 1853 company were Peter Sr. and Betsy, Jane, William and his wife, Mary Muir, Ann, Frank, Christina, Janet, and David.

31. See my "Bound for Zion: The Ten- and Thirteen-Pound Emigrating Companies," *Utah Historical Quarterly* 70:4 (Fall 2002): 300–25.

onto the ground. Unsurprisingly, such preaching led to incidents of violence. In March 1857 outside the city walls of Springville in Utah County, William Parrish and his son Beason were murdered for trying to go to California. Aaron Johnson, Springville's local LDS leader, wanted to cleanse the town of apostates. Duff Potter, a spy pretending he too wanted to leave, was also murdered when he was mistaken for a younger Parrish son. These murders—known as the Parrish-Potter murders—were perpetrated six months before the Mountain Meadows massacre. In the latter some 120 Arkansas emigrants, passing through southern Utah heading for California where they intended to establish ranches, were betrayed and killed. The McAuslans were increasingly horrified. The murders in Springville, six miles from Spanish Fork where they were living, especially frightened them as they too no longer believed in Mormonism and wanted to go to California.

What about Davy? The story of his being disappeared fits right into the fearful atmosphere of the Reformation. But who was he? The Mormon shipping records for the ship *International* on which the McAuslans sailed in 1853 had in their roster or mentioned in journals four Davids: one aged 11, one 16, one 80, and the ship's captain David Brown. The sixteen year old looks the most likely, but he was traveling with his parents and three siblings.[32] That leaves the possibility of a crew member, for which there is no roster. If Davy were part of the crew and traveled with the McAuslans, he would be listed in the Jacob Gates Overland Company with them. Those rosters show four Davids age 12 or under, and one aged 76.[33] None of those fit. I then checked the overland company in which Peter and Agnes traveled the next year, but with no better results.

It is possible Emily got the name wrong. I went through the names of single men from Scotland on the Jacob Gates Overland Company. Three were possibilities, but two are found in the 1880 census, so obviously they had not been disappeared. That left one,

---

32. See www.mormonmigration.lib.byu.edu/mii/voyage/180?sweden=on&mii=on&scandinavia=on&netherlands=on&europe=on&keywords=ship+International.

33. See www.history.lds.org/overlandtravel/companies/124/jacob-gates-company-1853.

James Forsyth, a baker from Edinburgh, Scotland. He does not appear in the 1880 census. That name does turn up in newspaper articles in the Deseret News, but it is impossible to know if it is the same James Forsyth as the one on the 1853 overland company.[34]

In the end, the Davy story, dramatic as it is, seems unlikely. There may well have been a large barn built by the McAuslan men after son Peter and his wife joined the family in 1854, for father and son Peter had adjacent city lots.[35] In December 1856 Brigham Young ordered the Salt Lake bishops to take in the starving and frostbitten handcart pioneer survivors and house them in their wards.[36] In the 19th Ward, where the McAuslans lived, Bishop Alonzo Raleigh took in seventeen, so it is possible that he took the barn to house some of them.[37]

The McAuslans did move south to Spanish Fork, where the animals would have had a better chance of surviving the winter.[38] But the story of Davy being taken away and disappeared probably comes from the anti-Mormon novels of the late nineteenth and early twentieth centuries. Emily was known to be a voracious reader, her mother was known to be anti-Mormon after the family's experiences in Utah, and so it is likely Emily consumed many such stories.[39] There were also the writings by T. B. H. Stenhouse and his wife, Fanny, Bill Hickman, John Hyde, and Ann Eliza Young, which included stories of avenging angels, murder, and abuses of priesthood authority.

Perhaps initially the McAuslan women were left in Salt Lake City—Peter's wife Agnes was seven-and-a-half-months pregnant, and William's wife Mary had a daughter who was one and a half. The men may have gone south to Spanish Fork first to build houses or make other living arrangements. As for whether Emily's

34. "List of Letters," *Deseret News*, July 8, 1857, 8, and July 29, 1874, 16.

35. Aird, *Mormon Convert, Mormon Defector*, 145.

36. Brigham Young, "Remarks by President Brigham Young, Tabernacle, Nov. 30, 1856," *Deseret News*, Dec. 10, 1856, 8.

37. Alonzo Hazelton Raleigh, Journal, 151, Church History Library, Church of Jesus Christ of Latter-day Saints, Salt Lake City.

38. Aird, *Mormon Convert, Mormon Defector*, 169n37.

39. Arthur Conan Doyle's *A Study in Scarlet* was first published in 1887, and Zane Gray's *Riders of the Purple Sage* came out in 1912.

mother Mary ever became a seamstress for Brigham Young's wives, it is possible even though women in that period knew how to sew. Mary was known in the family to be a fine seamstress. If she worked there, she was most likely paid in tithing script and was able to exchange the scrip for food from the Lion House's store. However, I have not found her listed in any of the store records. Perhaps she worked there for just a short time. As for Emily's account of the family's escape at night to the protection of the army, that is probably correct, but it was from Spanish Fork, not Salt Lake City and took place in June 1859.[40]

The McAuslans, with their faith shaken to its depths, dared not tell anyone of their wish to go to California for fear of a fate like the Parrishes. After the army established Camp Floyd in Cedar Valley west of Utah Lake in the summer of 1858, the McAuslans asked for an escort out of Utah. In the late spring of 1859, as soon as the grass was high enough for the animals and the snow melt stopped swelling the rivers they needed to cross, a detachment of 162 military under Major Isaac Lynde led a total of forty families out of Utah by the northern route until they were well on their way to California. It is the only time I know of in America when the army escorted fearful religious refugees to safety.[41]

A sense of satisfaction began to settle over me as I realized that finally, after many years of research, I had pretty much separated the wheat from the chaff in Emily's story. I now had a good grasp of what had happened to the McAuslans: It was faith and the belief in the Mormon Gathering that pulled them to find a new home in Utah. Changes driven by the Industrial Revolution also drove them out of Scotland, for calico printing work was increasingly mechanized and in five years they would have been without jobs. It was both loss of faith and fear that drove them out of Utah with the help of the army. Like scientific research where one learns from failed experiments, so I too had learned from failed lines of research. Those dead ends brought me greater knowledge and

40. Aird, *Mormon Convert, Mormon Defector,* chap. 17.

41. Polly Aird, "Escape from Zion: The United States Army Escort of Mormon Apostates, 1859," *Nevada Historical Society Quarterly* 44:3 (Fall 2001): 196–237; Aird, *Mormon Convert, Mormon Defector,* chap. 17.

understanding of Scotland in the 1840s and early 1850s, of the grinding journey to Utah, and of what the McAuslans found in the Zion of their dreams. My time had not been wasted, and my ladder was a little closer to the moon.

In the meantime, I had been going through the papers of Peter McAuslan that he had left in Live Oak, California. They consisted of draft letters and scraps of writings where it appeared that some thought had captured him and he needed to get it down on paper, any paper, sometimes a heavy felted material, before it drifted away. There was the notebook kept by Peter as they left Scotland, but seasickness overtook him and the journal ended after three days. There were letters from others—his brother-in-law John Allan and his old friend Robert Salmon, both still in Scotland but planning to emigrate; his sister Christina who stayed in Salt Lake City after the family left for California; and his brother-in-law William Cunningham in Scotland who usually asked for money for his growing family. Peter's marriage certificate and citizenship papers were there, and on and on, some sixty items in all. Most important was the draft letter Peter wrote to Robert Salmon giving his reasons for why he left the Mormon faith.[42]

Lavina Fielding Anderson, then the editor of the *Journal of Mormon History*, lured me further and further into Mormon history. In 1999, she asked me to do my first book review. The next year she invited me to join the board of editors for the *Journal*. In her generous way, she wrote that my name had come up in an executive committee of the *Journal*, she had then taken it to the MHA Board of Directors meeting where it was "greeted with unanimous enthusiasm" and that those who knew me delivered "spontaneous seconding speeches."[43] Lavina knows how to persuade. But I was honored and thrilled. The usual term on the editorial board is for three years, but I ended up serving three terms. MHA had become my Mormon home.

As mentioned earlier, I met Will Bagley early on at an MHA

---

42. The Peter McAuslan Papers are in the Polly Aird Papers. Peter's letter to Robert Salmon is in the epilogue of Aird's *Mormon Convert, Mormon Defector.*

43. Lavina Fielding Anderson, Email to Polly Aird, Nov. 28, 2000, in my possession.

conference. He was the one who introduced me to William "Bill" MacKinnon who was working on a documentary history of the Utah War. And at the Utah Historical Society, I met David Bigler whose work coincided with some of mine, particularly his article in the *Western Historical Quarterly* (Winter 2007) on the Aiken murders. The Aiken party of six men, named for two Aiken brothers, rode into the Salt Lake Valley from California in May 1857 expecting to find the army. They most likely hoped to set up gambling houses and brothels to profit from the 2,500 soldiers stationed there. But the army had been delayed by heavy snow and did not come into the valley until the next year. Brigham Young, suspecting the six were federal spies, eventually made sure they were each relieved of the gold they carried and, according to Bigler, were one by one killed. The article was further evidence of the violence of that period. In addition to the Aiken Party paper, Bigler and Bagley were working on a book of the collected documents of the Mountain Meadows massacre, one of the crimes that frightened the McAuslan family.

I began to be asked to do more book reviews. And I got into writing papers. I realized that without a PhD, I was at a disadvantage for finding a publisher or being considered a historian. I decided that I could establish my credibility by publishing papers and not all in a single journal. By now I had real reasons for writing papers, as the subjects were part of my research into what would become my hoped-for book. The first paper was "Why Did the Scots Convert?" published in the *Journal of Mormon History* in the spring 2000 issue. Then came "Escape from Zion: The United States Army Escort of Mormon Apostates, 1859," in the *Nevada Historical Society Quarterly* in their fall 2001 issue. That was followed by my paper about the half-price scheme the main McAuslan family traveled on to Utah: "Bound for Zion: The Ten- and Thirteen-Pound Emigrating Companies," in the *Utah Historical Quarterly* in the fall 2002 issue. That won the Dale L. Morgan Award from the Utah State Historical Society for the best scholarly article of 2002.

Next came "'You Nasty Apostates, Clear Out': Reasons for Disaffection in the Late 1850s," in the *Journal of Mormon History* in the fall 2004 issue. That article won an award as one of two "Outstanding Articles in Mormon History," presented by the Mormon History Association in 2005. It has been the article most read and cited as it analyzes the reasons seven Mormon immigrant converts gave for leaving Utah in the late 1850s. It details the Parrish-Potter murders and captures some of the fearfulness of the times. Next came "Without Purse or Scrip in Scotland" about local (that is, newly converted Scottish) missionaries who traveled around the countryside trying to convert others. It was published in *Dialogue: A Journal of Mormon Thought* in the Summer 2006 issue, and won "Best Article of the Year" by the Mormon History Association in 2007.

By this point, I had learned a lot about life in Scotland in the early nineteenth century, Mormonism in Scotland and Utah, about reasons for conversion and disaffection, and I had a set of primary documents related to the McAuslan family. I had a role in the Mormon History Association, had published papers that had received awards, and had made many Mormon and non-Mormon friends. Now I had to actually write the book. That is a much bigger project than a paper. Where to start? How much background of the McAuslans in Scotland to give? Should I go into depth about the dislocations of the Industrial Revolution and the breakdown of the former authority of the Church of Scotland?

In trying to find my way through these questions, I read a book my brother gave me titled *Writing Great Screenplays for Film and TV* by Dona Cooper. In the note that came with it, my brother said, "This is the best book I've read so far on what makes a good story. ... It is very good on what the audience is looking for and getting you to think how you want to present your story."[44]

Indeed, it proved invaluable. I was not writing a screenplay, but I had a story that had all kinds of drama. It would have distorted Peter McAuslan's life to write the narrative as a one-dimensional sequence of events: This happened, that happened. It demanded much more, some way to tell the story that would get readers to travel with Peter through the dramatic events of his life. Although

---

44. Bruce Aird, Note to Polly Aird, Jun. 6, 1997, in my possession.

Cooper's book covers some of the usual elements of writing that I had hoped to find in the nine-month-long writing course, such as plot, setting, character, point of view, and theme, Cooper takes a different approach. She compares the story line to a roller coaster that captures the emotional ups and downs the audience (or the reader) experiences. The challenge is to discover where those peaks and valleys are in the story. Although Cooper is discussing a script for a fictional film, the same principles can apply to a biography. She describes possible shapes for the structure: Is the story like a simple triangle, building up and up in intensity and then descending swiftly to a resolution? Or is it a series of high points and valleys, gradually building up to the highest point? Or maybe the story starts out with an introductory bang (a peak), but then descends into a valley and rises again to a higher peak, only to descend quickly to the end?

To figure out a story's structure, one needs to identify the dramatic center, the idea most vital to the story. For Peter McAuslan, I came to see the center as his seeking for God. Cooper's book forced me to think not only about what the dramatic center was, but also the pivotal moment of change in Peter's outlook when he began to feel betrayed after reaching Utah—it should have been heavenly there, but instead it was horrible and he was trapped by its isolation. I also had to think about what kind of character Peter was. He was the protagonist, but what was his type? An idol, an everyman, an underdog, a lost soul? By then I knew Peter was an everyman, a Mormon foot soldier. He did not do anything extraordinary, but he had sincere faith and then lost it. And he had the integrity to act on his changed feelings.

Once I had a feel for what kind of man Peter was and what he was looking for, then figuring out how much of his background in Scotland to include became much more obvious. Once I had a picture of what he found when he arrived in Utah that led to his loss of faith, I had a feel for how much of the Utah detail needed to be told. And similarly for what he and his family found in California. I could see that settling in California mattered much less than his decision to escape Utah.

Writing the book took a long time. I needed to stop doing

research and get started on it. I knew enough to see how the structure would probably go. As I went along, holes appeared that needed further research, but by this time I had built up a library of Scottish and Mormon history, which helped reduce delays as I filled in the missing pieces.

But a big problem appeared: How could I explain some of the pivotal moments about which Peter never left writings? For example, did he struggle with doubts before converting to Mormonism? He wrote that after he converted, he had a vision which confirmed his decision, but he did not say anything about exactly what led up to his leap of faith. Later, what was he thinking when he left Glasgow and his homeland on the coastal steamer? He wrote about steaming under a clear sky and that the stars were "shining most splendidly," but not about his thoughts as the outlines of the hills of southwestern Scotland faded from view.

Gary Topping, who had encouraged me all along, pointed me to a letter Wallace Stegner had written to Leonard Arrington after reviewing the manuscript of a biography Arrington was writing about the Scot David Eccles.[45] Stegner wrote, "I'd play up that missed train in Hannibal, and I'd play it up from David's point of view. If you haven't any record of how he felt to see that train pulling out and leaving him in a strange town in a strange country, guess. Put it in the subjunctive. ... Not 'David watched the train departing, ... etc.,' but 'David would have watched.'"[46]

The subjunctive, supported with what else is known about the person, can capture critical points in a narrative which might otherwise be missed. With Gary's and Stegner's encouragement, I introduced such portrayals with phrases like "One can imagine ...," "What were Peter's thoughts ...?" and "One can reasonably speculate ..." It is not ideal—primary sources would be best, or

---

45. The letter was the result of Eccles family member Nonie Eccles Harrison paying a stipend to Stegner to review Arrington's manuscript. For more detail, see Gary Topping, *Leonard J. Arrington: A Historian's Life* (Norman: Arthur H. Clark Co./University of Oklahoma Press, 2008), 153.

46. Wallace Stegner, Letter to Leonard J. Arrington, Apr. 25, 1973, copy in the Leonard J. Arrington Papers, Merrill–Cazier Library Special Collections, Utah State University, Logan.

contemporaries writing about the same thing—but sometimes I had neither of those.

As I approached the end of writing, I asked several people to read all or parts of it. They did willingly, and the book kept improving. Gary Topping read versions of the early chapters which kept me pointed in the right direction. He later carefully read the whole manuscript and suggested a number of beneficial changes. I had also come to admire the work of Ian D. Whyte, a professor at Lancaster University in England, who wrote *Scotland before the Industrial Revolution: An Economic and Society History, c. 1050–1750.* I decided to write to him and ask if I could pay him to review my chapters on early Scotland. He treated me as a colleague, refused payment, generously read the chapters, and corrected some inaccuracies in my interpretation. Ron Barney, a senior archivist in the LDS History Department, read all the Utah chapters, and Richard "Rick" Turley, then Assistant LDS Church Historian and one of the authors of *Massacre at Mountain Meadows*, reviewed the parts about that atrocity. All of them encouraged me and their suggestions made for a better book.

Through the years of MHA conferences, I had met some of the publishers of Mormon history, and when at last my book was done, I presented it to Robert "Bob" Clark of the Arthur H. Clark Company, then an imprint of the University of Oklahoma Press. He asked Lavina Fielding Anderson to review the manuscript and then Bill MacKinnon, both of whom agreed that it should be published, but they each made suggestions to improve it. Bob then accepted it for publication and asked Bill MacKinnon to write an introduction. Rosemary Wetherold became the editor and eventually proposed the title.

In 2009 the book was published, and the next year it won the Best Biography Award at the MHA conference. Not bad to have the foremost association in Mormon history honor a biography about a man who became an apostate. I hope it says something about the way I wrote it—trying to be fair and honest. It definitely says something about the Mormon History Association and its open-mindedness. I was gratified.

I had climbed to the top of the impossible ladder and truly

touched the moon. I had encouragement and help each rung of the way. The adventure, however, did not end with this book as more projects were calling.[47] There are still more stories that need to be told and cannot be put to rest.

---

47. Shortly after the publication of my book, Will Bagley asked if I would be one of the editors for a forthcoming book on Mormon dissidents. The result was *Playing with Shadows: Voices of Dissent in the Mormon West* (Norman: Arthur H. Clark Co./ University of Oklahoma Press, 2011), by myself, Jeff Nichols, and Will Bagley.

2

HISTORY NEVER STOPS
WILL BAGLEY

I have written many books on many subjects, but none has ever blessed and haunted my career as much as *Blood of the Prophets: Brigham Young and the Massacre at Mountain Meadows*. I should have long ago said everything I have to say about it, but I learn something new about the past every day, and often it involves the most controversial event in Mormon history. As interesting as the atrocity was, Juanita Brooks wrote, it was "such a ghastly thing that I shall be glad and relieved to feel that it is finally done."[1] As Brooks learned over the next forty years, once you engage with this human disaster, it is never done.

This essay tries to explain how *Blood of the Prophets* came to be, honor the mentors who contributed so much to it, and recall the reaction when the book appeared. I will complain again about the institutional history that, as I read it, seems dedicated to spinning the past and continuing the cover-up of a capital crime that has dragged on for too many decades across three centuries. It will examine some critical evidence that has emerged in the last two decades to celebrate the historical process that demands we continually update and revise what we think we know about the past, for history never stops.

At dawn on September 7, 1857, at Mountain Meadows, an alpine oasis on the California Trail's southern route, Utah territorial

---

1. Brooks, Letter to Leslie Bliss, June 5, 1946, Institutional Archives, Henry E. Huntington Library, San Marino, California.

militia major John D. Lee led some seventy of his men and a handful of Indian freebooters in an attack on a wagon train from Arkansas, known to history as the Fancher-Baker Party. The train consisted of a dozen large, prosperous families in eighteen to thirty wagons with as many as 900 cattle, all bound for California's Central Valley. The company totaled about 140 souls, but the women and children outnumbered the able-bodied men two to one. The initial assault killed or disabled about a quarter of the train's men, but the survivors stopped the frontal attack in its tracks, pulled their scattered wagons into a corral, and dug a trench to protect the women and children. Cut off from water and under continual sniper fire, the emigrants endured for five brutal days.

On Friday, September 11, hope appeared in the form of a white flag. Lee, who served as the federal "Indian farmer," claimed he had come to rescue the emigrants from the Indians and escort them back to the nearest substantial town, Cedar City. Uncertain if Mormons had participated in the attack, out of water and ammunition, the travelers agreed to Lee's strange terms. They surrendered their arms and divided into three groups: the wounded and youngest children led the way in two wagons; the women and older children walked behind; and the men, each escorted by an armed guard, brought up the rear. Lee led this forlorn parade for more than a mile to the rim of the Great Basin, where a Mormon officer gave an order: "Halt!" A shot rang out, and then the escorts turned and shot the men. Painted savages—a few of whom might have been Indians—cut down the women and children, while Lee handled murdering the wounded. Within five minutes, the atrocity was over. Everyone was dead except for seventeen orphans, all under the age of seven, whom under Mormon doctrine qualified as "innocent blood" and the killers deemed too young to be credible witnesses.

Utah's Superintendent of Indian Affairs, Brigham Young, knew about the attack before the massacre happened, but four months passed before he reported it to Washington. "Capt. Fancher & Co. fell victim to the Indians' wrath near Mountain Meadows," Young wrote. He attributed the atrocity to the evil acts of the emigrants who, he charged, had "cheated, and then poisoned and wantonly

slain untutored savages." He did nothing to recover any of the train's considerable property for the surviving children.

After investigating the case in 1859, federal officials discredited Young's cover-up. Based on participant statements, which furnished "an abundance of evidence in regard to the matter," Judge John Cradlebaugh issued warrants for the arrest of thirty-eight prominent men for "the cowardly, cold-blooded butchery and robbery at the Mountain Meadows." Young continued blaming the victims and the Southern Paiutes for a decade. Fifteen years passed before the arrest of any of the murderers. In the end, only a single scapegoat, John D. Lee, "faced the music." In March 1877, federal authorities executed Lee at the scene of the crime.

For the victims, it was over in seconds, but the men who committed the atrocity lived with memories they could never escape. For today's Mormons, nothing in their faith's history of suffering, sacrifice, and devotion explains such an outrage.

For generations, leaders and official historians of the LDS

Church have spent millions of dollars to create a cottage industry to justify an unjustifiable atrocity. An early highpoint of this
costly cover-up was Charles Penrose's 1884 public defense of the
sanitized fable Mormon historians crafted for western chronicler
Hubert Howe Bancroft. For the first time it made public the dis-
patch Young sent south the day before the massacre, telling Major
Isaac Haight he "must not meddle" with emigration trains, but "the
Indians we expect will do as they please." This letter has served as
Young's alibi ever since Bancroft accepted it.

In contrast, Brigham Young explained why he directed the
destruction of the Fancher Party when he visited Mountain Meadows in May 1861 to celebrate the start of the Civil War. He read
the verse from Romans American soldiers engraved on the cross
atop the cairn they raised over the grave of the victims in 1859:
"Vengeance is mine: I will repay, saith the Lord." Young said it
should say, "Vengeance is mine and I have taken a little."[2] Dudley
Leavitt recalled that the LDS prophet directed the destruction of
the monument so that all present could deny Brigham Young had
ordered the desecration. "He didn't say another word. He didn't
give an order. He just lifted his right arm to the square, and in five
minutes there wasn't one stone left upon another. He didn't have
to tell us what he wanted done. We understood."[3]

Had it not been for a March 1995 help-wanted ad in *The Salt
Lake Tribune*, I might never have written about the Mountain
Meadows Massacre: "Inquisitive Research Manager needed for 1
to 2 yr. full time project on the Fancher Wagon Train Party of
1859 [*sic*]. Generous salary plus expenses. High energy, enthusiasm, resourcefulness, and self-discipline must be proven via a
resume of your qualifications." I knew that the story would challenge any serious historian and feared that the evidence had been
so thoroughly corrupted it would be impossible to come up with a
reasonable reinterpretation of the crime. But it was an intriguing
proposal that would cut my ten-year plan to become a full-time

2. Scott Kenney, ed., *Wilford Woodruff's Journal*, 9 vols. (Midvale, Utah: Signature
Books, 1983), 5:577 (May 25, 1861).

3. Brooks, *The Mountain Meadows Massacre* (Rev. Ed., Norman: University of
Oklahoma Press, 1972), 183.

historian in half, so along with some thirty other historians, I tossed my resume into the ring.

Two facts distinguished my application: unlike all the others, I had no PhD, and I did not include an assurance that Brigham Young had nothing to do with the crime. In 1991 Dave Bigler had asked me to transcribe the diary of Young's Indian interpreter and brother-in-law, Dimick Huntington, at the LDS Church's Historical Department in downtown Salt Lake City. The diary's contents demonstrated that the depth of Young's involvement was an open question.

By May I had quit my job as a publications manager at Evans & Sutherland Computer Corporation and was an employee of Frank James Singer and the Eve Insurance Brokerage of Roseville, California. Singer was a swashbuckling entrepreneur, dedicated Republican, and gun-rights advocate who had acquired a consuming interest in western history after joining the LDS Church. He had built a $100 million business and decided to apply some of his fortune to his passion for history. In particular, he sponsored my two-year investigation of the 1857 Mormon massacre of 120 Arkansas travelers at Mountain Meadows in southwestern Utah. Singer said he planned to use the research in a novel and eventual movie.

For the first month on the job, I worked exclusively with Laura Buttrell, Singer's executive assistant. I do not recall ever speaking with him on the phone. In late June we scheduled an all-day meeting at a private terminal at the Salt Lake City airport. Singer arrived on a Lear jet with his wife and assistant, and we spent the day outlining the project's aggressive schedule. I listed the archives and libraries that held the most promising new material. I promised to write a report that would summarize and interpret the research and give him my findings as a historian based on the evidence. I told Frank that he might not be happy with my conclusions, but they would represent my best professional opinion.

The project faced two great challenges: mastering the vast array of sources and sorting through the contradictory evidence found in primary materials—diaries, reminiscences, sermons, church papers, trial records, survivor and participant accounts and affidavits, government documents, and newspaper reports. The integrity of virtually every contemporary account could be challenged for good reason. Save for the youngest children, "All were killed who could have had any certain memory of the circumstances," noted historian B. H. Roberts.[4] The story had to be assembled from the testimony of children, murderers, and passers-by.

For five decades Juanita Brooks's masterful 1950 monograph, *The Mountain Meadows Massacre*, had been definitive. My first (and last) task was to reread this classic study, which summarized scholarship up to 1970 when the University of Oklahoma Press published the book's third revision. This led to tracing her many pointers, which led to new discoveries and items Brooks had been unable to access. Her papers at the Utah State Historical Society and the University of Utah yielded new insights, sources, and clues.

Brooks was the Huntington Library's LDS expert and the source of its extensive "Mormon File." What puzzled me was that she never used a word from the trial records in the library's Jacob Boreman collection. Boreman was the federal judge who presided at John D. Lee's trial. He later persuaded W. L. Cook, his court clerk, to create a typescript for a share of the profits of the memoir Boreman hoped to write. The judge died without producing a memoir, but the Huntington paid the Boreman family tall dollars for his papers, including the trial typescript. Cook resented this and donated his carbon copy to the Library of Congress.[5] In 1996 I was the first person to look at them. I spent a day copying every page. I hoped the record would produce overlooked details and reliable dates for a timeline. I read every page and learned why Brooks never used them: they were a useless festival of falsehoods told by mass murderers lying as hard and fast as they could. Every word was based on twenty-year-old memories of an event the liars had worked hard to forget. Nobody could recall the day of the week the massacre happened, let alone the date, which court officials never figured out.

---

4. Brigham H. Roberts, *A Comprehensive History of The Church of Jesus Christ of Latter-day Saints*, 6 vols. (Salt Lake City: Deseret News Press, 1930), 4:139–40.

5. Lee Trial Transcripts, W. L. Cook Papers, Manuscripts Division, Library of Congress, Washington, DC.

Between 1995 and 1997, I visited the Huntington, Bancroft, and California State libraries, the California, Utah, Nevada, and Arkansas historical societies, special collections at the universities of Utah, Nevada, Arkansas, Brigham Young, Southern Utah, Weber State, and Dixie College. The Library/Archives of the Reorganized Church of Jesus Christ of Latter Day Saints (now Community of Christ) and the LDS Historical Department and Library (now Church History Library) provided fascinating material, including much that Brooks could never examine. I experienced the same denial of access that frustrated her, but I took comfort in her words: "I don't quarrel with them; I don't fight them, I don't criticize them; I can just laugh at them for many of the silly little things they do."[6]

Historical mentors guided me through the Mountain Meadows maze. Wilbur "Bud" Rusho advised me to paraphrase my many block quotes and observed that since the massacre sources were such a mess, I should simply use the evidence I considered reliable and ignore the rest. I followed his advice on paraphrasing but not on cherry-picking the evidence. Professor Brigham D. Madsen's essay "The Craft of History" became my north star. He believed the craft required "special skill and careful attention to detail"—which also be applied to what he called his "other calling": carpentry. When the Mormon History Association declined to consider his *Corinne: The Gentile Capital of Utah* for an award because it was not Mormon history, even though it was about the struggle "over economic and political control of Utah," Brig joked about forming a "Utah Gentile History Association." Madsen "did not understand the point of view of some of my colleagues who view themselves as 'Mormon historians,'" quoting one who announced he would "tell the truth and nothing but the truth but not necessarily the whole truth." Madsen found the statement incomprehensible. "Which part of the 'whole truth' is to be eliminated?" he asked. In a court of law, would this historian "declare that he intends to omit some essential information? Of such formulae, apologetic history is born." He pointed to a Mormon

---

6. A. C. Lambert Conversation Notes, Oct. 8, 1954, 3–4, Lambert Collection, Special Collections, J. Willard Marriott Library, University of Utah, Salt Lake City.

historian who devoted "fourteen pages to a discussion of the 'Utah War' without once mentioning the Mountain Meadows Massacre. I want no part of such sinning by omission," he wrote.[7]

I dedicated *Blood of the Prophets* to the two historians who most influenced the book. David Bigler inspired much of my evolving understanding of Mountain Meadows. Dave had a singular ability to look at the critical episodes in often-analyzed events and see what other historians had missed. He asked simple questions about favorite elements of the accepted historical mythology of the Mormon West. He advised me, "What is the simplest thesis that would best explain what happened?" When you find the truth, Dave said, you'll know it. A big problem with the subject involved the behavior of the Fancher party. Mormonism's most eminent historians had long blamed the massacre, in part, on the emigrants' provocative acts. These stories appeared years after the event, but there were enough of them to support a new branch of folklore studies. I wrote a draft chapter using much of the "evil emigrant" mythology to describe a confrontation in a Mormon town and asked Bigler to review it. Such "stories of wicked emigrant behavior generally fall into the realm of later justification," he noted. "Mormon settlements were never Dodge City at any time, much less fall 1857." My theory about "an 'explosion' at Cedar City" was "a necessary mainstay of 'blame the emigrants' apologists."[8]

These tall tales tried to shift blame from the killers to the victims.

Even before I began working on the Mountain Meadows Massacre in 1995, Floyd A. O'Neil, director of the American West Center at the University of Utah, would take me to lunch and patiently explain complicated issues. During ten days at the National Archives and the Library of Congress, he shared his invaluable knowledge of these records. O'Neil was an excellent anvil on which to hammer out a consistent interpretation of the story's

---

7. Brigham D. Madsen, "The Craft of History: A Personal View" (Salt Lake City: Utah Westerners, 1995), 18.

8. Bigler, Email to Bagley, Oct. 19, 1999, in Will Bagley Papers. The Will Bagley Papers, 1836–2007, Accn1937, are at Special Collections, J. Willard Marriott Library, University of Utah. The papers currently consist of 41.5 linear feet of 104 boxes of material. The collection includes a "History Never Stops" folder containing copies of the items cited in this essay.

contradictory sources. When I'd push the evidence too far, Floyd would chide me, "You can't stretch a rat's ass over a rain barrel!" He insisted that no matter how fond one might grow of a pet theory, without evidence it was only speculation. Over many years, Floyd taught me the craft of history—and how to deal with the contradictory and fabricated evidence that clutters up Mormonism's violent past. It was essentially graduate school training in history.

My research tried to find more reliable sources than the contradictory and self-serving murderers' accounts Juanita Brooks had relied on. A 1996 trip to Arkansas turned up interviews with five of the surviving children and provided the insights of descendants whose family members had been murdered at Mountain Meadows.[9] Plus I made friendships that endure to this day.

Research surprises included finding the August 1857 account of the widow of martyred LDS apostle Parley P. Pratt, calling on God's vengeance for the shedding of her husband's innocent blood in Arkansas; Brigham Young's discourses later that month threatening to turn the Indians loose on emigrants and blockade the overland wagon road; the autobiography of Ann Gordge, the last thirteen-year-old John D. Lee ever married; the narratives of James Gemmell, a frontier adventurer who blackmailed Brigham Young; folksinger George A. Hicks's letters to Brigham Young denouncing Lee and Young's curt response advising Hicks to try "a rope round the neck taken with a jerk" as a remedy; and "Discursive Remarks," apparently the earliest detailed Mormon account of the massacre. I was able to survey the "Mountain Meadows Massacre" subject file at LDS Archives, which historian Gene Sessions used in his posthumous edition of Donald Moorman's *Camp Floyd and the Mormons*. It included much southern Utah lore of little historic worth, but it also documented the LDS Church's struggle to deal with the history of the single most difficult event in its history.

Research is fun, writing is hard. As the project's end approached in 1997, I had collected dozens of images and maps, assembled

---

9. See David L. Bigler and Will Bagley, *Innocent Blood: Essential Narratives of the Mountain Meadows Massacre* (Norman, Oklahoma: The Arthur H. Clark Company, 2008), 425–40.

roughly a thousand pages of transcribed documents, created more than 1,300 computer files, and drafted ten chapters of a book.

I hoped to meet Frank Singer in spring 1997 to ask him to extend the project, but the last two years had not been kind to his financial empire. The proposed sale of his insurance business collapsed and his wife divorced him. Rumor said that the FBI and the FCC were investigating him. That spring a *Wall Street Journal* article chronicled his financial rise and fall. We scheduled many meetings to discuss how to wind up or continue the Mountain Meadows project, but Singer cancelled them all. On June 10, 1997, he walked out of his offices in Roseville and disappeared without a trace. In March 1999, a federal grand jury indicted Singer on four counts of tax evasion. The vast majority of people who try to disappear eventually give up, but Frank vanished. I saw him lounging on Cayman Islands beach, but his assistant believed he had been murdered. A California Superior Court judge agreed and declared Singer dead on February 7, 2014.

I received only one personal communication from Frank Singer during the two years I worked for him. It was about the doctrine of blood atonement, which he suggested Lee used to persuade the men to commit the Mountain Meadows atrocity. "This had to be an act performed by rational thinking people who were acting in consort with their values and a heart-felt sense of what was right and wrong," he wrote. The killers perceived "it was better to kill someone than allow them to live in sin." Sometimes it required shedding "another person's blood so that they could go to heaven … in the afterlife, they would thank you for doing it." Singer concluded, "These murderers were believers in the concept of blood atonement, they viewed themselves as carrying out a holy act. Otherwise, they would not have done it."[10]

Singer had come up with an excellent answer to the hardest question historians must ask about the Mountain Meadows Massacre: How could good people commit such bad act? We have no clear idea of how the doctrine was to be practiced and know that blood atonement meant different things to different Mormons,

10. Singer, Letter to Laura Buttrell, June 3, 1995, Bagley Papers.

so I did not want to wade into that swamp without sufficient evidence. The killers confessed to dressing up as Indians, but none of them ever uttered the words "blood atonement"—and why would they? If one of the murderers confessed to Assistant LDS Church Historian Andrew Jenson when he interviewed the surviving perpetrators in 1892 that they killed the Arkansans to save their souls, would Jenson have reported it? Singer, however, had come up with a compelling explanation of how zealots could persuade otherwise decent men to slaughter so many helpless women and children.

Singer's disappearance and unresolved issues about who owned the rights to the research and writing I had done as a "work for hire" complicated my ability to publish a book. Ultimately I signed an agreement with the insurance company running the ruins of Singer's financial empire that allowed me to publish *Blood of the Prophets*. In the course of these discussions, the company calculated the "burdened cost" of my two years' work amounted to $250,000. It was a staggering amount, but considering how much Singer paid in salary, benefits, travel, and office expenses, it was not far from the mark. That figure would be useful in estimating how much similar private historical investigations might cost: $125,000 per employee per year.

Now, how to finish the book on my own hook? The job was more complex and time consuming than I'd estimated—and I still had any number of difficult questions to resolve. By 1997 I believed the massacre was exactly what Brigham Young said it was in 1861—an act of righteous vengeance. In his diary, John D. Lee recorded how Young told him in May 1861 that the "company that was used up at the Mountain Meadowes were the Fathers, Mothe[rs], Bros., Sisters & connections" of the men who had slain Mormon prophets. Murdering the women and children troubled the prophet, Lee wrote, but, Young had told him, "under the circumstances [it] could not be avoided."[11]

A tough question remained: Was it, as LDS historians have long argued, an event driven by circumstances, in which one damn

---

11. Robert Glass Cleland and Juanita Brooks, eds., *A Mormon Chronicle: The Diaries of John D. Lee 1848–1876*, 2 vols. (San Marino, California: Huntington Library, 1955), 2:314 (May 30, 1861).

thing led to another, or was it a calculated act of revenge? After years of wrestling with the evidence, I concluded that there were any number of enigmas I'd never resolve.

Making a living and editing three volumes for the Arthur H. Clark Company series, "Kingdom in the West: The Mormons and the American Frontier," occupied much of my time over the next three years. Consulting work added a surprising number of key documents to my quest, and some of them resolved what I'd long considered insolvable mysteries. The inadvertent discovery in 1999 of the remains of twenty-eight victims by a backhoe digging the foundations of a monument at Mountain Meadows provided something not available since 1859—physical evidence of the massacre.

I completed drafting the book in 1998 and began revising it more times than I recall. By spring 2000 the submission draft was done. Finishing the book required resolving paradoxes and drawing conclusions. The ambiguity of the surviving evidence still allows many alternative interpretations. I tried to present that evidence fairly, so that others could draw their own conclusions. In the end, I felt I understood what happened—and why it happened—at Mountain Meadows.

I later came across an observation attorney Andrew Hamilton made at the trial of printer John Peter Zenger in 1735: "I will beg leave to lay it down, as a standing rule in such cases, That the suppressing of evidence ought always to be taken for the strongest evidence; and I hope it will have weight with you."[12] Like almost everything connected to this mass murder, the historic record has been purged. After convicting John D. Lee, US Attorney Sumner Howard observed that whatever orders Brigham Young had sent about the Fancher party had "long since been taken care of." No one ever accused Young "of being either a fool or so indifferent to his own safety as to allow written evidence of his own guilt to remain in the hands of men over whom he has had supreme control for all the time since this crime was committed, now about twenty years."[13] The destruction of evidence speaks for itself.

12. Anonymous, *The Trial of John Peter Zenger, of New-York, Printer* (London, J. Almon, 1765), 26.
13. "Howard's Defence," *New York Herald*, May 9, 1877, p. 4, col. 1.

The story of Mountain Meadows is an awful tale, drenched in blood. The nature of such history requires looking human evil in the face and asking unanswerable questions, but they are questions we must ask that provide lessons we need to learn.[14] Despite its harrowing and horrific subject, the project was in many ways an adventure. As any historian knows, the profession's greatest reward is the people you get to know. You don't meet many lowlifes studying history, historian Stan Kimball once told me, and, Lord knows, nobody's in it for the money. Many of these new friends have been dead for generations, but it has been a joy to tell the stories of forgotten heroes such as Nancy Saphronia Huff Cates, Sally Baker, Rebecca Dunlap, George Calvin Williams, John Hawley (the Mormon Ulysses), Josiah Gibbs, George A. Hicks, Laban Morrill, and Charles W. Wandell.

The context in which I wrote the book influenced it dramatically, as it always does: a competent interpretive history begins with what is known at the time and seeks to build on that foundation. *Blood of the Prophets* inevitably reflected the state of official LDS history at the time of its creation. As I reminded my friends who worked for the LDS Church, the mere fact that it denied access to so much material showed it was hiding something: Brig Madsen said he loved it when the Brethren—LDS Church officials—censored the materials he wanted to see, because it showed where he could find critical evidence. Archival realities, the size and inconsistent access provided to scholars, the LDS Church's own publications, and the federal government's vast record of Mormon history printed in executive documents and public records, meant it was almost always possible to find items the church wanted to hide.

The problem that confronts all censors—what are you trying to suppress?—led church officials to deny access to thoroughly benign material. In 2001 the archives review committee would not let me see an innocuous but entertaining George A. Smith letter describing an 1856 meeting with Sam Houston. In less than a month, they provided a copy of the epistle to Ardis E. Parshall, a faithful

---

14. Much of this essay first appeared in Bagley, "Looking Evil in the Face," *Oklahoma* 2, 1 (Spring 2002): 2–3.

LDS historian. Ardis eventually shared it with me, and William P. MacKinnon published the letter in 2013, but the unjustified censorship terminated my pursuit of truth at LDS Archives.[15] I had already noticed that something suspicious was going on in the reading room where I reviewed the archival materials. Archivist friends asked odd questions about Mountain Meadows sources, and I saw flocks of volunteers capturing screen shots of restricted documents I was not allowed see. I suspected something was afoot, but the drama surrounding its announcement leapt from the shadows and surprised me.

In May 2002 the advance copies of *Blood of the Prophets* arrived in Tucson while I was attending the Mormon History Association's annual meeting. LDS Church History Department director Richard E. Turley Jr. gave the plenary address about the church's future publication plans. He began with a defense of the department's attempt to seize many of former Church Historian Leonard J. Arrington's papers at Utah State University (recently opened to the public). He gave his annual explanation of the church's bureaucratic reshuffling and rebranding, and announced an "expanded effort to publish" the papers of the faith's founding prophet, Joseph Smith, before his 200th birthday in 2005.

Rick then invited colleagues Ronald Walker and Glen Leonard to join him on stage to announce their new project, *Tragedy at Mountain Meadows.* They distributed a press release claiming it would offer "the definitive account of a dark chapter in American history" and appear "in 2003 from Oxford University Press!" They eventually used *Massacre at Mountain Meadows: An American Tragedy* as their title, even though the atrocity was, in fact, a premeditated criminal act. The three men had spent almost a year doing research, but Walker already claimed "the heavy weight of evidence" made some points clear: LDS apostle George A. Smith did not carry "secret orders during his August tour of southern Utah that set in motion the crime at Mountain Meadows." He asserted, "the charge that Brigham Young ordered the massacre

---

15. William P. MacKinnon, "Into the Fray: Sam Houston's Utah War," *Journal of Mormon History* 39, 3 (Summer 2013): 204–205.

remains the canard that it always has been."[16] With this proclamation, Dr. Walker revealed that whatever the project discovered, the church had its story and was sticking to it, as one of my archivist pals put it.

My life changed forever on Wednesday, July 31, 2002, when antiquarian book wizard Ken Sanders sponsored a launch party at his downtown Salt Lake City store for *Blood of the Prophets: Brigham Young and the Massacre at Mountain Meadows.* "First, let's get one thing clear," I began. "I am the world's luckiest historian." Historical research is detective work, and I recalled how an archivist at the LDS Church Historical Department had asked me, "What are you trying to prove?" "I'm not trying to prove anything," I replied. "I'm trying to figure this out." My mentors had taught me to seek the simplest thesis that would best explain the evidence, and the trick is to ask hard questions.

I doubted I would ever find definitive answers to the most important questions, such as, *How did Eleanor Pratt, whose ex-husband had killed LDS apostle Parley P. Pratt, her current husband and whose death may have helped to precipitate the massacre, get from St. Louis to Salt Lake in less than six weeks in mid-1857?*

As often happens, serendipity provided the answer while looking for something else. Bill MacKinnon asked me to copy the unpublished 1857 journal of federal judge "Pious Elias" Smith, Joseph Smith's cousin. On July 23 Smith's diary revealed Orrin Porter Rockwell delivered the widow Pratt from Fort Laramie to Salt Lake in an amazing five days and three hours. "All at once I knew what had happened," I said at Ken's that night.[17] This "might appear to be an unimportant detail," I later wrote, "but the fact that historian Harold Schindler, who spent more than forty years relentlessly researching Rockwell's career, never learned how Pratt's widow arrived in Utah indicates how scrupulously this information was suppressed." I am no longer as convinced as I was twenty years ago, but that discovery galvanized the interpretation

---

16. "What's New in Latter-day Saint Church History?" *Journal of Mormon History* 28, 2 (Fall 2002): 1–3, 21.

17. "Wrestling with the Devil," Ken Sanders Rare Books, Wednesday, July 31, 2002, presentation notes in Bagley Papers.

presented in *Blood of the Prophets*. I have written better books since, but probably none that will have the enduring power of the book we introduced that night has had.

Before I spoke, my friend Jane Beckwith approached me with a manila folder in her hand. Jane was the granddaughter of Frank Asahel Beckwith, publisher of the *Millard County Chronicle*. I had shared my copy of the Huntington Library's manuscript of his book, "Shameful Friday: A Critical Study of the Mountain Meadow Massacre," with her. Jane had a remarkable tale to tell. The previous fall, a friend of mine who worked at LDS Archives visited her in Delta, 135 miles by car southwest of Salt Lake City. He asked about some papers her grandfather had collected related to the Mountain Meadows Massacre. The archivist claimed he was working on a personal project about the Utah War and was looking for information about Frank King, who recalled traveling with the Fancher Party. Jane said something did not quite add up: she thought he might be lying. She told him she did not have anything that would interest him, but that night at Ken Sander's bookshop she handed me a sheaf of her grandfather's papers. "This is what he was after, I think," she said.

Years later I had lunch with the archivist who had been ordered to visit Jane and disguise what he was really doing. He had been assigned to search the Beaver County courthouse for records of the John D. Lee trials, which I had already surveyed. On his way home he was to stop and see if Jane Beckwith had any records that might shed light on her grandfather's investigations into the massacre. He said he was tired when the day began and after reaching Delta High School, where Jane taught journalism, he was worn out. "It was the worst interview I've ever had," he said. "I could tell she knew I was lying," he said. When he returned to Salt Lake City, he said, he told his boss, "I'm not lying anymore."[18]

Ken's event sold a hundred books and was a big success. By academic press standards, so was *Blood of the Prophets*. It won six big best book awards, including a Spur from Western Writers and the best book prize from the Western History Association. My

---

18. "Ends and Means," essay, May 2007–Aug. 2009, copy in Bagley Papers.

publisher's royalty statements would baffle Einstein, and the press provides random numbers, but it seems to have sold more than 10,000 copies in cloth, paper, and e-book format.

People who build their lives on their religion resent having their beliefs questioned, so any historian who challenges the flimsy foundations of faith should expect a heated response. Decades ago Hal Schindler, longtime journalist with the *Salt Lake Tribune*, told me he expected the oatmeal would hit the fan when he published *Orrin Porter Rockwell: Man of God, Son of Thunder* in 1966. I was unprepared for how much oatmeal the machinery of Mormonism flung hither and yon to greet my massacre book.

The *Deseret News* unloaded on it in an over-the-top review on September 1, 2002, helping to make *Blood of the Prophets* a local best seller: manager Dennis Evans said Sam Weller's Books alone had "sold more than 400 copies."[19] Critics who did not depend the church for their paycheck praised it. "Will Bagley's definitive *Blood of the Prophets*," wrote historian David Roberts in 2007, "amasses a powerful circumstantial case against Brigham Young." Its contents proved "so disturbing to the faithful that during the last five years, a triumvirate of high church officials has spent millions of dollars and collected bookshelves full of 'evidence' in support of a book intended to refute Bagley at every turn." Roberts's endnote credited the statement to "Richard Turley, personal communication, August 2006."[20]

When the first volume of the church's response to *Blood of the Prophets* arrived in 2008, readers discovered that its narrative ended the day after the massacre, making clear that the cover-up that began before September 11, 1857, was still grinding on. Knowing your conclusion before you begin your research is a fundamental flaw of faithful history. In September 2002, Turley told the *Chicago Sun-Times* he already knew "that Young did not plan the murders"

---

19. Dennis Lythgoe, "'Massacre' Book Has Ax to Grind: Anti-Mormon 'Tract' Compares Young to Hitler," *Deseret News*, Sept. 1, 2002, at www.deseretnews.com/article/print/934467/Massacre-book-has-ax-to-grind.html; C. G. Wallace, "Book Blames Massacre on Mormon Leader," *Chicago Sun-Times*, Sept. 22, 2002; both accessed May 18, 2019.

20. David Roberts, *Devil's Gate: Brigham Young and the Mormon Handcart Tragedy* (New York: Simon & Schuster, 2008), 316.

and had "no part in the massacre, calling it an independent plan by an isolated group of settlers."[21]

Powerful people can try to obstruct justice or suppress the truth for a variety of reasons, but guilt drives most cover-ups. Attempts by some LDS historians to refute Juanita Brooks's conclusion that "Brigham Young was accessory after the fact, in that he knew what happened, and how and why it happened," are foolhardy. She observed, "Evidence of this is abundant and unmistakable, and from the most impeccable Mormon sources." To insist that Young investigated the massacre repeatedly over fifteen years yet somehow never figured out whodunit may comfort the faithful, but such denials start with insisting Lee lied to his adopted father when he reported the massacre in late September 1857. (At the time, Lee had been ceremoniously "sealed"—or adopted—to Young as a son.) If Lee and *all* the senior LDS leaders who carried out the murders lied to Young, this raises a question apologists never ask: Why did the man Lee called "the Old Boss" keep protecting him long after the entire country knew Lee was guilty? Young knew the names of the Saints who had participated in the wholesale atrocities, Robert Glass Cleland and Juanita Brooks concluded more than fifty years ago. "Brigham Young was not a credulous simpleton: he was not duped or hoodwinked: he was not misinformed."[22] Despite this reality, for many, denial of the cover-up has remained a party line.

Over the years I've spilled a lot of ink critical of the first installment of the church's history of its worst crime. Since David Bigler and I attended the September 15, 1990, dedication of a granite monument atop Dan Sill Hill listing the names and ages of the victims and surviving children of the 1857 massacre, I have visited Mountain Meadows almost annually. In 1995 I began seriously searching for the actual site of the massacre but never found it. Neither did the church's representatives, though they claimed they had. In 2011 the National Historic Register declared the property the LDS Church now owned a National Landmark. It is unfair to classical Japanese dance-drama, but Americans have co-opted

---

21. Wallace, "Book Blames Massacre on Mormon Leader."
22. Cleland and Brooks, *A Mormon Chronicle*, 1:xiii–iv.

the word Kabuki to characterize any overly formal and ritualized event. I have participated in seven such rituals to dedicate monuments or commemorate anniversaries related to the Mountain Meadows Massacre. They often seek to promote "healing" and achieve "closure," but the atrocity is still a suppurating wound for relatives of the murdered and for Latter-day Saints who care about their faith's history. History cannot be stopped, but it can become a chronic disease that defies healing.

Blood of the Prophets described LDS Church President Gordon Hinckley's dedication of the most elaborate monument. It rebuilt the original 1859 cairn US Major James Carleton raised when he buried the remains scattered across meadows eighteen months after the murders. Its hurried construction unintentionally discovered the original burial, but on September 11, 1999, the 142nd anniversary of the massacre, Hinckley conducted another ritual in front of more than 1,000 white folks and a handful of uninvited Southern Pauites. "No one can explain what happened in these meadows 142 years ago," he said. "It is time to leave the entire matter in the hands of God. ... Let the book of the past be closed."[23]

When I heard those words, I was committed to prying open that book. I had already explored the site on November 27, 1995, to test my evolving theories about where the massacre happened. It was a beautiful day, but windy as hell and damn cold. I tried to trace the swales of the Spanish Trail pack road and the wagon road to Los Angeles from the rim of the Great Basin to see if erosion had "captured" the trail traces at the head of Magotsu Creek. I was looking for the spot where Charles Kelly photographed Frank Beckwith standing on the *east* side of an old dirt road during the 1930s at what they believed were the remnants of an 1859 army monument marking the massacre site. If I could find rocks similar to the one shown in Kelly's photo, it should identify one of the graves, so walking 570 yards up or down the trail trace would take me to the second grave.

As usual, what's easy in an armchair is complicated on the

23. Bagley, *Blood of the Prophets*, 373–76; Hart, "Let the Book of the Past Be Closed," *LDS Church News*, Sept. 18, 1999, digital copy at https://archive.sltrib.com/article.php?id=52558655&itype=CMSID.

ground: I found *several* rock piles scattered across the field. I recall searching a ravine I took to be the eroded trails, now the head of Magotsu Creek, at least on the rare occasions when water actually flows in the dry creekbed. I remembered a wide wash that had been used as a dump for worn-out washing machines. I may have walked right by the actual sites. Memory. Meh.

What I did not know was that in 1999 President Hinckley had instructed the church's real estate agents to buy and preserve as much of the meadows as possible. Over the next decade, the LDS Church acquired the sites it considered significant from the landowners using life-hold purchases and land swaps. Once it owned the land, the church nominated Mountain Meadows for National Landmark status. Paula S. Reed and Associates, Inc., of Hagerstown, Maryland, prepared the original nomination in 2010, credited to Reed and historian Edith Wallace. The original draft reflected Mormonism's tradition of "persecuted innocence" and its historical perspective of victimization, which evoked this response from a veteran public historian and member of the Nevada Writers Hall of Fame, who was serving as chair of the national historic sites board:

> The idea that this example of mass murder needs to be seen in the context of the victimization of the LDS members is weak and on occasion repugnant. Innocent people were the victims of cold-blooded mass murder, and it is inappropriate to repeat an assertion that it is understandable or somehow justified. We don't interpret Wounded Knee by discussing how Euro-Americans had suffered at the hands of Native Americans during centuries of warfare. When at the site of a mass murder, the point of view of the murderers is made invalid by the cold-blooded nature of the crime. The perpetrators of such a heinous act forever abdicate their right to be understood when interpreting that historic site. Germans suffered terribly under the onerous terms of the Versailles Treaty, but we never bring that up at Auschwitz. That would be a tasteless affront to the victims of mass murder.[24]

In June 2011, Mountain Meadows became a national historic landmark. Next to Highway 18 that September, the LDS Church unveiled a "new memorial where it is believed the boys and men

---

24. Will Bagley, Email with the chair of the Advisory Council on Historic Preservation, Oct. 26, 2010.

of the group were murdered, a little more than a mile north of the siege site"[25] After it acquired more acreage, church employees produced a revised draft credited to Chad Orton, Historian, and Benjamin C. Pykles, PhD, Historic Sites Curator, Church History Department, The Church of Jesus Christ of Latter-day Saints. Their revisions included pictures of the purported "Women's and Children's Massacre Site, Washington County, Utah" and the "Men's and Boy's Massacre Site."[26] The nomination included maps showing the "Trail Trace" of the California wagon road closely following State Route 18. I never saw a trace of any such trace.

On September 10, 2014, the three organizations representing different perspectives on the atrocity, the Mountain Meadows Association, the Mountain Meadows Massacre Descendants, and the Mountain Meadows Monument Foundation (MMMF), conducted joint ceremonies to dedicate two "newly-erected monument complexes purporting to show the locations of the two massacres and associated graves." The Church of Jesus Christ of Latter-day Saints constructed both monuments on land the Corporation of the Presiding Bishop owned.

After the 2014 rites, some of us returned to our campsite, drank gin and tonics, and pondered the solemn, sacred, and sometimes silly ceremonies of the morning. Everett Bassett made better use of his time and spent the afternoon searching for the true traces of the Spanish and California trails. To the trained eye of this talented field archeologist, the "newly-erected monument complexes" appeared to "be in an unlikely landscape for the massacres to have occurred and contradicted much of the historic record." Bassett had "uncovered a number of errors and misinterpretations" in the Mountain Meadows National Historic Landmark nomination. "An unavoidable side effect of stating where something occurred is that other possible locations can then be discounted. This is re-enforced when, as in this case, those conclusions are literally writ in stone," he noted. His concern that the atrocity's

---

25. Mark Havnes, "Mountain Meadows Group Walks Path of Victims for First Time," *Salt Lake Tribune*, Sept. 12, 2011, available at https://archive.sltrib.com/article. php?id=52558655&itype=CMSID, accessed 9 May 2019.

26. This draft is available at www.mtn-meadows-assoc.com/MountainMeadows %20NPS.pdf, accessed May 16, 2019.

actual locations and physical remains could be destroyed motivated Bassett to "attempt to identify the actual locations of the massacre sites and mass graves."[27]

A year later, in Harrison, Arkansas, Bassett described what he found to the annual gathering of the Mountain Meadows Monument Foundation: the sites of the two military graves the US Army built in 1859 to protect the scattered bones its troops had collected along the trail between the two killing grounds. All of us had been looking for a pile of stacked rocks, but Everett had followed the California/Old Spanish Trail traces on private ranchland and "was sitting on a pile of boulders when he realized that the rocks were the top layer of a tumulus," the technical term for a burial chamber or sepulcher. "It was like getting hit in the stomach," he said that night in Arkansas.

Brevet Major James Carleton "caused the distance to be measured from point to point on the scene of the massacre." His Dragoons probably carried a portable Gunter surveyor's chain and a Burt solar compass, tools that "would have enabled them to make measurements to within just a few feet over several miles." From the siege site where the Arkansans fought off a terrorist assault for five days, "to the point upon the road where the men were attacked and destroyed, and where their bones were mostly found," was 6,975 feet, about a mile and a third. The "grave where Capt. Campbell's command buried some of the remains" was here. The spot "where the women and children were butchered; a point identified from their bones and clothing" was 1,710 feet east of the first burial, Bassett observed. Here the Dragoons created a second military grave. He found both sites within five feet of the distances Carleton reported.

He found the 1859 US Army reports, which gave the distance from the siege sites to within five feet of the burials. He showed that the 2011 monument for the male victims was 2,196 feet from the actual site, and that the 2014 women and children's marker

---

27. Everett J. Bassett, "The Mountain Meadows Tumuli: The Spatial History of a Massacre Site," forthcoming in *The Journal of Historical Archeology*, draft in my possession.

was about 1,000 feet from their 1859 burial.[28] Except for the location of the siege, Bassett concluded, the other sites "have been interpreted and memorialized some distance from where they actually occurred" so the "actual locations are currently unprotected by any National Landmark status."[29]

A year later, Everett Bassett led an onsite tour. On September 10, 2016, he explained how he found the graves. My wife, Laura Bayer, observed he had "a real gift for explaining everything anybody needs to know to understand a complex issue." He led us to a solitary cedar tree standing near the edge of the ravine that had once been the Spanish Trail. Bassett estimated the tree was 400 or 500 years old and perhaps provided a landmark to begin the 1857 massacre.[30] He explained how he had used the contemporary 1859 eyewitness reports of the military burials to cut through the clutter and assumptions that had long kept the sites hidden.

"Why is it important to identify the right place?" Bassett asked. "Because if someone says something is at some place, they are also saying where it's not." If you identify the wrong place, it leaves the right place open to disaster and destruction. If you find the right place, you can learn details you would never otherwise suspect. In hindsight, little about the officially monumented sites rings true—neither the vegetation nor the distances reported in primary sources. In contrast, Bassett's analysis carefully matched the evidence.[31]

Bassett's field trip did not prepare us for the impact of anthropologist Shannon Novak's presentation that evening. Novak matched Bassett's rational professionalism. Its subject matter was even more disturbing, for it dealt not with bones hidden in mass graves, but one particular bone: the skull of a six- or seven-year-old child. Now at the National Museum of Health and Medicine, it arrived at the US Army Medical Museum in 1864, probably via

---

28. Bill Bowden, "Resting Places of Victims in 1857 Massacre Found," *Arkansas Democrat-Gazette*, Apr. 13, 2015, at www.nwaonline.com/news/2015/sep/13/resting-places-of-victims-in-1857-massa-2/, accessed May 9, 2019.

29. Bassett, "The Mountain Meadows Tumuli."

30. Higbee, Statement, in Brooks, *Mountain Meadows Massacre*, 230.

31. "Monumental Mistakes: Mountain Meadows, 1999 to 2017," Will Bagley notes, Sept. 10, 2016, Bagley Papers.

contract surgeon Charles Brewer, and was long displayed on the third floor of Ford's Theater in Washington, DC. Novak traced the artifact's impeccable provenance. Her images showed the round entry wound from a large caliber weapon and its jagged exit wound. Novak's dispassionate, professional but profoundly troubling presentation raised a question I have spent decades trying to answer: How do you persuade a religious person to put a musket or pistol against a child's temple and pull the trigger?[32]

In 1765 Voltaire answered the question: *"Certainement qui est en droit de vous rendre absurde est en droit de vous rendre injuste,"* which is often translated as "Those who can make you believe absurdities can make you commit atrocities." A more literal interpretation is "Certainly anyone who has the power to make you believe absurdities has the power to make you commit injustices."[33] It required convincing the deeply religious men who carried out the murders they were doing God's work.[34] As John D. Lee firmly believed, those who carried out the murders "considered it a religious duty to unquestioningly obey the orders which they had received. That they acted from a sense of duty to the Mormon Church, I never doubted."[35]

The men who destroyed their own lives on September 11, 1857, "were True Believers who thought they were doing God's work." I later ended presentations about the massacre with this thought: "God save us from men doing God's work."[36]

After meeting with more than two dozen Paiute elders at Santa Clara, Utah, early in February 2004, Edwin Brown Firmage, a distinguished law professor emeritus, humanitarian, and ethnic Mormon, told author Logan Hebner he had dreamed on

---

32. Novak wrote *House of Mourning: A Biocultural History of the Mountain Meadows Massacre* (Salt Lake City, Utah: University of Utah Press, 2008), which won the Society for Historical Archaeology's James Deetz Best Book Award.

33. Norman Torrey, *Les Philosophes. The Philosophers of the Enlightenment and Modern Democracy* (New York: Capricorn Books, 1961), 277–278.

34. Will Bagley, *Blood of the Prophets: Brigham Young and the Massacre at Mountain Meadows* (Norman: University of Oklahoma Press, 2002), xv, 380–381.

35. John D. Lee, *Mormonism Unveiled; or the Life and Confessions of the Late Mormon Bishop, John D. Lee* (St. Louis: Bryan, Brand & Company, 1877), 213–14.

36. "Big Trouble: The Legacy of Mountain Meadows," presentation at the Bennion Institute, Utah State University, Aug. 7, 2007, copy in Bagley Papers.

Easter Sunday of "a river of blood, with various ghastly historic events bobbing along, but finally with the bones of MM [Mountain Meadows] pulling together, walking and talking." Said Ed: "The answer to yesterday's questions are here today and will reveal themselves tomorrow. The bones are beginning to walk."[37] Firmage's vision proved prophetic. As Geoffrey Chaucer wrote long ago, "Murder will out," and so will the truth.

When powerful organizations want to exert their power in the provinces that they rule, they can bend federal authorities to their will. They can even acquire and manage the site of a notorious mass murder, put it on the National Historic Register as a National Historic Landmark, and mark the sites they own with monuments. What happens when they mark the wrong locations? They buy the right ones.

On November 2, 2018, archeologist and LDS Church Historic Sites Curator Benjamin Pykles notified the board of the Mountain Meadows Monument Foundation that the church had completed its purchase of the Kay Robert Ence family property bordering Utah Highway 28 at Mountain Meadows.[38] This meant that the church now owned all the land within the National Historic Landmark the National Park Service established at Mountain Meadows in 2011, and more, including the sites of the two 1859 burials Everett Basset discovered. "The months-long endeavor is a great win for our collective goal of preserving the grave sites located on the Ence land," the December 2018 MMMF newsletter announced. "Next steps include working with the National Park Service and the Utah State Historic Preservation to ask for their counsel on protecting the tumuli, and to obtain their support in order to add this site to the National Historic Landmark."[39]

What compels people to commit such horrific acts? At the trial that convicted John D. Lee, when asked why he had participated in mass murder, Nephi Johnson said, "I didn't think it

---

37. Logan Hebner, Communication with Will Bagley, Sept. 15, 2016.

38. Ence died on September 26, 2017. For his obituary, see *Spectrum and Daily News*, Sept. 30, 2017; digital copy at www.legacy.com/obituaries/thespectrum/obituary.aspx?n=kay-ence&pid=186795904, accessed Dec. 14, 2018.

39. *Newsletter*, Mountain Meadows Monument Foundation, Dec. 2018, 3.

was safe for me to object." What did he fear? Cedar City's leaders made him afraid *not* to do what they told him to do.[40] Visiting Mountain Meadows always begs even the casual tourist to stare evil in the face. Thirty years and dozens of visits haven't blunted the difficulty of facing the hard questions, and the shape-shifting nature of this embattled history is still a ghostly phantom. By 1880 virtually every possible explanation, account, interpretation, elucidation, excuse, or rationalization had appeared in the territory's independent newspapers, the *Valley Tan, Union Vedette*, and *Salt Lake Tribune*, or in the LDS-managed *Mountaineer, Deseret News*, or *Salt Lake Herald*. Both perspectives framed the story as part of a conspiracy to promote, avenge, or destroy the Latter-day Saints and their prophets. Yet when Juanita Brooks summarized her conclusions in *The Mountain Meadows Massacre*, number one was: "While Brigham Young and George A. Smith, the church authorities chiefly responsible, did not specially order the massacre, they did preach sermons and set up social conditions that made it possible."[41] Having identified those who were morally responsible for the atrocity, is everything else inside baseball?

The longer I've studied at Mountain Meadows the more I'm convinced that our best guesses about what happened are the only answers we'll ever have. Whatever took place is probably much worse than the known awful elements of this "awful tale." Much of what we "know" is based on the artful lies of fanatics who made lying a way of life. Only a few bones of truth—such as Nephi Johnson's statement that "White men did most of the killing"—project from the dusty earth of lies that cover the meadows.

How much has corporate Mormonism spent on its twenty-first century Mountain Meadows project? The Acknowledgments in the first installment, which extended "special thanks" to fifteen colleagues in the Family and Church History Department, provided enough evidence to make an informed guess. Multiplying $125,000 (my "burdened cost") by fifteen yields $1,875,000 per annum, even without counting the expense of visiting archives in

---

40. Testimony of Nephi Johnson, Second Trial of John D. Lee, Lee Trial Transcripts, W. L. Cook Papers.

41. Brooks, *The Mountain Meadows Massacre*, 219.

thirty-one states or the salaries paid the three lead authors, all senior church employees.[42]

It took seven years to produce volume one. Estimating the
project had an annual cost of $2 million means by 2008 the cor-
poration had spent at least $14 million to produce a book that
ends the day after the massacre. Mountain Meadows has cost the
Church of Jesus Christ of Latter-day Saints some $20 million in
the twenty-first century. Sadly, the Mormon historical establishment has yet to produce a single thesis Charles Penrose did not
propose in 1884.

At a symposium commemorating Wallace Stegner's hundredth
birthday in 2009, historian Richard White said when he heard
about how much money the LDS Church had spent to counter
Blood of the Prophets, he thought, "What greater validation could
a historian want?" I'd love to say right on and shut up, but it is in
my nature to write on. The scope and occasional nastiness of the
church's response to my work makes me crazy. I know it shouldn't,
but it does. I admire the dispassionate history and anthropology
my professional colleagues produce, but I am a passionate historian and react to attacks on my work and character passionately.

Since history never stops, historians will find new evidence
about Mountain Meadows as long as they keep looking. Consider
independent researcher Connell O'Donovan's discovery of what
may be a document written by a member of the extended Brigham
Young family describing the massacre by September 21, 1858.[43]

Blood of the Prophets asked a key question about the Mountain
Meadows massacre: What did Brigham Young know, and when
did he know it? During John D. Lee's 1876 trial, Mormon zealot
Jacob Hamblin testified he told "President Young and George A.
Smith" about the crime "pretty soon after it happened." He gave
them the facts and provided more details "than I have here, because I recollected more," Hamblin recalled. Thanks to the LDS

42. Ronald W. Walker, Richard E. Turley, and Glen M. Leonard, *Massacre at Mountain Meadows: An American Tragedy* (New York: Oxford University Press, 2008), 233–241.

43. Connell O'Donovan, "The Earliest Written Account of the Mountain Mead-ows Meadows Massacre?" *Journal of Mormon History* 39, 4 (Fall 2013): 144–57.

Church's decision to "open all of its records," we now know when Brigham Young learned everything he needed to know about the crime. On June 19, 1858, a stormy Saturday "with heavy rains," Hamblin visited LDS Church Historian George A. Smith "in regard to the Santa Clara Indians [and] gave an account of the Massacre at Mountain meadows."[44]

Some old arguments will never change. As bookman Ken Sanders observed. "I don't believe any faithful Mormon will ever believe that Brigham Young knew about or caused the Mountain Meadows Massacre, and there's no gentile [non-Mormon] that thinks otherwise."[45] Historians will argue these points to the end of human time, but the last word about the bloodbath is best left to Eleanor Tom, a brave Southern Paiute elder: "Now, nobody'd listen to an Indian anyway. The whites, they won that story."[46]

44. Bagley, *Blood of the Prophets*, xiv, 136–137, 304–305, 382; Historical Department Journal, June 19, 1858, p. 2, Box 2, Folder 21, CR 1234, LDS Church History Library.

45. KUER Radio West Podcast, "Summer Reading," June 7, 2017, 39 minutes, 22 seconds.

46. Qtd. in Logan Hebner and Michael L. Plyler, *Southern Paiute: A Portrait* (Logan: Utah State University Press, 2010), 79.

PLURAL ACCIDENTS
WRITING IN SACRED LONELINESS

TODD COMPTON

3

In Sacred Loneliness: The Plural Wives of Joseph Smith, published by Signature Books in 1997, was written as the result of a series of odd accidents. Before starting to learn about the wives of the founding prophet of the Church of Jesus Christ of Latter-day Saints (also known as the Mormon Church), I had no particular interest in Mormon polygamy. In fact, I had no interest in ever writing about any subject in Mormon history. I did enjoy Mormon history, and had dipped into it a bit. At annual Sunstone symposiums, I thoroughly enjoyed history sessions, and though a fairly conventional, if liberal-tending, Mormon, I enjoyed edgy subjects. Problems in Mormon history were *interesting*. We had Juanita Brooks's *Mountain Meadows Massacre* on our bookshelves at home when I grew up, and I later read books and articles by Samuel Taylor and D. Michael Quinn. While living in southern California as a graduate student at UCLA, I attended the periodic meetings of the Miller-Eccles Study Group, which invited Mormon scholars and historians to speak, so heard memorable presentations by people such as Leonard Arrington, Paul Edwards, and Stanley Kimball.

Nevertheless, at LDS Church-owned Brigham Young University in Provo, Utah, I had been a follower of Hugh Nibley—arguably, the church's best-known defender of Mormon scripture as ancient texts—and was studying ancient languages, ritual, myth, apocrypha, and the history of religion. After I got my BA in English in 1979, I changed my major every three months for a while, but finally settled down in Classics, ancient Greek and Latin. I got a master's in Classics at BYU, then went to UCLA for my PhD, starting in 1983. I chose the UCLA Classics department because it had a professor, Jaan Puhvel, who specialized in comparative myth.

Just as Nibley wrote a few books on LDS history, so my fellow Nibley-acolyte friends and I had an interest in LDS history, with its quirks, contradictions, and drama. But that definitely was not a research focus for me.

There is also a component of history in Classics—Herodotus, Thucydides, Livy, Tacitus. I studied as well palaeography and textual criticism, which gave me a deep respect for primary documents. And there would be a history component in my doctoral dissertation—titled "The Exile of the Poet: Bardic Expulsion and Death in the Archaic Greek and Indo-European Traditions"—which dealt with stories of poets who came to act as scapegoats and exiles in myth, legend, and history. But none of this led me to work with *modern* history—say, history after 1500 CE.

So there was nothing logical or predictable that would lead me to write *In Sacred Loneliness*. Circumstances in our lives are sometimes the result of mysterious, odd accidents. Here's how this particular chain of unlikely occurrences took place.

After finishing my PhD at UCLA (in 1988), I taught Classics for a year across town at USC. I knew it was not a permanent job—it was something that might help me get an appointment someplace else. But as my time at USC came to an end, my employment prospects were not looking good. Jobs in Classics were scarce. One heard stories of seventy-five or more applications for every job opening in the field, and applicants from Ivy-league schools back east, as well as from Chicago and Berkeley, enjoyed a big advantage. It was a difficult time in my life, as it was starting to look as if everything I had been working for would not come to fruition. It was emotionally devastating. I would somehow have to find some non-teaching job. I began doing temp jobs in Los Angeles to get by.

I was single, attending singles wards in the L.A. and Santa Monica area. I had a friend in the LDS L.A. First Ward, Janet Ellingson, who ended up moving back to Utah, then, out of the blue, started a doctoral program in American history at the University of

Utah. As a history student, she applied for, and received, a summer grant from the Henry E. Huntington Library, back in southern California, in San Marino, near Pasadena, which has a marvelous collection of documents in American history and a sizable collection of Mormon documents. They had acquired the diaries of John D. Lee, one of the perpetrators of the infamous Mountain Meadows Massacre, which led to historian Juanita Brooks visiting the library in 1944 and editing the diaries, in the early 1950s. As a result, Brooks began collecting documents from southern Utah for the Huntington.[1]

So in summer 1991 Janet was back in our small group of friends in L.A. First Ward, and the Huntington was paying her to go read Mormon documents full time in their library and archives every day for a couple months. As for me, I was trying to get my doctoral thesis on scapegoat poets into shape so I could get it published. I

1. Levi S. Peterson, *Juanita Brooks: Mormon Woman Historian* (Salt Lake City: University of Utah Press, 1988), 147, 212.

thought that if a good university press accepted it, I *might* be able to find a job in Classics.

At this point Janet suggested that I apply to the Huntington Library to receive a summer fellowship. The Huntington had the overland diaries of Eliza Snow, she said; apply to work on them. (Snow was a well-known leader in the early LDS Church, a brilliant woman, a poet, the second president of the LDS women's organization, the Relief Society. She had been a plural wife of Joseph Smith in Nauvoo, Illinois, and later, after Smith's death in 1844, a plural wife of Brigham Young, the second LDS prophet-president.) Janet followed this up by sending me a letter and suggesting things that I could write in the application: "here's the info for the Huntington fellowships. I've been thinking about the E R Snow diaries and have decided the project would be worth doing (not that my opinion matters much) and hope you seriously pursue the project. ... I think Snow's experience would work well to identify gender boundaries and issues of male/female authority."[2]

Now, I thought this was a crazy idea. I still think it was a crazy idea. I had no background in Mormon history; I had no background in women in Mormon history. My research interests centered on ancient myth, ritual, the history of religions. I had no real inclination to work on the Snow diaries, and no real qualifications for getting the fellowship.

But I looked the application over. It didn't look like it would take too much work. And Janet had almost written it for me. I spent an hour or so finishing the application, wrote some quick letters to people I knew for recommendations, and sent the application in. I wouldn't get it, I knew. I had no background in Mormon history.

We have now had two improbable events—one, that Janet would come up with the idea to encourage me to apply for a grant to work on the diaries of Eliza R. Snow, and, two, that I would actually take her advice and apply for the grant. After I sent off the application, I completely forgot about it, as I *knew* that I would not receive a summer fellowship from the Huntington to work on Mormon history.

---

2. Janet Ellingson, Letter to Todd Compton, undated, in my possession.

And then, of course, the third improbable event happened: To my complete surprise, a few months later, out of the blue I got a letter from the Huntington that informed me that I had been awarded a summer grant to work on the diaries of Eliza R. Snow. I was floored. But happy.

In summer 1992 I entered the Huntington Library as a visiting fellow. The Huntington is known as a paradise for scholars—a fabulous repository of literary and historical documents and rare books, surrounded by the gorgeous Huntington Gardens. And by some mysterious quirk of fate, I was being paid to go there and read all day, for a couple months. Janet's bizarre plan that I knew would never work somehow had succeeded.

Of course, I realized, now I would have to do something with the Snow diaries.

It was a great moment when I entered the reading room of the Huntington, with its long desks and bookcases with rare books, set up my primitive grey laptop computer, and ordered Eliza R. Snow's diaries. (More specifically, these were her overland diaries, written as she crossed the plains to the Great Salt Lake Valley in 1847—there were also Nauvoo diaries by Snow in the archives of the LDS Church.) I had already tracked down some non-scholarly transcriptions of these diaries published much earlier in the LDS Church's monthly periodical for adults, the *Improvement Era*. But when I was given one of the two little volumes and sat down to read them, it was exciting. Snow had sat by the campfire at night and written her daily report in these very notebooks. The entries were in her neat, precise handwriting, and in her inimitable literary style, so different from the great majority of the Mormon documents I would read later (which were in a more idiomatic, less grammatical and formal style).

For example, here is one day from that diary:

Mo. [August] 23 [1847] This mor. sis. P. broil'd some buff. meat which Capt. M. kill'd yes. but it seem'd to have been the father of all buffalos & uneatable. We start at 8 with Capt. N. in front and Prest. Y. & Capt. G. in the rear. In about 3 ms. cross a stream—come onto the Platte in about 8 ms., which seems like meeting an old friend—find an inscription "90 ms. to Ft. Johns"—go 2 ms. cross Deer Creek, bait & dine—a dish of tea is very acceptable—The day clear—the road pretty smooth but very hilly & barren. A windy thunderstorm before night. Trav. 15 ms.

When you read the works of Homer, say, or Herodotus, you are reading copies of copies of copies, manuscripts dating to the Middle Ages, long after the author had lived. Here I was reading an actual handwritten manuscript made by the author herself, on the actual day that the events had occurred. It was an exciting contrast.

I began typing a transcript of the diaries from the printed version, so I could correct the transcript, and start to annotate it.

It was at this point that *In Sacred Loneliness* began. When you annotate, I knew, you must try to explain words and cultural elements that are unclear to modern readers, which includes identifying all the people mentioned in the text. So there were many entries in Snow's journal that identified people in a kind of shorthand—instantly understandable to Snow herself, or to her friends, but to a modern reader with no knowledge of Snow's life, incomprehensible. For example:

> tu. June 1st [1847] This is truly a glorious time with the mothers & daughters in Zion altho' thrust out from the land of our forefathers & from the endearments of civiliz'd life. This forenoon made a cap for sis. Pierce in the afternoon visited at sis. Miller's in com. of Priscinda Zina, sis. Chase, Cristene &c. after supper sis. Whitney, Kimball, Sessions came in and we had a spiritual feast in very deed

Sometimes she would simply give an initial, such as "Sister C."

To understand the people mentioned in passages like this, I found that lists of related people were very useful. For example, the list of the church's twelve apostles and their wives at the time of the diary was helpful. On the overland journey, there were lists of leaders of companies. For women, I knew that Snow had been a plural wife of Joseph Smith and was at the time of the overland diary a plural wife of Brigham Young. Therefore, it would be helpful to get good, reliable lists of Smith's and Young's wives. I also knew that Snow had many friends among the plural wives of Heber C. Kimball, Young's right hand man and counselor in the governing First Presidency. These lists would intersect, as many of Smith's widows married Young and Kimball.

So I went to the secondary literature in search of such lists. For Young, I found lists and analyses of wives and families by Jeffery Johnson, Dean Jessee, and Leonard Arrington.[3] For Heber C. Kimball, I found an excellent description of his families in a long appendix to Stanley Kimball's biography *Heber C. Kimball: Mormon Patriarch and Pioneer* (published in 1981 by the University of Illinois Press).

The only scholarly list of Smith's wives that I could find was the long appendix to Fawn Brodie's controversial biography, *No Man Knows My History: The Life of Joseph Smith* (first published by Alfred A. Knopf in 1945). While Brodie's list of forty-eight women was useful, it was also problematic. It was half a century old, compiled in 1945, long before the recent modernization and partial opening of the LDS Archives in the 1970s. As a result, it lacked many primary sources now available, and sometimes used sources that did not seem reliable.[4] Some women were listed as Smith's wives who weren't reliably documented. In one case, because of the complexity of one woman's marital history—Elizabeth Davis Goldsmith Brackenbury Durfee Smith Lott, with her five marriages—Brodie listed her twice, once as Mrs. Durfee, number 11, and once as Elizabeth Davis, number 38.

I've criticized the mistakes Brodie made in preparing a list of Smith's wives that was not always reliable. However, we also need to bear in mind that the LDS Archives was not open at the time of her research. You also have to respect Brodie's pioneering, if sometimes flawed, accomplishment, as she was the only LDS scholar to attempt a scholarly list of Smith's wives.[5] The fact that the topic

---

3. Jeffery Ogden Johnson, "Determining and Defining 'Wife': The Brigham Young Households," *Dialogue: A Journal of Mormon Thought* 20, 3 (Fall 1987): 57–70; Leonard J. Arrington, *Brigham Young: American Moses* (New York: Alfred A. Knopf, 1985), 420–21. Dean C. Jessee, "Brigham Young's Family," *Brigham Young University Studies* 18, 3 (1978): 311–27, and "Brigham Young's Family: The Wilderness Years," *Brigham Young University Studies* 19, 4 (1979): 474–500, at 476. See now Colleen Whitley, ed., *Brigham Young's Homes* (Logan: Utah State University Press, 2002).

4. See my "Fawn Brodie on Joseph Smith's Plural Wives and Polygamy: A Critical View," in *Reconsidering* No Man Knows My History: *Fawn M. Brodie and Joseph Smith in Retrospect*, ed. Newell G. Bringhurst (Logan: Utah State University Press, 1996), 154–94.

5. Andrew Jenson, an assistant church historian, had published a list of Smith's wives in 1887, see below. However, at this time I was looking for modern scholarship on the subject.

had not been treated by "traditionalist" LDS scholars in half a century shows that the subject of Smith's Nauvoo polygamy, or plural marriage, had become a "taboo" subject of sorts.[6]

Therefore, I started making my own list of Smith's plural wives. At first this was purely to help me identify the women in Snow's diary. I realized I would need, as a basis, good evidence that the woman married Smith during his lifetime. (This would disqualify many women who plurally married—"sealed to" is the term members of the church often use—Smith after his death.) Ideally this evidence would include the date of marriage to Smith. (I defined marriage as a union with a marriage ceremony of some sort.) Then I would need the birth name of the woman, her birth and death dates, and her full marriage history, with names of husband(s), marriage dates, and dates of divorce or separation. Marriage history was important because in diaries often a woman was referred to as Sister [surname], and many women married men civilly before their marriage to Smith, and after. Names and birthdates of children would help in solidifying the marriage history.

For example, in the Snow diary entry quoted above, "sis. ... Kimball" was Vilate Murray Kimball, born Vilate Murray to Roswell Murray and Susannah Fitch Murray on June 1, 1806. She married Heber C. Kimball on November 7, 1822, and had a large family with him. He subsequently married approximately forty-three plural wives. Vilate died on October 22, 1867.

In the case of Elizabeth Davis Goldsmith Brackenbury Durfee Smith Lott, she was sometimes referred to in contemporary records as Sister Goldsmith, Sister Brackenbury, or Sister Durfee. This led to Brodie's understandable confusion. Just to add to the historical complexity, Elizabeth went back to using her Brackenbury surname in her later life (as I eventually learned, see below).

---

6. I've been told that during this time period some graduate level religion students at BYU wanted to do theses on Smith's polygamy but were told that the subject was too controversial and thus off limits. As one administrator reportedly said, "There are three things you can't write about here: blacks and the priesthood, the Mountain Meadows Massacre, and Joseph Smith's polygamy." D. Michael Quinn would publish a list of Smith's wives in 1994, which was helpful but was not footnoted: *The Mormon Hierarchy: Origins of Power* (Salt Lake City: Signature Books/Smith Reseaerch Associates, 1994), 587–88.

Often a woman's polygamous marriage to a man was secret, especially in the Nauvoo period (1839–46), and so in contemporary diaries she is not known by the "polygamous" marriage name. Smith's plural wives were never known as "Sister Smith" in contemporary records. In the Snow diary entry above, "Priscinda Zina" were Presendia Lathrop Huntington Buell Kimball and Zina Diantha Huntington Jacobs Smith Young, sisters, both plural wives of Smith, and later, respectively, of Heber C. Kimball and of Brigham Young. Both sisters were close friends of Snow.

Snow is an interesting case. Technically, her name was Eliza R. Snow Smith Young. She was known throughout her life as "Eliza R. Snow," despite her marriages to Smith and Young, but sometimes signed her name Eliza R. Snow Smith.

To understand a woman's marriage names, I found that you needed to do more than simple genealogy—you needed to find the stories behind the marriages. So I began to collect any autobiographies, diaries, or biographies of these women, along with standard historical sources, such as birth or marriage records or newspaper stories that mentioned the women. I found that creating a residence history for each woman was also helpful.

Every one of these steps was fraught with peril for the careless historian. For example, simply establishing that a woman married Smith during his lifetime was not easy. Unfortunately, there is no known, extant contemporary record of Smith's plural marriages kept during the Nauvoo period. A few Nauvoo plural marriages are mentioned in contemporary diaries. If a non-eyewitness, late source mentioned a woman as a wife of Smith, I accepted that as a guide for further research, but not as a final, certain source.

Andrew Jenson, an LDS Church historian, published a list of twenty-seven plural wives of Smith in 1887.[7] I found this to be an excellent, though incomplete, start for further research. Jenson knew some of Smith's plural wives personally, and they helped him locate and contact other wives. In addition, Joseph F. Smith, the son of Joseph Smith's brother Hyrum, had collected affidavits from some of his uncle's plural wives, in his attempts to counter

---

7. Andrew Jenson, "Plural Marriage," *Historical Record* 6 (May 1887): 219–40.

the position championed by the RLDS Church that Smith never practiced polygamy. (The Reorganized Church of Jesus Christ of Latter Day Saints was a branch of Mormonism that stayed in the Midwest and is now called the Community of Christ. The RLDS Church did not believe that Joseph Smith practiced polygamy.) I did not have access to the originals of Joseph F. Smith's affidavits, but Danel Bachman, an LDS Church educator, had listed and discussed them extensively in an important thesis he wrote on Smith's polygamy.[8]

As I began to work on my list of Smith's plural wives, the list turned into little biographies, and the little biographies turned into bigger biographies. I eventually came up with thirty-three women whose plural marriages to Smith during his lifetime were supported by solid evidence, in my view. In a separate list, I compiled ten or so names of women who were reputed to have married Smith, but who didn't yet have evidence solid enough for me. I regarded them as topics for further research. However, in excluding them from my list of thirty-three, I was possibly operating from an excess of caution.[9]

Sometimes there were knotty tangles of documentation regarding these women's marriages and lives. The riddles were not just secret polygamous marriages. I found that many of these women did not have death dates or birth dates. An equally annoying problem was women who had two or three birth dates or death dates—which I thought was too much of a good thing. There were also puzzles related to these women's children and husbands. Puzzles simply led to more puzzles.

One fascinating element in Smith's plural marriage practice was polyandry, in which a woman was married to Smith but stayed married to her "first husband" after the plural marriage ceremony

---

8. Danel Bachman, "A Study of the Mormon Practice of Plural Marriage before the Death of Joseph Smith," MA thesis, Purdue University, 1975.

9. Quinn's list of Smith's wives included forty-six women, *The Mormon Hierarchy: Origins of Power*, 587–88. George D. Smith, in his *Nauvoo Polygamy: "... But We Called It Celestial Marriage"* (Salt Lake City: Signature Books, 2008), lists thirty-seven plural wives. Brian C. Hales adds two plural wives to my count of thirty-three: *Joseph Smith's Polygamy*, 3 vols. (Salt Lake City: Greg Kofford Books, 2013), 1:24–25. Richard Lyman Bushman has thirty-two in his count: *Joseph Smith: Rough Stone Rolling* (New York: Alfred A. Knopf, 2005), 644n1.

to Smith.[10] I was not the first person to write about this subject. Danel Bachman and Richard Van Wagoner had already written pioneering treatments of it.[11] But the practice greatly complicated my attempts to come up with full names clearly reflecting marriage histories for these women.

For example, in the Snow entry quoted above, "sis. ... Sessions" was Patty Bartlett Sessions Smith Parry. She had been born Patty Bartlett to Enoch Bartlett and Anna Hall Bartlett on February 4, 1795. She married David Sessions on June 28, 1812, at the age of seventeen, and they had a large family. She married Joseph Smith (polyandrously) on March 9, 1842, but continued to live with Sessions. She became a widow in the Smith marriage on June 27, 1844 (when Smith was killed), but her marriage to Sessions remained. She became a widow in her Sessions marriage on August 11, 1850. On December 14, 1851, she married John Parry, who died sixteen years later, on January 13, 1868. Patty herself finally died on December 14, 1892. (It is difficult to write her name in a way that captures her marriage to David Sessions: Patty Bartlett Sessions Smith Parry makes it sound as though she married Smith after parting from Sessions.)

I had to struggle to make sense of the ideology of Smith's polyandrous marriages. Working from the pioneering treatments of Bachman and Van Wagoner, I collected any references to the reasons for polyandry in the historical record. I found that it was rarely discussed. Perhaps this was one of the reasons that Smith's polygamy had become a taboo subject for the institutional LDS Church.

---

10. Some scholars, such as Lawrence Foster, reject the term polyandry for Nauvoo "complex" marriages. Lawrence Foster, "Why 'Polyandry' Isn't the Right Term to Describe Joseph Smith's Marriages to Women Who Remained Legally Married to Other Men: Personal Reflections On a Difficult Issue and How It Might Be Resolved," talk given at Mormon History Association Conference, June 29, 2012. I think the term "polyandry" is valid as long as one recognizes that a woman was married to two men at the same time with different kinds of marriages. One was a legal marriage for time only; the other was a "sacred" marriage for both time and eternity.

11. Bachman, "A Study of the Mormon Practice of Plural Marriage"; Richard S. Van Wagoner, "Mormon Polyandry in Nauvoo," *Dialogue: A Journal of Mormon Thought*, 18:3 (Fall 1985): 67–83, and Van Wagoner, *Mormon Polygamy: A History* (Salt Lake City: Signature Books, 1986), 38–44.

I also wanted to understand what the dynamics of these marriages might be. I found that in all the cases I could identify, the woman continued to live with her "first husband." To document this, I had to pursue "residence" histories of the women and their husbands to the extent it was possible to do so.

So my research at the Huntington was split in two related compartments. One was transcribing and annotating Snow's diaries; the second was continuing to compile this collection of thirty-three short biographies.

Any genealogist or historian will understand the excitement I felt as I tracked down clues to give substance to these often forgotten women. Just to get a good birthday and birth name for a lesser-known wife was exhilarating. Finding obscure marriages and marriage dates was always a triumph. I also began to take an interest in siblings of the wives and the wives' children. This was exciting detective work, putting pieces of complex puzzles together. Working out the details of the polyandrous marriages was also fascinating.

I began to find diaries, letters, and autobiographies of these women in the Huntington. One that stood out for me was the diary and autobiography of Eliza Partridge Smith Lyman. (A daughter of early LDS leader Edward Partridge, she and sister Emily as teenagers lived in the Joseph Smith household in Nauvoo as maids/nannies. He married both secretly. After Smith's death, Emily married Brigham Young, and Eliza married Amasa Lyman, an apostle.) It was a beautiful, haunting diary, written in a gentle, precise style, documenting a struggle for survival in south-central Utah, and a husband who was often absent.[12] One example of Partridge's style: Her sons Platte and Joseph settled San Juan country via the famous Hole in the Rock route over the Colorado River, one of the epic adventures in Utah history, and the next year Platte came back to take her to San Juan. Eliza wrote, "We had a very cold and uncomfortable time on the first part of the journey, but more pleasant and comfortable after we crossed the Colorado. The road was as bad as could possibly be and be traveled over at all,

---

12. This was later published as *Eliza Maria Partridge Journal*, ed. Scott H. Partridge (Provo, Utah: Grandin Book Co., 2003).

but the Lord preserved us from accident and we arrived in safety at our journey's end." Her daughter Lucy Zina adds a few details: "We camped at the 'Hole-in-the-Rock' on the Escalante Desert for the horses and cattle to rest. We made bread for a week's travel using only 'shad scale' [saltbush] for wood. I put a loaf under my pillow at night to keep it from freezing but next morning it was frozen solid."[13]

After reading diaries and similar documents (including the diary of Eliza R. Snow), I started to develop an attachment to these women. And I started writing longer biographies than I had at first expected. I realized that I wanted to research the entire lives of these women, not just their time as wives of Joseph Smith in Nauvoo.

I should mention that during my time at UCLA, I was impacted by a number of sources that led me to be seriously interested in women in history. One influence was the New Testament classes of S. Scott Bartchy, who showed how social justice, concern for minorities and the poor, was a central concern of the early Christian church. He also emphasized how women had a significantly higher status in the early New Testament church than is commonly understood. In addition, some of my good friends in the Classics department were women interested in women's issues, and they recommended books and articles for me to read. These influences led me to be interested in telling the stories of Joseph Smith's plural wives more fully, from their own points of view, not viewing them simply as appendages to famous men (in this case, Smith, Young, Kimball, and other male church leaders).

The Huntington also had the extensive diaries of Oliver Huntington, the brother of Zina and Presendia Huntington, on microfilm. I had the time, because of the summer grant, so I read through these diaries and took notes. They did give insights into the enigmatic complex marriages of his two sisters, and were eye-opening for many reasons.

When I was about halfway through my time at the Huntington, I received a gentle shock—I was contacted by Maureen Ursenbach

---

13. See Compton, *In Sacred Loneliness*, 450.

Beecher, *the* authority on Eliza R. Snow in the LDS historical community. It turned out that Janet and I had been naïve in thinking that the Eliza R. Snow diaries at the Huntington had simply been ignored. Maureen was far along in the project of editing all of Eliza's diaries and life writings for publication with the University of Utah Press.[14] She had heard through the Mormon history grapevine that I was starting to work on such a project too. So I agreed to turn my focus entirely toward Joseph Smith's plural wives. As it turned out, Maureen and I were able to help each other in our separate but related projects. I helped her check and correct some parts of her transcription of the Snow diary against the originals at the Huntington; and she was generous in sharing many documents related to Smith's plural wives. I visited her in her office at BYU once (Provo is my home town) and found her to be expansive and friendly. We went to make some copies at one point, ran into Leonard Arrington, and she introduced us—a memorable moment for me, and I'm sure instantly forgotten by him!

———————

By the time I finished my time in the paradise for scholars, the Huntington, I was committed to writing a book about the plural wives of Joseph Smith whom I had identified. I was now engaged in an all-consuming historical detective quest—quick, Watson, the game's afoot!—combined with a strong emotional bond with thirty-three remarkable women.

Readers will readily appreciate what a brilliant career move this was—writing a book on early Mormon polygamy was the perfect way to get a job teaching ancient Greek and Latin.

My next step was clear: I had to visit important libraries for Mormon history, especially the mother lode of Mormon documents, the LDS Church library and archives in Salt Lake City.

People often ask: Where do you find your sources? The answer is easy: The great majority are from archives and reading rooms of libraries. In a different generation, historians such as Juanita Brooks would often track down documents privately held by descendants of early LDS Church figures. I did very little of this

---

14. Eventually published as Maureen Ursenbach Beecher, ed., *The Personal Writings of Eliza Roxcy Snow* (Salt Lake City: University of Utah Press, 1995).

kind of thing. I wasn't living in Utah, and I didn't have the contacts that Brooks had. But there were many documents relevant to my interest that were in libraries with Mormon collections. (I did get some documents and feedback from descendants of Smith's wives and others.) I should mention that the Internet was undeveloped at that time. Today, many primary documents are available on-line in digital collections of archives and libraries, and sites like *Internet Archive* (which has many rare Mormon books and magazines) and *Utah Digital Newspapers* with searchable runs of the *Deseret News* and *Salt Lake Tribune*; but back then, there were none of these resources. I was just delighted that the Huntington had many nineteenth-century Utah newspapers on microfilm.

I worked with libraries in California and prepared for a research trip to Salt Lake City. Curiously enough, two of my thirty-three women, Elizabeth Davis Goldsmith Brackenbury Durfee Smith Lott and Agnes Moulton Coolbrith Smith Smith Smith Pickett, had lived in California. Agnes's first marriage was to Joseph Smith's brother Don Carlos, and their precocious daughter, Josephine, became a famous poetess in California, taking her mother's maiden surname as her pen name—publishing her poems as Ina Coolbrith. (Another example of how widely-used names can be problematic for family historians: I would construct her real name as Josephine Donna Smith Carsley.) She is well known in California's literary history, a friend of Bret Harte, Joaquin Miller, John Muir, and Jack London. Ina had had a painful marriage with Robert Carsley, which ended in divorce in Los Angeles, and I went to L.A.'s downtown civil archives and, to my surprise and delight, found her divorce papers, written in a difficult legal handwriting style. There were collections of Ina Coolbrith papers in the Huntington and in the California State Archives in San Francisco, and in the Oakland Library, where she had been a librarian. In her letters Ina often mentioned her mother.

When it came time to go to Utah, I informed the temp agency where I worked that I would be gone for a couple months, and took off. (As I did not have formal employment, this was not a problem.) I visited my parents in St. George on the way up, then stayed with my sister Tammy and her kids, Brittany and Jacob, in

Salt Lake City, sleeping on a couch in her kitchen, being awakened periodically through the night by her cat playing with toys on the slick kitchen floor. (At other times, I stayed with my sister Tina in Salt Lake's Avenues neighborhood.) While I was researching and writing *In Sacred Loneliness*, I was living in what could reasonably be described as poverty, in a small studio apartment in Santa Monica, without health insurance, without a steady job. If I'd have gotten a job teaching Classics, I never would have applied for the Huntington fellowship, and might have been living anywhere in America. In a way I was lucky that my academic career had foundered, though it was certainly depressing during those years, and I lived with a constant sense of insecurity. This gave me freedom, in a way; I was able to be more adventurous in my research. Without that complete failure to find a college-level teaching job, I never would have had the privilege, honor, and pure fun of researching and writing *In Sacred Loneliness*.

One day, in late 1992 or early 1993, I showed up at the LDS Church Library and Archives, on the first two floors of the east wing of the towering Church Office Building on North Temple Street. (The present Church History Library building, across the street, came later.) I didn't know what to expect. I had decided to be completely forthcoming regarding the focus of my research, and I didn't know how the people in charge would respond.

As it turned out, I had a great experience at the Church Archives. I decided not to ask for the more controversial, restricted documents, such as the William Clayton Nauvoo diaries, but instead to focus on diaries, letters, and autobiographies of the women on my list. Among the exciting documents I found there were the heartbreaking letters of Louisa Beaman Smith Young, which told of the loss of her children in early Utah and her own approaching death by cancer.[15] Here is her account of the death of one of her twins:

> I am led to think at times their is not much else but sorrow and affliction in this world for me, the next day after I arrived in the valley my babes were both taken sik with the bowell complaint the canker set in

---

15. I later edited these for publication as "'Remember Me in My Affliction': Louisa Beaman Young and Eliza R. Snow Letters, 1849," *Journal of Mormon History* 25, 2 (Fall 1999): 46–69.

and on the 11. of Oct I was called upon ᵗᵒ give up the oldest one and his litle spirett took its flight to join with his brothers and father in Heaven, my anxiety was all turned towards the other that was living.

I also found the diary and autobiography of Emily Partridge Smith Young, which were as memorable as her sister Eliza's writings. Her difficult experiences as a wife in the large Brigham Young family were certainly arresting. She also wrote a remarkable memoir telling the story of her and her sister's marriage to Joseph Smith. It ends with a jaunty question, "A strange way of getting married, wasn't it?"[16]

Usually I read a document on microfilm, taking notes on my laptop computer placed to the right of the microfilm reader. (If there was a problem with the microfilm image, I could ask for the original document.) If the document was short, such as a letter or a brief autobiography, I transcribed the whole document. If it was longer, I only had time to transcribe excerpts. However, if a particular long document seemed especially important, I would take the time to transcribe it entirely.

Every day I would receive my microfilms from the reading room archivist, Linda Haslam, who, I found out, was doing research on the companies in the Mormon overland migration. Whenever I found a word that was hard to read, I'd ask her to take a look. Often she could decipher the problem word. Her help was invaluable. One day I came to the archives with a bad cold—I should have stayed home, but losing a day at the archives was unthinkable. Linda shared some cold medicine with me—which I thought was going the extra mile for an archivist.

The archivists at the LDS Church Archives were unfailingly helpful, despite my working on a subject that some may have considered to be "taboo." However, I was approaching the subject from the perspective of writing the lives of the women, from birth to death; I wasn't focusing only on the marriages to Joseph Smith in Nauvoo, though I was dealing with that part of their lives fully and frankly. Therefore, I usually didn't need to request "controversial" documents. I later learned that some historical department

16. Compton, *In Sacred Loneliness*, 408.

administrators were concerned about my research interests, but I didn't feel any pressure.

Some archivists were kindred spirits. Bill Slaughter, the photo archivist, learned that I had given a paper at the annual Sunstone Theological Symposium on "The Spiritual Roots of the Democratic Party," dedicated to the (self-evident) proposition that no good member of the LDS Church could possibly be a Republican. He told me stories of what it was like being a Democrat in his Salt Lake City ward. He said that one of his fellow ward members called him up one day, told him he was giving out "Orrin Hatch for Senate" yard signs, and asked when he could bring some over for the Slaughter front lawn. Bill replied, "I'm sorry, I belong to the same political party as Elder James E. Faust" (a member of the church's First Presidency). Stunned silence on the other side of the line. Another archivist, Randy Dixon, was researching the Brigham Young homes, so we sometimes talked about residence history of the Smith-Young wives such as Emily Partridge Young.

If you are researching a subject in Mormon history, and need to work with primary documents, you simply go to all the major libraries with Mormon collections and spend time in the archives at each library. In addition to the Church Archives, I visited other important archives: the J. Willard Marriott Library at University of Utah, the Harold B. Lee Library at BYU in Provo, the library at the Utah State Historical Society, the LDS Genealogical/Family History Library, and the Stewart Library at Weber State University in Ogden. As I would find out later, I made a mistake in somehow missing the Merrill-Cazier Library at Utah State University in Logan.

At every archive you get to know archivists, sometimes researching subjects related to your own, and fellow researchers, many of whom give you leads to documents you might never otherwise hear of.

I had the names of thirty-three women; at each archive I would type the names into the electronic catalog and see what came up. In addition, I would type in the names of parents, siblings, children, and friends of those thirty-three women. At the Utah State Historical Society, I found an autograph autobiography by

Mary Elizabeth Rollins Lightner Smith Young, one of Smith's polyandrous wives, that gave a remarkably frank account of how she remembered Smith approaching her. It was also a striking collection of stories in its own right. In addition, the Historical Society had the papers of Stanley Snow Ivins, who decades earlier had collected material on Smith's plural wives. He was an interesting example of someone who conducted vast researches, made copious notes, but published little (one article, to the best of my knowledge, though it's a classic).[17] Ivins was fascinated by LDS polygamy and, naturally, by the beginnings of the practice. (His father, Anthony W. Ivins, a counselor to President Heber J. Grant in the First Presidency, had been an important player in the endgame of authorized polygamy, solemnizing many plural marriages in Mexico after the issuance of the 1890 Manifesto ostensibly ending the practice.)

At University of Utah, in the Marriott Library, I found more important writings by Emily Partridge Smith Young.

One of the pleasures of spending time in archives is reading the correspondence of scholars of different generations. Pursuing some reference to one of my thirty-three plural wives at the Utah Historical Society library, I stumbled upon the correspondence of Juanita Brooks. What fun it was to read her letters to contemporary scholars such as Dale Morgan, Wallace Stegner, Charles Kelly, and others. I had to exercise considerable self-control to stop reading these, and return to my main research focus.

I began constructing chronologies for these thirty-three women, and inserted important and moving quotes from documents I had found. During this period, often I took notes until 5:00 p.m. when the Church Archives closed; grabbed a bite to eat somewhere; then moved to the Church Genealogy library and worked there till it closed at 9:00 p.m. Then I would drive to my sister's apartment and insert my notes from the day into the chronologies.

One memorable discovery at the Church Archives came about because I tried always to get to the most primary source possible

---

17. Stanley S. Ivins, "Notes on Mormon Polygamy," *Western Humanities Review* 10 (Summer 1956): 229–39; available in D. Michael Quinn, ed., *The New Mormon History: Revisionist Essays on the Past* (Salt Lake City: Signature Books, 1992).

for any document I used. For example, if a diary had been edited and printed, even by a reliable scholar, I tried to check important passages in the original autograph manuscript. Good scholars often disagree on interpretations, and they can disagree about the readings of words in an original manuscript.

Some Mormon documents have been published by non-scholarly authors. These kinds of publications were handy, gave you access to the text, so it seemed, without having to spend precious time taking notes in the Church Archives. But were the texts reliable? Aside from possibilities of "edited" transcriptions, leaving out problematic paragraphs or pages, these printed transcriptions seemed very grammatical and "cleaned up." But I love transcriptions with all of the characteristic misspellings of the nineteenth-century writers reproduced faithfully.

The autobiographies of Levi Hancock and his son Mosiah were examples of this. (Levi left an autobiographical sketch; Mosiah continued his father's story.) These were widely available as booklets published in a non-scholarly way. Levi was the uncle of Fanny Alger, whom I accepted as Joseph Smith's first plural wife, married to him as a teenager in Kirtland, Ohio. There was a brief reference to Fanny in the published Levi Hancock autobiography. One day at LDS Archives, I decided to find the original autograph versions of these well-known texts. In fact, I found the autograph texts in the archives catalog, ordered them, and waited for the microfilms to be brought down. When I had the microfilm loaded onto the reader, I checked the text of the Levi Hancock memoir, then moved on to Mosiah Hancock and started reading. I read this and nearly fell off my chair:

> As early as Spring of 1832 Bro Joseph said "Brother Levi, the Lord has revealed to me that it is his will that righteous men shall take Righteous women even a plurality of Wives that a Righteous race may be sent forth upon the Earth preparatory to the ushering in of the Millenial Reign of our Redeemer["] ... Therefore Brother Joseph said ["]Brother Levi I want to make a bargain with you—If you will get Fanny Alger for me for a wife you may have Clarissa Reed. I love Fanny" "I will" Said Father. "Go brother Levi and the Lord will prosper you" Said Joseph—Father goes to the Father Samuel Alger—his

Father's Brother in Law and [said] "Samuel[,] the Prophet Joseph loves your Daughter Fanny and wishes her for a wife what say you"—Uncle Sam Says—"Go and talk to the Old woman about it twill be as She says" Father goes to his Sister and said "Clarrissy, Brother Joseph the Prophet of the most high God loves Fanny and wishes her for a wife what say you" Said She "go and talk to Fanny it will be all right with me"—Father goes to Fanny and said "Fanny Brother Joseph the Prophet loves you and wishes you for a wife will you be his wife?" "I will Levi" Said She—Father takes Fanny to Joseph and said "Brother Joseph I have been successful in my mission"—Father gave her to Joseph repeating the Ceremony as Joseph repeated to him.

That was *not* in the published version! Whoever made that transcription of the Mosiah Hancock autobiography left it out. It was clearly an important record of the very beginning of Joseph Smith's practice of polygamy.[18] That was an exciting day for me.

I have mentioned that I found lots of documents to read at the Church Archives without asking for controversial documents. However, I decided I should take a look at the Joseph F. Smith affidavits on Joseph Smith's polygamy.[19] There were at least three or four tiers of document accessibility at the time at the archives. The majority of documents were open to researchers (and now many of these are scanned and freely available on the Internet); some documents were listed on an in-house catalog that employees, but not the general public, could access; some were explicitly restricted for various reasons; and some were in the First Presidency's office vault (the highest level of practical inaccessibility). The Joseph F. Smith affidavits were restricted. However, you could fill out a special form and ask to be given access. This request would go up

18. This text contradicts the argument that Smith's relationship with Alger was an extramarital affair. I realize there are questions about the accuracy of Mosiah Hancock's account, but I leave out the analysis such a late source requires as not germane to this particular story. However, I do accept Hancock's account as generally reliable. See Compton, *In Sacred Loneliness*, 29–31.

19. In 1869, Joseph F. Smith collected affidavits from the living wives of Joseph Smith and from other Nauvoo polygamy insiders (LDS Church History Library, MS 3423). They are recorded in four books, two of which seem to be a copy of the other two (though there are discrepancies between the originals and the copies; book 4 seems to be a copy of book 1, and book 3 a copy of book 2). They are invaluable for recording Nauvoo plural marriages, dates of marriages, and the names of people performing or witnessing the marriages.

the ladder to administrators and possibly committees to decide if you may see the documents or not. Then, as now, sometimes you are allowed access to restricted documents, and sometimes not. So I filled out the form, described the collection, told why I was interested in reading these affidavits, what my research focus was. Sometimes you can argue points to strengthen your case—in this case, I mentioned that Danel Bachman had had full access to the affidavits and had described them in detail, and I merely wanted to check his research.

I turned in my request and waited. There was no quick response.

Finally, my last week in Salt Lake City came. I mentioned my request to an archivist, reminding him that my last day was Friday. Then I would return to California. He looked worried. The jury was still out on my request, apparently.

Friday morning came, and the archivist told me they were working to get me access to the affidavits that day. An hour before the archives closed, I was given permission to see them. I did what I could in an hour, checking the data from selected affidavits. An hour was not enough. However, it looked like Bachman had adequately reproduced data about the affidavits.

In California, I began working temporary jobs again. I worked as a security guard, as a typist in a law firm, as a data inputter in a stockbroker's office, as an administrative assistant in a property management firm. I didn't want to get a full-time job because such a job would not allow me to make research trips to Utah. I continued to visit the Huntington, and also the California State Historical Society in San Francisco, the Oakland Library, and the Bancroft Library at UC Berkeley.

Another exciting day occurred when I was back home in Santa Monica. I was trying to piece together the marriage history of Elizabeth Davis Goldsmith Brackenbury Durfee Smith Lott (as I reconstructed her full name later). She was not a woman who had left an autobiography or diary. We had a Mrs. Durfee (or Durphy) in Nauvoo; who was she? What was her birth name? We also had a Sister Goldsmith in earlier Mormon history and a Sister Brackenbury, but at first I didn't know about them or their connection to Sister Durfee. And after Nauvoo, Sister Durfee was mentioned once or twice in Utah. After those late mentions, she seemed to have dropped off the face of the earth. I had no death date for her.

Frustrated in my efforts to obtain the basic facts about Elizabeth's full life history, I resorted to a high-tech research instrument called the telephone. I knew she had children with her second husband, John Brackenbury, so, in theory, if her children stayed with the LDS Church, there might be Brackenbury descendants in Utah with more information about her. In addition, Brackenbury was a fairly rare name, which would make it easier to research. So one day I called Utah phone directory assistance and asked them if they had any listings in the state under the name of Brackenbury.

They found a Brackenbury and gave me a phone number to call.

I called, and a man answered the phone. I told him I was researching a pioneer woman named Elizabeth Brackenbury and asked if he was related to her or had any information concerning her. He said he had a relative who might be able to help me and gave me a name, Ethel Jo Christopherson, and a phone number. I called the number and the sprightly voice of an older lady answered. I told her I was interested in learning more about a woman named Elizabeth Davis Brackenbury who had lived in Nauvoo as Mrs. Durfee but then disappeared. Could she help?

Yes, she said. Elizabeth followed her Brackenbury sons to southern California and went back to using her Brackenbury name. Then they converted to the RLDS Church and moved back to the Midwest, settling in or near Independence, Missouri.

Again, I nearly fell out of my chair.

You don't have a death date for her, do you? I asked.

Yes, I do, Jo said. Let me get my book. When she returned to the phone, she read out: Died on December 16, 1876, at White Cloud, Kansas, in a railroad accident.

Starting with that, we had a great talk about Elizabeth. She also knew more about her first husband, Gilbert Goldsmith, than I. She generously sent me a packet of priceless documents and photographs related to Elizabeth and her sons. One key document was the original record of her marriage to Jabez Durfee in Missouri. That was a key link in the chain of identity in Elizabeth's life.

Finally, I could write out Elizabeth's full name. And knowing that she went by Mrs. or Sister Brackenbury the final years of her life would allow me to research her later years. It seemed odd but somehow fitting that she had lived in southern California, where I was doing my research. Putting together the pieces of Elizabeth's marriage history was intensely satisfying.

I should mention that this is one example of many in which people whom I didn't know personally helped me in my research. I was in St. George one day, and either my parents or family friends told me that there was one local person I ought to contact. I called him up, he invited me over to his home, we chatted, and he pulled out a document relating to Nauvoo temple marriages from his files. He allowed me to go to a nearby copy center and photocopy it. It turned out to be a key document in my research. I remain greatly indebted to him.

I might mention the time I spent researching women who did not end up on my list of thirty-three. This was not wasted time, but it was time that did not directly contribute to my book. Historians often have to act as detectives, pursuing leads that go nowhere. (Or, for the time being, leads that seem to go nowhere. New evidence can change the situation at any time.) As an example, I quote from a letter I wrote to Maureen Ursenbach Beecher, who was wondering who an "Olive" who appeared in the Eliza R. Snow diary on September 9, 1846, might be. I mentioned as a possibility Olive Andrews, who had married Brigham Young in a Nauvoo proxy marriage, with Young standing in the stead of the deceased Joseph Smith. An early proxy marriage to Smith was good evidence that Andrews might have married Smith during his lifetime, but not certain evidence, so I had to try to find corroborating documentation. I wrote to Maureen:

> Now, when I started working on Olive, I had two documents that gave some information about her: First, the sealing record, a proxy marriage to Joseph Smith, Brigham Young as proxy, with a sealing to Brigham for time. This took place on Jan. 15, 1846, Heber Kimball officiated. According to this record, she ("Olive Andrews") was born in Livermore, Oxford, Maine on Sept. 24, 1818. She was 27 at

the time of the proxy sealing. ... Second, [is] the Nauvoo Temple endowment register ...

Those are the two pieces of solid information that I started out with. One day when I was in Utah, I set aside some time to find out more about Olive. I searched diligently in the LDS Genealogical Library for hours. I ended up with those same two solid pieces of information, and nothing else. I checked several other sources and data bases, including censuses, but found nothing helpful.

I found people who might have been relatives of Olives in the censuses, but no certain documentation on her.

So I had a maddening time with Olive. A wife of Brigham Young, and she is just a shadow. She doesn't show up on many of the standard lists of his wives.

What happened to her? Perhaps she died between Nauvoo and Salt Lake City. Having had no children, no one took much notice of her. Maybe the proxy marriage didn't "take," and Andrews quickly married someone else. Maybe she stayed behind in Nauvoo and married someone else. Maybe she stayed behind in Nauvoo and didn't marry. One thing is for sure: she didn't end up as one of Brigham Young's well known wives.[20]

Here's another anecdote about a lead that I couldn't confirm. I have a friend who had spent time researching in the LDS Archives in the "early days," long before it became more professional. He and a friend had been given access to many documents. One day he requested something, and the woman who was delivering documents came into the room with a number of them in her hands. She stumbled, the documents fell on the floor, and my friend helped her pick them up. He said as he was gathering them, he noticed something about Zion's Camp, the quasi-military Mormon group that traveled from Kirtland to Missouri in May–June, 1834. He asked if he could take a look at it, and the clerk said yes. So he read through it. According to a Zion's Camp participant, Joseph Smith had brought Fanny Alger, his first plural wife, with him on the expedition, and she was staying with him in his tent. This caused an uproar among the other members of the

---

20. Letter to Maureen Ursenbach Beecher, Jan. 29, 1993, in my possession.

expedition, most of whom hadn't heard of Smith's doctrine and practice of plural marriage, and Alger was sent home.

As Fanny Alger is one of the most controversial of Joseph Smith's wives, I wanted to read this account and assess the author's reputation and writing style. My friend had told me this story long before I had started researching Smith's plural wives. So I called him up to see if he could help me locate the document. However, he didn't have the specifics on it.

I spent time in the archives, reading memoirs of Zion's Camp, seeing if I could track down that document, but without any success. So the story could not go into my Fanny Alger chapter. Hopefully someone will be able to track it down someday, if it still exists.

I should mention the challenges of writing collective biography, as opposed to individual biography. For an individual biography, one might select a subject who left a number of primary documents, perhaps a diary, letters, and so on. However, for a biography of a number of persons, one finds great variation in documentation. In my case, some women left diaries, some left letters, some left both. Some left hardly anything. In such cases, you do the best you can with the documents available. You might find an "under-documented" woman mentioned in someone else's diary. (Though here, she would be doomed to be a "bit player"—the diary writer would be primarily focused on her or his own life.) Sometimes, you can find standard genealogical information in censuses or birth, death, or marriage records. Sometimes the woman wrote a diary, but only long after Nauvoo, as was the case with plural wives Emily Partridge Young and Helen Mar Whitney.

Then you find women, such as Eliza R. Snow and Zina Huntington, who did write Nauvoo diaries but did not specifically mention their marriage relationships to Smith in their diaries.

Another challenge was simply having to write about thirty-three individuals, instead of one person. Sometimes you were enjoying researching a certain women, but then you looked at your schedule and realized that you had to work on other women. It was hard to switch easily from one subject to another.

As I progressed with my research and thought about publication, I realized that my project could be problematic for conservative Mormons. I began to tell some of the stories of these women to my friends and family. The story of Zina Huntington Jacobs Smith Young was especially strange. She had married Henry Jacobs and had two children with him. But she married Joseph Smith for time and eternity soon after her civil marriage to Jacobs. As was customary for Smith's polyandrous marriages, Zina continued to live with the first husband. After Smith died, she eventually married Brigham Young, who acted as a proxy for Smith in the Nauvoo temple—Young felt a special calling to marry many of the plural widows of Smith. Henry Jacobs acted as a witness as Young stood "proxy" for Smith in the marriage ceremony; at the time, Zina was pregnant with her second Jacobs-fathered child. Then Jacobs and Zina started to cross Iowa, in a covered wagon, in rainy weather, on their way to Winter Quarters and eventually Utah. Chariton Jacobs was born in a wagon, in the rain, near the Chariton River, in southeastern Iowa. After his birth, Zina, Henry, and their two boys continued on the overland trek.

However, while Smith was generally content to allow his polyandrous wives to continue to live with their "first husbands," Young now called Jacobs on a mission to England, then brought Zina into his household as his de facto wife while Jacobs was gone.

After his mission, Jacobs continued to stay in touch with Zina, and wrote longing letters to her from California, seeming to want to reunite with her. But it was not to be.

It's a tragic story, at least from Jacobs's point of view, and the two church presidents involved played roles that appear to be less than entirely sympathetic.[21]

---

21. According to descendants, when Zina told the story of her separation from Jacobs, years later, she described him as not suitable for her. (Often polyandrous wives "adjusted" chronology, portraying or implying divorces with the first husbands before the marriage to Smith.) She may have fallen out of love with Jacobs, but contemporary documents, including her diary, don't support this. It is certain that Zina continued to live with Jacobs and have children with him during her marriage to Smith and during the first part of her marriage to Young. She later had a child with Young, Zina Presendia Young Williams Card. See, in addition to my book, Martha Sonntag Bradley and Mary Brown Firmage Woodward, *Four Zinas: A Story of Mothers and Daughters on the Mormon Frontier* (Salt Lake City: Signature Books, 2000).

I once told the late B. Carmon Hardy, author of two classic books on Mormon polygamy, that I had transcribed Jacobs's letters to Zina and would be happy to share them with him. He groaned; no, he said, it was a subject so painful he didn't want to read the primary documents.

I remember telling my orthodox LDS mother a couple of the stories of Smith's polyandrous marriages. "Well, if he did marry the wives of other men," she said, "he shouldn't have."

Did I want to be the bearer of bad news on a subject the church regarded as taboo? I did not take this issue lightly. Though I was a somewhat liberal Mormon, with a healthy sense of the humanity and limitations of church leaders, the LDS Church was my community. I had close ties with many conservative Mormons among family and friends. The local leaders (called bishops) I'd had in southern California had been not just good people, but great people. (Bob Rees, former editor of *Dialogue: A Journal of Mormon Thought*, had been my bishop in the L.A. First Ward.)

Nevertheless, I came to the conclusion that I should continue my research and share my findings. Joseph Smith was a major figure in American history. It would be absurd for conservative Latter-day Saints to tell his story and leave out his marriages. These thirty-three women were authentically his wives, married to him with marriage ceremonies. It would be irresponsible for a good historian—which I wanted to be—to leave them out of the story.

In addition, some of these women were major figures in Mormon/Utah history—particularly Eliza R. Snow and Zina Huntington Young, who were the second and third general presidents of the church's all-female Relief Society in Utah. These were not "lesser-known" wives whom one could sweep under a rug. When they traveled through Utah as church leaders and talked to local women (and men) about their past lives in Ohio, Missouri, and Illinois, they retold the story of their marriages to Smith as important events. The responsible historian would have to treat the marriages to Smith as significant occurrences in their lives. (And in the case of Zina, this requires a full treatment of an especially "complex" marriage.)

I was fully convinced by the statements of historians such as

Juanita Brooks and D. Michael Quinn that the only effective way for faithful historians to treat problem subjects is to research them thoroughly, then write about them in a full, frank way. As Brooks said, "I feel sure that nothing but the truth can be good enough for the church to which I belong."[22] Even if LDS leaders decided that no good church member should publish on a problem area such as the Mountain Meadows Massacre, does that mean that non-LDS historians would politely ignore it? Far from it. And discouraging LDS historians from dealing with these problem subjects would keep them from looking at these events from the perspective of sympathy, compassion, and even faith. (And for "partisan" conservative LDS historians to treat such problem areas in less than full, frank ways would eventually be damaging to the LDS Church, especially if it adopted such sugar-coated versions of history, which would subsequently be proved wrong.)

Of course, one way that some conservative church members have dealt with LDS historians writing about problem subjects has been to label them as "critics" and as anti-Mormons. I knew I could face something like that.

———

At one point, I was planning a trip to the Midwest, to see family and friends, and decided to stop in Missouri and Illinois and visit some library-archives there, in particular the RLDS archives, located in the RLDS temple in Independence, Missouri. So the day before I arrived in Independence, I called the archives and was connected to Ron Romig, the main archivist. He welcomed me to the archives and asked what my research focus was. I told him I was researching the plural wives of Joseph Smith. Hmm, he said. I don't think you'll find much about that here. I thought he didn't sound too enthusiastic about my visit.

Fortunately, when I got to the archives and started working, Ron was friendly and helpful. I told him the story of Elizabeth Davis Brackenbury, and he helped me trace the story of her life and the lives of her sons in east Kansas, near Independence, and

___

22. Brooks, *The Mountain Meadows Massacre* (Norman: University of Oklahoma Press, 1962), xxvi; Quinn, "150 Years Of Truth and Consequences About Mormon History," *Sunstone* 16 (1992): 12–14.

93

then in Independence. (Her son Joseph Wesley Brackenbury became one of the early RLDS pastors in that city.) We found a
date for Elizabeth's baptism into the RLDS Church, in November
1869. Ron was an authority on Mormon historical places in Independence, and he helped me understand Emily Partridge Smith
Young's memoirs of growing up in Independence, and of seeing
her father, Edward Partridge, tarred and feathered, when she was
nine years old.

I found other friends and kindred spirits in Missouri, both
at this time and during subsequent visits: Michael Riggs, who
had published a good paper on early Mormon polygamy; Dale
Broadhurst, the creator of a wonderful website on early Mormon documents; Andrew Bolton, from England, later an RLDS
apostle; Mark Scherer, who would become official Community of
Christ Historian. I'd already met historian Bill Russell, who became a solid supporter of the *In Sacred Loneliness* project.

Finally, it was time to turn my chronologies into narrative,
something people might read. Writing the chapters called for
checking many details, so research continued as I wrote. I sat at
my computer in my small studio apartment in Santa Monica and
hammered out the book. I often wished I could write like noted
western writer Wallace Stegner, but had to work with my own
style. Though I told the stories of these women from birth to
death, I tried to combine my narrative structure with their own
words, from diaries, letters, and memoirs.

At that time, I was corresponding with the late Gene Wolfe, a
brilliant fantasy/science fiction author who was deeply interested
in ancient Greece and Rome, and he gave me a piece of advice that
directly influenced *In Sacred Loneliness.* He said it was a good idea
to "Kill the sheriff in the first paragraph" of your story. In other
words, immerse the reader in the story immediately. I tried to start
every chapter with a dramatic or memorable moment from the
life of the woman that would lead readers to continue to relive and
understand her full life.

When I had a manuscript, I began exploring publication op-
tions. Signature Books, a Salt Lake City-based independent press
specializing in Utah/Mormon history, biography, and fiction, was

always the most interested in the book. I remember talking to Gary Bergera, Signature's managing director, on the phone when I finally decided to go with Signature (in 1994, I recall). He was enthusiastic, and I've always appreciated his support through the publication process and afterwards. I'd known Gary and Ron Priddis (Signature's marketing manager) since their *Seventh East Press* days at BYU. (The *Seventh East Press* was an independent student newspaper that Ron had helped to found and that flourished during the early 1980s before being banned from campus for publishing an interview with noted LDS philosopher Sterling McMurrin.) Now fate had cast us together again. I've also been grateful for the support of Signature's publisher George D. Smith; one of his research interests was Nauvoo polygamy, and sometimes historians are touchy about other people working in their territory. There was none of this feeling from George.

In Sacred Loneliness was a risky book for Signature; aside from questions of content, it was long. I think many publishers would have asked me to compress it to 300 pages. The book was much richer, I believed, at 700 pages. Each woman's voice could be fuller, with many quotes from diaries, letters, memoirs, and autobiographies.

Early on I came up with a title—at first, *Sacred Loneliness: The Plural Wives of Joseph Smith* (Signature suggested adding "In" to make *In Sacred Loneliness*).[23] As I read the life stories, the diaries and autobiographies, of these women, I found I had compiled a revealing cross section of Mormon polygamy. I was struck by how separated from their husbands plural wives often were. Of course, if you are a plural wife in a large family (in Brigham Young's case, about fifty-six wives), you can't have your husband's undivided attention, time, emotional focus, and economic support. While this seems an obvious conclusion, the emotional impact of documenting and retelling the story of a woman's life in polygamy was often moving and troubling. So LDS polygamy was paradoxical; it was widely seen by nineteenth-century Latter-day Saints as a higher

---

23. I had the title in mind by August 19, 1994, when I gave a talk at the annual Sunstone Symposium called "Sacred Loneliness: The Ordeal of Presendia Lathrop Huntington Buell Smith Kimball."

marriage, a sacred marriage, the only path to complete exaltation; and on the other hand, for the women, it often led to loneliness and financial struggle. Certainly, different families and wives had contrasting experiences, but it seemed as though the very institution of plural marriage, especially in larger families of elite church leaders, led to female isolation.

At some point my friend Terry Szink gave me as a birthday present a copy of *Solemn Covenant: The Mormon Polygamous Passage* by Carmon Hardy (released in 1992 by the University of Illinois Press), one of the great books in Mormon history, and this introduced me to Hardy's work. Then my friend Jan Eyring told me she knew him—he taught just down the hall from her at Cal State Fullerton. She introduced me to him, and he loaned me a master's thesis he had helped with: Suzanne Adel Katz, "Sisters in Salvation: Patterns of Emotional Loneliness Among Nineteenth-Century Non-Elite Mormon Polygamous Women" (1987). This gave additional support to my book's central thesis.

I turned in a version of *In Sacred Loneliness* to Signature in mid-1995, but kept working on it. Signature sent the manuscript to at least three readers, one of whom was Richard Van Wagoner,[24] and he sent me a number of helpful comments. Occasionally I disagreed with him, but this caused me to research those areas further, which I hope made the relevant passages stronger. I remember how much I enjoyed meeting Richard at a Sunstone conference, and he sent me an email expressing how delighted he was to know that a younger generation of LDS historians was carrying on the torch of good scholarship. (Actually, I think I looked younger than I was.)

At one point Gary Bergera suggested that I consider sending a copy of my manuscript to Michael Marquardt, a thorough, meticulous researcher, to review. I contacted Mike, and he generously agreed to read the entire manuscript. When he finished, he also sent me a number of helpful comments. In particular he pointed me to a key document (or part of a document) I had no idea existed. As I had been researching the life of Helen Mar Kimball

---

24. Lavina Fielding Anderson was another reader (though I didn't know it at the time); the third reader remains unknown to me.

Smith Whitney, Joseph Smith's youngest wife and daughter of Heber C. and Vilate Kimball, I found two diary notebooks by her at the LDS Archives, covering her years in Salt Lake City when she was an older woman, one from November 1884 to September 1885 and one from December 1887 to May 1888. Marquardt told me that at the Utah State University Merrill-Cazier Library there was a Helen Mar Whitney collection which included more diaries by Helen, and many Kimball-Whitney documents, including letters by Helen and by her children. He let me know that someone named Charles M. Hatch was editing Helen Mar Whitney's diaries for the USU Press.

I contacted Hatch and told him of the LDS Archives diaries by Helen. It turned out that the LDS Archives diaries filled gaps in the sequence of the eleven diary notebooks at USU. We traded our transcriptions, and Hatch's transcribed diary sections opened up a new world of Helen's later life for me. It is certainly the longest diary written by a plural wife of Joseph Smith, and, I believe, is one of the great diaries in LDS history.[25] The Whitney diary was probably the last major document I used to finish my manuscript.

During this period I was giving talks on my research at Mormon History Association meetings and Sunstone conferences. Two articles that were basically chapters from my book were published in 1996, "Fanny Alger Smith Custer, Mormonism's First Plural Wife?" in *Journal of Mormon History* and "A Trajectory of Plurality: An Overview of Joseph Smith's Thirty-Three Plural Wives" in *Dialogue: A Journal of Mormon Thought.*[26] This latter article was essentially the first chapter in my book, a general explanation of how Joseph Smith practiced polygamy in Nauvoo, an analysis of marriage ages, and an explanation of polyandry to the best of my ability to explain it. This chapter was not in my original manuscript, which was all biographies. But someone—perhaps

---

25. Hatch and I eventually edited and published the complete set of diaries as *A Widow's Tale: The 1884–1896 Diary of Helen Mar Kimball Whitney* (Logan: Utah State University Press, 2003).

26. "Fanny Alger Smith Custer, Mormonism's First Plural Wife?" *Journal of Mormon History* 22 (Spring 1996): 172–205; "A Trajectory of Plurality: An Overview of Joseph Smith's Thirty-three Plural Wives," *Dialogue: A Journal of Mormon Thought* 29 (Summer 1996): 1–38.

Maureen Beecher—requested it, thinking that the book needed that kind of explanatory chapter so that readers would have a basic idea of Smith's rationale for polygamy as they read the biographies. I agreed. As published in *Dialogue*, it won an award from the Mormon History Association as best article of the year.

The publication process did not move as quickly as I'd expected (which I've subsequently learned is usually par for the course for any book). But eventually I started to get edited chapters back from Signature and, later, typeset proofs.

My memory of this period of writing, editing, and correcting is that it was difficult for me. When you've first written something, it's exciting to edit it three or four (or six or eight) times, improving it each time. Finally, it seems as though you've completed your final edit and feel more or less satisfied and exhausted mentally. Then your manuscript comes back in the mail with lots of reworking by editors, and you have to examine and weigh those changes in detail, accepting some, rejecting others, and rewriting.

In addition, this was my first book, so I really didn't know what to expect.

Authors sometimes have little sense of what goes on behind the scenes at a press to support their work. Ron Priddis recalled an intense, but also fairly typical time of work on *In Sacred Loneliness* at Signature:

> The project occurred over a period of about 6–9 months, everyone's involvement staggered somewhat but overlapping in the middle. In other words, Gary [Bergera] did his thing and passed the ms. [manuscript] on to me but didn't discontinue his involvement. I passed it on to [designer and typesetter] Connie [Disney] and Brent [Corcoran], but I didn't discontinue my involvement in editing ad copy and so on. It went to Jani [Fleet], who afterward continued to proof other things related to the book, and then to Boyd [Payne] for marketing and Greg [Jones] for shipping review copies and filling orders. But if you see my point, for a couple months it was all hands on deck, everyone working to produce and promote your book.[27]

I remember one day working on some of the final edited texts,

---

27. Email to Compton, July 20, 2018.

sitting at a table in the open air near the cafeteria of North Campus at UCLA, reading through the pages, making final rewrites, rereading sentences and paragraphs to make sure their rhythm was right to me. I was feeling psychologically at the end of my rope. Joanna Brooks, whom I knew in L.A. First Ward and later wrote the best-selling memoir *Book of Mormon Girl* (2012), walked by, saw me, came over, and said hello. I fear I did not brighten her day as I described the challenge of final edits.

In a book editing process, there are usually varied changes suggested by editors: they help the author correct errors or factual mistakes, simplify unclear sentences, tighten and strengthen the narrative.[28] As published, my book ended up at 788 pages (including the index); as submitted it might have been at least a thousand pages, probably more. As usually happens, I was amazed at the minor (but embarrassing) errors that had slipped by me in my multiple readings of the text.

People have asked about my footnoting method, which does not use numbers in the text but instead has sections in the back matter corresponding with key words in the main text. This happened because I once gave my father a chapter to read with many numbered footnotes, and he complained that the chapter was hard to read because there were so many numbered notes in the text. (I had about twenty notes in the first paragraph, I think!) So I developed this non-number system to make the book more readable. Of course, the unintended consequence was that readers who wanted to check my sources sometimes found them hard to use, as they were not the numbers readers customarily encountered in history books.[29]

Some people have referred to the book as non-scholarly because I used this system, but I, of course, disagree. It is a different method of doing notes; it isn't a non-scholarly lack of notes and documentation. In addition, I've found that some other historians and publishers have used similar methods.[30] I do regret that the

---

28. Signature's edits were entirely stylistic.

29. I remember Gary Bergera once, and maybe more than once, expressing reservations about this method of documentation.

30. See, for example, J. S. Holiday, *The World Rushed In: The California Gold Rush Experience* (New York: Simon and Schuster, 1981); David McCullough, *1776* (New York: Simon & Schuster, 2005); Barbara W. Tuchman, *The First Salute: A View of the*

method has bothered some people, but I hope the book has been more readable because of that choice.

I remember Gary Bergera gave me an unexpected shock just as I thought the book's editing process was coming to an end. "You'll need pictures," he said.

Pictures? I hadn't even thought of pictures. I groaned.

He gave me the technical specifications I would need for usable pictures, gave me a budget, and wished me good luck.

Once again, we see how inexperienced I was. I've learned since that you need to collect photographs on your subject as you do your research, as the photographs are often in the same archives as the manuscripts. Now, for *In Sacred Loneliness*, I had to collect the pictures quickly. I'm grateful to the individuals who generously shared photographs with me, descendants of some of the plural wives such as Clark Layton, Maxine Willoughby, and Ethel Jo Christopherson, and historians such as Nelson B. Wadsworth, Richard Van Wagoner, and Josephine DeWitt Rhodehamel, co-author of a biography of Ina Coolbrith.

As it turned out, collecting the pictures was an exciting experience, though complying with the technical requirements was a challenge for me, as were the time constraints. Photographs are authentic historical documents and work together with written documents to supply a unique depth of historical reality (I found out). I was lucky enough to be able to collect a marvelous, haunting group of photographs of the women I wrote about.

At one point Gary asked me if I knew any historians who would be willing to read some of my book and provide promotional blurbs for the dust jacket. Asking friends and acquaintances for blurbs is never a comfortable job. But I turned to two historians I'd gotten to know: Newell Bringhurst, author of biographies of Brigham Young and Fawn Brodie, and Irene Bates, whom I knew from mutual friends in my L.A. ward, co-author of an important history

---

American Revolution (New York: Alfred A. Knopf, 1988); and Stephen Oates, *With Malice Toward None: The Life of Abraham Lincoln* (New York: Harper & Row, 1977). See also *Chicago Manual of Style*, 16th ed. (Chicago: University of Chicago Press, 2010), 14.48, "Notes keyed to text by line or page numbers."

of the general patriarchs of the LDS Church.[31] They generously agreed to help. I am still enormously grateful for their willingness to read under the time constraints. They wrote marvelous blurbs. Newell said that the book was a "carefully-written, engaging presentation" and a *tour de force*. Irene wrote, "This is a magnificent achievement—a truly scholarly work that reaches the heart."

All the time I had researched at LDS Archives, I had been open with the archivists about what my research topic was. So I knew that general information about my project had probably filtered upwards to church administrators. I had also been publishing articles and giving talks. However, I felt that I would like the LDS Church to have full knowledge of the contents of my book. My parents had known a general church authority when he had been in the bishopric of their home congregation, so I sent him a letter, mentioned my parents, and asked if he would be interested in reading the manuscript. He replied that he would, so I sent him an in-progress copy of *In Sacred Loneliness*, mentioning that it would be published by Signature Books in the near future.

His response, while not wildly enthusiastic, was measured and courteous. This general authority was not a "hard-liner"; but I knew that he might inform other church leaders, who were not sympathetic to what had become known as the "New Mormon History," a more balanced, less partisan approach to the Mormon past. In any event, I felt that at least they would not feel blindsided when the book appeared.

One of the final events of the publication process was the dust-jacket cover. My memory is that I was visiting Signature one day during which Ron showed it to me. I had asked for a certain photograph on the cover: Zina Huntington Jacobs Smith Young, Emily Partridge Smith Young, and Eliza R. Snow Smith Young, seated, in beautiful pioneer dresses. Signature had asked Ron Stucki, a graphic artist, to design the cover, and he had done a beautiful job. It had mainly a reddish-purple background, with a photograph of Zina, Emily, and Eliza in that same color. Above them was a photograph of Joseph Smith in a circular frame, standing out

---

31. Irene M. Bates and E. Gary Smith, *Lost Legacy: The Mormon Office of Presiding Patriarch* (Urbana: University of Illinois Press, 1996).

with a bright white color, and in front of them was a cushioned altar, again in a bright white color with purple shadows. The title, in archaic cursive golden type, was to the left, sideways. I was a bit startled by this cover at first, though I've come to really like it. However, I did ask for the three women to be more visible, brought out somehow. Signature could not do this fully for the first edition, but the women stood out more in the "second" edition. So you can distinguish between the two "editions" by comparing the visibility of the three women.[32]

The book appeared for sale in mid-December 1997. The series of improbabilities and accidents that had made it possible for me to receive a Huntington fellowship in 1992 had led to my creating tentative lists of Joseph Smith's plural wives, brief biographies of the wives, then longer biographies, marvelous hours of research at many libraries, generous help and encouragement from many friends, editors, historians, archivists, and descendants, later fleshed-out narratives of the wives, and now an edited, compressed, corrected, published book. My own five-plus-year intense involvement with the text of *In Sacred Loneliness* had ended; it was now appearing in bookstores, and I would soon see if readers experienced what I had, to some degree.[33]

---

32. After the first edition sold out, I made a few corrections to the second, which appeared in late February or early March 1998. See www.toddmcompton.com/correct.html.

33. The scholarly and other responses to the book, following publication, are probably best left to a future essay.

JOSEPH SMITH'S POLYGAMY
HISTORY AND THEOLOGY
BRIAN C. HALES

4

One of the most common questions I've been asked over the years involves my motivations for studying Mormon polygamy. Back in 1989, as I was finishing up my anesthesia training at the University of Kansas Medical Center, Kansas City, I learned that a relative had been excommunicated from the Church of Jesus Christ of Latter-day Saints for entering into a plural marriage. (Though the church once practiced plural marriage, it abandoned the practice completely at the turn of the twentieth century and expels any members who practice it today.) I contacted her with both curiosity and concern. She explained that her prayers had led her to join a Mormon fundamentalist polygamist group. (All such groups are disavowed by the LDS Church.) She shared with me the same documents that she had studied, and I sought additional books and pamphlets to read.

After graduation I moved to Layton, Utah, to practice medicine and soon was able to study the fundamentalist materials in greater depth. Some of the claims I read seemed valid, but, through it all, the issue of priesthood keys—God's power and authority to perform salvific ordinances in mortality—was paramount. I believe in the LDS Church's truth claims and take church founder Joseph Smith's July 12, 1843, revelation (canonized as LDS D&C 132) at face value when it states that there is "one" man—the presiding prophet—who holds the keys and "there is never but one on the earth at a time on whom this power and the keys of this priesthood are conferred" (v. 7). The lines of priesthood authority promoted by the fundamentalist groups were never believable to me. Frankly, I never seriously felt to join my relative in her new lifestyle and convictions.

Though untrained and naive, I jumped into the Mormon polygamy controversy with both feet. Through my research, I met Max Anderson, who published, in 1979, *Polygamy Story: Fiction and Fact.* He and I subsequently collaborated on the book *The Priesthood of Modern Polygamy: An L.D.S. Perspective* that was printed in 1992 by the subsidy press Northwest Publishing (which later went bankrupt). That same year Max and I presented our research at the annual Mormon History Association meeting in St. George, Utah. The year previous I had presented some of it at the annual Sunstone Symposium in Salt Lake City. At this time, Fred Collier, a practicing independent Mormon fundamentalist, began calling me, trying to persuade me to join his group. Once we talked for over two hours, but I never found his answers to the priesthood authority questions fully satisfying.

The 1990s found me distracted with other projects and writing. By the end of the decade, I teamed with Cedar Fort Books to publish non-polygamy titles, including *The Veil* (2000), *Trials* (2002), and *Light* (2004). During these years various Mormon fundamentalist churches were making a stir, and I knew that no one had written a detailed history of the Mormon fundamentalist movement. So the time seemed right to unbox all my polygamy research and focus my writing on fundamentalism. With the help of Greg Kofford Books, my *Modern Polygamy and Mormon Fundamentalism: The Generations after the Manifesto* was printed in 2006. (LDS Church President Wilford Woodruff issued a "manifesto" in 1890 to end the practice of plural marriage.)

Publishing with Kofford Books introduced me to the most amazing editor I've ever worked with, Lavina Fielding Anderson (Lavina worked on a freelance basis for Kofford Books). During the early 2000s, she didn't email so she would send the multi-page chapter drafts via the US Postal Service to me, and I would make changes on the pages in pen and drop them in the Winder Diary milk box on her front porch in Salt Lake City. One day I parked in her driveway and jumped out of my car leaving the door open

to quickly drop off the completed chapter in the box and return. As I approached her porch, Mike Quinn was just leaving to get something out of his vehicle. To make a long story short, I was invited in for dinner with Lavina, her husband, Paul, and Mike. We had a most enjoyable evening as I picked Mike's brain for fundamentalist details. He has such an amazing history database stored in his memory. When I left hours later, I found my car door still wide open. Glad the crime rate in Lavina's neighborhood was low.

Focusing on Joseph Smith's Polygamy

Shortly after I published *Modern Polygamy and Mormon Fundamentalism*, my longtime friend Alex Baugh, who taught religion at LDS Church-owned Brigham Young University, asked me which of the book's chapters I thought was the most popular. I drew a blank as he responded, "The first," which provides a brief summary of the beginnings of polygamy in Nauvoo, Illinois, under Joseph Smith's direction. He pointed out that the full story of the introduction of Mormon plural marriage had yet to be told. There were books like *Mormon Polygamy: A History,* by Richard Van Wagoner, and *In Sacred Loneliness: The Plural Wives of Joseph Smith,* by Todd Compton. Each contributed to polygamy historiography in its own useful way, but no scholarly telling of the early unfolding of the practice in Kirtland, Ohio, and later in Illinois had been written.

In addition, once my book on fundamentalist polygamy was out, questions through emails and letters were launched my way. Many of them involved Smith's plural marriages, which I could not begin to answer. I felt a desire to dig deeper into that early phase of plurality.

A January 20, 2007, entry in my journal mentions a conversation I had that day "about Joseph Smith's polygamy" that ended with me writing: "Perhaps I'll have to do something with that topic." A few weeks later I wrote: "Worked all day on my polygamy stuff. I love writing and researching. Very enjoyable day." By the end of March, I had spent at least a hundred hours writing and produced a 100-singled-spaced-page "very rough draft." Three months later I printed off an expanded version that was almost double the length.

Despite some progress, I knew that I could not personally research the required caches of documents while working full time as an anesthesiologist. The three most important collections included:

1. Joseph F. Smith's affidavits collected primarily in 1869–70 and, at the time, restricted at the LDS Church Archives;

2. Andrew Jenson's 1887 twenty-seven page article, "Plural Marriage," published in his monthly *Historical Record* and any associated documents at LDS Archives; and

3. The 1892 Temple Lot litigation depositions that were microfilmed and available at LDS Archives. (The Temple Lot legal case involved competing claims, not directly involving the LDS Church, regarding the ownership of some important land in Independence, Missouri.)

It became quickly obvious that I needed skilled help in the form of a research assistant.

Don "Sherlock Holmes" Bradley

A literal answer to prayer came on July 29, 2007. I recorded: "Spent a couple of hours with Don Bradley. He has done some great research in the past." This wasn't the first time I had asked Don to help me. In the early 1990s I hired him to investigate some fundamentalist historical issues, and he had identified important sources that were new to me. Don is a writer, editor, and researcher with a deep interest in Latter-day Saint history. In 2017, he obtained a master's degree in history from Utah State University. Don's first book, *The Lost 116 Pages: Reconstructing the Missing Contents of the Book of Mormon*, was published by Greg Kofford Books in late 2019.

While Don's rates were very reasonable, $35.00 an hour, I was not immediately comfortable with the idea of paying someone to research a topic if it was purely for my own personal interest. I did realize that without Don's sleuthing nothing I could produce on my own would be comprehensive enough to constitute a useful contribution to the topic. On October 10, 2007, after having paid Don a few thousand dollars for his excellent labors, I told him that "I hoped 30–40 hours more might do it."

The next month, on November 16, my journal entry recorded: "I met Don Bradley and he had more good stuff for me. We strategized too. I can see the end of this project and am excited, although a lot of work remains to be done." I really couldn't see the end— that was wishful thinking. Don kept finding significant historical sources throughout 2007, logging over 250 hours, more than 750 hours in 2008, and a few dozen more hours in 2009.

Sometime in 2008 I realized that if we continued, Don and I could possibly identify every known manuscript source dealing with Joseph Smith's polygamy so I could quote or at least reference them in what book or books resulted. Our goals changed at that point from merely surveying the topic to trying to find and collect everything available. Then, if ten years after publication, we could look back and say that we had identified 90-plus percent of all available documents, we'd be satisfied with our efforts. Today (2020), a handful of important new documents have surfaced, but that's all. I was pleased to note that while post-publication criticisms were plentiful, none complained that *Joseph Smith's Polygamy: History and Theology* (published in 2013 in three volumes) left important documents out.

Generally Don and I divided our focuses. I would review published sources during the week and glean references that I would place on a growing list called "Documents to Obtain or Review." I would email this to Don who would use it to guide his searches. In truth, Don found most of the best stuff on his own. Sometimes, the references I would copy from other authors' notes were not accurately described. For example, Danel Bachman listed in the text of his 1975 master's thesis on Joseph Smith's polygamy a letter written by Mary Elizabeth Rollins Lightner that was supposedly addressed to "John A. Young," but the note listed "John A. Smith." Richard S. Van Wagoner cited the letter's recipient as "John R. Young." Don discovered that the actual addressee was John Henry Smith. Throughout the written text, I seldom quoted a source secondhand. One of our goals was to identify and cite firsthand every reference and to create a comprehensive bibliography to benefit future scholars.

During those years, our interactions were fairly predictable as Don lived in Salt Lake City and I was in Layton, twenty miles north. I was singing with the Mormon Tabernacle Choir (now called the Tabernacle Choir at Temple Square), which practiced and performed on Thursday nights and Sunday mornings. Don and I would arrange to meet right after practices at the LDS Conference Center near the underground parking lot entrance. We'd exchange copies of documents and discuss their possible significance. For example, in late November 2007 I journalized: "I met Don Bradley after [choir practice] and got 100s of pages of research materials." I often referred to him in my journal simply as "Sherlock" because of the remarkable manuscripts and data he was accumulating.

One recollection from 2008 remains clear in my mind. On a cold Thursday evening, at about 9:45 p.m., we were standing by the elevator in the hallway inside the LDS Conference Center door 13. Don had given me some information regarding Fanny Alger, whom Joseph Smith had reportedly married in the mid-1830s in Ohio, and I asked him whether anyone had accused Smith of polygamy prior to John C. Bennett in 1842. (Bennett had left the church in 1842 and before the end of the year had written a book attacking Smith and the Latter-day Saints.) Writers such as Fawn Brodie and Jerald and Sandra Tanner had asserted that throughout the 1830s Smith was deflecting polygamy allegations. We both paused and pondered for a few seconds. We then realized that our research didn't support this. It seemed that no one had accused Smith using that specific word (or anything similar implying a plurality of wives) throughout that decade or in connection with Alger. I asked Don to search for any contemporaneous charges of polygamy, which both he and I were never able to find in the historical record.

There is no denying that Don Bradley is the single most important adjunct to the creation of the *Joseph Smith's Polygamy* books. The first two volumes list me as the author with the clarification "with the assistance of Don Bradley."

The Andrew Jenson Papers

One of Don's most remarkable documentary finds involved Andrew Jenson, the publisher of the *Historical Record: A Monthly Periodical Devoted Exclusively to Historical, Biographical, Chronological, and Statistical Matters,* printed between 1882 and 1890. Although Jenson is best known as an official Assistant LDS Church Historian (1897–1941), he was an independent researcher during these eight years.

Don reviewed Jenson's personal journal (at LDS Archives), which recorded visits he made in 1886–87 to the few Nauvoo polygamists who were still alive to get information about Joseph Smith's wives. Reading those accounts prompted the question: "Where were the documents that he made during those visits?" The Church History Library (previously LDS Archives) catalog contained no obvious references to where those manuscripts might be located. Don later related how the problem was solved: "The still small voice of Church History Library employee Robin Jensen" told him to access a collection just recently re-catalogued.

Don requested the document collection and found it contained previously unpublished data. It is probable that he was the first non-church employee to look at those manuscripts since they had been filed with the archives. They contained important recollections dealing with topics such as polyandry and the identity of Joseph Smith's wives.

As Don was evaluating a list of names that Jenson compiled, he noticed a shift in the handwriting midway down one of the pages. Puzzling over what this change might represent, he invited me to meet with him and historian Jill Mulvay Derr, an expert on the life and handwriting of Eliza R. Snow, one of Smith's plural wives. Don was testing his theory that during an interview with Snow in late 1886, Jenson was writing names and then turned the paper over to Snow to finish the list. Derr verified that, in her opinion, it was clearly Snow's handwriting. Afterwards Don did his own comparison, concluding that Snow had indeed penned the final half of the names on the list.

Discovering Snow's handwriting added validity to the all the names on the list. Probably only Joseph Smith knew all of the names of his wives, some, in my opinion, for time and eternity, and others for eternity only. But among those plural wives, Snow may have been the best informed.

Binders

The acquisition of an ever-increasing number of documents created a problem for me—how to file and maintain them? Without any formal archival training, I initially just spread them all out on the floor of my office. Soon the number became too great for such a rudimentary filing system. Years earlier I had acquired a binding machine that used plastic combs to keep pages together. It would punch the slots and could assemble nearly 150 pages in one binder. I took up the papers from the floor and bound them into binders of around 100 pages each. Some contained dozens of individual documents, while others may have been full of excerpts from a single source. In the end I had 95 bound volumes with probably 10,000-plus pages. I kept a running catalog of each book's contents. (All of these binders are now available on-line at MormonPolygamyDocuments.org, with the originals now housed at the Harold B. Lee Library at Brigham Young University.)

I am embarrassed to say that during 2008 I always carried copies of documents with me. Whenever a spare minute arrived at work or even while attending church services, I had copies with me that I was reading and marking. My annotation system began with an initial reading where I would mark important sections with a yellow high-lighter and those worthy of transcription with both yellow cross-throughs and yellow stars in the margins. Next, I would review the document a second time and reread the yellowed portions, transcribing those excerpts into a computer database. While inputting the information, I would always include a full citation, so if I chose to use the quote later, I wouldn't need to spend any time finding the reference information. I know some people write and later add footnotes. I think that would be such drudgery to have to search out footnote reference information after writing the body of the text that I avoided it at all costs.

The last step was to print out, read, and reread the excerpts to familiarize myself with them to the point where I could implement them into the manuscript I was writing. I was always careful to use a quotation only once while composing. If I did feel the need to repeat it in the text, I advised the reader and explained my reasons for including it a second time. This did not apply to volume 3 of *Joseph Smith's Polygamy*, which I treated as a separate book from volumes 1–2.

Temple Lot Depositions

As discussed above, the 1892 Temple Lot litigation depositions constitute a primary source of Nauvoo polygamy information. I did not feel comfortable delegating all that research to Don, so I dove in myself. I quickly learned that references to Nauvoo plural marriage in the 606-page version sold by the Reorganized Church of Jesus Christ of Latter Day Saints (now Community of Christ) were too redacted to be useful to my research. What I didn't know at the time is that the original manuscript is over 1,700 pages long, divided into four sections.

I had no problems getting access to the microfilm to view the depositions on the old microfilm readers in a dimly lit portion of the library on the first floor of the LDS Church Office Building. I'd never used a microfilm reader before, but with the help of the staff, I got the film loaded. As I tried to understand what I was reading, I found myself repeatedly spinning the handle as the frames of microfilmed pages rolled in front of my eyes. After less than an hour, I found myself experiencing serious motion sickness that limited my ability to continue. Such nausea was a problem for me as a boy, and now it prevented me from enjoying my microfilm adventure. Although I had my computer with me and transcribed a couple of pages of notes, I knew something was going to have to change if I were ever to understand the contents of the Temple Lot proceedings. Dosing myself with an anti-emetic every time I sat at a microfilm reader didn't seem practical.

I searched the Internet and even called the Eighth District Court in Kansas City, Kansas, to see if I could get a copy of an original. They couldn't locate it based on the information I gave them. I also contacted the Community of Christ archives. While they wanted to help, giving me a full copy was beyond their ability. Eventually I explained my problem to a senior church historian in Salt Lake who told me that if I would fund the photographing of the document at five cents a page, they would make me a high resolution copy on a CD-ROM. So within weeks I had my own digital pages of the entire document for less than a hundred dollars. I loaded the scans onto my laptop computer and was reading the depositions everywhere I went for the next several weeks. Even when traveling to my daughter's apartment in California for Christmas, I remember deciphering the typed copies on the plane and during minutes of down time. Eventually I printed off about 400 pages that seemed more important. These I bound into their own booklets and added them to my binder collection. (All 1,700-plus pages of the Temple Lot litigation are available today at Archive.org.)

Joseph F. Smith Affidavits

The third important database of Nauvoo polygamy activities, and perhaps the most important, includes a set of affidavits compiled by Joseph F. Smith (Joseph Smith's nephew) in 1869–70. When he finished, he had forty-four affidavits recorded in his four books and thirteen on separate sheets for a total of fifty-eight separate first-hand accounts. Fifteen of these were from Smith's plural wives. At the time, these were listed as "restricted" in LDS Archives.

I applied for access, which was granted, but I could only view them when the archives was open. In the meantime, I had purchased a set of CDs and DVDs from a long-time history scholar who was refocusing his research. They contained copies of old newspapers, dissertations, and theses. Tucked within the digital files was a complete set of the affidavit books. Someone had copied and removed them from the archives. I was pretty sure my copies were not authorized, but my vendor may not have realized they were there. I must confess experiencing a tinge of guilt as I reviewed them at my leisure in my home. (Now they can all be viewed at Archive.org.)

I'll never forget the night I compared the two unfinished affidavits that mentioned plural wife Sylvia Sessions. The first used an 1842 date for her sealing to Joseph Smith, which date had been popularized by Todd Compton in *In Sacred Loneliness* and was commonly cited as reliable. As I read a similar affidavit in another affidavit book, I was startled to see it included the year 1843. As far as I could see, neither date was necessarily more reliable than the other. I could hardly sleep that night thinking how the different dates affected some otherwise accepted assumptions. Months later I asked Compton about the discrepancy. He told me that his time in Salt Lake City to research the affidavit books was limited to one week. He applied for permission on Monday, but didn't receive it until Friday and so only had a few hours to review the books' contents and must have missed the inconsistency.

Copying Michael Marquardt's Files

At the 2007 meeting of the John Whitmer Historical Association in Kirtland, Ohio, *Modern Polygamy and Mormon Fundamentalism* received the "Best Book of 2007" award. I was grateful to the awards committee, to Greg Kofford, and to Lavina Fielding Anderson for helping to get the book published. There I also met H. Michael Marquardt and learned of his massive files, many of which dealt with plural marriage. He mentioned he was donating them all to the J. Willard Marriott Library at the University of Utah. A couple of weeks later Don Bradley and I met with him at his home in Sandy, Utah, to view the file boxes that were everywhere throughout his basement. We made arrangements with him to allow me to copy-scan all of his polygamy-related items before they left his possession. I knew Don couldn't find everything Marquardt had accumulated and was elated that he permitted me to copy those files prior to delivering them to the university.

Weeks later in mid-December I returned to Marquardt's home with my desk-top scanner for three solid days during which I copied thousands of pages of documents. It was a treasure trove of manuscripts I couldn't wait to devour back in my own home.

During those hours, Marquardt and I had many opportunities to chat, and I grew to appreciate his goodness and remarkable scholarship. We would continue to meet whenever a question came up that I knew he could help me with. One issue in particular was the chronological sequences surrounding the approval of the article on "Marriage," section CI (101) in the 1835 Doctrine and Covenants. I remember Marquardt's methodic approach to the evidence. He insisted we lay the pertinent documents out across his couch in his basement (the file boxes were long transported to the library). After a few hours, the apparent sequence of events seemed to emerge to our delight and satisfaction.

Working with the LDS Church Archives, Historians, and Leaders

On several occasions between 2007 and 2012 Don and I met with church historians to seek permission to use photographs and to access documents. In every case our requests were granted with only one exception. When I asked to see William Clayton's personal journals for Nauvoo, LDS Church Historian Marlin K. Jensen of the Seventy met with me personally. He explained that Clayton's journals were located in the First Presidency's office vault and that the Church History Library had no control over it. As he spoke, I must confess to thinking, "How about asking them for me?" But I didn't voice that request. Instead, he told me they had an accurate typescript of the journals and would be happy to check all Clayton quotations that I was going to use against the typescript. They verified all the Clayton quotes prior to my using them. (I understand the Clayton journals are scheduled for future publication by the Joseph Smith Papers historians.)

As discussed above, while researching and writing, Don and I received what seemed to be unrestricted access to the documents we desired to review. Members of the Church History Library were always willing to read through the latest draft or offer an opinion or suggestions concerning specific issues we confronted. Frankly, I did not always accept the recommendations I received, but usually I would make some modifications to the text causing concern. While singing with the choir at the 2010 October general conference, I approached Elder Jensen standing on the rostrum below the choir loft. His first words to me were, "When is your book coming out?" I wrote in my journal that night: "I interpret that as unofficial support. I hope he will feel the same when it finally is printed."

Editing and Publishing

At the end of March 2007 I gave a copy of my manuscript, which, at the time, totaled 100 pages single spaced, to Greg Kofford to see if he might be interested in publishing a longer version. While he obviously needed a finished manuscript before making a decision to publish, he was always supportive as the number of pages continued to grow. He even attended a book signing at Barnes and Noble in south Salt Lake for *Modern Polygamy and Mormon Fundamentalism* on November 28. I arrived with excitement and saw my book on the poster by the front door. The chairs in the back were all arranged in a half-circle, and I was poised to read a few sections and field the questions that were to flow from dozens of attendees. Nobody else came. I got to keep the poster, though, and later tacked it on the wall of my library.

I wrote feverishly throughout 2007 to 2009, at least twenty-to-thirty hours a week, including when on vacation. Eventually I decided to split off any theological discussions of Smith's plural marriage doctrine into its own volume, so by July of 2008, the working title of the primary volume became: "Joseph Smith's Polygamy: History." I then printed off a copy that topped 400 single-spaced pages. Other printed drafts came in October, and then January, April, and September 2009.

I don't recall precisely why I spent the time and money to print out these 500-plus page volumes, but I think it was so I could share what I had accumulated with various readers and friends. Their feedback was always welcomed. Sometimes, I would simply send a chapter or two. Reviewers of various portions included Todd Compton, D. Michael Quinn, Michael Marquardt, Daniel Bachman, Ron Barney, and several other friends in the Church History Department.

Finally, on March 13, 2010, I sent a copy to Lavina Fielding Anderson that I thought was ready for final editing. Unfortunately for me, the Kofford Books publishing schedule had had to push publication back a few months, which turned into a couple of years. As I impatiently waited, I continued to tweak specific chapters so that when we finally did start editing in 2012, the text was tighter and better documented. In February 2012 I wrote: "I'm so glad that we didn't go to press a couple of years ago because the research has continued and this chapter updates have greatly strengthened the discussion."

When we finally reached the editing stage, I found Lavina to be a kind taskmaster. By this time, she had adopted all the modern "track changes" approach to editing. As an accomplished historian and writer herself, she often guided me to ideas and sources that, frankly, I had missed. Her reworking of my prose was a constant blessing. More than once she typed "no more passive verbs!" in the comment section. I can't help wondering if my writing style about drove her crazy. Needless to say, her investment in getting the final text "right" involved far more than what a traditional editor might have expended, and I will be forever grateful to her.

Years later I told Lavina's husband, Paul, that I'd been having an online romance with his wife with multiple emails and one-on-one meetings. The back-and-forth sometimes seemed like a literary dance. Lavina recently edited a short article I was working on, an early version of "Curiously Unique: Joseph Smith as Author of the Book of Mormon," and I told her it was great to hear her voice in my head again. (The article was published in *Interpreter: A Journal of Latter-day Saint Faith and Scholarship* in 2019, and is available at www.mormoninterpreter.com/curiously-unique-joseph-smith-as-author-of-the-book-of-mormon.)

Once we started editing in early 2012, there was talk of having published copies of the book available for sale by the June meeting of the Mormon History Association, but we weren't close to publication by that time. On July 29, 2012, I recorded: "I went to lunch with Lavina and we talked all about the book. It will take some time, but I think we can have advanced readers copies by [the annual conference of the] John Whitmer [Historical Association, less than two months away]. I just finished the 7th (of 48) chapters." Again, that timeline was far too optimistic, but at least things continued to move along.

By the time I was ready to send the final edited manuscripts, "Joseph Smith's Polygamy: History," and "Joseph Smith's Polygamy: Theology," to Greg Kofford Books, Kofford had hired a talented director, Loyd Ericson. To speed things along, Ericson edited the "Theology" volume rather than Lavina and was very knowledgeable regarding the steps needed to get the manuscripts into book form.

However, when Ericson received the 322,196-word "History" manuscript along with its 47,691 words of appendices, he got back to me the next day saying the volume would be massive. He even tried expanding the page format. We discussed splitting the manuscript into two volumes and received Kofford's approval. Instantly the project became a trilogy—sometimes I call it my "triple combination," a term LDS members use to refer to the one-volume edition of The Book of Mormon, The Doctrine and Covenants, and The Pearl of Great Price.

The trilogy was released on March 23, 2013, and sold out its run of about 1,200 sets within a year or so. Kofford Books reprinted it and a few years later came out with a paperback edition which is still available. An ebook edition may also be purchased online.

Moving Beyond Polygamy

Looking back to 2007, I recall that due to surrounding controversies, research into plural marriage often brought some eyebrow-raising from some church members who heard of my projects. Sometimes people wondered if my interests might blossom into actual practice, but at the time I was divorced and single. My response was simply that I couldn't successfully "monog," so they didn't need to worry about me trying to "polyg." Later, after I remarried in 2013, Don Bradley observed that I had finally moved beyond "zerogamy."

There is no denying the ambiguity and contradictory nature of many of the accounts presumably documenting Joseph Smith's introduction of plural marriage among the Latter-day Saints. The good news is that all known manuscript data is available, most of it on the Internet, for any interested inquirer to investigate.

While critics may contend libido, power, control, or ego drove the process, that is not what I found. Through my research, I concluded that the principle of plural marriage was adopted by Joseph Smith and other church members as a religious practice. Participants contracted those marriages because they felt God required it. Supernatural influences, dreams, visions, and even angelic visitations were sometimes reported supporting its expansion among the most devout Latter-day Saints. I also learned through this project that Smith was not perfect, and I should not expect him to be. With that said, I found nothing to convince me he was ever unworthy to exercise the spiritual gifts required of God's prophet on earth. Lastly, I concluded I personally don't like polygamy. It is unequal, that is, unfair and even sexist. I'm glad my God does not command such challenges of me today.

Even though polygamy is controversial and its practice has undermined the faith of more than one Latter-day Saint, through the entire research and writing process, I felt sustained by an unrelated belief regarding the Book of Mormon. I believed that Joseph Smith, as a twenty-three-year-old farmer, did not possess the skill set needed to generate all 269,320 words recorded by scribes in 1829. Perhaps it is no surprise that now that I've said all I care to say about polygamy, I've decided to test that theory regarding Smith and the Book of Mormon. Stay tuned.

WRITING MORMON HISTORY

MELVIN C. JOHNSON

5

The art of writing New Mormon History and its post-modern successor(s) fascinate me. All good history writing, because we conceptualize and interpret our lives in narrative, must be first-rate narrative. Another way to express this is that we live as our own first-person characters. We recount our adventures that way.

Humans communicate to one another their unending roles in families and groups, with a cast of characters, friends and enemies and strangers, in all sorts of social interactions. From my youngest days in my family and on the school grounds at Commonwealth Elementary, people have been telling their lives in story form.

I think the girls were much better than we boys in telling the days of their lives. Their ability to embellish stories about the marvelous worlds they inhabited made us boys seem like dolts. LDS youth in Southern California engaged in telling self-stories endlessly, I remember, ongoing stories with their companions from Primary through MIA and priesthood quorums and scouting. Many of us embraced ourselves as the latest actors in the ongoing dramas of the Mormon "Us" versus the "Them" of everyone else. We were the next generation of LDS persecuted yet privileged *Saturday's Warriors*. On social media I follow many enduring friends and acquaintances as well as newer contacts. They are still telling stories, now with flashbacks and much editing.

Our existences, in other words, are breathing, living narratives, and telling our stories enlightens us as well as our listeners and readers in making sense of our lives. As historians, we bring that ability to spin tales to our profession.

Writing Biography and History Is Hard

Narrating and describing the lives of Lyman Wight and John Hawley,[1] I have found to be anything but easy. Being a good biographer can be more challenging than writing a good biography, as the crafting of the latter flows from the understanding the former, and that will challenge inevitably the writer's pre-conceptions. Noted biographer Scott Donaldson has defined the art of history as "the impossible craft." And it's a matter of judgment where to draw the line between "necessarily tough" and "unnecessarily tough." Donaldson explains, "There's a blurb from Peter Matthiessen on the back of my Fenton book that says I was tough where I needed to be. And that's good. You want to be honest and tell the whole story; you don't want it to be wrapped in any more concealments than are necessary, if any are. And let's say that the most important reason of all it's an impossible craft is that you cannot know what someone else's life was like. You can try to come close."[2]

Writers will draw the lines differently. The good biography will be inevitably molded as part of "the impossible craft" and will be incomplete to some extent. All one can do is to try to come close.

Because biography is an art that cannot rummage thoroughly the subject's soul, conclusions will be imprecise. Gathering data remains critical, but much of the quality will come from the laborer's growing skill over the decades in mining, appraising, and interpreting data that fashion story.

All evidence possible—no matter how contrary or opposed or kindly or reassuring—that can be must be quarried and assayed

---

1. *Polygamy on the Pedernales: Lyman Wight's Mormon Villages in Antebellum Texas, 1845–1858* (2006). The book can be obtained at no cost online at https://digitalcommons.usu.edu/usupress_pubs/43; and *The Life & Times of John P. Hawley: a Mormon Ulysses of the American West* (Salt Lake City, Utah: Kofford Books, 2019).

2. Bill Morris, "Scott Donaldson on the 'Impossible Craft' of Writing Biography," in *The Millions Interview*, posted Feb. 27, 2012, www.themillions.com/2012/02/scott-donaldson-on-the-impossible-craft-of-writing-biography.html; accessed July 1, 2014. The Fenton book is *Death of a Rebel: The Charlie Fenton Story* (2011).

fairly. Because all evidence will not be found about a complex subject, the inexactness of biography or history can be minimized only to the extent of the writer's professionalism and experience and talent and fairness.

Below are some guidelines in writing Mormon history and biography. They are, of course, not definitive; they worked for me and might be of use to others.

1. Create and use a database for entering research and querying questions from it.

Databases and their uses for research and writing were introduced by Jonathan Gerland and me at the Texas Forestry Museum in the early 1990s. (Gerland is senior archivist of the History Center in Diboll, Texas, and foremost historian of the East Texas forest culture and industry fields.) Carol Riggs, the museum director, was the brain child who figured out that we should create and use databases to record and query the East Texas forest industry information that we discovered. I have upgraded since then from ClarisWorks 2.0 to the latest versions of FileMakerPro because of its relational capability and programmability. FMP is very powerful, easily handing all my digital database needs (see www. filemaker.com).

Gerland and I began creating databases to archive and interpret material in the East Texas milieu of mill towns, lumber operations, and logging rail and tram roads. The entered data and narratives of the peoples and companies revealed how a world was transformed in East Texas from a limited, subsistence society of family farms to a growing, dynamic, and increasingly industrial modern society based, first, on the railroads and the lumber industry, and then oil. Gerland had gone on to the Tyrrell Public Library in Beaumont by the time I completed the databases in May 1996. We had entered and could query several tens of thousands of sourced entries and information on hundreds of logging rail and tram roads and thousands of mill towns and logging sites. The program received national and state awards, and we ended up writing a professional article of some notice on industrial transportation in East.[3]

My research for the Texas History Museum, at Lufkin, Texas, from 1994 to 1996, laid the foundation of *Polygamy on the Pedernales: Lyman Wight's Mormon Villages in Antebellum Texas, 1845–1858*. That research has led to various subjects including John Hawley, the Zodiac Temple, and the Mormon community in Pine Valley, Utah Territory, as well as others.

2. *Record the research on a manipulated timeline.*

Building a database (DB) narrative on a time-based order permits the historian to more easily record, store, and ask the DB to query questions. Let it do a Henry Adams DB flash back after your imagination suggests the questions you wanted answered. For instance, I queried the data about marriages at Zodiac, Texas, in the Lyman Wight Colony, and the DB gave me easily processed

---

3. See www.treetexas.com/research/sawmill. The project was recognized by and won awards from the American Historical Association and the Texas State Historical Association. Melvin C. Johnson and Jonathan K. Gerland, "Tapping 'Green Gold': The Steam Rail and Logging Tram Roads of East Texas," *Environmental History* 1, no. 4 (Oct. 1996): 46–65.

information to produce a chart identifying married individuals living in Zodiac in 1850 according to residence, household heads and spouses, age, and marital status.[4]

During my East Texas research, I kept encountering references to the "Mormon millers" of the Texas Hill Country west of Austin and north of San Antonio during the 1840s and 1850s. I dutifully entered the material but kept their increasingly interesting narrative in the back of my head. Eventually, the lure grew so great that I created a specific database for these Texas Hill Country pre-Civil War Mormons and began entering information.

3. Find the theme or "heart" that will emerge and beguile you.

The book's theme or heart will emerge from the material in the DB, at least it did for me. I wanted to figure how to explain Lyman Wight's quest for meaning in a way that would purposefully and worthily authenticate and place his character and biographical narrative within the Latter Day Restoration of Joseph Smith.

In Wight's case, his discipleship to Smith obviously defined his identify. Once I grasped Wight's motivation, the partisan values of his followers emerged. Their loyalty to Wight and antipathy toward Brigham Young cored the spiritual and emotional identity of the Texas Colony. The colony's central body of families began in the Black River lumber mission in Wisconsin Territory. They worked for Lyman Wight, Bishop George Miller, and Henry W. Miller in logging, milling, and supplying the economic boom of Mormon Nauvoo, Illinois, with finished timber for building the temple, the Nauvoo House, and local housing needs. The colony then trekked to the Republic of Texas in 1845 and lived on the frontier until its remnants merged at the death of Wight into the greater population of the State of Texas.

4. Make the narrative as clear and simple and entertaining as possible.

The Lyman Wight story was arranged chronologically as a narrative and written as a story. As our lives are narratives, so were the Wight members as well as colony itself, its own being full of

---

4. This chart is on p. 78 of *Polygamy in the Pedernales.*

life and fraught with death. I committed myself to tell the stories of Wight, his colonists, their communities, and their lives on the American borderlands. In doing so, I had to learn about the ins and outs of genealogy, family history, and community history. And "ins and outs" will sometimes reveal the most amazing life tales of people you think virtually unimportant.

One story was the romance of John Hawley's commendable love for his wife of almost sixty years, which to an extent mitigated his lack of writing about and, apparently, his gender's general acceptance and expectation of the women to labor and sacrifice on the wagon road and frontier. The subject of women and the frontier, their overwhelming and unique challenges and challenges in the American West, continues to be a major area for historical enquiry.[5] However, every magnificent story of a Sylvia Hawley is balanced by that of a Sarah Hadfield Wight Hawley Earl, a sister-in-law of John Hawley.

5. Be sensitive to secondary personages and themes that emerge from the narrative and research.

Sarah Earl beggars the heart's capacity to clutch her story. Born in 1827, christened in the Cathedral Church of England in Manchester, Sarah immigrated as a young LDS convert with her family to Nauvoo in 1841. The girl then went to the wild pineries of western Wisconsin. She sheltered in the rudest of frontier shacks and shanties for more than twenty years, suffering lack of food and enduring desperate winters and being the plural wife of three husbands. A teenage plural wife of Orange Wight, Lyman's son, she walked and rode and floated 1,500 miles down the American borderlands to the Texas frontier. She bore Orange three children: Martenisia, who would be a plural wife herself and die in

5. For a distinctive presentation of the sacrifice and challenges unique to womanhood, consult Lillian Schlissel, *Women's Diaries of the Westward Journey* (New York: Shocken; rpt. ed., 2004). Her footnotes on p. 87 are worth noting here: William R. Taylor and Christopher Lasch, "Two 'Kindred Spirits': Sorority and Family in New England 1839–1846," *New England Quarterly* 36 (1863): 25–41. Also Charles E. Rosenberg, "Sexuality, Class, and Role in Nineteenth-Century America," *American Quarterly* 25 (May 1973): 131–53; and Carroll Smith-Rosenberg, "The Female World of Love and Ritual: Relations Between Women in Nineteenth Century America," *Signs* 1 (1975): 1–28.

1910; Hyrum, who was buried as a toddler in the Mormon Mill Cemetery of Hamilton Valley, Texas, in 1851; and Joseph William, who survived until 1881.

Sarah then joined George Hawley as his second plural wife along with her sister Ann (Hawley's first wife), when the Hawley clan moved to the Cherokee Nation. Sarah bore a daughter named either Amy or Emma, who died as an infant. George took a teenage girl, Jeanette Goudie, as his third wife. The family immigrated to Utah Territory, settling in Ogden then Lehi, then Washington, and finally in Pine Valley, where the Hawleys scrabbled for a rude back country life. Sarah, before her death, left George and married an Earl, bore a daughter who carried her own name, and within a year both were buried in the Old Pine Valley Cemetery.[6] John Hawley, George's brother, does not mention Sarah or her sister neighbors' travails other than the deaths of his children. Sarah was thirty-nine when she was interred in Pine Valley's cemetery.

Sarah's incredible tale would not have come forth without asking the DB about her, and reinforces that important secondary themes and characters will be discovered.

Another character was John Pierce Hawley.

The emergence of John Hawley's character grew on me. The more I worked on Wight and his colonies in Wisconsin and Texas, the more the Hawley family and John focused the story in ways more poignant than I would have thought. I wondered if he might someday become keener a subject than Wight. And, as time went by, John Hawley grew more intriguing to me. His record in the west and his interaction with major sects of Mormonism rival those of Bishop George Miller, Zenos H. Gurley Sr., Richard Hewitt, and John Kelting. Hawley became to me the Everyman of the Latter Day Restoration in the mid-nineteenth-century American West. I discovered he had his own secrets as well and did not easily share them. I came to realize I would write about him as well as Wight.

6. Ancestral File, database, FamilySearch, familysearch.org/pal:/MM9.2.1/M75N-QRV, accessed: Feb. 20, 2014, entry for "Sarah HADFIELD," and Ancestral File Number:2PFT-TL, files.usgwarchives.net/tx/burnet/cemetery/mormills.txt, accessed Feb. 20, 2104; Johnson, *Polygamy on the Pedernales*, 84; Hawley, "Autobiography," 20; Old Pine Valley Cemetery, 1.

The Hawleys with the Wightite community built the first Latter Day temple west of the Mississippi, in Zodiac, Texas. John recorded that "Lyman told us we must build a house for to attend to the baptism for the dead and also the ordinance of washing of feet and a general endowment in the wilderness. So we ... built a good little Temple to worship in ..." On the second floor of the large, two-story log building, Hawley received his temple endowment and was sealed to Sylvia for time and eternity. He also officiated as proxy in sealings and baptisms for the dead. More than forty years later, in a deposition as a witness in the Temple Lot case (to determine the legal ownership of some land in Independence, Missouri) and in other writings, he compared the Zodiac temple ritual and regalia to that of the LDS Church's Endowment House in Salt Lake City. His commentary adds insight about the LDS first and second anointings in territorial Utah.[7]

John Hawley's search for the authentic Restoration finally found its rest in the mid-west with the RLDS Church. John is little remembered today in the history of Pine Valley or in Utah or at Mountain Meadows. This book of Hawley's faith odyssey through the American West covers his life until the age of forty-four. He

---

7. *Autobiography of John Pierce Hawley,* ed. Robert Hawley (Privately printed, 1981), 7. This is a typescript copy of the unpublished handwritten John Hawley manuscript in the Community of Christ Archives, Independence, Missouri. Although the RLDS *Journal of History* published an autobiographical sketch of Hawley in its April 1911 issue, the editors deleted his portion when he lived in southern Utah during the 1850s. For the suppressed section, see the 1885 transcript, entitled "Autobiography of John Hawley," in the Community of Christ Archives. Robert Hawley placed the 1911 article of John P. Hawley "Experiences of John Hawley," *Journal of History* 4, no. 2 (Apr. 1911): 223–45, toward the end of the Autobiography. See also John and Dorothea (Weinehiemer) Cotter, comps., "The Mormon Colony (Zodiac) Near Fredericksburg, Texas," Unpublished Manuscripts, Cotter Collection, Pioneer Heritage Memorial Library, Fredericksburg, Texas; and William Leyland Journal, in Heman Hale Smith, "Lyman Wight Colony in Texas," 21, 25, a manuscript prepared for the Reorganized Church of Jesus Christ of Latter Day Saints, 1920, Community of Christ Archives. Heman H. Smith (son of Heman C. Smith, grandson of Spencer Smith, and great-grandson of Lyman Wight, all members of Zodiac), an apostle, member of the Seventy, and historian for the RLDS Church, prepared the manuscript from the Lyman Wight Journal, Spencer Smith Journal, and William Leyland Journal, all later destroyed by fire. He wrongly insisted that polygamy was limited to the families of Lyman Wight, Orange Lysander Wight, and Ezra Chipman. *United States Census, Social Statistics Schedule, Census of 1850, Gillespie County, Texas.*

would live another thirty-nine years, more than half of his adult life, actively in the service of RLDS Mormonism.

6. Create a modern information platform to record what you research, and ask your DB questions that can be more easily relationable and searchable on a digital platform.

I concluded that I was to write about Wight, his colony, and their journeys through the American borderlands from Wisconsin Territory to the Republic of Texas, their lives on the Lone Star frontier, and their dispersals after his death. So was the book to be a biography of Lyman or a history of the colony? That is when I made a monumental discovery.

Following the Henry Adams's guide of asking oneself questions to which one does not know the answers, I began querying the DB, and I began writing, and, in the process, found more and more questions to which I needed to find more and more answers. So I researched more and kept collecting sources, entering the data, and correlating the answers to my questions. The program became a symbiotic process of questioning and researching and answering and questioning. A great strength of the FileMaker Pro DB is that the constructed fields can be opened fully to see what has been recorded in that field with the sources for the information. For example, I was able to create a Lyman Wight Colony DB covering the colony's stay in Zodiac, Texas, that included specific fields for terms, places, year(s), individuals, commentary, and bibliography. Each field contained all the information that I entered and could be easily opened for present and future use.

Here is an example of a question I wanted answered. How many Wightite marriages were polygamous versus monogamous? Did the information suggest more polygamous marriages than previously thought? Creating a specific field for marriages led to questions about divorces and births and deaths, cross-referencing them by year and community (for example, Zodiac or Mormon Mill), thus adding considerable depth to colony history as well as to the lives of individual colony members. Being able to correlate a spectrum of information, stored in the DB fields, brought community and individual history to life.

Model of Zodiac, Texas.

7. Fine history writing encompasses good literary skills.

These last decades, a remarkable assembly of writers and researchers has stepped forward in our fields of Restoration Studies. They have been producing wonderful narrative interpretations. They are aware of the roles of objectivity and fairness in theme and conflict, as well as being proficient in the art of diction, syntax, tone, and semantics.

Plagiarism and Recognition

Be careful to avoid plagiarism, the great wickedness of professional writing. The good writer does not need it. The emerging writer cannot afford it. The FM Pro program makes research easily accessible (through indexes and lists) so that (1) you can find the source you want and (2) you can attribute it correctly. Jealousy assails all historians at one time or another, I believe. Act rather than react to it. I know of a historian of some repute who was unhappy that a peer working in the same area was gaining some renown. The first writer eventually published in the same area, used many of the same sources, yet failed to acknowledge the other writer and his works or his use of the same sources. The first writer's work was incomplete, inaccurate, and unimportant, in the end. Don't be guilty of pettiness. Give credit where credit is due.

The student of Mormonism is fortunate that John Hawley, despite his lack of formal schooling, recorded his life. He was literate and wrote well for a man born, raised, and survived on the American back country and borderlands and frontiers. He wrote more than fourteen years after leaving Utah Territory, and at times he was recounting events more than five decades earlier. However, mostly after he joined the RLDS Church in 1870, some of his comments became disingenuous and even false, particularly about Restoration leaders, issues, and controversies, including the doctrine of and who practiced plurality of wives. I note where I think Hawley deliberately obfuscated on these subjects.

Dualism, Us v. Them, Faithful History, and History of the Faithful

Many historians have to overcome a tendency to dualistic interpretation of belief and experience, suppressing the desire to separate "us" from "them." Dualism regrettably does satisfy many readers, particularly in our field of studies. Avoid being the kind of historian who accepts that evidence should be screwed onto a preconceived position, rather than alter the viewpoint to fit the data and information. A history of the faithful should not be faithful history. John Hawley, unfortunately, himself wrote faithful history by the end of his life. I believe such a concept of barrel and hoops (for example, Hawley thinking priesthood ordinances produced eternal consequences) should not constrain the arts of history and biography. Mormon writers and readers alike must avoid being trapped in corners of classification that warp interpretation. They should keep in mind the counsel of Paul M. Edwards, a Community of Christ theologian and historian, who wrote, "History which is dependent on an individual's faith is a statement of convictions, not a statement of the convictions of his or her inquiry. If we are interested in the former rather than the latter, then we should be searching for a pastor—not a historian."[8]

Research and narrative can be crafted on an axial integration of opposites: for example, liberals/conservatives; east/west; true believer/no believer; democratic/republican; Dodgers/Giants; Mormons/gentiles; fundamentalist Mormons/everybody else. Wight could not exist in a religious community dominated by his apostolic peers. He turned his back on Nauvoo and created a new Mormon kingdom in the Republic of Texas. Hawley, on the other hand, stayed with the Twelve Apostles for fourteen years and struggled in a polygamous society of conferred authority, while being beckoned by a monogamous society of patrilineal authority. He weaved those antitheses and their data points along the axis into patterns and perspectives ever more complex and nuanced. I have tried my level best to come close as possible to "knowing" Lyman Wight and John Pierce Hawley and what their lives were like, being sympathetic where sympathy is due, being honest about human failings, willing to adjust the emerging themes to the data.

We all journey our trails and encounter our travails. Judy Nolte Lensink offers a cautionary note on the importance of our heritage: "If we kill off the sound of our ancestors, the major portion of us, all that is past is history, is human being, is lost and we come historically and spiritually thin, a mere shadow of who we were, on the earth." The narratives of Lyman Wight, Sarah Hadfield Wight Hawley Earl, John Hawley, and thousands of others are touchstones from which we try to capture their sound and tone and voice, to reveal their humanity, as they all journeyed the west in search of an authentic Latter Day Faith.[9]

---

8. Paul M. Edwards, "The Irony of Mormon History," *Utah Historical Quarterly* 41 (1973): 394–95.

9. Emily Hawley Gillespie, *"A Secret to Be Buried": The Diary of Emily Hawley Gillespie, 1858–1888*, ed. Judy Nolte Lensink (Iowa City: University of Iowa Press, 1989), quoted from Alice Walker, "Finding Celie's Voice" (72), XI.

ENLISTED FOR THE DURATION

DISCOVERING THE UTAH WAR, WRITING AT SWORD'S POINT

WILLIAM P. MacKINNON

6

The historian does not know what he has decided until he writes it. The act of writing is an essential part, then, of the process of research, of evaluation, of deciding about the significance and truth of any inquiry. It is writing — finding the words to express the assessed as well as the felt meanings — that brings research to its point. ... To write is to know.

> —Robin W. Winks, *Cloak & Gown: Scholars in the Secret War, 1939-1961* (1987)

When Joe Geisner asked me to write this essay, I was concerned about its relevance and the extent of reader interest. Thirteen years ago, before the first volume of *At Sword's Point* appeared, I wrote an article for *Dialogue: A Journal of Mormon Thought* to explain the reasons for my then half-century of research about the Utah War and to summarize my main findings to date. Shortly thereafter the internet blog *Dave's Mormon Inquiry* published an essay describing this piece under the heading "The Utah War: Nine Conclusions" and invited comments. One reader, styling himself "Matt W.," responded with a less-than-flattering reaction: "It would be helpful if MacKinnon hadn't spent the entire first third of his article talking about himself and how he came to write about this subject. Dude, you're not [LDS Church president] Gordon B. Hinckley. I really couldn't care less about your personal journey. Put a sock in it, and talk about the subject at hand already!" With this advice still in mind more than a decade later, I wondered about the wisdom of Joe's invitation. On the other hand, upon reflection, I realized that this anthology was explicitly dedicated to the proposition that readers indeed want to know who historians of the Mormon past are and why they write as they do. And so, with my admiration for Joe Geisner in mind and in the company of distinguished colleagues, I "proceed onward" but with sock at the ready.[1]

The "Why" and "How" Questions: A Personal Odyssey

Why has a Presbyterian Air Force veteran born in upstate New York during 1938 spent much of his life probing the history of a nineteenth-century army campaign in Mormon Utah? The answer is complex, loaded with tales of serendipity and colorful discoveries unearthed over the past sixty years. And so, with a tip of the hat to the title of novelist Tobias Wolff's wonderful anthology, our story begins.[2]

One might think that, as a native of Schenectady, New York, not far from Palmyra and the Burnt Over District, my first awareness of Mormonism came in childhood almost by osmosis.[3] The truth is that it was not until junior year in a Massachusetts preparatory school that I browsed the stacks of the school library and impulsively dipped into an early biography of Brigham Young while in search of a term paper topic. Why I pulled that particular book in 1955 is an unknown, although I was intrigued to discover later that my twin brother, Dick, had read the same book a few weeks earlier for the identical purpose. Spooky.

On one level, I think what drew me to Brigham Young's

---

1. *Dave's Mormon Inquiry: The Utah War: Nine Conclusions*, May 28, 2007, at www.mormoninquiry.typepad.com/mormon_inquiry/2007/05/the_utah_war_ni.html (accessed June 6, 2007). The article to which this blog essay relates is MacKinnon, "Loose in the Stacks: A Half-Century with the Utah War and Its Legacy," *Dialogue: Journal of Mormon Thought* 40 (Spring 2007): 43–81.

2. Tobias Wolff, *Our Story Begins: New and Selected Stories* (New York: Alfred A. Knopf, 2008).

3. For years I thought that my first book about Mormonism was Carl Carmer's biography of Joseph Smith, *The Farm Boy and the Angel*, and that I had read it while in elementary school in Schenectady around 1950. Only in preparing this essay did I realize that Carmer did not publish his book about Smith's early years until 1970, another reminder of the pitfalls awaiting historians relying on memory rather than documentation.

life's story was the realization that he was a near-contemporary of my school's founder, Protestant evangelist Dwight L. Moody (1837–99), and physically resembled Moody down to their shared beard and portliness. Young, like "D. L.," had a charismatic but rough-hewn platform style, lacking formal education because of the demands of his parents' hardscrabble farm near the Vermont-Massachusetts border, where Moody also toiled in the fields before heading to Boston to find God while selling shoes in the 1850s. And then there was the exotic element to Young's later life and surroundings—the same appeal that prompted Arthur Conan Doyle to enliven the first of his Sherlock Holmes stories, *A Study in Scarlet*, with a fictive murder that spilled from polygamous Utah into fog-shrouded Victorian London.

Thus introduced to nineteenth-century Mormon history in the American West, I went on to other interests and priorities, including college and a running dialogue with my draft board in the aftermath of the Korean War. What then prompted an interest in the Utah War of 1857–58 was an epiphany in the stacks of another library, this time in New Haven, Connecticut, during 1958, my sophomore year of college.[4] There, amid Yale's Gothic spires, gargoyles, and moats, I chose a history honors major. I then needed a topic for my senior essay, a required paper that was to approach the character of a PhD dissertation. In return for this commitment, Yale largely exempted me from attending my last two years of classes. A lot was at stake with this trade-off, including my very graduation.

Seeking advice on a topic, I turned to my hero and unofficial mentor at Yale. That man was Howard R. Lamar, then a young assistant professor from Alabama, whose wildly popular History 37 course on the frontier—dubbed "Cowboys and Indians"—would have a profound effect on me as it has on several generations of historians and others. Unknown to me then was a future in which Lamar would become a lifelong friend and Yale's Sterling Professor of History, dean, and president, as well as a founder of the Western History Association and authority on Utah's territorial period.[5] After I made several false starts on my own, Lamar suggested a topic, new but intriguing to me. It was one for which the

---

4. By way of contrast, see the story of how Jan Shipps, a Methodist housewife, began her long fascination with Mormon history on the campus of Utah State University in Logan. Shipps, *Sojourner in the Promised Land: Forty Years among the Mormons* (Urbana: University of Illinois Press, 2000); Klaus J. Hansen, "The Long Honeymoon: Jan Shipps among the Mormons," *Dialogue: A Journal of Mormon Thought* 37 (Fall 2004): 1–28.

5. As yet there is no full-length biography of Howard Roberts Lamar, age 96, and he has not written his reminiscences. Nonetheless, over the decades a rich body of anecdotal and chapter-length material about him has sprung up to describe his teaching skills, sense of humor, seminal role in the study and interpretation of Western Americana, willingness to mentor more than sixty graduate students, including large numbers of women, and ability to calm turbulent faculty/alumni waters at Yale. See essays in honor of Lamar by his former graduate students in George Miles, William Cronon, and Jay Gitlin, eds., *Under an Open Sky: Rethinking America's Western Past* (New York: W. W. Norton, 1992); and Lewis L. Gould, "Howard Roberts Lamar," in *Clio's Favorites: Leading Historians of the United States, 1945–2000*, ed. Robert Allen Rutland (Columbia: University of Missouri Press, 2000), 84–97. One assessment of Lamar's work by his peers took the form of multi-paper panels devoted to this subject at the 2003 and 2005 annual meetings of the Western History Association and Organization of American Historians, respectively. In 2005 the Mormon History Association honored Lamar with its Thomas L. Kane Award. His most recent book is *Charlie Siringo's West: An Interpretive Biography* (Albuquerque: University of New Mexico Press, 2005).

library's manuscript collection had extensive, unexploited primary sources: the Utah War.[6]

This suggestion propelled me to the "Mother Lode"—the Yale Collection of Western Americana—where I introduced myself to its curator, Archibald Hanna Jr. Archie Hanna was a Massachusetts Yankee and a veteran of World War II's Pacific theater, then in the early stages of an extraordinary thirty-year run in making Yale the leading force that it is today in the study of the American West. As formidable as this archivist-marine then seemed to a teenager, Archie, too, was to become and remain a friend.[7]

After Hanna's guided tour through the collection's Utah War materials—acquired in the 1940s as part of the enormous trove donated by William Robertson Coe—I concluded that this topic was indeed both fascinating and manageable.[8] Once the Yale Department of History sanctioned this choice, I hurtled into the strange new world of the 1850s, territorial Utah, military history, and antebellum Washington politics. Two years later I emerged from this daunting experience with a senior essay that won the Yale Library's Water McClintock Prize while helping me to grad-

---

6. The Utah War of 1857–58 was the armed conflict between Mormon leaders and US President James Buchanan over power and authority in Utah Territory. Ultimately the struggle pitted nearly one-third of the US Army against Brigham Young's territorial militia in a guerrilla campaign until a non-violent settlement resolved the military aspects of the affair. For the most recent scholarship on the war, see MacKinnon, ed., *At Sword's Point: A Documentary History of the Utah War* (Norman, Oklahoma: The Arthur H. Clark Co.), *Part 1, to 1858* (2008) and *Part 2, 1858–1859* (2016); David L. Bigler and Will Bagley, *The Mormon Rebellion: America's First Civil War, 1857–1858* (Norman: University of Oklahoma Press, 2011); Ronald W. Walker, Richard E. Turley Jr., and Glen M. Leonard, *Massacre at Mountain Meadows* (New York: Oxford University Press, 2008); Norman F. Furniss, *The Mormon Conflict, 1850–1859* (New Haven, Connecticut: Yale University Press, 1960).

7. A description of Archibald Hanna Jr. and his archival career appears in MacKinnon, "The Curator Retires from the Old Corral: Where the East Studies the West," *Yale Alumni Magazine* 45 (Oct. 1981): 33–37.

8. For a description of this collection and the author's interactions with Messrs. Lamar and Hanna, see MacKinnon, "Yale's Collection of Western Americana as Mother Lode," unpublished lecture, Mar. 31, 2017, Sterling Memorial Library, Yale University. During the 1970s, one of Yale's PhD candidates researching in this collection was Jeffrey R. Holland, later president of Brigham Young University and now an apostle of the LDS Church, who comments: "Like you, I hold Archie and Howard in high esteem—both legends in their time." Holland, Letter to MacKinnon, June 15, 2018, copy in my research files. See also Holland, "A Note on Mormon Americana at Yale," *BYU Studies* 10 (July 1970): 386–88.

uate with a BA degree in history magna cum laude and election to Phi Beta Kappa.[9]

Although still intrigued by the West and its Utah War, I chose, for a variety of personal reasons, as my vocation business and finance. Accordingly I moved immediately from Yale to the Harvard Graduate School of Business Administration in Boston to pursue an MBA degree. I barely realized that George Albert Smith Jr., son of the LDS Church president and great-grandson of a Mormon apostle, then taught at the Harvard Business School. But from this base—on weekends—I mined Harvard College's own substantial manuscript collection across the Charles River at Houghton Library.

With Howard Lamar's long-distance encouragement, I also used precious spare time while studying business to convert part of my Yale senior essay into a journal article. During the winter of 1961–62, he urged me to submit this piece to his Salt Lake City friend, Everett L. Cooley, then director of the Utah State Historical Society and editor of its *Quarterly*. Cooley was then quartered in the Kearns Mansion, now the official residence of Utah's governor. Although I did not know it until years later, the title of Cooley's 1947 master's thesis at the University of Utah had been "The Utah War." He accepted my manuscript submission; and in the spring of 1963, the article—my first published one—appeared in *Utah Historical Quarterly*. In retrospect, the publication of this article was a key motivator for the life-long immersion in Utah War studies to follow.[10]

---

9. MacKinnon, "President Buchanan and the Utah Expedition, a Question of Expediency Rather than Principle" (unpublished senior essay, Yale Department of History, 1960, available in Senior Honor Essays of Yale Students, RU 118, Box 25, Manuscripts and Archives, Sterling Memorial Library, Yale University, New Haven, Connecticut). Also of substantial help during a crucial point in my research for this paper was William H. Goetzmann, then a Yale associate professor and later a lion of the faculty at the University of Texas, Austin. Either by intent or oversight, neither Lamar nor Hanna mentioned to me that, while I was working on my senior essay, Norman F. Furniss, a Yale PhD then teaching at Colorado State University, was finishing a book on the Utah War. The week I handed in my paper, the Yale University Press published Furniss's *The Mormon Conflict, 1850–1859*, a complete surprise and temporary blow to my morale from which I soon recovered with the prospect of graduation before me.

10. MacKinnon, "The Buchanan Spoils System and the Utah Expedition: Careers of W. M. F. Magraw and John M. Hockaday," *Utah Historical Quarterly* 31

By 1963 I had graduated from Harvard, had been on active duty with the Air Force in Texas, and had started six years as an air reservist in New York State while simultaneously working as a financial analyst in General Motors' Manhattan corporate treasurer's office. The year before, while I was finishing my business studies in Boston, Yale had conferred an honorary doctorate on President John F. Kennedy, who famously quipped that he then had the best of both worlds—a Harvard education and a Yale degree.[11] As I started out in the world of work in New York, I shared JFK's pride, but also had a distinct feeling—worrisome yet exciting—that I was very much at the bottom of life's ladder and facing a lot of unknowns: how would I adjust to life in the big city, what kind of career would I have, whom would I marry, would my air squadron be called back to active duty for whatever was bubbling in distant Laos (Vietnam was not then even on my radar), and to where would my interest in the history of the American West take me?

At General Motors, the reaction to the *Utah Historical Quarterly* article was quizzical. Thomas A. Murphy and Roger B. Smith—my young bosses, both of whom would become GM's chief executive officer and board chair—asked why I was spending so much of my spare time on such an obscure subject.[12] Notwithstanding skepticism from the business types, but never from the former Ann T. Reed, whom I married in 1965, I quietly pressed on with historical research at ragged intervals.

(Spring 1963): 127–50. Although I was not paid for this article, my delight at its publication was no less than nineteen-year-old Arthur Conan Doyle's 1878 joy upon seeing the sale of his first published story, "The Mystery of Sasassa Valley," to an Edinburgh magazine: "After receiving that little cheque I was a beast that has once tasted blood, for I knew that whatever rebuffs I might receive–and God knows I had plenty–I had once proved I could earn gold, and the spirit was in me to do it again." Quoted in Daniel Stashower, *Teller of Tales: The Life of Arthur Conan Doyle* (New York: Henry Holt and Co., 1999), 30–31.

11. John F. Kennedy, Yale University, Commencement Address, June 11, 1962, www.jfklibrary.org/Historical+Resources/Archives/Reference+Desk/Speeches/JFK/003POF03Yale06111962.htm (accessed Nov. 8, 2006).

12. Notwithstanding my six demanding years at Yale and Harvard, it was in this business office that my writing skills underwent their most rigorous test. For a description of the atmosphere and work style in this unusual staff operation, see MacKinnnon, "Developing General Motors' Chairmen: The Extraordinary Role of GM's New York Treasurer's Office since World War I," *Automotive History Review* 33 (Fall 1998): 9–18.

To the extent that a grueling work style at General Motors permitted, I began to draft a unit history of the Utah Expedition's virtually unknown volunteer battalion.[13] Everett Cooley's earlier editorial confidence in my work as well as the subsequent use of my first article during the mid-1960s by Howard R. Lamar, Juanita L. Brooks, James B. Allen, and Glen M. Leonard was highly motivating.[14] On Saturdays I worked my way through the New York Public Library's wonderful manuscript collections as well as many of those in Washington, DC, at the National Archives and Library of Congress. With the invention of the Xerox 914 machine, the world was my oyster. I was able to extend my research range by obtaining photocopied materials by mail from almost anywhere. Clearly I had fallen victim during the 1960s not only to the Utah War's powerful mystery, complexity, and color but also to the aptness of the comment by historian Dale L. Morgan, "I find the more I find out, the more I need to find out."[15]

Coincident with this civilian activity, the war in Vietnam welled

13. The unit history for this four-company infantry organization remains unfinished. I intend to complete it and have provided a few snippets about this battalion and its homicidal sergeant-major in MacKinnon, ed., *At Sword's Point, Part 1*, 196–203 and 459–66. Interestingly, when I visited Dixie State University's library in St. George, Utah, on April 17, 2018, the staff of its special collections presented me with a photocopy of a long-forgotten letter that I had written to Juanita Brooks on November 16, 1965, seeking information about the volunteer battalion's officers. In 2018 this letter captured my imagination for two reasons: I wrote it only days after returning from my honeymoon; and I had addressed it to Mrs. Brooks only at "St. George" without street address or zip code. When I mentioned the latter point to Douglas D. Alder, president emeritus of Dixie State, he chuckled and noted that Brooks's husband, Will Brooks, was then the town's postmaster and probably just took my letter home with him.

14. Howard Roberts Lamar, *The Far Southwest, 1846–1912: A Territorial History* (New Haven, Connecticut: Yale University Press, 1966), 337–48; Juanita Brooks, *On the Mormon Frontier: The Diary of Hosea Stout, 1844–1861*, 2 vols. (Salt Lake City: University of Utah Press and Utah State Historical Society, 1964), 2:553–54; James B. Allen and Glen M. Leonard, *The Story of the Latter-day Saints* (Salt Lake City: Deseret Book, 1976), 676.

15. This classic Morganism has been adopted by Will Bagley as the tag line for his Salt Lake City research and publishing firm, Prairie Dog Press. The entire quote is: "In the last four years I have amassed several million words about Mormons, including about 650 life sketches, journals, and autobiographies, which range from a page to eight 600-page volumes, but I find the more I find out, the more I need to find out." Dale L. Morgan, Letter to Robert Allen, Apr. 12, 1942, Morgan Papers, microfilm 01:0795-0804, Bancroft Library, University of California, Berkeley, courtesy of Will Bagley and Richard L. Saunders of Southern Utah State University, Cedar City.

up unexpectedly, then grew in ferocity. For years my squadron—activated and assigned to Germany for the Berlin Wall crisis of 1961–62—prepared monthly to support jungle warfare in Southeast Asia for which, mysteriously, we were never called. Instead we deployed to such far-flung but improbable operational locations as the sands of the Mojave Desert and Cape Cod, my ancestral ice-bound home in Newfoundland, and again to the lush, pastoral hilltops (radar sites) of southern Germany in proximity to Soviet MiG traffic into the Czech airfields. I sometimes wondered what Brigham Young would have thought about this Catch-22-like federal military experience.[16] Soon after the 1968 Tet offensive, I was offered but declined a commissioning opportunity and was discharged from the reserves as a staff sergeant, unscathed except for a minor encounter with a gasoline explosion.

The years turned into decades, and I continued to research and publish in a variety of journals throughout the West and even in England. After Everett Cooley moved to the University of Utah and its J. Willard Marriott Library, my editor at the *Utah Historical Quarterly* became Stan Layton. He, like Cooley, became a long-time friend. General Motors transferred me from New York to Detroit in 1972, I switched career fields from finance to human resources, and in 1982 I became a GM corporate vice president in charge of

---

16. Although my unit, NYANG's 106th Tactical Control/Direct Air Support Squadron, had no officer named Major Major, as did Captain Yousarrian's fictive World War II bomber unit in Joseph Heller's *Catch 22*, its troops did have some ironic names: a mess sergeant bearing the name [Robert] Hash and a first sergeant whose last name was [Barney] Bombay. As a historian studying the Vietnam War a half century after my discharge, I was unnerved to read the de-classified transcripts of the secret tape recordings made in Lyndon B. Johnson's Oval Office during a July 1965 debate between the president and his military chiefs of staff over whether to escalate the American presence in-country by activation of reserve units, increasing monthly draft calls, or both. A few weeks later six squadrons of us from NYANG's 152nd Tactical Control Group flew from a naval air station in Brooklyn to an American air base in Canada to await the broadcast of a presidential press conference to announce his decision, one that would determine whether we would proceed to Saigon to set up a Direct Air Support Center or fly to Germany to establish radar sites for maneuvers there. This was LBJ's "guns or butter" announcement, one that I heard over the CBC's television network on July 28, 1965, at Ernest Harmon AFB, Newfoundland ("Gateway to the North"). It was a decision of high interest to me since I was scheduled to be married two months later in Pennsylvania. Reviewing the aging records of all this through the hindsight of the twenty-first century was vaguely like watching grainy films of one's own colonoscopy.

the Personnel Administration and Development Staff—a sort of managerial dean and advocate for the organization's 200,000-person salaried workforce during the stunningly turbulent leadership of Roger Smith and, briefly, of H. Ross Perot. Increasingly, I came to the unsettling feeling that my role at GM was akin to running a damage control party aboard a smoldering ammunition ship adrift in the Philadelphia Navy Yard. The leadership shortfalls that unthinkably brought the company to bankruptcy in 2009 were evident to me by the mid-1980s and even earlier.

In 1987 I left the company at age forty-eight after twenty-five years of service to found my own management consulting firm, MacKinnon Associates.

Although I did not think of my GM years in quite this way at the time, what I took with me included an intimate, valuable understanding of the leadership and travails of an organization that in some ways was as structured, sprawling, and complex as the US Army and LDS Church, albeit one with a quite different mission. Armed with the lessons learned amid the complexities of General Motors (as well as Yale, Harvard, and USAF), I was equipped to advise the chief executive officers of other businesses about the organizational issues that kept them awake at night. I was also prepared to understand both sides of the Utah War with a perspective different than perhaps any historian who had approached this subject other than Col. Hamilton Gardner, the distinguished Utah attorney-soldier who, unknown to me, was finishing his extensive research on the war as I was starting mine.[17]

Two years later, both my wife and her mother died of cancer, and I did my best to guide our two children, Tom and Kate, through high school and college into adulthood. Partly to cope with this turmoil, I immersed myself in not only consulting work but in the design and organization of a conference in Pennsylvania to examine James Buchanan's presidency at the bicentennial of his birth.[18] At about the same time, I also embarked on plans for

17. Hamilton Gardner's research files, like mine, have been donated to the Utah State Historical Society (Mss B 1913). Except for several first-rate journal articles, his work on the Utah War remains largely unpublished.

18. James Buchanan Bicentennial Conference, Sept. 20–21, 1991, at Lancaster (Franklin and Marshall College) and Carlisle (Dickinson College), Pennsylvania.

a narrative history of the Utah War to be written collaboratively with friend Richard D. Poll, then a retired history professor and university administrator living in Provo, Utah, who, like Hamilton Gardner, had published several seminal articles about the war. When Dick Poll died unexpectedly in 1994—another heavy blow—I shelved our narrative history project, although to honor him I did complete a journal article on the Utah War's origins which we had started together.[19] In 1993, I married again and for-tuitously to a very positive, supportive Patricia M. Hanley.

During 1996 I was re-motivated with the serendipitous discovery that the Arthur H. Clark Company of Spokane, Washington, was planning to commission a documentary history of the Utah War. This book was to be part of the firm's exciting new, multi-volume series *Kingdom in the West: The Mormons and the American Frontier*. A telephone call to Robert A. Clark, the firm's third-generation owner-president, established that the series had not yet identified either an author-editor or a title for its Utah War volume but was open to suggestions.[20] By coincidence—but not without symbolism—Bob was a non-Mormon descendant of Lt. Gen. Daniel Hanmer Wells, the Nauvoo Legion's Utah War commander, as well as of the LDS Church's seventh president, Heber J. Grant. Although I had previously considered writing only a narrative history of the Utah War—a volume to build on Norman F. Furniss's classic 1960 study—the quite different challenge of editing a documentary compilation intrigued me. A book in this format struck me as a logical way-station for a subsequent narrative study of the type that I had originally planned

---

Many of the papers given at this symposium subsequently appeared in Michael J. Birkner, ed., *James Buchanan and the Political Crisis of the 1850s* (Selinsgrove, Pennsylvania: Susquehanna University Press, 1996). Other than design of the conference's format, content, and speakers, my contribution was an unpublished paper titled "James Buchanan's Western Military Adventures."

19. Richard D. Poll and MacKinnon, "Causes of the Utah War Reconsidered," *Journal of Mormon History* 20 (Fall 1994): 16–44.

20. I had been an admirer of the Arthur H. Clark Company and its indispensable, elegant books since my Yale days. I subsequently befriended Bob Clark, first through telephone calls as a book-buying customer and then occasional meetings in the Pacific Northwest and Salt Lake City. After my wife's death in 1989, I toyed with the notion of becoming a part-owner of the Clark Company, but the notion never progressed beyond the fantasy stage.

with Dick Poll. Bob Clark liked the idea and urged me to introduce myself to William Grant Bagley, his *Kingdom in the West*
series editor and an independent Salt Lake City historian (descended from at least one Nauvoo Legionnaire) of whom I had
virtually no prior awareness.[21]

From our first telephone call on July 3, 1996, Will and I hit
it off. After reexamining LeRoy R. and Ann W. Hafen's 1958
documentary history of the Utah Expedition—published by Bob
Clark's father—I realized that there was indeed need for a new
such compilation. I submitted a formal proposal to Clark and Bagley, calling for a study that would use the Hafens' book as a point
of departure rather than one to rehash or deconstruct it.[22] My
intent was to take advantage of the intervening decades of scholarship and to present, through unexploited documents unknown
to the Hafens, an account of the Utah War that would be considered by my contemporaries as well as subsequent generations to be
fair, even-handed, complete and—above all else—revealing. They
accepted this proposal in August 1996, and I contracted to edit a
volume bearing the working title "At Sword's Point: A Documentary History of the Utah War of 1857–1858."[23] My expectation
was that I could complete my manuscript by the end of 1999. For
the third time, I moved deeper into a commitment to the fascinating world of Utah War studies while juggling the other demands
of my professional and personal life.

---

21. I did not meet Will Bagley until 1997; my first awareness of him was as a
fellow commentator (filmed separately) for *The Tops of the Mountains: An Illustrated
History of Utah*, a videotape produced in 1995 for the January 1996 centennial celebration of Utah statehood. Although over the decades it has become apparent that Will
and I do not always share the same approach to Utah and Mormon history, I continue
to admire his inquiring mind, ferocious dedication to research in unexploited primary
sources, big heart, and generosity in sharing information.

22. LeRoy R. and Ann W. Hafen, eds., *The Utah Expedition, 1857–1858: A Documentary Account of the United States Military Movement under Colonel Albert Sidney
Johnston, and the Resistance by Brigham Young and the Mormon Nauvoo Legion* (1958;
rpt., Glendale, California: The Arthur H. Clark Co., 1982).

23. The title "At Sword's Point" was one that I had originally planned on using for
a manuscript begun in the 1970s to describe the conflicts among the senior uniformed
and civilian leaders of the antebellum US Army. When the Utah War project arose, I
could not resist transferring this title from my incomplete work–still unpublished–to
the book for the Clark Company, although I had to fend off the forces of editorial
intervention that argued for use of "bayonet" rather than "sword" in the title.

Since I had decided to tell the Utah War story through the heretofore unheard "voices" of the participants on both sides, letting them largely speak for themselves, I immediately started to gather the documents foundational to this approach. In so doing, I chose a non-traditional definition of "document." I included not only letters, diaries, newspaper dispatches, reminiscences, memoirs, other personal narratives, military correspondence and orders, congressional reports, poems, stage dramas, religious discourses, and patriarchal blessings, but also commemorative quilts, the lyrics to hymns and folk songs, and images such as photographs, paintings, sketches, maps, and even rock inscriptions.

Over the years I had already collected a substantial body of unexploited primary sources from the rich holdings of Atlantic Coast repositories like Yale's Beinecke Library, the New York Public Library, National Archives, and Library of Congress, but I needed much more as this material largely related to the federal side of the war. I was acutely aware that I was a non-Mormon located in Michigan more than 2,000 miles from Utah with a limited travel budget and little experience in navigating the intricacies of the treasure trove in Salt Lake City then known as LDS Church Archives. If I had come to regard the Yale Collection of Western Americana as the "Mother Lode," I knew enough to realize that mining the holdings of LDS Archives, Utah State Archives, the voluminous Thomas L. Kane Papers at Brigham Young University's Harold B. Lee Library, and the Richard D. Poll research files at the University of Utah's Marriott Library would be essential to producing a complete, even-handed history. The advent at this juncture of technical advances (principally fax machines, e-mail, and Internet search engines) was a boon to this process, but, having earlier lost Utah-based Dick Poll as a collaborator, I still needed "boots on the ground" steeped in the arcane world of Mormon sources and culture. Enter Will Bagley and Ardis E. Parshall.

I had, of course, first met Will in the role of series editor for *Kingdom in the West*, but I soon realized that he had other talents. Other than being a musician and cabinet maker, he was a data software expert, a published author, and a remarkably resourceful researcher in the formative stage of building a career as an independent historian and proprietor of the Prairie Dog Press. Like me, he was doing so without the credential of a PhD degree, but with the examples of Dale Morgan and Allan Nevins before him, he moved forward without inhibitions. Bagley was also what he called a "cultural Mormon," i.e., someone belonging to the church but not active religiously while maintaining a pride in his LDS heritage.

Accordingly, I engaged Will to serve in the invaluable but unglamorous role of documents scout extraordinaire. As such, he responded energetically to my countless what-if questions, ferreting out and copying manuscripts (some in private rather than institutional hands) to which I had no prior access, connection, or even awareness. He also was generous to a fault in sharing, when appropriate, sources encountered during the course of his non-MacKinnon research. Accompanying this activity, he conducted by e-mail a virtual tutorial on Mormon history and sources and, in the process, introduced me to dozens of other researchers, manuscript collectors, and bookpeople who became friends as well as professional colleagues.

This process went on for several years, but as Will became more deeply engaged with the burgeoning troupe of other *Kingdom of the West* author-editors and their output, devoted more time to his pending book on the Utah War's Mountain Meadows Massacre (*Blood of the Prophets: Brigham Young and the Massacre at Mountain Meadows*), and assumed the self- appointed role of "burr under the saddle" to many Mormon historians, faculty members, and archivists, I realized that I needed to broaden my resources.[24]

The answer to this need was Ms. Ardis E. Parshall of Orem (later Salt Lake City), Utah, a faithful Latter-day Saint whom I had known as a former legal secretary and crack typist. She, like Bagley, was transitioning from a life of an employee at an established organization to the risky but more satisfying role of an independent,

---

24. For an example of Bagley in full bloom as provocateur (calling Brigham Young and other Mormon leaders at various levels in various eras "murderers," "goons," and "troglodytes"), see Bagley, "Conan Doyle Was Right: Danites, Avenging Angels, and Holy Murder in the Mormon West," in Leslie S. Klinger, ed., *A Tangled Skein: A Companion Volume to the Baker Street Irregulars' Expedition to the Country of the Saints* (New York: Baker Street Irregulars, 2008), 3–29.

self-supporting solo professional. In Parshall's case, her field was genealogy and family history. Coincidentally, Parshall, like Bagley and Bob Clark, had ancestral connections to the Nauvoo Legion side of the Utah War. Her family linkage came through Pvt. James Parshall Terry, a distant cousin and one of Maj. Lot Smith's cavalrymen who burned Fort Bridger, Fort Supply, and two trains of US Army supply wagons in early October 1857. Parshall's sensitivity to Mormon heritage, coupled with superb document hunting instincts as well as transcription skills guided me into the daylight of wonderful Utah manuscripts, out of the dark tunnels, blind passages, or potential cultural pitfalls/sensitivities awaiting unwary Wise Men from the East, and away from the bogus materials plaguing some Mormon sources. Parshall also performed a valuable service in constantly reminding me that there are at least two sides to every story, including the Mormon perspective. Later, until 2013, she transformed my chapter drafts faxed west from the Detroit area into a form with which Messrs. Bagley and Clark could eventually work their editorial and publishing magic.

With all these document discoveries and my awareness that the Second Millennium was approaching, I turned to the wisdom of Bagley's advice that the key to transforming a plethora of documents into a publishable history was the process of struggling to winnow and determine a sensible arrangement for this material. Bagley believed that "all documentary collections [compilations] have a natural organization that only becomes apparent after an editor has wrestled with them long and hard ... [to provide] a coherent, logical structure to the volume."[25] For Bagley, such a struggle or total immersion by the author-editor yielded a form of organization that virtually suggested itself, after which the writing process could begin. He was right. I also discovered that once into the drafting of chapters, there was a predictably high probability of additional rearrangement of the material prompted by a clearer understanding of heretofore unforeseen relationships between people and events.

The organizational challenge was especially complex for the Utah War because many of its important events did not unfold

---

25. Bagley, Email to MacKinnon, Apr. 24, 2005, copy in my research files.

Where it all began: Yale's libraries. In two March 2017 lectures at the Beinecke and Sterling Libraries, I described their impact on my research and writing about Utah since 1958. (Event poster courtesy of Yale's Howard R. Lamar Center for the Study of Frontiers and Borders.)

in what I call linear fashion with a clear, orderly sequence. Some aspects of the war took place nearly simultaneously and in different regions of the United States (or even other countries), while other incidents were multi-year in character. For this reason my construction of a detailed chronology for the war became invaluable to revealing the relationship between seemingly unconnected events that played out at widely separated locations.

By the spring of 2004 it became clear to me that perhaps the most important organizational decision to be made for my Utah War study was a need to change the original concept of a single book to a two-volume history. Even after an intense, even ruthless, culling process, the remaining bulk and appeal of unexploited documents was such that an expansion of our scope was essential to match the plethora of available information I had surfaced. I proposed this expansion to Bagley and Clark, and, to my delight, they accepted and vigorously supported the change. For their flexibility and farsightedness, I was and remain thankful.

We made the decision to split the war's action at year-end 1857, the point at which Thomas L. Kane prepared to leave Philadelphia for his messianic 6,000-mile mediating mission to Utah and back. That structural change permitted me to shift to the second volume several multi-year thrusts that began in 1857 and lapped into 1858: Capt. Randolph B. Marcy's trek to New Mexico to remount and resupply the Utah Expedition, Lt. Joseph C. Ives's ascent of the Colorado River in search of an invasion route into southern Utah, Benjamin F. Ficklin's expedition to the Flathead country of Oregon Territory to buy cattle and Indian ponies, the evolution of the Mormon Standing Army of Israel, the formation of volunteer military units throughout the United States to reinforce the Utah Expedition, and the Mormons' pleas for the intervention of US Senator Sam Houston of Texas.

Principal exceptions to this organizational design were to be the chronologically sprawling stories of Thomas L. Kane's mission, Ben McCulloch's several quite different wartime assignments for first Secretary of War Floyd and then President Buchanan, and the atrocities or provocations committed by both sides. I would present various aspects of these subjects in both volumes. In 2005, as the early chapters began to take shape, Bagley told me, "I'm also delighted that we decided to deal with the subject in two volumes, since the material is simply too good, too complex, and too vast to try to put within a single cover—and the division by year is a simple and natural structure."[26]

Even with this decision, the troubling problem of length—an embarrassment of riches—remained, and Bagley cautioned, "My main concern at this point is one that's now commonplace [for me] as series editor: every volume so far has simply had Too Much

26. Ibid.

Good Stuff to print it all. But you're obviously addressing this, and until we have a complete draft, we can wait till we see the scope of the problem before making those painful decisions of what stays and what goes. You're clearly moving under a good head of steam and the only advice I can offer now is, plow ahead! And of course, keep up the good work."[27]

Meanwhile, in the Pacific Northwest the sands were shifting at the Arthur H. Clark Company. On July 1, 2006, Bob Clark and the University of Oklahoma Press announced that to ensure his company's continued operation after 104 years of successful independence, Clark had sold the company. While no longer independent legally, the Clark Company would retain its identity and continue to publish first-rate foundational books about the West as an identifiable imprint of OUPress. Clark would become a senior member of the parent organization's editorial-management team; he and his wife, Sheila, would move from Spokane to Norman, Oklahoma. To me, the change seemed logical in view of the absence of a family successor to Clark and the century-old western focus and premier reputation of both organizations. As the transition unfolded, it appeared essentially seamless, although from my management consulting experience I realized that for Bagley and Clark there was more heartburn than I could see from my less exalted outside perch as a mere free-lance author-editor in the *KITW* series.

As this change was announced, I experienced a twinge of regret that back in the early 1990s I had not bought some or all of the Clark Company. That reaction passed with the realization that, had I done so, many other good things that subsequently unfolded for me might not have taken place as they did. Years later, when Bob Clark read a draft of this essay, he wrote to me, "Your comment about your interest in The Clark Company ... was bittersweet. Had a melding of our interests been accomplished, I know I would have gained so much from you. As if I haven't benefited greatly already!" After these generous comments, he completed the thought with a typical Bob Clark touch, a quote from Robert Frost's 1916 poem "The Road Not Taken."[28]

---

27. Ibid.
28. Clark, Letter to MacKinnon, Jan. 28, 2019, copy in my research files.

Given this background, though, I was pleased in December 2007 when Clark wholly unexpectedly dubbed me a Field Acquisitions Editor, a non-employee role recognizing my past efforts to steer appropriate manuscripts and authors his way. I asked for his expectations for the future, and Clark explained, "Because of your special connections within the world of Mormon, Great Basin, Utah, and military studies, I know you are aware of numerous projects that might find a ready home with Clark. Your recommendations to authors and editors to contact us, or your advice to me in regards to contacting them, would be of great assistance to me [as Clark Company publisher]."[29]

After a difficult siege to whip the completed manuscript into shape during 2006–2007—I remember cutting its length by 47 percent near the end of the process—the Clark Company published *At Sword's Point, Part 1* in April 2008. Because of the two-volume character of the study, it bore a title slightly altered from the original and was styled *At Sword's Point, Part 1: A Documentary History of the Utah War to 1858*. As with the earlier debate over the wisdom of using "bayonet" rather than "sword" in the title, Bagley worried about advice he was receiving from elsewhere in the publishing world that the use of the word "documentary" in a book title is a marketing negative, but I preferred documentary, and he in his statesmanlike fashion again supported me. One of the things that pleased me about the painful concluding phases of the editorial process was that Richard E. (Rick) Turley Jr., Assistant Historian of the LDS Church, had agreed to serve in the critical role of outside reader for the entire manuscript, and gave it a highly positive assessment.

The book was designated volume 10 in the *Kingdom in the West* series. In a tremendous vote of confidence in my ability to complete this project and with some risk, OUPress, Clark, and Bagley decided to reserve the series volume 11 designation for what I began calling *ASP2* even though we knew that it would be years before this book would be published, with several more *Kingdom in the West* volumes to appear in the interim. *ASP1*'s first printing

---

29. Clark, Email to MacKinnon, Dec. 17, 2007, copy in my research files.

sold quickly, and inventory of the second printing is nearing depletion. Fortuitously, the book received best documentary history awards from the Utah State Historical Society and the Mormon History Association. I had the distinct feeling that this was good recognition for a Presbyterian lad from upstate New York.

During *ASP1*'s twelve-year gestation period, I kept hearing the same questions: when is the book coming out, and why is it taking so long? The two most obvious and easiest explanations for this timing ran to the scope and complexity of the Utah War. There were a lot of moving parts to this conflict and a very large cast of characters. Compounding the impact of these factors was the reality that, by design, I had taken on the task of trying to tell the war's story through a series of documents which were unpublished and, in some cases, not yet located—what US Secretary of Defense Donald Rumsfeld later called "the known unknowns."[30]

As I have thought about this long slog to completion, there were additional reasons for its duration, including my own inexperience. By this I mean that this project was my first book-length effort and one in a format (an edited documentary history) new to me. Since 1963 I had been writing narrative journal articles, some running to fifty pages, but that work was a far different matter than the marathon-like road I started down with optimism in the summer of 1996. At the heart of the matter, I suppose, is the fact that without any background in producing such a study, my original estimate of 1999 as a completion date was hopelessly unrealistic.

Equally impactful were the limitations on my available time and resources, including financial support. I was essentially working alone on this major study with only a part-time researcher-typist (paid by me) for day-to-day help and a distant, over-burdened series editor to whom I could turn for guidance to the extent his time permitted. I received no financial assistance in advance for this project, and the very modest royalty payments would not start

---

30. See "DoD News Briefing–Secretary Rumsfeld and Gen. Myers[,] Presenter: Secretary of Defense Donald H. Rumsfeld[,] February 12, 2002 11:30 AM EDT," at www.archive.defense.gov/Transcripts/Transcript.aspx?TranscriptID=2636 (accessed May 16, 2019).

flowing until after publication and then only to the extent the book sold. In effect I was financing the entire project through sweat equity, while covering years of out-of-pocket expenditures for office rent and equipment, utilities, travel, research costs, and typing from funds generated by my even more time-consuming management consulting practice. I mention this not as a complaint, but simply to point out that this was a far different working model than the methodology by which, at the same time, other narrative and documentary histories dealing with Mormon history were being written by multi-person teams of editor-historians supported by substantial research and clerical staffs and the expenditure of hundreds of thousands (perhaps even millions) of dollars provided by academic and church history departments.

The time schedule also slipped because of my protracted but successful bout with prostate cancer in 2002–2006, Pat's and my delightful but disruptive relocation from Michigan to California in 2007, and because of my decision to publish during 1996–2008 a series of articles and book reviews in journals such as *Dialogue: A Journal of Mormon Thought*, *Journal of Mormon History*, *Utah Historical Quarterly*, *New Mexico Historical Review*, *BYU Studies*, and *Journal of Arizona History*.

To some extent I made these writing commitments because of my difficulty in saying "no," but to a greater degree they were a deliberate, strategic effort to research and produce polished essays that could later serve as building blocks for all or part of chapters in my Clark Company project while stimulating advance reader interest in what would be coming. I refer to *ASP1*'s chapters 5 ("'It's a Hell of a Place': The Decision to Intervene") and 12 ("'Lonely Bones': Violence and Leadership") and *ASP2*'s chapters 6 ("'To Mask the Real Movement': Pacific Adventures, Presidential Intrigue") and 9 ("'Remedy Worse than the Disease': Raising Regulars, Volunteers, and Sam Houston") as well as that volume's conclusions and epilogue sections. Whether the same can be said to justify my three years committed to service on the board of the Mormon History Association, my four years as chair of the Yale Library Associates' Board, several years spent in organizing and mentoring the Utah War Sesquicentennial Commemoration

Committee, and my chairmanship of Children's Hospital of Michigan is a judgment call.

I believed that most, if not all, of these efforts were relevant to *ASP* rather than simply distractions, and, in some important ways, I did indeed say "no." For example, because of my focus on fulfilling my obligation to Bob Clark, I deflected OUPress's offer to engage me to write a narrative history of the Utah War of the type that in the early 1990s I had planned to produce with Dick Poll as co-author. This decision created a publishing vacuum of sorts that David L. Bigler and Will Bagley filled with their book *The Mormon Rebellion: America's First Civil War, 1857–1858*, published through OUPress in 2011. Along with this decision I also put on the back burner two monographs that I had long been marinating that focused on Utah War newspaper correspondent Albert G. Browne Jr. and Franklin R. Grist, one of the sketch artists accompanying the Stansbury Expedition of 1849–50. With the completion of *ASP*, these projects are now back at the top of my writing priorities.

With the publication of *ASP1* in 2008 and the completion of a time-consuming, ten-stop promotional visit to various historical societies, book shops, and archivist groups in Utah, I returned to California to resume work on *ASP2*. As with *ASP1*, this second volume was to benefit from a close reading of the entire manuscript by Rick Turley as well as historian David H. Miller. Again the process to completion took longer than I expected—eight years. *At Sword's Point, Part 2: A Documentary History of the Utah War, 1858–1859* emerged from the Clark Company in November 2016.

This time the slippage in schedules was for familiar but also unexpected reasons. Among the latter was the unsettling (for me) departure of Bob Clark from Oklahoma in 2012 to an assignment as editor-in-chief of Washington State University Press in Pullman. Responsibility for the Clark Company imprint and *ASP2* gravitated to OUPress's editor-in-chief, Charles E. (Chuck) Rankin, whom I had known since his days at the Montana Historical Society, and one of his talented editorial lieutenants, Steven B. Baker. Both men are consummate professionals; in the wake of Clark's loss, I considered myself and my work to be in good hands, but there was the inevitable sorting-out process before roles clarified.[31] Chuck never asked me to turn in my Field Acquisitions Editor badge, but then he may never have been aware that it existed. Then there was the death of two of my four siblings. There followed more of my "building block" journal articles as well as leadership roles with western-oriented historical groups in Utah and California that included the presidency of the Mormon History Association and the sheriff's assignment with the Santa Barbara Corral of Westerners International.

In the introduction to *ASP2* I acknowledged this publishing delay without going into all the reasons, but I did try to explain to readers that since 2008 "a plethora of additional documents have welled up through [my] discoveries in ten countries on six continents. It is a diaspora illustrating one of my principal findings—that the Utah War was an event with international as well as regional sweep, rather than a conflict confined to Utah Territory and Washington."[32] This was a substantial understatement.

The fact is that if I had completed *ASP2* several years earlier than I did, I would have missed the discovery of key documents that either altered or reinforced my understanding of the latter stages of the Utah War. This unexploited material included the trove of diplomatic dispatches sequestered at Oxford University's Bodleian Library written by Sir William Gore Ouseley in Washington to

---

31. Before Clark left OUPress, he reviewed and commented on the first five chapters of *ASP2*, a wonderful continuity of editorial support with the first volume of this study, to which Bob contributed so much.

32. MacKinnon, ed., *At Sword's Point, Part 2*, 17. I took some solace in the fact that I was not the only historian writing a multi-volume study who has had to deal with the "when" question. The most recent notable example is Robert A. Caro, now at work on the final book of his five-volume biography of Lyndon Johnson. His loyal but increasingly impatient readers have sometimes raised this question in angry tones, especially when he paused during the early stages of writing the fifth volume to publish a small volume (*Working: Researching, Interviewing, Writing*) to reprise his writing career and methodology. The first of his gargantuan books about LBJ was published in 1982, thirty-eight years ago, and it has been seven years since his fourth and most recent volume appeared. In a recent interview, Caro commented, "If you ask me how many years to go, I can't answer you." During the 1960s–70s, the late Shelby Foote had to field similar queries before completing his acclaimed three-volume study titled *The Civil War: A Narrative*. Jeffrey A. Trachtenberg, "Robert Caro Has Chronicled LBJ for Decades. Fans Fret He'll Never Finish," *Wall Street Journal*, Feb. 23–24, 2019, A1/3-6 and A10/1-6.

Lord Clarendon, Britain's foreign secretary. Once I became aware of them, Ouseley's reports of confidential conversations with his friend President Buchanan enabled me to understand the linkage between "Old Buck's" quirky plans for opening a second front for the Utah War from the Pacific Coast and Buchanan's concept of American Manifest Destiny, as he hoped it would play out through military gambits involving California, Utah, northern Mexico, and Cuba.[33] Ditto for my location of the "lost" letters of Bvt. Maj. Thomas Williams, Fourth US Artillery, as well as the discovery and use in *ASP2* of photographs of previously unknown Utah War participants such as Lafayette Shaw (Fay) Worthen, the volunteer battalion's Sgt. George Austin Beardsley, and 2d Lt. Robert L. Browning, the US Marine Corps' one-man contribution to the Utah Expedition.[34]

In 2017 *At Sword's Point, Part 2* was co-recipient of the Utah State Historical Society's award for that year's best documentary history. The book's first edition is almost entirely sold.

Although vastly relieved at seeing the publication of the second volume of this study in 2016, I confess that it was a bittersweet experience. Parting with this completed project reminded me of 1st Sgt. P. G. Lowe's leave taking from the First US Dragoons at Fort Union, New Mexico, upon completion of his five-year enlistment in 1854: "The day of my departure came, my last roll call was made at reveille, and I passed from right to left of the troop and shook hands with every man. I was obliged to nerve myself to the utmost to meet this trial, one of the greatest of my life. My work was done. I had turned my back upon my best friends. I would never make better."[35]

Summing Up

And so for sixty years one irresistible Utah War challenge has led me to another. Each of these adventures has been reinforced by a wonderful series of interconnected historical and documentary

---

33. MacKinnon, "Hammering Utah, Squeezing Mexico, and Coveting Cuba: James Buchanan's White House Intrigues," *Utah Historical Quarterly* 80 (Spring 2012): 132–51.

34. MacKinnon, ed., *At Sword's Point, Part 2*, 447, 302, and 479.

35. Percival G. Lowe, *Five Years a Dragoon ('49 to '54) and Other Adventures on the Great Plains* (Norman: University of Oklahoma Press, 1965), 140.

discoveries—one leading to the next. For me these linkages suggest the prophet Ezekiel's vision of the valley of the dry bones (37:1–10) or at least the lyrics of the American black spiritual it inspired.

Since 1958 this interest has produced articles, essays, and book reviews in more than thirty journals and encyclopedias, the two volumes of *At Sword's Point*, and my delivery of invited lectures at the US Naval Academy at Annapolis as well as in Logan, Provo, and St. George in honor of war mediator Thomas L. Kane and Mormon historians Leonard J. Arrington and Juanita L. Brooks.[36] Perhaps my most unusual such talk was a staff briefing on the Utah War that I gave at Camp Floyd State Park in August 2015 at the invitation of Utah's adjutant general, Maj. Gen. Jefferson S. Burton. It was fun to do this on the site of the Utah Expedition's largest garrison amid a group of the Utah Guard's most senior officers and NCOs whose ancestors—including one of General Burton's—served with the Nauvoo Legion during 1857–58.

At the end of the Camp Floyd session, I ran through a number of observations about the Utah War that I described for my military audience as "Lessons Learned" and "Surprises Encountered." It is a long list, and so, rather than rehash this material here, I will refer you to several places where it is available in published form.[37] I also refer you to my observations about the war's character, its leaders' accountabilities, the conflict's winners and losers, and the significance of their armed struggle as they appear in the "Conclusions" section of *At Sword's Point, Part 2*.[38]

When I submitted my completed manuscript for *ASP2* to the Clark Company, it did not have a "Conclusions" section, and the

---

36. For published versions of these lectures, see MacKinnon, "James Buchanan's Neglected Expedition against the Mormons: The Decision to Intervene in Utah Territory," *English Westerners' Tally Sheet* 27 (1980): 3–12; "'Full of Courage': Thomas L. Kane, the Utah War, and BYU's Kane Collection as Lodestone," *BYU Studies* 48, no. 4 (2009): 89–119; *Predicting the Past: The Utah War's Twenty-First Century Future*, Leonard J. Arrington Mormon History Lecture Series, No. 14 (Logan: Utah State University Press, 2009); and *Across the Desert in 1858: Thomas L. Kane's Mediating Mission and the Mormon Women Who Made It Possible*, 35th Annual Juanita Brooks Lecture (St. George, Utah: Dixie State University Library, 2018).

37. MacKinnon, "Loose in the Stacks: A Half-Century with the Utah War and Its Legacy," *Dialogue: A Journal of Mormon Thought* 40 (Spring 2007): 48–81.

38. MacKinnon, ed., *At Sword's Point, Part 2*, 599–622.

book essentially was to end with the Utah Expedition's peaceful march through Salt Lake City on June 26, 1858. My thought was that the book was already overly-long, and the meaning of the two volumes would be evident from the material itself. In effect, readers could draw their own conclusions without my "voice" intruding. Fortunately, Will Bagley convinced me that, for a study of this length and significance, the author-editor should provide readers with a summation of its meaning as he sees it. By the time the book came out about a year later, I was glad that Bagley had urged this change, and readers have agreed. One laudatory book reviewer commented that *ASP2*'s "Conclusions" section was worth the price of the entire book, while another wrote that he wished he had started with "Conclusions" instead of reading it in sequence.

I close with the thought that a complete, accurate understanding of this extraordinary territorial-federal conflict still beckons those interested in the history of Mormon Utah, the American West, and even international relations in a wide range of unlikely places. I have written as I have driven by the realization that the Utah War has been a large, unexplained, and lamentable gap in the history of our nation's antebellum era. For 160 years the conflict has languished in obscurity because of the twin forces of neglect and obfuscation as well as the overshadowing impact of our nation's fascination with the Civil War. It has long been a subject needing probing and understanding. I am not a latter-day Thomas L. Kane with a keyboard, but, like him, I recognize a need and an opportunity to contribute when I see one.[39] For sixty years, the conflict has remained as colorful and exotic an episode as I have encountered. It is one during which my grandfather was born, and it is a war my nine grandchildren now seek to understand in their own way.

Sustaining me during this long immersion in the Utah War's story has been my awareness that I have been in good company with strong support. Recently Howard R. Lamar, my longstanding mentor and Yale's president emeritus, made it all worthwhile by commenting, "Bill MacKinnon, now a westerner, likens his effort

---

39. In the interest of full disclosure, in 2008 the Mormon History Association honored me with its Thomas L. Kane Award.

to understand the Utah War to a military enlistment and campaign stretching over nearly two-thirds of a century. If so, I—in my ninety-fifth year—claim the role of his recruiting officer and comrade-in-arms."[40]

---

40. Howard R. Lamar in Introduction to *A Sixty-Year Hitch with the Utah War: Writing "At Sword's Point,"* an essay printed in an edition of seventy-five copies upon the occasion of the author's eightieth birthday and Christmas 2018.

7

LIVING THE JOURNEY, REAPING THE WHIRLWIND
REFLECTIONS ON WRITING EMMA HALE SMITH'S BIOGRAPHY
LINDA KING NEWELL

On October 4, 1984, I held the first copy of *Mormon Enigma: Emma Hale Smith* in my hands and smelled the aroma of fresh ink. For my co-author, Valeen Tippetts Avery, and me, this day culminated nine years of labor to document, understand, and interpret the life of Emma Hale Smith. Emma had long been neglected, even shunned as dangerous, by the Church of Jesus Christ of Latter-day Saints. She had virtually been written out of its history except for an occasional reference to her as the Prophet Joseph's wife and first president of the Female Relief Society. Emma's life was heroic in many respects, the stuff of sagas; in other ways, it was a round of quiet domesticity and private charity.

My husband, Jack, met Valeen and Charles (Chuck) Avery at Duke University in Durham, North Carolina, three years before I did. The two men were both graduate students—Chuck in forestry and Jack in American history. Jack was showing interest in joining the LDS Church at that time and was attending the Durham Ward, as did the Averys. They were kindred spirits and became fast friends. Jack and I married that next summer of 1963; the Averys had moved to Laramie, Wyoming. Two years later, in the fall of 1965, we were on our way to Deep Springs College, located on the California–Nevada border, where Jack had agreed to teach for the next two years. Our route west took us through Laramie where we called on the Averys. Val and I liked each other immediately, and we felt we had known each other for years. Our conversation was easy and fast paced. In the ensuing ten years, our two families kept in close touch through phone calls, letters, and visits in various places.

During that time we lived three years in New Hampshire, where Jack taught American history, then moved to Columbus, Ohio, where he finished his PhD at Ohio State. My own journey with Emma Hale Smith began there in 1973. I attended a BYU Education Week where Jaynann Payne from Provo, Utah, was one of the speakers. Her topic was "My Friend Eliza R. Snow." Dressed in a long, ornate black silk dress with matching hat—an exact copy of the one Eliza R. Snow wore in her famous photograph—Jaynann spoke eloquently of Eliza, often comparing her with Emma: Emma was not as faithful as Eliza; Emma abandoned her faith and church by not going west when Eliza did; Emma kept the prophet's sons from the church; and Emma did not love Joseph as much as his plural wife, Eliza, did. I was puzzled.

Instinctively, I felt the comparisons were unfair and pledged to find a good biography of Emma that would balance Jaynann's rhetoric. There wasn't one—only a small, twenty-five page pamphlet called *Judge Me Dear Reader*, by Erwin E. Wirkus, and a biographical novel, *Emma Smith: The Elect Lady*, by RLDS writer Margaret Gibson. The latter was truly a work of fiction. And Wirkus asked us to forgive Emma's transgressions because she suffered a "mental breakdown."

When my dad died the next spring, I flew to Utah for his funeral. Afterwards, I went to the old Deseret Book store in Salt Lake and asked if they had a biography of Emma. The clerk said, "Oh, let me think ... ," and she disappeared in the stacks and Returned with *The Elect Lady* by Margaret Gibson. She said, "This is all I have."

"That's by someone in the Reorganized Church. Isn't there anything by an LDS author?"

She said, "Honey, I've worked here for forty years and this is the only thing I've ever seen on Emma Smith." I just thought, *Somebody needs to make this right. Someone needs to write her biography.*

When Jack joined the faculty at the University of Utah in 1974, I viewed the proximity to LDS Church history documents and decided this might be an opportunity for me, too. Even though I didn't know much about Mormon history, nor had I written anything beyond a college term paper, I believed I could

write a better biography of Emma Smith than Margaret Gibson. I could do the research if I found someone with writing experience to work with me.

We moved in June. A year later, I gave birth to our last child Heather. That fall Val called us from Flagstaff, Arizona, where they were living and Chuck was teaching forestry at Northern Arizona University. She said she and Chuck would be in Salt Lake for October's general conference and asked if we could we get together. By the time the Averys left for home, the Newells had an invitation to spend Thanksgiving with them in Flagstaff.

After our fill of turkey and all the wonderful things that go with it, Val and I talked in front of the Averys' fire. I began to tell her of my frustration that there was not a legitimate biography of Emma Hale Smith, and about going to a BYU Education Week two years earlier in Ohio and listening to Jaynann Payne unfavorably compare Eliza Snow with Emma. I explained that since there were a number of repositories of LDS Church history in and around Salt Lake, I wanted to start researching Emma's biography, and that I had been looking for someone to write it with me.

As I finished my story, Val turned to me and said, "Why don't we do it together?" Without hesitation I said, "You're on!" What I didn't know is that Val had never written anything beyond a college term paper either.

The task would not be easy. Neither of us had an advanced degree and neither of us had studied history. Val had a degree in foreign languages from Rocky Mountain College in Montana. I had an art education degree from Utah State University. We each had four children. Val had three boys, ages thirteen, twelve, and seven, and a girl, ten. I had three girls, ages nine, six, and four months, and a boy, three. And we lived in separate states.

We would need a division of labor that allowed each of us to contribute while also doing justice to our families. We agreed the primary research would fall to me because of my access to LDS Church Archives and those at the University of Utah, Brigham Young University, Utah State University, the Utah Historical Society, and eventually the Daughters of the Utah Pioneers. Val would start by reading secondary sources and taking notes and building a chronology. We began with a simple desire to know Emma Smith. We had no other agenda—no theories, no preconceived thesis, and we believed we would have a completed manuscript in two years.

I made my first visit to the LDS Church Office Building, which then housed the Church History Library and Archives, in late December 1975. I met Church Historian Leonard J. Arrington[1] and other historians who worked with him: James B. Allen, Davis Bitton, Dean Jessee, Ronald Esplin, Maureen Ursenbach (later

---

1. Arrington was called by LDS Church leaders as Church Historian in 1972. It was the first time a professional historian had served in this position. He formed a team of scholars who worked in the History Division of the church. It was a time of openness and exploration. They all encouraged new writers–particularly women. As more controversial publications appeared, some church leaders became increasingly concerned and released Arrington from his position in 1982, at the same time moving the History Division to Brigham Young University and renaming it the Joseph Fielding Smith Institute of Church History. Previous to his position as Church Historian he had founded the Mormon History Association, which included historians from the RLDS Church, along with members from other splinter groups, and non-Mormons of every stripe. He died at age eighty-one on February 11, 1999.

Beecher) and Jill Mulvay (later Derr). When I said I wanted to co-author a biography of Emma Smith, no one laughed—for which I am deeply grateful. Later Ron Esplin told me their attitude was, "Well, let's see what they can do."

That day I asked Ron where he thought we should begin. He said, "The first thing you need to do is join the Mormon History Association."

"How do I do that?" I inquired.

"I'm chair of the membership committee. I can sign you up right now." Before I left the building, both Val and I were members of MHA.[2]

By the first week in February 1976, I had lined up a baby sitter one day a week for our two preschoolers and began research in the church archives where I experienced my initial shock. The card catalogue identified only one thin folder of Emma material. It contained a photograph mislabeled "Emma Smith," which was actually of her adopted daughter Julia, taken a few months before her own death. With it were a few scraps of information about Emma. There were no books, articles, or conference talks about her. I found only the occasional references to her as Joseph's wife, the first president of the Relief Society, or as the recipient of "Elect Lady" revelation. The Elect Lady had virtually been written out of LDS history. Val and I would eventually write the first article about Emma Hale Smith for an LDS Church publication in 115 years. We were delighted, even though Correlation (the LDS Church committee assigned to "standardize" all publications) redacted the original manuscript to where the *Ensign* published a piece half the size we submitted.[3]

I soon discovered "treasures" hidden in other collections. And, of course, one source leads to another—and another. I loved researching, the thrill of the hunt, the elation of being able to solve a vexing historical problem. Every time I stepped onto the elevator that took me to the second floor archives of the Church Office

2. Val would become the president of the Mormon History Association in 1987–88; I would hold that honor in 1996–97.

3. Valeen Tippetts Avery and Linda King Newell, "The Elect Lady: Emma Hale Smith," *Ensign*, Sept. 1979, 64–67.

Building, my stomach fluttered with excitement. The next year I was able to research two days a week, and, once all the kids were in school, I could spend several days a week in the archives. After each sojourn I stopped at a copy center and copied everything I had gleaned and sent it to Val. Sometimes there were as many as two or three thick manila envelopes a week. At home whenever I could squeeze in spare minutes, I organized my research and began building a chronology of Emma's life.

The University of Utah's Special Collections yielded a number of important sources. In the 1940s, Vesta P. Crawford and Fay Ollerton began researching and writing a biographical novel of Emma Smith. Crawford's papers, including the unfinished manuscript together with voluminous notes and correspondence, are housed there. When the two women first visited the LDS Church Archives (which was then called the Church Historian's Office) to begin their research, they were told that there wasn't enough material for a book on Emma. Undeterred, they contacted Mary Audentia Smith Anderson, daughter of Joseph Smith III and granddaughter of Joseph and Emma. Audentia had published *Ancestry and Posterity of Joseph Smith and Emma Hale* in 1929.[4] Vesta and Audentia began corresponding. Audentia freely shared stories and other information with the two Utah women, including personal recollections of her grandmother. Crawford's collection was a gold mine of information about Emma's personal and family life.[5]

Our initial encounter with historians from the Reorganized Church of Jesus Christ of Latter Day Saints (RLDS)[6] came that first spring of 1976 when Val and I attended the Mormon History Association meetings in St. George, Utah. We met Alma Blair, who taught church history at the RLDS-owned Graceland College in

---

4. Mary Audentia Smith Anderson, *Ancestry and Posterity of Joseph Smith and Emma Hale* (Independence, Missouri: Herald House, 1929).

5. Vesta P. Crawford, Papers, including unfinished manuscript on Emma Hale Smith (with Fay Ollerton), correspondence and notes, Special Collections, J. Willard Marriott Library, University of Utah, Salt Lake City.

6. Now the Community of Christ. For the purpose of this essay, and in keeping within the historical time frame in which Val and I were working, I will refer to it as the RLDS Church.

Lamoni, Iowa; Bill Russell, also a historian at Graceland; Richard Howard, RLDS Church Historian; Ken Stobaugh, Director of Historic Sites; and Paul Edwards, also a faculty member at Graceland, who is a great grandson of Joseph and Emma Smith. Paul was President-Elect of MHA that year—the first RLDS scholar to lead the organization in its eleven-year history. These introductory acquaintances were cordial. If any of them viewed us with skepticism, we were not aware.

In the winter of 1977 Val and I decided to go together to research at the RLDS Archives in Independence, Missouri, and visit the Joseph Smith properties in Nauvoo, Illinois, as well as Graceland College in Lamoni, Iowa. In preparation for the trip I wrote letters to archivists Madeline Brunson and Pat Roberts, as well as Mark McKiernan, to tell them the dates we would be in Independence. Mark sent a note back inviting us to have lunch with him while we were there. I also wrote to Ken Stobaugh, about when we would be in Nauvoo, and to Alma Blair to say we were going to be in Lamoni and what days. Alma kindly offered us lodging at his and Kay's lovely home, and said he would inform others of our coming so they could offer their assistance.

We approached our upcoming journey with some trepidation. We had both heard stories of historic animosity between the two churches and hoped we would not do anything to kindle those feelings in our hosts. I had become friends with Robert D. Hutchins, a master's student at BYU, who had been raised RLDS and converted to the LDS Church. His thesis, "Joseph Smith, III," centered on proving that Joseph Smith Jr. *did not* give his son, Joseph Smith III, a blessing naming him his successor—which most RLDS Church members accepted as fact. Bob's undergraduate work had been at Graceland College and his research in the archives in Independence, so he knew virtually all the people we hoped to see. It was he who had told us who the archivists were so we could write to them in advance of our arrival. At the beginning of the research, we were meeting so many new people that we began keeping cards with notes on each of them to remember their names, addresses, telephone numbers, research interests. Robert's descriptions of various RLDS people were helpful. I remember particularly that he described Madeline Brunson as a smart, quick-witted, white-haired woman who was a bit of a "libber," and Bill Russell as very bright, a runner—something of a "jock."

On our arrival in Kansas City, we rented a car and drove to our hotel near the RLDS Auditorium in Independence. I had butterflies in my stomach as we trudged up the green ramps of the Auditorium to the archives room. Madeline and Pat greeted us warmly and made us feel welcome. We soon were bantering as old friends.

Word of our being there soon got around, and people like Church Historian Richard Howard, Grant McMurray (who would later become president of the Reorganization), and Mark McKiernan dropped by to visit. Mark upped the ante of his earlier lunch invitation by inviting us to dinner at what he said was "the best steak house in Kansas City." He picked us up as the archives closed for the day and drove us into the city where we parked about a block from the restaurant. As we were walking down the street, with Mark between Val and me, he quipped, "This is every Reorganite man's dream, to be walking down the street with a Mormon woman on either arm!" The steaks turned out to be superb.

While we were in Independence, we made an appointment to see Lynn E. Smith, the only grandchild of Emma's last son, David Hyrum Smith. We knew that he had correspondence between David and Emma as well as other documents and artifacts. He and his wife, Lorene, welcomed us cordially and showed us a number of historic items they had spread out on the table for us to see. Among them was a diary of David in which someone had pasted some of his pen-and-ink drawings over the writing on many of the pages. We wondered what lay beneath the sketches that someone apparently wanted to cover up.

To our delight Lynn brought out a lovely topaz ring that had been Emma's and invited each of us to try it on. Later, back at the archives, we told Madeline of our visit with Lynn and Lorene and gushed that we even tried on Emma's ring. "Well," she shot back, "I hope it wasn't her wedding ring—we already have four of those in the vault!"

The RLDS Archives produced the first major shock of our research—the William McLellin letters to Joseph Smith III of

January 1861 and July 1872. In these letters he talked about a number of "irregularities" among church leaders, including Samuel Smith getting drunk on sacrament wine in the balcony of the Kirtland, Ohio, temple and throwing up on the floor, and what McLellin called the Joseph Smith/Fanny Alger "transaction" that he said Emma witnessed through a crack in the barn door. There was more. Before we finished we, both felt as though we had been kicked in the stomach. The next morning at breakfast, Val slipped a piece of paper across the table to me. On it she had written a quote from Huck Finn: "and so there ain't nothing more to write about, and I am rotten glad of it, because if I'd a knowed what a trouble it was to make a book I wouldn't a tackled it, and ain't a-going to no more."[7]

Later that day, we treated ourselves to an hour at a hair dresser. Val's hair was long and thick and took longer to dry than mine, so I decided to go next door to a pharmacy to pick up a few things we needed. Her list included dental floss, a new toothbrush, and Kleenex. Then she added, "You might also see if you can purchase redemption, salvation, peace of mind, and something to ease the whole general ache this thing causes."[8]

When we left Independence after nearly a week of research, we had far exceeded our expectations for what we might find by way of sources and friendship. My continuing friendship with Madeline has been a great pleasure. Years later, when Jack was president of Deep Springs College, we needed someone to help the college establish our newly-built archives and invited Madeline to come and do that. She worked with several students, taking thousands of documents pertaining to the school's history from card board boxes and organizing them into an accessible archive.

From Independence we drove to Nauvoo where Ken Stobaugh welcomed us. He gave us an informative attic-to-basement tour of the Joseph and Emma properties and opened historical files for us to peruse and copy as we pleased. That winter had been

7. At www.gutenberg.org/files/76/76-h/76-h.html.

8. Valeen Tippetts Avery, Handwritten note (unsigned), Jan. 27, 1977, Independence, Missouri, Linda King Newell Papers, Special Collections, J. Willard Marriott Library; hereafter LKNP.

extremely cold, and once again the Mississippi River froze from bank to bank. In what could have been a pretty dumb thing to do, Val and I decided to walk out on the ice to try to envision what it might have been like that winter of 1846 when wagon after wagon crossed over to the ice to safety in Iowa. When we turned to start back, we could see all three of Emma's homes: the Homestead, the Mansion House, and the Riverside Manson all shrouded in sparkling winter white. We were both quite taken with the scene.

Alma and Kay Blair hosted us in Lamoni with the same warmth we had begun to expect. Alma was in the middle of restoring Liberty Hall, the beautiful old home on the outskirts of Lamoni that had belonged to Joseph III. He enthusiastically gave us a tour, tramping through sawdust, up and down partially restored stairways, giving us a running commentary of what used to be and how they would restore it. He invited us to sit in on his church history class at Graceland. We readily accepted. Both Val and I would have loved to have been his students for the entire term.

Paul Edwards showed us around Graceland and saw that we would be given access to whatever historical material the college had that might be of interest to us.

Val and I had decided early on that, in addition to attending annual MHA meetings, we needed to write and give papers to test our scholarship as well as our insights on various issues. We chose tough problems so we could get the best feedback on our scholarship and writing. In the nine years the book was in preparation, we presented seven different papers at MHA meetings. We got excellent feedback from the commentators and enough praise to assure us that we were on the right track and that our work was competent. The first of these papers was in progress when we made our sojourn to the land of the Reorganization. Our proposal had been accepted by the program committee, chaired by non-LDS historian Jan Shipps, for the 1977 MHA Conference in Kirtland, Ohio.

In Independence, we had heard stories of two RLDS women presenting a paper together at the annual John Whitmer Historical Association conference meeting the year before, to which Paul Edwards had responded with little mercy. (The John Whitmer Historical Association was the RLDS equivalent of MHA.) At an evening gathering hosted by the Blairs, Paul, with a hint of skepticism in his voice, said, "I understand you are planning to give a paper at MHA in Kirtland."

"That's right, we are." Val said.

"Could you tell me just how the two of you plan to deliver your paper?" he asked.

"Well," I replied, "I am going to dress up like Emma, curls and all, and read our paper while Val plays her violin in the background." That broke the ice, and everyone had a good laugh. Val, who was not musical at all and never owned a violin, was unable to go to Kirtland, so I delivered the paper without fanfare—or costume.

This trip, one of only three research trips that Val and I took together, became one of the highlights of our nine-year partnership. We flew home through Denver, where I boarded a plane for Salt Lake and she boarded one for Flagstaff. As we said goodbye before taking our separate flights, Val gave me a note to read on the plane:

> Some events in life are enough in themselves—and whether this book ever goes to press or not ... these two weeks together have been such an intense experience that it will always be a milestone to measure other events by. The association with the RLDS—Madeline, Patricia, McKiernan and his super-ego, Grant Mc Murray—then the weekend in Nauvoo with Ken Stobaugh ... all these impressions finally came together with Alma Blair & Kaye and the fact that we were able to feel a genuine love and association between these two churches.
>
> The lunch invitation from Madeline and Pat seemed to sum it all up, but as a sleepy, tired, home-sick, nearsighted analysis of the whole trip, I feel now that excited as we are about what information we collected ... about Emma, you and I came home from this stay knowing more about each other, about the substance of the modern Reorganization and about the true brotherly (and sisterly) relationship between the *individuals* of the two churches than we ever learned about Emma Smith![9]

As the research began to put Emma's life together for us, it became increasingly clear how controversial this story was becoming. Once when Val was in Salt Lake City for one of our work sessions, we went up to the LDS Church Archives and Historical

---

9. Valeen Tippetts Avery, Letter to Linda King Newell, Feb. 5, 1977, Denver, Colorado, airport, LKNP.

Department and visited with Maureen Beecher. In 1974 she and Davis Bitton had published in *Dialogue: A Journal of Mormon Thought* an interview with Juanita Brooks,[10] whose ground-breaking account of the Mountain Massacre caused her to be shunned by her local church leaders and members. We asked Maureen if she thought our book might cause a negative reaction with church leaders. She thought a moment then said, "No, I don't think so. There is a new, more open climate now with Leonard Arrington as Church Historian. But, I would be prepared if I were you."

Each summer our family drove across the country to visit Jack's father in Ohio and spend a couple of weeks at the Newell vacation cottage in the Georgian Bay of Lake Huron in Ontario, Canada. With the indulgence of my family, we took detours which enabled me, over several summers, to visit every place that Emma lived. The next July after Val and I took our research trip, Jack and I and the kids detoured through Nauvoo on our way home from Georgian Bay. While the kids entertained themselves at a playground within our sight, I helped Jack lift our red canoe off the top of the car and slip it into the water. The two of us paddled through lily pads in full bloom and out into the river. Jack took photos of the scene that had enthralled Val and me the previous winter. From those pictures, I painted a 24" x 36" oil painting of the three mentioned homes as a gift to Val.[11]

At about the same time, Val had purchased as a gift to me a print of the classic painting of Emma—cascading curls in front of her ears, gold beads hanging gracefully over a white lace collar.[12] That painting hung over our bed for a number of years, causing Jack to quip: "I believe I am the only polygamist in good standing in the LDS Church. Every day I live with Linda and Emma and even share a bedroom with both of them."

---

10. Davis Bitton and Maureen Ursenbach Beacher, "Riding Herd: A Conversation with Juanita Brooks," *Dialogue A Journal of Mormon Thought* 9 (Spring 1974): 22–33.

11. After Val's unexpected death in 2006, her children returned the painting to me. I believed it should be in Nauvoo. I approached Lach MacKay, who oversees all the Community of Christ historical properties. He liked the painting and agreed that it should be in Nauvoo as well. It now hangs in the Visitors Center at the Joseph Smith Properties.

12. I eventually gave that portrait of Emma to the Garden Park Ward in Salt Lake, where it hangs in the Relief Society room—which would have been unthinkable when Val and I began our journey with Emma.

By the end of the second year of collaboration, Val and I had established a routine of working together. We were both able to carve out small blocks of time to write, but with four kids in each of our households, that often proved difficult to accomplish. Occasionally, we were able to get away to a friend's condo or cabin to work uninterrupted. The first draft of the manuscript came together in a two-week period at a friend's condominium in Park City. Each of us took a section and started typing. When we each finished our part, we leap-frogged over to a new section until we reached the end of Emma's life. It was a primitive start, but we had a draft to work with. When we returned to our separate homes, we each began rewriting what the other had produced in Park City, expanding the narrative by plugging in more research and insights. About every two months, I went to Flagstaff for a week (sometimes on an overnight Trailways bus with our youngest daughter Heather) or Val drove to Salt Lake. We reworked and edited the manuscript as we sat side by side. Neither of our egos was highly invested in what we had written, which allowed us to blend our styles and accept each other's word changes. It became my favorite part of our partnership as we slowly produced what we were told was a readable, engaging narrative.

One summer going east with the family, we dipped south off I-90 to visit Fulton, Illinois, where the riverboat *Uncle Toby* took Emma and her children when the mobs drove the last of the Saints from Nauvoo. While Jack showed the kids what happens to pennies when you put them on a railroad track before a train passes by, I went in search of information about Emma. I ended up in the living room of a ninety-year-old retired newspaper man, who had a collection of old clippings, a town history, and other accounts having to do with Emma's few months there. He graciously let me copy everything. He also gave me the name and address of a woman who had recently purchased a diary which had a detailed description of Emma on her arrival in Fulton and told where she lived and several other nuggets about her and her family.[13]

After Jack and the kids pocketed their newly flattened pennies,

---

13. Abbey Jenks Rice, Diary, 1838–83, owned by June Gustafson, who graciously shared excerpts with me.

we headed a few miles east to Amboy, Illinois. Over the years, several of Emma's siblings had moved to that area from Pennsylvania. Since I had done well with a newspaper man in Fulton, I decided to start at the newspaper office in Amboy. I told the woman behind the first desk who I was and what I was looking for. Her face broke into a wide smile. "Well," she said, "you have certainly found the right person. I have been interested in the Mormons and particularly Emma Smith's family all my life. I have gathered every newspaper account and other documents that mention any of them. I would be happy to share them with you." I offered to pay her, which she declined, but she did accept a $20 bill for copying and postage. When I arrived home, there were two thick manila envelopes waiting for me—a treasure trove of information that filled many gaps in the research of Emma's early life and that of her extended family.

Near Harmony, Pennsylvania, I found the foundation of the house where Emma grew up, walked among the dogwood trees and maples behind the crumbling ruins where Emma had her own experience praying in the woods. I sat next to the tiny grave of her first-born child and dipped my hand in the current in the Susquehanna River where, as a girl, Emma maneuvered a canoe along its banks. In Kirtland I stood in pouring rain over the graves of Emma's own twins and the adopted baby, Joseph. I walked in the quarry where men cut limestone for the temple, visited the Johnson farm where a mob dragged Joseph from the house and tarred and feathered him, and walked from room to room in the Newell K. Whitney store and other places Joseph and Emma stayed in Ohio. With MHA tours I did similar excursions in Missouri and Nauvoo.

Eventually the research took me to other archives with extensive Mormon history holdings: Stanford University's Special Collections, the Bancroft Library at the University of California–Berkley, and twice to the Beinecke Library at Yale University in New Haven, Connecticut. Val and I were able to go together to the Huntington Library in San Marino, California. She made a follow-up trip later, where she also arranged to meet descendants of Lewis Bidamon, Emma's second husband, and secured access to two different collections of his papers, which several collectors had previously tried by purchase. Val's persuasiveness convinced the family that the papers belonged in an archive, and they are now in the LDS Archives.[14]

Through friends and history contacts, word started to travel around Salt Lake that I was working on a biography of Emma Smith, and I began to get invitations to speak at book clubs, firesides, Relief Society meetings, and discussion groups. I always took questions, and when I didn't know the answer, I focused on finding it the next time I was in the archives. The most frequent question I got was: "Did Emma push Eliza R. Snow down the stairs?" Eventually, the two of us coauthored an article with Maureen Ursenbach Beecher, who was working on a biography of Eliza. We presented it as a panel titled "Emma, Eliza and the Stairs" at an MHA conference and later published it as an article in *BYU Studies*. An audience member asked if we believed that Emma had, indeed, pushed Eliza down the stairs. In unison, we answered, "Yes" (Val), "No" (Maureen), and "I don't know" (me). After all our research and publishing an article on the alleged incident, we had each reached a different conclusion. There are several versions to the story. The most common accounts say that after catching Eliza and Joseph in an embrace in the upstairs hall, Emma (who did not know the two had secretly married) flew into a rage and pushed her down the stairs. Another says she dragged her down by her hair. Still another claims she turned her out into the dark in her nightgown. I believed there was enough evidence to conclude that there was a physical altercation, but we were unable to determine what exact form it took. Had it been me, I would have pushed her down the stairs.

As an aside to this, neither Val nor I was an accomplished typist. Val believed a good typo could be a work of art. One day she called me laughing so hard she could hardly talk. When I asked

---

14. Emma Smith Bidamon and Lewis C. Bidamon Papers in Marcia Vogel Collection, and the Nancy Kalk Historical Collection (including Emma Smith Bidamon and Lewis C. Bidamon Family Papers), Church History Library, Church of Jesus Christ of Latter-day Saints, Salt Lake City.

her what was so funny, she said, "I've been working on the Emma, Eliza and the Stairs issue and I just typed 'Eliza R. Snot!'"

This was the era Val and I called BC—Before Computers. We each hired a typist to do finished copy. Marilyn Dameron White worked with me in Salt Lake City, and Maxine Wood Campbell with Val in Flagstaff. They had identical typewriters, and both were absolutely wonderful to work with. We each developed a life-long friendship with these two amazing women.

Val also began getting invitations to speak about Emma. One occasion in particular stands out in my mind. She was a member of the Flagstaff Westerners Corral, a branch of the International Westerners, which was founded in 1944 and now has over sixty chapters (or corrals) in the United States, and twenty outside the country, representing over 4,000 members internationally. Corrals have monthly programs on all aspects of western US history. Val was elected "Sherriff" of the Flagstaff Corral. During this time, she received an invitation to speak to the Utah Westerners in Salt Lake City about the relationship between Emma Smith and Brigham Young. At that time the Utah Westerners was male only, as was the Alta Club, where the group met. Wilbur "Bud" Rusho, who Val had met earlier, had issued the invitation and accompanied her to the Alta Club the evening she spoke.

As they approached the front door, Bud told her, "You can't go in that door, it is only for members. I will take you in the side door."

Val shot back, "The hell you say!" and marched up the front stairs and into the lobby, much to the consternation of the door guard.

"Hey, you can't come in this door," he confronted.

"I already did," she said, and walked right past him.

When Bud introduced her to the group, he told of her position as a woman sheriff in the Flagstaff Westerners and of her grand entry into the Alta Club. This being the one meeting a year that wives were invited to attend, she received resounding applause. Her talk that night, "The Lion and The Lady", became the basis for a chapter in our book.

In March 1978, our family drove across the country to New York, where we would fly to London for Jack's three-month exchange professorship in England. When Bill Russell heard we were driving east, he invited me to speak at Graceland College. After that I wrote the following to Val about our time there:

Our stay in Lamoni, Iowa, was such a pleasant experience. Val and Bill Russell took all six of us right in stride and made us feel so welcome. They even let their two girls (Chris and Jennifer's ages) stay home from school on Monday, then hired a baby sitter ... to be with all the kids so Jack and I could have a tour of the campus, lunch with faculty, ... and a grand tour of Liberty Hall with Alma and Kay Blair.

Alma is still as delighted with Liberty Hall as he was last year. Some of the rooms are now finished and furnished, though not all, and Alma has done a nice slide show on the steps of restoring the home. I was amazed at how much they had accomplished in a years' time. We could have spent hours there listening to Alma tell every detail of the reconstruction, but we had to get back to dinner.

My presentation was at 7:30 Monday evening. ... The first people I saw when I walked into the lecture hall ... were Madeline Brunson and Pat Roberts. They drove up and back from Independence that night. They both gave me a big hug and we had a few minutes to visit before it started. Chris and Jack were there so they got to meet them. Alma and Kay, Paul Edwards, and others we have met were all there. I felt, as I looked out over the group that I was among friends.

My remarks were called "The Many Facets of Emma Smith" and were quite similar to what I gave at the "woman's symposium" in Provo last February. I began with background, her birth, description, marriage and a little about her children, the role she played in the restoration (hymns, scribe, etc.). I told the Ann Scott story about protecting the inspired version of the Bible. I then talked about the relationship between Joseph and Emma, read from their letters as illustrations of different aspects of their relationship. I used Lucy and Joseph's tribute to Emma (and Charlie Bidamon's later on).

Except for maybe 10 people ... they had not heard Bob Flanders remarks on Brigham and Emma. I used excerpts from "The Lion and the Lady" including the section on plural marriage, which I cut some and softened just a bit. (I also brought in the *New York Sun* letter, which surprisingly was new even to Paul.) I had really struggled over using anything on polygamy. Finally, I decided that if I ignored it completely I would not be credible with the scholars in the group and would probably get questions on it anyway. I did get a lot of questions at the end and a number of them were on polygamy—a couple were just a tiny bit

177

hostile but for the most part, good questions. The students there (Alma required his class to be there) asked a number of questions.

Paul Edwards had a nice man come up to him after and say, "Is what she said true?" Paul, with a sad but kind look on his face, nodded slightly. The man said, "I was afraid so," and walked away.

Two LDS missionaries and the Mission President and his wife were there—no one is sure how they knew about it except Bill had written mission headquarters way last fall about my coming. ... Paul told Bill that when I [said] I was not giving a formal paper, he was afraid it was not going to be much. Then he said, "Once she got into it, it was clear she was prepared—and well prepared. ..."

One feeling I [had afterwards] is ... sadness. I was reminded of my conversation with Vesta Crawford two years ago when I asked her how Emma's granddaughter, Audentia Anderson, reacted to her man-uscript and she said sadly, "It broke her heart; it just broke her heart."[15] There is no triumph in that and Vesta knew it well. You and I know it, too. Perhaps knowing that there were those in the audience who might react as Audentia did, is what left me with a feeling of melancholy.

Alma has a sign in his office that says, "The truth shall make you free, but first it hurts like heck."[16]

Early on in the research we discovered Jane Manning James, the free African American convert from New England who led a contingent of her people from Connecticut to Nauvoo, walking most of the way. In 1978 when blacks were given the priesthood and full access to LDS temples, I immediately called Lavina Fielding Anderson, then an editor for the LDS Church's *Ensign* magazine, and asked if she thought there would be an interest in an article on Jane. Lavina responded enthusiastically.

Jane had petitioned five church presidents[17] to receive her tem-ple endowment. Joseph F. Smith finally arranged a special temple ceremony, which Jane was not allowed to attend, wherein she was sealed to Joseph Smith as a servant. "Aunt Jane was not satisfied with this," he later reported in a meeting of the Council of the Twelve

---

15. Linda King Newell, Notes on a conversation with Audentia Anderson, n.d., LKNP.
16. Linda King Newell, Letter to Valeen Tippetts Avery, Mar. 28, 1978, LKNP.
17. Brigham Young, John Taylor, Wilford Woodruff, Lorenzo Snow, and Joseph F. Smith.

Apostles.[18] I was determined that before the article was published, her temple work would be done. I got the name of someone as high up in the Church Temple Department as I could, and set up an appointment. I told the man (whose name I have forgotten) Jane's story and asked if I could do her temple work. He said, "If you had come in here a week earlier I would have said no, you can only submit work for your own family line. However, the Brethren just made a rule that members can submit names and do the work for special friends. I would consider you Jane's special friend."

In July 1979, Jack and I were joined in the Salt Lake temple by Ron and Judy Esplin, Lowell Bennion, Andy and Lori Ehat, and two members of the Genesis group,[19] Ruffin Bridgforth and Lucile Bankhead, to participate in the ordinance work for Jane and her family. I did Jane's endowment, and Ruffin and Lucile were proxy for the sealing of the family. It was a remarkable experience.

In the spring of 1978 while the Newell family was still in England, MHA held its meetings in Logan, Utah. Val went without me. On June 16, she wrote to me: "When I came home from MHA, Chuck … told me, 'The kids and I got along just great when you were gone. We didn't need you to come home.' He meant it. But he also meant it as a tool and a threat so that I will 'stay home and be a good wife.' I have not understood the depth of his jealousy and frustration with the 'Emma' project and the *success* of it is what is most threatening."

---

18. "Minutes of a Meeting of the Twelve Apostles, 2 January 1902," reprinted in Henry J. Wolfinger, "A Test of Faith: Jane Elizabeth James and the Origins of the Utah Black Community," in *Social Accommodation I Utah*, ed. Clark S. Knowlton, 126–72, and cited in Quincy Newell, *Your Sister in the Gospel: The Life of Jane Manning James, a Nineteenth-Century Black Mormon* (New York: Oxford University Press 2019), 116.

19. The Genesis group was formed in 1971 as an LDS Church organization for African American members. Members attended their own neighborhood LDS congregations for regular Sunday meetings, but held special Relief Society (for women), Primary (for children under age twelve), and Young Men and Young Women meetings without priesthood authority. Ruffin Bridgeforth led the group (1971–78) until after church leaders lifted all priesthood and temple-related restrictions on June 8, 1978. It was discontinued in 1987. But in 1996 the group was reorganized with Darius Gray as leader (1997–2003), based on the perception that African Americans had unique issues and could benefit from opportunities to affiliate with one another. Leaders of the group include Darius Gray (1997–2003), Don Harwell (2003–18), and Davis Stovall (2018–present).

Her letter went on to assure me that Emma is not the cause of the problem, but only a manifestation of long-time, deep-seated issues that they had not solved earlier.[20]

Unbeknownst to Val, the Flagstaff Stake president had called Chuck into his office to talk to him. He told Chuck that Val had no right to be delving into Church history. "The Church has its own historians," he said, "and if Church leaders want history written about Emma Smith or anything else, they will tell those historians to write it." Then he told Chuck, "You must control your wife. She needs to stay home with her family—where she belongs."[21] He did not tell Val of his encounter with the stake president until many months later. Caught between his wife and priesthood authority, Chuck chose to tread a middle ground of passive resistance. Among other things, he did not support the project financially, and Val took jobs hanging wallpaper to earn money for our joint research account.

Prior to that, Val also had a run-in with her local LDS ward bishop, who was a close friend of the stake president. She was asked to give a talk on Joseph and Emma's children at a fireside for the youth of her ward. In what was probably a lapse in judgment on her part, Val ended by talking about the possibility of children by Joseph's plural wives. In a letter to me she wrote: "My Bishop was so affronted that he was rude at the fireside, challenged my statements, took the RLDS position that we do not know that Joseph Smith had wives other than Emma! And would not listen when I sought him out privately to explain."[22]

Somewhat later when the ward Gospel Doctrine teacher asked Val if she would teach the lesson on Emma and the "Elect Lady" revelation, she declined, saying that she would be a resource, but she didn't think she had better teach the class. On the appointed Sunday morning, Val was gathering up her papers to leave for church when the phone rang. It was her bishop. "I understand you are going to teach the Gospel Doctrine class on Emma Smith

20. Valeen Tippetts Avery, Letter to Linda King Newell, June 17, 1979, LKNP.

21. Linda King Newell, Notes on a telephone conversation with Valeen Tippetts Avery, n.d., LKNP.

22. Valeen Tippetts Avery, Letter to Linda King Newell, Mar. 8, 1977, LKNP.

this morning." Val told him no, that she was only going to be a resource. "You will not go into that class," he said. "As long as I am bishop of this ward, you will not talk about that woman in my church!" He hung up.

When Val arrived at the ward house, she saw the bishop in the foyer and tried to talk to him. He turned and walked away, so she followed him into his office and shut the door. He told her he had nothing more to say to her and she replied. "Either you talk to me now or I will go down the hall, get all four of my kids and take them home. And we will not be back." So they talked. They agreed to disagree about Emma if Val would not talk about her in church.[23]

I ached for her and what she was going through, and felt guilty because I had none of those experiences. My ward leaders and members were fully supportive of what I was doing. Jack and I taught the Gospel Doctrine class together during most of those years.

When both Val and I began our marriages, we followed fairly traditional female gender roles (although they were starting to crumble). We experienced a dramatic change over those years. Both families had to make adjustments and sometimes it was hard. I had basically been a stay-at-home mom—more so than Val. As I became more involved with the research and writing, I was gone a lot, sometimes for a week or more. Jack and the kids adjusted to accommodate these changes.

Jack and I agreed that this Emma work was important. I had no outside income, and there were expenses involved. I practiced frugality in my travels and dealings, but when finances got a little tight, the long distance phone bills with Val became a point of contention. In one letter to Val, I complained that I had spent nearly four hours on a long, detailed letter to her, something we could have done in a $5 phone call. "Instead," I said, I saved $1.25 an hour by writing it down. I believe my time is worth more than $1.25 an hour!"[24]

So it was a bit hard for Jack at first. I remember buying a blazer

23. Linda King Newell, Notes on a telephone conversation with Valeen Tippetts Avery, n.d., LKNP.

24. Linda King Newel, Letter to Valeen Tippetts Avery, Aug. 7, 1978, LKNP.

to wear at MHA in Kirtland, and I said, "Look what I got to wear when I give our paper!"

"Well," he said, "you have your professional woman's haircut and now your professional woman's *uniform*."

After the first MHA conference we attended together, he commented, "I hardly knew anyone."

"Well" I said, "that's how it has been for me when I've gone with you to professional gatherings all these years."

It became an enlightening experience—getting an idea of what my role was like supporting him in his profession and then figuring out how to fit in with mine. Finding our way through these changes proved stressful at times, and eye opening at others, but we did it and it worked. Jack enjoyed having full responsibility for the kids when I was away, and it wasn't easy to juggle childcare with his demanding deanship[25] and teaching responsibilities at the university. His relationship with each of our children expanded, and at the same time gave him a new appreciation for my role as a mother.

Because of where each of us lived, and our very different family situations, Val and I had much different experiences during these years—not just with our families, but as we worked on the book. On a weekly basis I had contact with any number of historians whom I could bounce ideas off at any of Utah's archives. I soon discovered a network of scholars working on their own projects who were also interested in sharing relative information with others. If I had questions or frustrations, I had only to turn to a friend at a table nearby or walk down the hall to the Church Historian's office. One day I remember marching into Ron Esplin's office and blurting out, "Everybody is lying about polygamy! Joseph and other church leaders are lying! Emma is lying!

Ron looked at me and calmly said, "You don't know about the code words do you?" Then he explained that church leaders were answering the public accusations of polygamy with denials "of polygamy in the Asiatic sense," or "spiritual wives," but they privately called it "the new and everlasting covenant," "celestial marriage," or "a man's privilege."

---

25. Jack served sixteen years as the dean of Liberal Education, completely redesigning the university's undergraduate program.

A lie is a lie whenever you knowingly lead someone to a conclusion that is false, even if what you say is true. But my point is this: I had someone who would listen to my frustrations and defuse my anger. Val had no one in Flagstaff to deflect those moments.

One day when I called her, I noticed that her voice seemed strained and far away. I asked if something was wrong. "I'm sick," she whispered, "sick to my stomach. I have been lying on the floor so I won't throw up." I expressed my concern and asked if she ate something that could have caused it. "No," she said, "I'm just working in the polygamy section of Nauvoo where Joseph has taken Helen Mar Kimball as a wife—Linda, she was only fourteen! That is how old Maureen is." Maureen was her only daughter.

Not surprisingly, we sometimes drew different conclusions as we wrote. On an almost daily basis, I worked with primary sources. I read them carefully when I found them and again as I filed them. Val placed the copies of my weekly archival gleanings in her files in no particular order (later we actually hired someone to organize her files into a usable form). Meanwhile, she read the secondary sources and formed opinions and conclusions from them. Likewise, when I sent drafts to her, she would find that my conclusions sometimes differed from hers, and this was mainly because we were writing from different sources. It became frustrating for both of us.

Val had a wonderful sense of humor and quick wit that carried us through many difficult times. Her fine mind and devotion to good scholarship added greatly to our understanding of Emma. We each brought different skills to the task and learned from each other. We edited and sometimes rewrote each other's drafts as many as five or six times. As the manuscript evolved, so did we. Our close friendship sparked a variety of interactions and emotions. Once when we were arguing about some aspect of the manuscript, I started to laugh. Val said sharply, "What are you laughing about?"

I said, "We are fighting like a married couple."

"Well, I don't want a divorce," she shot back. Then we both laughed.

Several people asked who our publisher would be. Of course, we wondered that, too. A casual writer friend of mine was a member of the League of Utah Writers. Each year the organization

Val and me at work on our manuscript, ca. 1980.

invited publishers from across the country to meet with authors and review their manuscripts for possible publication. Because Doubleday in New York had published Donna Hill's *Joseph Smith: The First Mormon in 1977,* she volunteered to talk with one of their editors on our behalf. She reported back that he dismissed our work with: "Donna Hill's book on Joseph Smith has sold well, but I can't imagine who would want to read a book about his *wife.*"

Undeterred, my friend said, "I know he is wrong. Who you need to talk with is Doubleday's regional sales representative." She gave me the telephone number of Dell Jenks of Alpine, Utah. I called him and asked if I could go down and talk with him about our biography of Emma Hale Smith. He sounded skeptical, but said he could spare a half hour. We set time and date. Val flew up from Arizona for the meeting. We initially got a fairly cool reception from Mr. Jenks, then as we talked, he started to ask questions, then more questions. Two hours later, he told Val to contact another sales rep, Robert Brienholt, in Phoenix to see what he thought. Maybe he and Bob could approach the editors at Doubleday together and convince them that they could market the book and it would sell well.

After we left Alpine, Val said she thought she had met Bob Brienholt. His mother, a member of the LDS Church, had a serious car accident outside of Flagstaff and had to be hospitalized there. Val was the stake Relief Society president and visited Mrs. Brienholt in the hospital regularly, running errands for things she needed and generally taking the place of her family, who could not be there. She met Bob when he drove up to Flagstaff to take his mother home. Val contacted him as soon as she got back to Arizona and asked for a meeting, without telling him of their earlier encounter. When they got together, she told him about our meeting with Dell Jenks. After they had talked, Bob eyed Val, "I feel like I know you from someplace." Val smiled and told him they had met and where. "Why didn't you tell me right away," he asked. She replied that she did not want him to meet with her out of any obligation. She wanted our work to stand on its own.

We provided Dell and Bob with an outline of the book and other material about the research. They presented our case to the Doubleday acquisitions people. We ended up with a contract. Dell retired not long after that, and Bob absorbed his sales area into his own. He became a good friend to both of us, prodding us, encouraging us, and scolded us for taking so long to finish the book. In the end, he arranged book signings for us and pushed the sale of our book.

One of the most difficult times in our partnership occurred when we were writing the Nauvoo period. I had done the first very rough draft, and Val had the responsibility of rewriting and fleshing out those chapters. When she sent them to me, I could hardly find Emma. The focus was Joseph and plural marriage. There were major holes—nothing on the beginning of temple endowment or Emma's central role it, or what she did in the Relief Society. There was nothing on Joseph III's succession blessing (that is when we thought we had one—compliments of Mark Hofmann).[26] The narrative had become so strident that I could hardly recognize the story. By this time it was apparent to me that Val was transferring her anger at her ecclesiastical leaders and Chuck onto Joseph

---

26. In the mid-1980s, all of Hofmann's major "finds" would be later proven to be forgeries, but not until after he had killed two people with home-made bombs trying to distract attention from those who were beginning to question the authenticity of the papers he was selling to the LDS Church and others. He was sentenced to life in prison.

Smith. She had begun speculating and moving events out of their chronology to reach her conclusions.

I remember saying, "Val, we can't go beyond our sources. We have to give the relevant information and let the readers draw their own conclusions." It hit home much later, for in the introduction to her award-winning biography of David Smith, *From Mission to Madness: Last Son of the Mormon Prophet*, she writes: "I avoid imposing interpretations that would preempt the feelings and conclusion of those whose story this is. I keep my own voice muted when their voices can be documented and I avoid speculation when evidence is inadequate."[27]

This is not to say that my own writing was without problems, but, for the most part, I did my own rewriting after Val added her comments and corrected spelling or grammar (I am dyslexic and sometimes drop or reverse letters in a word). Her writing could be eloquent and her reasoning deft. We were eventually able to critique each other's work in a way that our styles flowed together seamlessly, but getting to that point was difficult for both of us.

In the end we joked about what we would say if someone criticized a section of the book. Val would say, "Oh, Linda wrote that, I didn't." and I would say, "Oh, Val wrote that I didn't."

———

By 1981 we were nearing the end of the writing and would soon begin sending the manuscript to several readers, then edit the entire manuscript to include their corrections and suggestions. Just when we thought we could see the end, I wound up in the hospital with a hysterectomy. Afterwards, my doctor refused to prescribe an estrogen supplement, and within two weeks I hit menopause like a brick wall. While I was dealing with the repercussions, I got a phone call from Val. She had been in a serious car accident and was in the hospital with several injuries, including a broken arm. "It's my right arm—my *write* arm," she said. I was so grateful that she had not been hurt worse. I told her to concentrate on healing for now, we would get through this. Maxine Wood Campbell had already been to the hospital to see her and said, "I will be your

———

27. Avery, *From Mission to Madness: Last Son of the Mormon Prophet* (Urbana: University of Illionois Press, 1998), xi.

186

right arm. I will be with you to do whatever is needed to get this book finished!"

From the beginning, we agreed that we would flip a coin to decide whose name went first. When that time came, we asked our friend and fellow researcher and writer E. Gary Smith to flip the coin for us. We did it over the phone—Val in Flagstaff, I in Salt Lake, and Gary in Los Angeles. One of my daughters said, "Mom, choose heads. Heads are smarter than tails."

With the three of us on the phone, I said, "Val, you call it.

"Tails," she said.

"Here goes," Gary chimed in. Then, "Heads!"

The finished manuscript tallied 1,000 double-spaced pages (again, this was before computers). When we mailed it to Doubleday, we experienced euphoria, relief, and reluctance at letting it go. It did not take long to bring us back to earth. Our Doubleday editor, Jean Ann Vincent, sent it back with instructions to cut it by one third. By now Val had earned both her master's and doctorate degrees and was teaching history at Northern Arizona University in Flagstaff. Jack and I were co-editors of *Dialogue: A Journal of Mormon Thought*, which was a full-time job for me. To have the manuscript back in our laps was a blow. The other disappointment was Doubleday's decision only to market the book regionally in several western states, rather than nationally (according to our editor, this was something they later regretted as we and the book drew national attention).

Some have asked where they might be able to read the uncut manuscript. "I want to read the good stuff," they would say. That always sounded odd to me. If you had to trim a manuscript, why would you take out the "good stuff"? We agreed on some rules. We would not cut any information about Emma, or any new historical material, and we would take out stories that were common knowledge and didn't relate directly to Emma's story. Then we looked at each page and said: "One third of this page needs to come out." We divided the manuscript in half. We deleted words, cut sentences and an occasional paragraph—we extracted the "lard." When we finished, we traded halves and went over each other's work, cutting even more.

The manuscript moved better, and the narrative was crisper. A number of well-known, faith-promoting stories about Joseph came out. The new material that we left in tended to be more controversial, but it was there because it added to Emma's story.[28]

By this time (speaking of controversy), document dealer Mark Hofmann had become well known in Mormon history circles. We were all amazed at the frequency he found documents pertaining to the history of the LDS Church, many of which served to embarrass the Church. Several of his "finds" had direct implications for our book. One was the long-rumored succession blessing that Joseph Smith pronounced on the head of his son Joseph Smith III. Just before the publication of *Mormon Enigma*, rumors surfaced that he had discovered a collection of William McLellin's papers and was in the process of purchasing them. He had already promised to sell them to the LDS Church. McLellin was an early leader in the church who served on the first organization of the Quorum of the Twelve Apostles. In Missouri, he become disillusioned with Joseph Smith Jr.'s leadership and was excommunicated. After Joseph's death, McLellin made contact with Emma and her eldest son, Joseph Smith III. Several of his letters to the young Joseph are housed in the Community of Christ Archives, which Val and I saw when we researched there several years earlier. We were quite sure that a collection of McLellin's papers would have letters to, from, or about Emma. We were also convinced that if the documents held any controversial information; the LDS Church leaders would not make them available to researchers.

We decided it would be a good idea to talk to Hofmann about the collection and see if he could be persuaded to sell it to a repository other than the church. He accepted an invitation to talk over lunch, at which time I expressed my concerns over the accessibility of the McLellin papers. When I asked if he would consider selling them to the University of Utah, Sam Weller's bookstore, or any number of other places where they would be available to

---

28. Copies of the uncut manuscript are in the special collections departments of the library at Brigham Young University (Provo, Utah), University of Utah, Utah State University (Logan), LDS Church History Library, and the Community of Christ Library/Archives (Independence, Missouri).

historians, he replied, "Linda, I'm not in this for the historians, I'm in it for the money."

Then Mark had a question for me. He had heard the story about my contacting a woman in Montana, Kelly Overton (not her real name), who claimed she had a diary of Emma Hale Smith. He asked me to tell him about her. I explained that Kelly claimed to be a descendent of Emma and Joseph through an illegitimate child of their son Frederick, and was making the rounds as a speaker in LDS Church meetings. I was able to contact her and ask her about the diary. In our telephone conversation, she said she actually had a small trunk that had been Emma's and it contained several of her diaries and journals, plus letters from various early church leaders. It also had some mementos that Emma had apparently kept— several baby teeth and locks of hair, an eagle feather with a note saying it had been a gift from Chief Keokuk, a leader of the Sauk tribe. The chief lived much of his life on the Illinois River near to-day's Peoria, a little over 100 miles directly east of Nauvoo. I told Kelly that I would pay her bus fare if she would bring the chest to Salt Lake City where I could introduce her to several people who might be interested in purchasing her collection. She agreed. A few days later, she arrived—without the trunk. She did have a list of the items in it, explaining that she was afraid to take it on the bus, fearing something might happen to it.

Over the next two days, I took her to see Everett Cooley at the University of Utah's Special Collections, Sam Weller, and to the archives at BYU. They all studied Kelly's list and asked good questions, which she fielded convincingly. Everyone we talked with agreed that a collection like that was worth around $1 million. Kelly seemed astounded.

We talked about where she might want the papers to be archived. She leaned heavily toward BYU. I pressured her to name a date when she could bring the trunk down. I was as eager as anyone to see its contents. But first things first: Kelly was a member of the National Guard, and had to leave for summer training camp in North Carolina. She promised to get back to me as soon as she returned. When she did call, she sounded as though she were in tears. "Linda," she sobbed, "someone broke into my house while I was gone and the trunk is missing." I asked if she had contacted the police. She had. They told her that whoever took the trunk did not leave any trace, so they felt there was nothing more they could investigate.

A few weeks later, after being questioned by an FBI agent, she got scared and confessed that she never had a trunk or any papers that had belonged to Emma. Neither was she a Smith descendent. She said other church people's accounts of their pioneer heritage had made her feel left out and inferior. She found an old diary of someone named Emma in Iowa and decided to tell people it belonged to Emma Hale Smith. That sparked a lot of interest, and she began getting invitations to speak in a number of LDS wards in the area. After I contacted her, she decided to invent the trunk and its contents. Then the whole story took on a life of its own, and she felt trapped, so she made up the break-in story.

At the end of my telling this to Mark Hofmann, I said, "You know, I think at one point, when she thought the papers were worth so much money, she considered forging the documents on her list. Could someone actually forge an entire collection?"

Mark looked thoughtful, then said, "No, I don't think so. The science of detecting forgeries is so advanced and so precise, you would have be crazy to try."

One year after the publication of the Emma biography, Mark Hofmann attempted to cover up his forgeries by murdering two people with homemade bombs: Steven Christensen, Salt Lake businessman and document dealer who was helping Mark negotiate with LDS Church leaders in the proposed McLellin Collection sale, and Kathy Sheets, the wife of his former business partner, Gary Sheets. Mark was maimed when a third bomb blew up as he was taking it out of his car. In the days between the first bombing and Mark's eventual arrest, fear gripped the community of historians who were writing Mormon history. Were they at risk, too, as rumor and speculation suggested? Was there a crazy person out there trying to protect the LDS Church from historical controversy? A few people left town for safety. We were all unnerved. After Mark's arrest, police found a locked room in his basement filled with his forgery equipment and tools as well as bomb making materials. He was later convicted of murder and forgery and sentenced to life in prison.

Finally, on October 4, 1984, *Mormon Enigma: Emma Hale Smith* arrived at bookstores. The response was heady. The Doubleday sales agent, Bob Brienholt, had set up autograph parties for us at Sam Weller Book Store and Deseret Book in Salt Lake City. Utah State University history professor Doug Alder arranged a signing for us at Needham Books in Logan, Utah, and had us speak to a large group of his friends that same evening. Many of my friends held autograph parties and invited me to speak to various groups.

Curt Bench, who ran the rare book department of Deseret Book, was as excited as anyone to see the book come out. One day he watched as an older woman gazed at the dust jacket of our book, then turned to him quizzically, "Can you tell me what a 'Mormon Enema' is?"

Val and I were grateful to the many scholars who had encouraged us, given us advice, shared sources with us, and suggested places to look for other material. Soon after the book was released, we had a party at our house to celebrate. We invited those scholars and friends who had been so supportive throughout the long process of researching and writing *Mormon Enigma*. One of our guests looked down at nine-year-old Heather, my youngest daughter, and said, "Tell me, how long did it take your mother to write this book."

Without hesitation, she rolled her eyes and said, "My whole life!" She had been only six months old when Val and I began. She practically cut her teeth on discarded manuscript pages.

Reviews of the book were laudatory. One exception, however, was Hal Schindler's review in the *Salt Lake Tribune*. He latched onto the short paragraph in the introduction that said our publisher had required us to cut the manuscript by a third and spent most of the review saying how terrible that was. He finished by writing that there was little new in the book and that we had relied mostly on secondary sources. We were stunned. He later admitted to a mutual friend that he just didn't have time to read the book, so he focused on the cutting then looked through the bibliography and found that the primary sources listed covered less than a page. What he didn't know is that the *Chicago Manual of Style* and Doubleday required that we only list the *repositories* and the *collections* that we used in them, rather than each individual source (which were cited in full in the endnotes.) Our primary sources consisted of seventy-five single-spaced, type-written pages of individual entries.[29]

The book would soon win best book awards from the Mormon History Association, the John Whitmer Historical Association, and the David W. and Beatrice C. Evans Biography Award for Western Biography. Sales of the book were brisk: within a month, the first printing of 10,000 was gone, then another 10,000. By spring we were in the third printing.

We knew that some readers would experience discomfort by what we found, particularly as we sorted through the controversial era of polygamy in Nauvoo; but we hoped church leaders and members alike would recognize the importance of facing difficult issues, rather than leaving them buried. We were wrong. What happened in the year following publication of our book revealed an unwillingness by church leaders to evaluate our book on the basis of its scholarship or to respect our efforts to interpret Emma Smith's life as objectively and sensitively as we could. Instead, we confronted a pattern of secrecy, non-communication, and misrepresentation that was utterly distressing to us and to our families.

Sometime during the first week of May 1985, LDS bishops in Idaho, Utah, and Arizona received telephone instructions not to invite Val or me to speak in church meetings. We were later able to reconstruct the chain of command: the action originated with the Quorum of the Twelve Apostles (just below the First Presidency in church hierarchy) in response to several letters asking questions about or criticizing various aspects of *Mormon Enigma*. One or more members of the Twelve Apostles contacted the area presidents, who phoned regional representatives, who called stake presidents, who either instructed stake high councilors to notify ward bishops or called them personally. Except for parts of Arizona, and perhaps Idaho, nothing was transmitted in writing, resulting in some appalling discrepancies and exaggerations of the

---

29. A list of these primary sources is in LKNP.

instructions.[30] Val and I were not informed of the decision to silence our voices nor of the instructions passed through priesthood channels to implement the decision.

Just before noon on Sunday, June 9, I first received news of the ban from a friend, Fred Esplin. His bishop (to whom he served as a counselor) had announced in their early Sunday bishopric meeting that "two girls" (Val and I were both over forty) had written a book about Emma Smith. Ward leaders were told to discourage the purchase and reading of the book by not inviting the authors to speak in any church-related meetings. Before the day ended, I had received several calls from other friends along the Wasatch Front who served in stake presidencies, on high councils, or in bishoprics. All were baffled and upset. That evening, I called Val in Flagstaff. She expressed concern and dismay but had heard nothing of such reports. No church leader from the local to the general level had called either of us, including our bishops and stake presidents. I initiated contact with my own.

That first Sunday evening, I called our bishop and asked if he had received any instructions about my not speaking in church meetings. He had. When I asked why he hadn't told me, he answered, "Because the stake president told me not to tell anyone." I then called the stake president, Eugene Hansen. Someone was in his office at the time so, rather than talk with me over the phone, he asked if I could meet with him at 7:00 the next morning. I agreed and told him I would like my husband Jack to be there, too.

President Hansen began our conversation Monday morning by affirming that he supported the Brethren (that is, the church's governing authorities), whether he understood their reasons or not, but he also expressed his concern for me. "You are my parishioner, and I care about you. I will see you through this issue—no matter how long it takes." And he did.

I asked a long list of questions, few of which he was in a position to answer. For instance: if Val and I could not speak in church, did this mean we could not offer a prayer, conduct a meeting, comment in class, read a scripture, sing in the choir, or hold a calling?

---

30. Direct quotations from this section are, with thanks to my husband, L. Jackson Newell's, from his detailed journal covering this period.

Had Val and I by this restriction, in fact, been disfellowshipped? Was this action a prelude to further sanctions? Why and on what grounds was it taken? How long was the ban to last? Who had originated the action and why?

More specifically, I asked when President Hansen received his instructions about me and why he didn't ask if anyone had talked with me? Why hadn't he called me himself? Did he have any idea what this would look like for the church when the press got hold of the story? At this point, he seemed concerned that I might go to the press. I assured him that was not my intent, but when this sort of instruction is given so widely, I pointed out, inevitably someone will eventually tell a reporter. It is just a matter of time.

I still believed, or at least hoped, that there had been a misunderstanding of some sort. I felt confident that if I could just talk with those who made this decision, we could clear the matter up and resolve the issue.

Jack was insistent at this point in our conversation. "You're a lawyer," he said, "And you know the importance of due process principles in a free society. Linda has a right to meet with her accusers." President Hansen said this was not necessarily the case in church affairs, but he would try to find the answers to my questions and see if he could arrange for us to talk to someone who could explain what happened and why.

"I'm not interested in talking with someone who can explain it," I said. "I want to talk to the person or persons who initiated it." He agreed to do the best he could. The meeting ended cordially, with all three of us expressing our hope that something could be worked out quickly and fairly.

Word of the ban spread so rapidly that, within days, people had called from Washington, DC, Detroit Michigan, Los Angeles, California, and many points between. By the end of the week, individuals I didn't even know were calling to offer support and express their own alarm about the reports they had heard. We were buoyed by the concern and affection of our friends even while we felt helpless to stem the rising rumors. As the gossip mill began churning, ridiculous stories began to surface—rumors that Val and I had been disfellowshipped or excommunicated; that one of us had had an affair; that Jack had left me and taken the children; that I had a cult following.

My next contact with President Hansen came on Thursday. He had talked to high church authorities and said he had answers for some of our questions. Jack and I met with him the next evening. He began the conversation by saying that he understood why we wanted to talk with someone higher up than he, but, unfortunately, he was "as high up" as we would get.

He then explained that the decision applied only to speaking on historical topics in any church meeting or in any church building. I commented, "So I can speak on any subject that I don't know anything about, but not on what I know best?" He nodded but acknowledged the irony with a smile. The decision, he explained, had been made in a meeting of the Quorum of the Twelve. The reason given was that Val and I had been using church meetings to promote our book. I replied that I was certainly aware of the line between an invited speech on a subject in which the audience seeks understanding, which I took pleasure in doing, and commercializing, which I scrupulously avoided. When invited to speak in church meetings, I had made every effort not to cross that line. For reasons explained earlier, Val had not spoken in any church meeting since her encounter with her bishop.

President Hansen acknowledged my judgment and showed compassion as I anguished over the accusations. Then he shared that he believed in the inspiration of the Brethren and that he had to sustain them even in this action. "If we don't maintain obedience in the church, I don't know where we'd be," he said.

"In cases like this I don't know where we'll be if we do," Jack interjected. "Couldn't you have responded to your superiors by saying, 'I'm sorry, but I can't act on these instructions in good conscience unless Linda has been informed of the action and given a chance to speak in her own behalf'?" President Hansen paused, looked at Jack, and agreed that such a response from him would have been appropriate.

Our discussion continued and ranged widely over topics of historiography, professional standards for historians, Val's and my goals for the book, responses to the book, and ethical concerns with the procedure taken by the Brethren. I described the number and geographical distribution of the calls we had been receiving and expressed my own concern that the press would surely be calling soon. It would be better for everyone if we could present reporters with a resolution. He agreed to continue his efforts to arrange an appointment for us with an apostle.

A week and a half after this meeting, I received a call from John Dart, religion editor for the *Los Angeles Times*. He wouldn't say how he had heard about the ban, but he told me he intended to write a story about it. I requested that he at least wait a few days, saying that I was hopeful the whole issue could be resolved soon. He said he would, then added, "Linda, there is a story here, and I will print it with or without your cooperation."

I hung up and called President Hansen with word of this development. He was relieved that I had not given Dart a statement and promised to redouble his efforts to arrange a meeting. He called the next day to tell me to telephone Apostle Dallin H. Oaks's secretary for an appointment with him and Apostle Neal A. Maxwell. The appointment was originally scheduled for Thursday (the usual meeting day for the Quorum of the Twelve), but was later rescheduled for Friday—the twelfth day of this ordeal.

Just before Jack and I drove to the meeting, I received a phone call from a friend who worked in the LDS Church Office Building in public relations. "You should know that you will not be talking with anyone who has read your book," he said. "In fact, to our knowledge, no one in the Quorum of the Twelve has read it."

We met at 2:00 p.m. in Elder Oaks's office. At my invitation, Gene Hansen accompanied us. Jack and I had previously known both Dallin Oaks and Neal Maxwell, from university and community events or through mutual friends. We were not strangers to one another. Elder Oaks had been ordained an apostle just a year prior, making him the newest appointee. Elder Maxwell's tenure had begun three years earlier. Both had extensive academic backgrounds.

Following initial greetings, Elder Maxwell offered an appropriate and thoughtful prayer. We began with an exchange of good will, then got down to business.

When I asked about the reason for the actions taken against Val and me, Elder Oaks handed me a copy of an old *Priesthood Bulletin* containing a warning against people who push commercial products in church meetings. He said this was the basis for the decision. I said I agreed with the statement, that I knew the difference between commercializing and being a resource for information, and that I tried scrupulously not to cross that line. Therefore, I didn't see how the statement applied to me.

The accusation that I had been hawking the book in church meetings hurt me deeply, and I explained that the charge was without foundation. If anyone had asked me about this, I explained, I would have told him or her that I had been speaking on Emma Smith for nearly ten years—since people first knew I was researching her life. By my own choice, the last sacrament meeting talk I gave on Emma was the Sunday after the book came out. I did not want someone to read the book on the basis of a sacrament meeting talk. I felt, and still feel, that it is improper to use a church meeting to promote sales of any product or publication.

I further explained that whenever I spoke to church-sponsored audiences I followed several guidelines. First, I asked to be introduced as a student of Emma's life, not as the author of a book. Second, unless I was asked to speak on a particular aspect of Emma's life, such as her role as mother or as the first Relief Society president, I usually spoke from a paper I had presented at the 1980 World Conference on Records that, ironically, had been reviewed and cleared by the church's own Correlation Committee. Third, whenever possible, I spoke in a format where people could ask questions if they wished. Fourth, I did not bring up controversial material (like Nauvoo polygamy) in my presentation itself, but I responded to questions about these subjects as objectively and as sensitively I could.

I then asked Elders Oaks and Maxwell if they believed that what Val and I had written was inaccurate. Jack added that he was puzzled that other scholars had recently written frank books and articles on Mormon history, but only Val and I had been singled out for this kind of action. Without responding to the scholarly accuracy issue, but in response to Jack's query, Elder Oaks offered a second reason for the sanctions against Val and me. He said that church officials had received calls from members asking if the LDS Church endorsed the book; some callers had complained about some of the contents of the book. By this time, *Mormon Enigma* had won the Mormon History Association's Best Book Award and the prestigious Evans Award for western biography (as co-winner with Richard Bushman's *Joseph Smith and the Beginnings of Mormonism*). Elder Oaks cited these prizes, then said that *BYU Today*, which had recently reported the BYU-administered Evans Award, went to 200,000 LDS homes. "We felt that we needed to do something to counter the impression that the church endorsed your book." I reminded them that the Evans Award was a privately funded award and that BYU just administered it.[31]

I suggested that the string of phone calls, whatever their reported source or accuracy, was surely one of the least defensible methods that could be used to justify official criticism of a book or its authors. Elder Maxwell, who to this point had said little, apologized that the ban had been implemented without our knowledge; he did not apologize for the action itself.

Then I asked a question which raised the third and, I believe, real reason for the ban. Had Richard Bushman been forbidden to speak because he had co-won the Evans Award and was mentioned in the same *BYU Today* article? Elder Oaks said, "No, your book represents a non-traditional view of Joseph Smith. The Brethren believe that the image of Joseph portrayed in your book undermines members' faith in his prophetic mission."

"That's the bottom line, isn't it?" I said. Elder Oaks replied, "Yes."

I asked at this point if either of them had read the book. I could see that Elder Maxwell had some photocopied pages of the book with him, although he did not refer to them at any point in the conversation. He did not answer. Elder Oaks said he had read some of the middle chapters which contained "problem areas"— the ones that had been pointed out in members' letters and calls to the church. If someone complained about a paragraph, he said

---

31. By the end of the year, the Evans family decided to insure future independence by moving the award from BYU to Utah State University to be administered by the American West Center.

he read the entire chapter. I asserted that, if that was his approach, he had read the "offending" material out of context. The middle chapters do present disquieting information, but we had made a conscientious effort to prepare readers to understand these historical realities in earlier chapters and had returned to the same issues in analysis in later chapters.

I said that anyone who read only selected chapters would not know this, nor would they have the benefit of our interpretation of the remainder of Emma and Joseph's lives. I referred to our reliance on some of Elder Oaks's own previous scholarship in that area of church history, mainly the distribution of Joseph Smith's private assets and those of the church after his death.

Elder Oaks took this opening to explain his position as a general authority. He said some may consider him an intellectual, given his academic background and professional history as a lawyer and judge, but his duty as a member of the Quorum of the Twelve is to protect what is most unique about the LDS Church—namely, the authority of the priesthood and the sacredness of members' testimonies about the restoration of the gospel and the Savior's divine mission. Everything else, he said, may be sacrificed in order to maintain these essentials.

At this point, Jack observed that it is impossible to manipulate historical facts to fit theological predispositions, and then explained his own conversion to the LDS faith as a college student. His interest in the church arose largely from then-President David O. McKay's affirmation of our embrace of truth wherever it may be found. Jack argued eloquently that church leaders might now consider the advantages of dealing openly and honesty with our entire history and begin by reconsidering the "unfortunate restrictions" on Val and me.

Elder Oaks asked if we had any ideas about how the damage to my reputation might be mended. Jack answered, "Certainly. Rescind the ban!" Elder Oaks said he was sure that wouldn't happen.

I asked how long this action was intended to last. "We all know that such oral communications expire eventually" was the unsettling reply. There seemed little point in further discussion. The meeting ended politely.

President Hansen rode down in the elevator with us. He expressed satisfaction at how well the two-hour meeting had gone. Jack and I looked at each other in disbelief. We had engaged in a candid yet civil exchange, but nothing, absolutely nothing had changed. We appreciated that Elders Oaks and Maxwell had met with us, that they treated us with courtesy and listened carefully, and that they had explained their rationale, even though it took probing on our part to get at some of the reasons for the church leaders' actions. It was deeply disappointing to us, however, that they were willing to defend what we believed were arbitrary, capricious, and unjust actions, and that they apparently had no qualms about subordinating historical evidence to institutional values and public pressure.

Jack and I had experienced other instances of church authoritarianism over the years, and we had been dismayed at official reactions to scholarship about the church in our continuing role as editors of *Dialogue*. Now, however, I was disillusioned in a way I had never been before, and so was Jack. I had entered the meeting with Elders Oaks and Maxwell, confident that reasonable people, committed to the gospel and the church, could find a way to resolve the matter. I expected that the procedural irregularities would be rectified, even if the ban was not lifted right away. Instead, I heard an unmistakable message: to protect the church's authority and its official interpretation of Joseph Smith, Val and I were expendable. The leadership regretted both the unfairness and our pain but accepted these conditions as necessary costs to achieve their purposes. We were effectively counted as "acceptable losses." If this meeting had been some kind of test, for the newest apostle, to see if he could defend the quorum's actions, then Elder Oaks passed.

On Tuesday, June 25, John Dart called again from the *LA Times*, as he said he would. Not wanting to be misquoted, I had prepared a statement which I read to him over the phone. In it, I gave a brief account of the ban and our meeting with Elders Oaks and Maxwell. I also sent copies to each of those men with a letter and to President Hansen. At the end of the statement I said,

> I believe in the ability of members of my church to understand and benefit from history. It may raise questions but questions are not bad. We grow by seeking answers and understanding. When we

attempt to bury aspects of our own past ... we only raise another set of disturbing questions and leave people prey to emerging historical information with no context in which to put it. The answers to many of the problems the Church faces today lie in our historical roots.

I have asked that the decision regarding my right to speak in LDS Church meetings be reconsidered by those who made it. I am hopeful that it will.

Dart asked why I was not angrier, more bitter than I seemed. I quoted Gandhi's response to his critics after the 1919 massacre of Indians by the British: "Do you want to punish them or do you want to change their minds?"

Dart broke the story in the *Los Angeles Times*, on Friday, June 28. It headlined the front page of the religion section with large photos of both Val and me. It covered over half the page. The Associated Press and United Press International wire services picked up the story, and it appeared in newspapers and news magazines across the country. The *Salt Lake Tribune* published an article by Dawn Tracy entitled, "L.D.S. Officials Ban Authors from Lectures on History."[32] My phone rang constantly. Friends sent clippings from their own newspapers from the *Sacramento Bee* to the *Boston Globe* and even a magazine in Paris. Meanwhile, Val, again isolated in Flagstaff, did not hear anything from her stake president or ward bishop or any church authority.

Jack and our oldest daughter, Chris, were leaving that morning for England to attend a summer program sponsored by the University of Utah's College of Liberal Arts, which he led as dean. I drove them to the airport, and we talked briefly, but really had no time to debrief or digest what was happening.

I had Eric and Heather with me in our yellow VW bug, and as we drove back toward town, I knew I did not want to go home and face the stream of phone calls that would inevitably come in. I asked the kids, "Hey, who wants to go to the arts festival?" I got an enthusiastic response from both.

---

32. Dawn Tracy, "LDS Officials Ban Authors from Lectures on History," *Salt Lake Tribune*, June 29, 1985, B-1, B-16; John Dart, "Mormons Forbid Female Biographers of Smith's Wife to Address Church," *Los Angeles Times*, June 29, 1985, Part 11–5. See also "Co-author Says LDS Ban Her Talks on History," *Deseret News*, June 30, 1985, B-4.

Face painting was first on the agenda, but we encountered huge lines of kids waiting for their turn and only three people doing the painting. I went over to one of the women and said, "I can do this. Can you use some help?" She gave me a grateful look and showed me where the paints and brushes were. I settled in, painting Eric's and Heather's faces first, then gave them some money so they could explore the festival. I spent the day creating butterflies, bumble bees, flowers, lions, bears, and every other imaginable image on beautiful little upturned faces. All three of us had a great day.

The next morning the phone woke me up at 7:00. The voice on the other end of the line said, "We have never met, but I am Maureen Whipple." Of course, I knew who she was—the author of *The Giant Joshua*, a novel published in 1941 about the settling of the LDS Church's "Cotton Mission" in southern Utah and the impact of plural marriage. She had been chastised by Mormon Church leaders, which affected her deeply. She continued, "I want you to know that this phone call represents dozens of people who have called *me* to express their outrage at what has happened to you and your coauthor and to give you their support."

After the call, I toyed with not going to church services that morning, but decided I should. I purposely went a bit late so I would not have to face the milling crowd in the foyer. As I walked in the front door, Steve Tyler, a counselor in the bishopric, saw me and gave me a hug. "How are you doing?" he asked.

"I think I am fine," I answered. "But it was hard to come this morning."

"This is where you belong, Linda, where people know and love you."

I slipped quietly onto the back row of the Relief Society room. As the closing prayer ended, quiet, shy, Sister Sorenson (now in her early eighties), who sat next to me, slipped her hand onto my knee and said, "I read your book, and I thought it was wonderful, and I think what they have done to you is terrible!"

Throughout the rest of the three-hour block of meetings, people caught my eye across the room and gave me a thumbs-up or squeezed my hand as they passed by me. It was bracing, and I was glad I had decided to attend.

The immediate impact of the newspaper reports was shatter-ing. Dozens of people called, some of them weeping with anger or sorrow. Letters poured in. Many (never at our request) wrote to church officials. They expressed their belief that the ban was un-fair. The questionable procedures for imposing and implementing it were particularly difficult for virtually everyone I talked with.

The ban continued. During those ten months, nearly anywhere I went I was asked questions about it. In my role as co-editor of *Dialogue,* the press frequently contacted me for comments on other issues touching on Mormon history or church-related news (the Mark Hofmann forgeries/bombings and church president Spencer W. Kimball's death occurred during that time), and re-porters would inevitably ask me about the ban.

In April 1986, as part of the publicity for the Mormon His-tory Association annual meeting being held in Salt Lake City that spring, I was asked to appear on the KSL program *Talk About* with Shelley Osterloh. (The KSL television and radio stations are owned by the LDS Church.) The show's format included audience participation. As the date drew near, I started to feel uneasy. My experience told me that no matter what the assigned subject for the telecast, the second or third question would be about the ban. I did not enjoy having conversation after conversation turn to that incident, and I was not happy to be a continuing source of negative press about the Church.

I remembered an earlier conversation with my college-age daugh-ter, Chris, and a family friend about her same age. Millie Whitman had been particularly perplexed by the ban, and I was touched by her concern for me. She had asked me how a situation like this could ever be resolved. When members are disfellowshipped or ex-communicated, there are positive steps they can take to regain full status in the church, but Millie could see no way out of this ordeal for me. Chris quipped, "Well, Mom can always get a lobotomy!"

While we laughed at the time, I thought again that there had to be some other resolution. With this in mind, I called President Hansen and told him about the upcoming TV appearance and that I knew the ban would be discussed. "It would be very nice," I suggested, "if I could say that the situation had been resolved."

He thought the timing was good and that it was worth a try. He agreed to make some calls and phoned me again late in the afternoon of Thursday, April 24, the day before the show. The Quorum of the Twelve had met that day. "I have good news," he said. "I have just been informed that you and your coauthor are no longer under any more restrictions than apply to any other member."

The next morning, the second audience question on *Talk About* came from a newspaper reporter and concerned the ban. I had not talked to anyone in the press about the lifting of the ban. I assumed that word would spread rather naturally and quickly as soon as the TV program was over, but I was very surprised that a reporter was present that morning. I explained to him that there had been a problem, but that the previous day my stake president had informed me that the issue was resolved and that Val and I were no longer under restrictions.

The story went nationwide immediately on both wire services and appeared in newspapers throughout Utah—with one glaring exception: even though the LDS-owned *Deseret News* had published a story on the original action ten months earlier, it did not report the lifting of the ban.

What were the effects of that whole episode? Initially, sales of the book tripled. Doubleday reprinted it in hardback seven times. The University of Illinois Press purchased the paperback rights from Doubleday and published a revised second edition in 1994. But many people who have never read the book felt that there must be something improper and dangerous about it because of the earlier church action against its authors. This, I am sure, was the intended result of the church officials involved in implementing it.

One long-term effect of the ban has been increased mistrust and cynicism toward the church hierarchy by an astounding number of church members. The resolution of the situation seemed grudging and forced, a concession to public relations rather than a clearing of our reputations, an apology for the injustice, and the placement of procedural safeguards to prevent such capricious action from happening again. If anything, the amount of secrecy in communication between general authorities and the field officers increased for several years afterwards, as did acts of intimidation aimed at legitimate

LDS scholars. The excommunications of the September Six (six historians and scholars were excommunicated from the church for their writings) in 1993 come to mind as do subsequent actions.

What about the impact on my family? Our two older daughters, Chris and Jennifer, were nineteen and sixteen at the time. They were bewildered that Val and I would be punished for trying to be honest and responsible, values they had been taught both in our home and at church. The first weekend Chris came home from her summer in England, the family all went to church on Sunday. Later we talked around the dinner table. Chris voiced her feelings. "I sat in the chapel looking at the line of men sitting behind the podium and thought, *my mother is not welcome there*, then I realized I don't feel welcome either. I'm not going back." Jennifer also eventually withdrew from the church, as did Heather after she left for college, something they might have done anyway, of course, but my treatment by authorities hardly endeared Mormonism to them. Today, our son Eric is the only one in our immediate family who still attends church.

From the very beginning of the sanction episode, I realized that I had no control over what anyone else did or said. I could only control my own reaction to the situation and therefore determined that I would not allow it to make me a bitter, angry person. Both Jack and I (as well as Val) redirected our energy to our families and to other worthy pursuits—which continue to be most rewarding and fulfilling.

It wasn't until several years later that I discovered that even though I was told we were no longer under any restrictions by the church, we were, in fact, blacklisted. We could not have participated in any forums at BYU (such as Education Week, history symposiums, etc.). More to the point, our work could not be quoted or cited in any church publication, not even in bibliographies, including anything published by church-owned Deseret Book. The one exception came when the editors of Deseret Book informed Jill Mulvay Derr of that rule when they were getting ready to publish her co-authored *Women of Covenant: The Story of Relief Society*.[33]

---

33. Jill Mulvay Derr, Janath Russell Cannon, and Maureen Ursenbach Beecher, *Women of Covenant: The Story of Relief Society* (Salt Lake City: Deseret Book, Co., 1992).

She simply told them that they had used us as a source and that it would be dishonest not to cite us. If they didn't want to do that, they should not publish the book. They relented.

The experience of researching and writing *Mormon Enigma* was clearly life-changing for both Val and me. When we began the journey, we had no idea of its breadth or length, or the toll it would take on our lives and families. Val's marriage did not survive. She and Chuck divorced in 1986. She married Bryan Collier Short in 1996. He died in 2003. Val died unexpectedly on April 7, 2006, at age sixty-nine.[34] Her death was a blow to all of us who loved her. She left a huge hole in Mormon history circles and in her community. I still think of her often and miss her.

It has been over three and a half decades since the publication of *Mormon Enigma: Emma Hale Smith*. Sales of our book remain steady. Doubleday sold over 40,000 copies in hardback. The University of Illinois Press published a second, revised edition in 1994, which enabled us to make a number of corrections (mainly associated with documents that were forged by Mark Hofmann), and to write a new preface which mentions the actions of church leaders to the book. Paperback sales today stand at around 25,000 and holds steady at just under 1,000 copies a year. Hopefully, it will remain a mainstay in Mormon history in the foreseeable future.

I treasure the many friends—including Val—whom Emma Hale Smith has brought into my life, enriching me significantly. I appreciate the opportunities to learn and develop new skills that both the experience of writing her biography and the aftermath gave me. Jack's and my marriage relationship has deepened, and our partnership has taken on many new dimensions. I am forever grateful for the experience of discovering and sharing the life of this remarkable woman with so many others. Thank you, Emma.

---

34. Val earned an MA in history at Northern Arizona University in 1981 and a PhD in history in 1984. She served as professor of history, with specialties in women's history and Colorado Plateau Studies at Northern Arizona until her retirement in 2005. Chuck Avery outlived her by ten years.

Genesis

I chose to write my first book, *Power from on High: The Development of Mormon Priesthood* (1995). My second book, *David O. McKay and the Rise of Modern Mormonism* (2005), chose me.

After a four-year tenure as an elders quorum president (1977–81), I had persistent questions about priesthood that weren't answered by any published references on the subject. So, in the late 1980s, I began an eight-year odyssey of discovery and writing.

During the time that I was researching the book in the LDS Church Archives, I dropped in on an old friend and former stake president, John Carmack, who was then a Seventy with supervision over church history. Knowing that I lived in the Washington, DC, area, he said the church had called a new president for the Washington, DC, North Mission, and his family was too large (eight children) to fit in the existing mission home. The church had identified a new home in Darnestown, Maryland, and John asked if I knew the neighborhood. Yes, it was in our ward. Would it be a good investment for the church? Yes, it was in a fine neighborhood. The church bought the home.

Nearly a year elapsed before I met the new mission president, Bob Wright, for the first time. It was early in June 1990, and I had been asked to teach the high priests group, so I chose to speak on the June 1978 revelation on priesthood. I gave some historical background on the revelation, including mention of the role that Lester Bush's seminal 1973 article in *Dialogue: A Journal of Mormon Thought* had played. At the conclusion of the lesson, Bob approached me and introduced himself. I first wondered if he would chastise me for discussing a controversial topic—after all, even then there was an abundance of denial within some church circles that there had ever been a restriction on ordination of blacks—but to my surprise he asked if I could introduce him to Lester.

Seeing that Bob was a bit different than most mission presidents we had known, my wife, JaLynn, and I invited him and his wife, Janet, over for dinner. We found them to be bright, refreshing, and open-minded. The second time they came over, I gave Bob a couple of chapters of the priesthood book, then still in the preparation stage. The third time they came over, having read the chapters, he asked if I knew who Clare Middlemiss had been. I said I knew she had been President David O. McKay's private secretary, but that was the extent of my knowledge. "She was my aunt."

He went on to say that she had spent countless hours, during the thirty-five years she served as McKay's secretary, in documenting his life, writing his diary, and assembling over 200 large scrapbooks. She had hoped to be his biographer, but while he was alive, she did not have time to begin the project (she did the diaries during evenings, weekends, and holidays, as the work flow during the day afforded no spare time), and after he died, her health declined quickly. Not long before her death in 1983, she told Bob she was leaving her papers to him. Although she did not ask him to promise he would write the biography that she had hoped to write, such an expectation was the clear impression that Bob had. Not knowing how to proceed, he asked if I would help him write it.

The Diaries

After Bob finished his mission, I flew to Salt Lake City (his home) and went with him to his brother's house, where Clare's papers had resided on two pallets in the basement for the prior three years. Bob had not prepared me for what I saw—all he had said was that there were two pallets of "papers." As I lifted the blankets covering the papers, I saw dozens of black notebooks, each with the following label on its spine: "David O. McKay Diaries."

I immediately felt a kinship to Joseph Smith, for to me, the note-books were as precious as gold plates.

Bob suggested that we ship the papers to my home in Maryland so that I would have continual access to them. The question was how to do the shipment. He was quite sure that the church, which had locked up the originals of the McKay diaries (some 40,000 pages of typescript) as soon as McKay died and wouldn't give access even to his children, was not aware of Clare's having made a copy for herself. Bob was savvy enough to know that premature disclosure of their existence could imperil the project. I came up with a solution that turned out to work flawlessly. For years, I had purchased out-of-print material from Sam Weller, owner of Zion Book Store, and I trusted implicitly his circumspection. He sent hand-picked employees of the store to Bob's home to box the papers, and then arranged to have a trucking company pick them up and carry them to Maryland. I held my breath until they arrived.

Upon their arrival, I had a dilemma. The temptation was to dive immediately into the diaries, but I was still in the process of writing the priesthood book. If I were distracted, I would have a difficult, if not impossible, time in finishing the book. So, I put them on the shelves and ignored them for the next two years.

The Interviews

I began to work on the biography in the spring of 1994. While the diaries were of paramount importance, I quickly saw that they needed to be supplemented with first-hand accounts. I bought a microcassette tape recorder and began a multi-year process of interviewing people who had known President McKay. These included friends, family, fellow LDS general authorities, other church employees, and historians. I quickly realized that not only would there have to be full-length transcriptions of each interview, but that I would have to do them. I had taken a typing class in junior high school several decades earlier, and I typed well enough that it was much quicker for me to do a one-and-done transcription than to correct one done by a secretary.

Before I began to write, Bob and I had conducted over 200 interviews—a surprising accomplishment given that McKay had died over twenty-five years earlier, at the age of ninety-six. While an earlier start would have opened the possibility of interviewing people who had since died, we found that the passage of time had actually worked in our favor, loosening the tongues of people who, in earlier years, likely would have been more concerned with shielding the church than telling the story. We began the project at the right time. Had we started earlier, people would have been less candid; had we started later, we would have missed some important interviews.

Recollections, particularly of events from decades earlier, can be inaccurate. In many instances, the interviewees told us things that had not been recorded elsewhere. In some instances, detailed below, there was no other living witness to the described events. I had to make judgment calls on the basis of other data that were among the historical record, and in some cases, my best guess as to authenticity. The fact that no significant statements in the biography have been challenged in the nearly fifteen years since it was published attests to the accuracy of the interviews.

Bob conducted some crucial interviews, including Gordon B. Hinckley, Thomas S. Monson, Marion D. Hanks, and Gunn McKay, but about two years into the project, he began to experience some troubling health issues. Months later (he was, as I recall, fifty-nine years old), he was diagnosed with early-onset Alzheimer's disease, which took his life nearly twenty years thereafter. Bob remained a crucial partner insofar as being able to read and critique the emerging manuscript, but I was largely on my own for the following nine years.

I cannot over-emphasize the importance of the interviews. Many crucial details in the biography came from them, and from no other source. Almost none of the interviewees had written any kind of record of their interactions with McKay or the church during his presidential years (1951–70), and so nearly all of the interviews constituted unique historical records. Since I used perhaps 5 percent of their content, much additional information awaits future historians. I include here some of the more interesting tidbits from those interviews, most of which were not included in the biography. Unlike the chapters in the biography, each of which tells a compelling story, the tidbits are an assemblage of vignettes with no plot line connecting them.

My very first interviewee was Sterling McMurrin. He was one of my most interesting and important. I had never met him, and reached out with a "cold call" via mail that included the only thing that I had published on Mormonism, a monograph on priesthood that later became the first chapter of *Power from on High*. Sterling gave me crucial information and insights, as well as encouragement from the start. He also told me that in the early 1980s he had gathered all of his notes relating to the period of 1952–54, when his self-described heresy had led senior apostles Joseph Fielding Smith and Harold B. Lee to attempt to have him excommunicated, only to have President McKay intervene and put a halt to the proceedings. He then spoke into a tape recorder for seven hours, giving detailed description and commentary. He had never had the recordings transcribed, and he offered to send me copies of the tapes if I had an interest in transcribing them. I welcomed the opportunity, and after transcribing all seven hours, I sent copies of the transcripts to the Marriott Library at the University of Utah to add to their collection of Sterling's papers. In return, I was able to fill gaps in his knowledge of the McKay years by sending him extracts of the diaries.

Sterling also opened doors to people who opened further doors. Before my second interview with him, he sent me a note that he was going to introduce me to his neighbor, Edward McKay. Bob Wright earlier had cautioned me against approaching any members of the McKay family too early in the process, as they had a reputation for not cooperating in anything having to do with chronicling President McKay's life. But I trusted Sterling, and my trust was amply repaid. Although Sterling had not been active in the church for decades, Ed had been his home teacher and close friend for many years. When Sterling walked across the street with me and said to Ed, "Greg is doing a biography of your father, and he is the right person to do it," I could do no wrong in Ed's eyes. He became my link to the McKay family and, when necessary, ran interference for me.

Ed's interview was one of many that opened doors to other interviews. At one point in our conversation, he asked to be excused for a minute. He went into the other room where there was a telephone, and made a phone call. When he returned to resume the interview, he said, "I just spoke to Arch Madsen"—who had been founding chief executive officer of Bonneville Communications, the church's broadcasting arm—"and told him you'd come over as soon as we are finished here." Because of Ed's endorsement, Arch held nothing back, and in the process gave me crucial insights into church broadcasting and, even more important, internal church politics.

Another early and crucial interviewee was Paul Dunn. Paul had been placed on emeritus status in 1989, and uncomplimentary reports of his having embellished war and baseball stories over the pulpit, published shortly thereafter, had left him bruised. This was another instance in which Bob played a crucial role. Because he had known Paul for many years, he was able to arrange for the two of us to interview him, whereas I likely would have been rebuffed if I had approached him alone. Within minutes during our three-hour interview, Paul and I realized that we saw the church in the same way, as an organization that on a good day could do great things, but one that was staffed by mortals who often had bad days. Neither of us felt that the long-term interests of the church were well served by covering up details of its past or present. On subsequent trips to Salt Lake City, I visited him and recorded more interviews, eventually some sixty hours. Much of what he told me concerned the nuts-and-bolts details of church government that allowed me to construct a backdrop of authenticity in my narrative without distracting from it. His interviews were particularly intriguing for their completeness. That is, he spoke in complete paragraphs, without verbal imperfections. Of over 800 interviewees that I have spoken to on a variety of topics, only two have this distinction, the other being Andrew Solomon, a contributing writer for the *New Yorker*.

When I met with LaRue Sneff, who served as secretary to N. Eldon Tanner when he was in McKay's First Presidency, she was very guarded in what she said about the McKay years. As we continued to converse, her comfort level gradually increased. Then, she asked that I turn off the tape recorder so that she could speak candidly about the time period when McKay added counselors to the First Presidency. I complied with her wish, and then proceeded to tell her what I knew about the schism that occurred within the First Presidency in 1965, when Tanner complained to McKay, in a First Presidency meeting attended also by Hugh B. Brown, McKay's first counselor, about McKay having brought Thorpe Isaacson in to manage financial affairs, in effect circumventing Tanner's portfolio. McKay was deeply offended—the word-for-word transcript of the meeting, likely recorded by Joseph Anderson, who was then secretary to the First Presidency, was included in the McKay diaries—and attempted to wall off Tanner and Brown by calling additional counselors, thus creating a schism that never healed completely. When I completed my summary, LaRue's countenance changed. She said, "Oh, so you know. Then let me tell you the story from where I saw it." She proceeded to confirm what I already knew, and add more to it.

Howard Anderson, who married one of McKay's granddaughters, and Michel Grilikhes, a broadcast executive who married

Hollywood actress Larraine Day, gave me exceptionally valuable and candid interviews, in large part because we had all been members of the church's Westwood Ward (Los Angeles) for decades. They were particularly helpful in constructing the inside story of the Polynesian Cultural Center (Laie, Oahu, Hawaii), which was built on orders of McKay in spite of unanimous disapproval from the Quorum of the Twelve Apostles.

Mike told me a story that extended beyond the McKay years. He was with Harold B. Lee when Lee visited Hawaii to speak at a stake conference. As they drove into the church compound in Laie, Lee saw a lot of construction and said to Mike, "What's that?" "It's the Polynesian Cultural Center"—which the Twelve had voted down. Lee had not been aware that construction had begun in spite of the down vote, and he blew his top on the spot— and in the stake conference the following day. But that was not the end of the story. Years later, when Lee became church president, Mike had a phone call from Arthur Haycock, secretary to the First Presidency. Art said, "Mike, are you and Larraine going to be in Salt Lake City anytime soon?" "Yes, Larraine has an engagement there in a few weeks." "When you're in town, please drop in. President Lee wishes to speak to you."

As Mike and Larraine entered his office, Lee extended his hand and said, "I need to apologize to you." He went on to say that he acted prematurely in condemning the center, which had quickly become the number one tourist attraction in Hawaii, because he was not aware of all of the facts. As Mike, Larraine, and Art left the office, Mike turned to Art and said, "What was that about?" "Mike, I've been here a long time, and I've seen men transform when they moved into the president's chair."

Ramona Bernhard was one of my mother's best friends. Her son Scott and I grew up together in Westwood Ward, and later served simultaneously in the Brazilian South Mission. With Ramona, as with Howard Anderson and Mike Grilikhes, there were no barriers to candid conversation. After Ramona and her husband, John, moved to Provo, Utah, in the late 1950s, Ramona became a best friend of Maureen Wilkins, who was one of the two daughters of Harold B. Lee. Ramona recounted a conversation with Maureen in which she said, "My father said that the Negroes will never get the priesthood as long as he is alive." Lee's words proved prophetic.

We attempted to interview all current and former general authorities who served during the McKay years, and for the most part were successful (although there were not many still alive). One who promised an interview but reneged was Boyd K. Packer. Bob and I approached him at a symposium on David O. McKay in which the three of us spoke, and he agreed to an on-the-record interview with both of us. But as soon as I returned to Maryland, he called Bob, asked if he could come to the office, and proceeded to interview Bob about me.

Later, Packer called Bob and asked if he could "send someone over" to his home to look at the Clare Middlemiss papers, which he knew Bob had, but whose content he did not know. Bob, who knew him well enough to see the motive, responded, "Elder Packer, as soon as we're finished with the book, I'd be happy to have someone come over." End of conversation.

Tom Parmley was a class act at the age of 97 when I interviewed him. A former professor of physics at the University of Utah, he was also the husband of LaVern, who for over two decades served as general president of the church's Primary Association for children. In spite of his age, Tom had a razor-sharp mind—and an expansive one. Since we were both scientists, much of our conversation veered that direction. At one point he said that if he were to live again, he would become a biologist rather than a physicist. Why? Because most of the interesting problems in physics had already been solved, whereas biology was still a great frontier. More than two decades later, his words resound in my mind as I have recently reentered experimental biology in what is, indeed, a new frontier.

Gabriele Baruffol was a delightful and saucy Swiss woman who had converted to Mormonism in her home country and immigrated to Utah. I had a double connection to her: her personal physician had been in my ward when he was in medical school, and two other converts from her Swiss town, with whom she had maintained contact, had been in my ward in Los Angeles. I got the feeling she was holding nothing back. She gave me two priceless stories. The first was that Thorpe Isaacson, who became an extra counselor in the First Presidency in 1965, ingratiated himself with Clare Middlemiss by giving her a mink jacket. In describing this, Gaby got up and strutted across the room, mimicking how Clare had shown off the jacket at the office.

The second was about a time, late in McKay's life, when the staff were told not to give anyone access to the president in his apartment in the old Hotel Utah. Ernest L. Wilkinson, then the president of BYU, felt he needed to see the president, and called the apartment from the hotel lobby. Gaby answered and told him that she was under orders not to allow visitors. "I'll give you $10 if you let me in." She did—and he paid up.

I interviewed Hugh Nibley in 1995, in his office at BYU. Nibley was probably the preeminent LDS scholar-apologist of the 1950s and 1960s. "Popcorn" is a good metaphor for the interview, for he popped from one subject to another, rarely completing one narrative before moving to the next. To get the essence of an important part of the interview, I include it verbatim: "I had a talk—I don't think I should even tell you about this. I had a real argument with David O. McKay. No, I won't tell you about it, because I have never told anybody about it."

He then asked me to turn off the recorder, which I did, after which he related a time in the mid-1960s when, upon returning from a trip to Israel to see the Dead Sea Scrolls, he made an appointment with McKay. He was excited to tell the president that the scrolls "will prove the historicity of the Book of Mormon," and shocked when McKay replied, "Well, we already know that Joseph Smith wrote the Book of Mormon." He blamed O. C. Tanner, a former LDS educator and very successful businessman, for polluting McKay's mind on the subject, and spent much of the rest of his career trying to reinstate the Book of Mormon as an authentic ancient record.

He then allowed me to turn on the recorder again, and a few minutes later, this time on the record, he retold the same story:

At that particular time, Brother McKay was under strong pressure from O. C. Tanner, I think, who was his very dear friend. They talked down the Book of Mormon, they didn't only neglect it. Of course, that group up there, they really talked it down. Well, the main thing, as we

[Tanner and Nibley] were driving back to the bus station, O. C. Tanner said to me, "We've got to get rid of the Book of Mormon. That's why we had this meeting. It's driving the best minds out of the Church. We can't have it any more. Now you don't understand this, but me, with my training and my education, I can see all these things." And then I [Nibley] started giving him some arguments. He [Tanner] got so mad, he could hardly control himself. We had a time. And I've never told anybody about that. That's the way it was. But I've always admired and loved President McKay. That's why I've never told anybody about it. But he said that, "Joseph Smith wrote the Book of Mormon."

Nibley said that he had never told anyone that story, and while that may have been the case, it is certain that he later told it to others. In May 2005, the Library of Congress hosted a two-day symposium on Joseph Smith, in commemoration of the bicentennial of his birth. In a dinner conversation between sessions, Noel Reynolds, a professor at BYU, learned of my interview with Nibley. He began to quiz me, tangentially moving towards a question he was hesitant to ask directly: Did Nibley tell me the story of McKay and the Book of Mormon? When I told him what Nibley had told me, he seemed a bit upset. He then said that one of his assistants had recently interviewed Nibley, who had told her the same story. But, he continued, he made sure that the account was "deep-sixed."

Arnold Friberg was one of the great Mormon artists. His paintings that once graced the Book of Mormon are iconic for Latter-day Saints, and his painting of George Washington kneeling in prayer at Valley Forge, a commission to commemorate the national bicentennial, is a national icon. Arnold was reclusive, and if I had not had an entrée to him, I would never have had an interview. But a woman who had been in his ward for many years, Lola Timmins, opened the door. After working in President McKay's office for several years, Lola moved to Philadelphia. One day, she received a phone call from Arnold, asking if he could stay with her for several days while he did sketches at Valley Forge—in the snow—for the commissioned painting. She readily welcomed him.

Deeply grateful for her generosity, Arnold enthusiastically consented to a visit from the two of us. During that interview, I asked Arnold if he would consider painting a portrait of President

McKay for the dust jacket of the biography. He said he had already painted such a portrait. I replied that I had never seen the painting, and he said that no one else had, either. He then proceeded to tell us the story. While Arnold was doing the artwork for Cecil B. DeMille's epic movie, *The Ten Commandments*, President McKay visited the set, at DeMille's request. While there, he asked if Arnold would paint portraits of the three members of the First Presidency for the Los Angeles temple, then under construction. Arnold turned to DeMille and asked what he thought, since he was Arnold's boss. DeMille consented, and told Arnold to go to the prop department, choose any chair he wanted, and ship it to his Utah studio for the sittings.

He told me he never used photographs for portraits, and so in between bursts of activity at the studio, he had each of the three men—David O. McKay, Stephen L Richards and J. Reuben Clark—sit in the chair in his studio. He completed all of the facial work from those sittings, but the crunch of the movie prevented him from finishing the paintings. The temple was dedicated, the paintings remained unfinished, and the church never paid Arnold anything. He had stored them in a shed for over forty years, and agreed to bring them into his studio prior to our next interview.

Lola and I invited Ed and Lottie McKay to that second meeting, so that they could see the portraits. Arnold had propped them against some cabinets, still unfinished. When Ed walked into the room, he began to cry, saying, "That is the best representation of Father that I have ever seen." Arnold agreed to finish all three paintings, and the finished images appear in the biography, with that of President McKay also on the dust jacket. Arnold's wife insisted that I purchase all three paintings, which I did. My wife and I later donated the portrait of Clark to the BYU law school that bears his name, and the portrait of Richards to the church's museum. The McKay portrait is on a prominent wall in our home.

An area where the biography broke new ground was the documentation of McKay trying, on multiple occasions, to change the exclusionary policy of the church towards ordination and temple attendance of blacks. Two years after the landmark *Dialogue* article on the subject by Lester Bush, my wife and I moved to

Maryland and, by sheer coincidence, into the ward where Lester and his family had moved a year earlier. After the 1978 revelation, Lester opined that the reason LDS President Spencer Kimball received the revelation was that he was the first president to have asked the question. No data points had suggested anything else. Indeed, there was not even a hint in the McKay diaries of him having asked.

As I conducted the interviews, however, I began to hear something different. Four people told me of four different occasions, ranging from about 1954 to 1968, where McKay did ask the question: Midene McKay Anderson (his granddaughter), Marion D. Hanks, Lola Timmins, and Richard Jackson. A fifth account was published four years after I began my research, in Leonard Arrington's autobiography (1998). All are fascinating (and are described briefly in the book), but Jackson's is a cut above.

Jackson, an architect, worked for just a couple of years in the church's building department, in the late 1960s. Lavina Fielding Anderson, a talented editor, referred me to him, as one of my chapters was on the building program. He gave me solid material on that subject, but then threw me the biggest surprise of any interview. One day, he said, President McKay came into his department and seemed upset, talking to himself. "That's it. That's the end of it." When Jackson asked what was troubling him, he said that he had approached the Lord many times about the issue of blacks and priesthood, and that he had done so again late the prior night. The answer was definitive: "No, this will not happen during your lifetime. Don't ask again." Richard then said that he had never written that account. "You are the only other person in the church who knows about it." But it was on the record, and my tape recorder was working fine.

I interviewed Reed Benson in his office at BYU. In earlier years, he had been national director of public relations for the John Birch Society. His father, LDS apostle Ezra Taft Benson, shared Reed's political views, and while never joining the society, he was one of its most fervent public advocates. The society's founder, Robert Welch, tried without success to talk McKay into allowing Ezra Benson to become a director of the society. His politics became so extreme that one LDS congressman, Ralph Harding of Idaho, denounced him on the floor of the Congress.

As deeply immersed as both Bensons were in right-wing politics, however, one would never know it from reading the elder Benson's biography. The reason? Reed told me that the family's instructions to Sheri Dew, who wrote the biography, were that there was to be no controversy in it. The book's index tells the tale: the words Communism, John Birch Society, and Robert Welch are absent. The book characterizes Benson's anti-Communistic activities as his "love of freedom." (I called the John Birch Society offices and asked if they had any photographs of Ezra Taft Benson. They were most gracious, and sent me a fine photograph of Benson posing with Robert Welch, along with authorization to include the image in the McKay biography.)

Ralph Harding was living in nearby suburban Virginia while I was working on the book, and agreed to an interview. He could not have been more cooperative; indeed, in addition to giving me a fascinating interview, he gave me copies of his speech regarding Benson (an off-print from the *Congressional Record*) and his correspondence with church leaders relating to Benson. In one of the letters, Joseph Fielding Smith, who later became church president, expressed the hope that Benson's two-year assignment to Europe in the mid-1960s would "purify his blood." But even though Harding had denounced Benson publicly, he bore the man no malice. In fact, he said, it had grieved him to have to make the denunciation, for Benson, a fellow Idahoan, had officiated at his wedding.

On the other side of the aisle from Benson, at least politically, was Hugh Brown, first counselor in the First Presidency. Brown died two decades before we began work on the biography, but I was able to interview his son Charles, who spoke at some length about the damage control that his father often had to do in the aftermath of a Benson address, particularly at BYU. He also spoke of his disdain for Clare Middlemiss, who bore a grudge against his father to the point of blocking him from seeing McKay in his later years when McKay was confined to his apartment. (Bob Wright told me that he witnessed a toe-to-toe shouting match between Brown and Middlemiss.) Then, he shared with me a ditty that he had written:

Little Miss Middlemiss was never ordained.
Little Miss Middlemiss was never sustained.
But of all of the Brethren, there's none can compare
With the line of authority of Little Miss Clare.

Alan Blodgett spent most of his career in the financial department of the church. Several years after McKay's death, Alan became the chief financial officer of the church—until he came out as gay, whereupon he was summarily excommunicated. He agreed to an interview, but in a different format than the others: so as not to run the risk of being misunderstood, he responded to every question by email. His very precise answers were of enormous importance to me in getting the story right, particularly about the chapter on the building program. After the book was published, he sent me a lovely note that included a regret that people in the building department, who were so hurt by the way things were handled when Wendell Mendenhall was summarily fired, didn't live long enough to learn the whole story—a story that he felt would have helped heal many wounds. (Mendenhall had headed the department for over a decade and oversaw the explosive, postwar growth of chapel construction throughout the world, but fell prey to suggestions to McKay by Thorpe Isaacson that cost overruns demanded the firing not only of Mendenhall, but those who had worked with him.)

Alan never betrayed a financial confidence, but still was able to steer me in the right direction on financial issues. Of particular importance was his insight in contradicting what others had sometimes claimed, that in the early 1960s the church was "near bankruptcy" because of the excesses of the building program. In fact, he said, the church had abundant assets in the form of real estate—buildings as well as land—but the overheated building program had resulted in a cash-flow problem. The solution, largely managed by Eldon Tanner of the First Presidency, was to put the building program on hold for one chapel-construction cycle, by which time revenues were able to catch up and again put the church in a positive cash flow.

Alan also played the role of general critic. He read every chapter in draft form and made comments as to content and tone.

Having been at the epicenter of church governance and politics for so many years, he gave invaluable insights and suggestions. It was a testament to the credibility of the other interviewees and the depth of my own research that he rarely questioned either a fact or interpretation.

Fred Buchanan, a Scotsman who spent his career as a professor at the University of Utah, gave wonderful insights and anecdotes regarding his home country and his proselytizing mission there. He also saved me from making an embarrassing misstatement concerning McKay's well-known emphasis on families. Most church members, including myself, had assumed that he originated his oft-stated aphorism, "No success in life can compensate for failure in the home." But McKay borrowed it from an early-twentieth-century American sociologist. The statement bore the same truth, and McKay's continual use of it had had an enormous and positive influence on LDS attitudes towards families; but Fred allowed me to give credit where it was due—and to escape later criticism from Internet-savvy fact checkers.

Ed Firmage is a professor of law and a grandson of Hugh Brown. He confirmed the observations of his uncle, Charles Brown, and added crucial insights into the release of his grandfather from the First Presidency upon McKay's death. The release was devastating to Hugh—and embarrassing, as it was the only time since the death of Brigham Young, nearly a century earlier, when a sitting counselor in the First Presidency was released. (The second—if you don't count Marion Romney, who had been totally incapacitated for several years—was Dieter Uchtdorf, who was released upon the death of President Thomas Monson in January 2018.) Ed said his grandfather's release came about because Harold Lee, the new first counselor (and de facto church president, given the failing health of Joseph Fielding Smith), was infuriated that Brown had tried to change the policy on ordination of blacks while McKay was alive but incapacitated.

Ed's mother was Mary Brown Firmage Woodward. She told me about the apostasy among missionaries in the French Mission in the late 1950s, which came to a head at the time of the dedication of the London temple. Her father accompanied McKay to London, both for the dedication and to resolve the apostasy. Brown, who was a newly called apostle, bore a heavy burden, and McKay said to him, "Hugh, I need you by my side." Three years later, he was called to the First Presidency upon the death of J. Reuben Clark.

The most memorable thing Mary told me was an account of a dream her father had about a month prior to his death: "One morning I went up, and he said, 'I've got something to tell you, Dot. Last night I was with the Savior.' I said, 'Oh, Daddy, can you tell me anything about it?' He said, 'There isn't much to tell. I was surprised at how comfortable I was. I was perfectly at home with him. But I was amazed at the great and marvelous quality of love that emanated from him, every part of him just enfolded me. The Savior loves me.' And he was surprised. It was a lovely moment."

Ed Kimball, son of Spencer W. Kimball, was researching and writing his father's biography during the same decade that it took me to write McKay's. When I interviewed him, we compared notes. I had assumed that since McKay had been so pro-active in trying to reverse the policy on ordination of blacks, and since Spencer Kimball had been the one who did reverse it, that the two men had had some communications on the subject. To my surprise, Ed said that he had not seen a single bit of evidence that there was any such communication. I was also surprised at the paucity of knowledge that Ed possessed regarding the meeting in the Salt Lake temple in which the 1978 revelation occurred. Our interview took place in 1995, and at that time he said he still did not have a clear idea of what occurred in the temple meeting. Shortly after the revelation, Ed asked Boyd Packer about it. Packer kindly but firmly told him it was none of his business.

Lynn Richards was a son of Stephen L Richards, who served as first counselor to David O. McKay from 1951 until his death in 1959. I interviewed Lynn when he was in his nineties. He had been in the general superintendency of the Sunday School (the title was later changed to general presidency) in the pre-Correlation era, and he opened my eyes to the independence the auxiliary organizations of the church had at that time. They decided their own curriculum, commissioned writers for their manuals, and published their own magazine (*The Instructor*), all without requiring approval from ecclesiastical authorities or coordination with other auxiliary organizations. When McKay resuscitated the idea of Correlation (which had begun in the first decade of the twentieth century) in 1961 and placed Harold B. Lee in charge of it, his intent was to eliminate the overlaps and contradictions among the auxiliaries. After McKay's death, however, Lee took it in a different direction and transformed what had essentially been a monarchy, with the church president being both head-of-state and head-of-government, into a constitutional monarchy, with the president of the Quorum of the Twelve becoming head-of-government. In the process, the auxiliary organizations were stripped of their autonomy, instruction manuals were written by committees, and the spices were removed from the stew.

Marie Moyle Wangeman was a daughter of Henry D. Moyle. When Stephen Richards died in 1959, McKay chose Moyle to replace him in the First Presidency. Moyle created some of his own problems by pushing for an over-heated building program and an over-heated missionary program that resulted in the tragic era of "baseball baptisms" in the British Isles, when young people were sometimes baptized without their parents' knowledge or consent. But one of his primary problems was not of his own doing. When Richards became the new counselor in 1951, he was second-senior member of the Quorum of the Twelve. But when Moyle replaced him, he was sixth-senior—and four positions junior to Harold B. Lee, who had been his close friend. The move damaged their relationship permanently. Marie said, "President Lee, I don't think, ever forgave him for going into the First Presidency over him. It really spoiled their friendship somewhat. President Lee just didn't feel that was right at all. There were such close friends before that, but they were never close friends after."

Milton Weilenman was Democratic State Chair in Utah in the early 1950s when one-term Republican Congressman Douglas Stringfellow was obliged, thanks largely to a meeting with David O. McKay, to withdraw from his bid for a second term because of misrepresentations of his war record. Milt had hoped that the timing would be such that the Republicans would not be able to replace Stringfellow with a strong candidate. "I'm trying to elect a Democratic congressman," he said, "and this is much too early to go down and see President McKay, because President McKay will have the authority to get this story released, and if it's released too early, they'll name a replacement, and the replacement will not be under the stigma that Stringfellow is under, and the whole plan will fail." He consulted with Spencer L. Kimball (oldest son of the apostle and later church president), who had been dean of his law school, and Kimball said, "We're after the truth. Truth doesn't wait until a week before an election." So Milt and Spence met with McKay, who subsequently met with Stringfellow. Concerned that the faith of young Latter-day Saints, who were enthralled with Stringfellow's war stories, would be destroyed by the knowledge that they were fabricated, McKay urged him to confess his misdeeds and withdraw. With only sixteen days left before the election, the Republicans replaced him with Henry Aldous Dixon, president of Utah State Agricultural College (now Utah State University), and the Republicans held onto the seat. Milt concluded the telling of the episode by saying, "This story has never been told, certainly not with President McKay's involvement. ... He demanded that the truth be told, let the consequences fall where they may."

T. Bowring ("Beau") Woodbury II spent a career in law, capped by several years as general counsel for Consolidated Edison Company in New York City. I met him in St. George, Utah, where he had retired. He was most gracious, not only granting me an interview, but also giving me access to a bound volume in his possession that contained all of the bulletins issued to missionaries by his father during his tenure as president of the British Mission (1958–62). It is likely that no other such collection exists. In reading it, I saw the evolution of what became known as the "Baseball Baptism Era." It began innocently, when missionaries asked their families to send baseball equipment that they could use on what was then called Diversion Day (later Preparation Day), the day during the week when missionaries were not expected to proselytize full time. When the missionaries began playing in public parks, British boys flocked to see—and then play—this strange American game that looked little like cricket.

Initially, the opportunistic missionaries used baseball to gain entrée to families, and many conversions followed. But the sequential bulletins showed increasing pressure from the mission home to increase conversion numbers. Each month's number became the baseline for the following month, during which there was expected to be an incremental increase. The innocence vanished, and the rest is history.

Usually I pursued interviews, but on occasion they found me. On one research trip to Salt Lake City, I dropped in to see Lavina Fielding Anderson. She introduced me to a houseguest, Marjorie Newton, an Australian who was in town to do research at the LDS Church Archives. When I told Marjorie of my project, she said she would put me in touch with a friend in Melbourne, Bill Delves, who had been a stake president in that city. Bill and I never met, but we exchanged correspondence for a couple of years. He gave me the account—which is in the biography—of his meeting southern Utah historian Juanita Brooks during a trip to LDS general conference in Salt Lake City, and being able to tell her of David O. McKay telling apostle Delbert Stapley to stand down from his attempt to excommunicate her for her biography of John D. Lee. (Brooks also wrote a near-definitive account of the infamous Mountain Meadows Massacre of 1857.)

In addition to conducting my own interviews, I was able to benefit from interviews conducted by others. These included several dozen in the LDS Archives, part of their oral history collection of over 6,000 interviews. Some of the oral histories to which I was given access were labeled "restricted." After going through the unrestricted ones that had content related to the McKay years, I approached Ron Watt, an employee in the archives with responsibility over the oral history collection. He suggested that I write him a letter and list the restricted interviews that I wished to see, with a justification for each. I did so, and he went to bat for me. I was able to get access to nearly one-third of them.

Another collection of interviews took a bit more effort to access. Historian Richard Poll had researched the life of Henry D. Moyle with the intent of writing his biography, but never completed the manuscript. (It was later completed and published by

Stan Larson.) Poll recorded many interviews, but rather than transcribe them, he merely played them back and made handwritten notes. After his death, his daughters donated his papers—which included the tapes—to the Marriott Library at the University of Utah. I made a proposal that the library leadership accepted: If they would make copies of the audiotapes and send them to me in Maryland, I would make full-length transcripts and donate copies to the library. There was much crucial information in the tapes, and I was astounded to see, when I compared the transcripts with Poll's handwritten notes, how much he did not transcribe.

Sometimes, interviews yielded unexpected information that didn't relate directly to McKay, but was nonetheless fascinating—and sometimes quite important. Bill Bates had been a counselor in the first stake presidency in Europe (London), and later presided over the same stake. While he was stake president, he became aware that a member of his stake had misappropriated tithing funds. When he reported the incident to church headquarters, apostle Bruce McConkie flew to England for the sole purpose of investigating the incident. He demanded that Bill excommunicate the man, but Bill refused. Because he and his counselors kept the matter confidential, the man repaid the money, and he and his family remained active in the church. Bill's comment to me as he concluded his telling of the story was, "The Savior said, 'Feed my sheep,' not 'Kill my sheep.'"

Jack Carlson was a dear friend and a member of my ward in Maryland. In 1976, he ran for the United States Senate from Utah, but was defeated in the primary election by Orrin Hatch. During the campaign, he met with Spencer Kimball and established a rapport that extended for several years thereafter. In the spring of 1978, he and his wife, Renee, met with Kimball, who said that he was considering reversing the policy regarding ordination of blacks. He said that he had not decided the matter yet, but asked Jack's advice on the politics of implementing a new policy. Jack said, "Do it quickly and move on, without explanation."

When I mentioned this story at a gathering in our home, John Baker, our stake patriarch, said, "Let me tell you a related story." He went on to say that in the same timeframe, the spring of 1978,

Merrill Bateman called him. John, a senior vice president of Mars, Inc., the candy company, had previously hired Bateman to head a cocoa research institute owned by the corporation. Now, Bateman told him the First Presidency had asked him to travel to Africa and make an assessment of leadership potential among African exchange students who had attended BYU. The trip was to be under the radar, and so Bateman asked if John would approach the Mars family with a request that he be given "cover" for the trip. The family agreed, and so the two men—John was invited along—toured several African countries as emissaries of the Mars company, rather than the LDS Church, reporting their findings to the First Presidency without realizing what was about to happen.

Yet another interview gave me an insight into the 1978 revelation. J. Thomas Fyans, a member of the First Quorum of Seventy, told me that in the early 1960s, when he was president of the Uruguayan Mission, Spencer Kimball visited the mission. One afternoon, as the two of them sat alone in one of the church's chapels, Kimball said to him, "Tom, some way we've got to solve this problem of 'the blood.' They are worthy people."

Sometime during the Vietnam War, the church authorized LDS servicemen to dye their garments to match the colors of their uniforms, for the practical reason that a white undergarment showing through a ripped uniform presented a bold target for the enemy. Later, the church began to sell to servicemen and servicewomen pre-dyed garments, either khaki or brown. I wondered if there was a record of the communication between the church and the army that documented the transition, so I submitted a Freedom of Information request to the Department of Defense. Several months later, I received a phone call from the Pentagon. The caller said that they had done a search and had found no documentation of the matter. "It was probably done with one or two unrecorded phone calls," he said. He went on to say that his boss, Colonel John Westwood, was LDS, and suggested that I speak to him.

A short time later, I spoke with Colonel Westwood by phone and described my project of writing the McKay biography. To my surprise, he said that he had grown up in the ward that McKay had attended, and thus he was very interested in my project. He then said that he had another garment story, one that I could not have anticipated. He said the army had just approved a black LDS garment. "For Special Forces?" I asked. "Yes," he said. The underwear, made by an army contractor using a special fabric that reduced the infrared signature of the wearer—a crucial feature given the frequency of nighttime missions and the existence of night-vision binoculars—would be sold to troops, who would then send them to Salt Lake City to have markings placed in them.

A few years later, I mentioned this to a cousin who had been an army pilot on a Chinook helicopter that had ferried Special Forces on missions in Afghanistan. He shrugged it off, but a few months later, as he was on his way to a new assignment, he came by the house and gave me a set of black garments.

The Scrapbooks

A major project by President McKay's office staff was to compile scrapbooks documenting his presidency—this in addition to the 40,000 pages of his diaries kept by Clare Middlemiss. Over 200 volumes of the scrapbooks reside in the church archives, and they contain much valuable information about the McKay years that is not available in other sources. The scrapbooks are not restricted, but I had a different problem with them. Whereas I had copies of the diaries in my possession and could take my time going through them, the task of trying to go through tens of thousands of pages of scrapbooks while on brief research trips to Utah seemed impossible.

Seeing my dilemma, Steve Sorensen, a church employee who oversaw the archives, offered a solution. Quietly, he instructed another employee to send me six rolls of microfilm at a time. I had a microfilm reader at home, and this allowed me to go through the entire set of scrapbooks at my own pace. If Steve had not intervened, I am sure that I would never have completed my research of the scrapbooks—and they contained crucial information.

Candid Views from Outside

The process of reading the diaries, marking passages of interest and then typing them into the computer verbatim took several years.

While I did some of the typing myself, most was done by my secretary, who willingly donated her time during off-hours. A Catholic, she had not known any Mormons prior to working for me. When she had finished typing the diary entries, I asked for her comments. "David O. McKay is my hero," was her first comment. What about the others? Her two-word response caught me off-guard, because she had no dog in the fight: "Power corrupts."

At the same time, I was host to my mentor in pathology at UCLA, Dr. David Porter. Recently retired from the faculty, he was spending a month in our laboratory to work with the younger scientists. In the evenings, he had little do to in his hotel room, and so I gave him several volumes of the diaries to read. After reading several hundred pages, he gave me a candid assessment that was as surprising as my secretary's: "If you change the names of the people, this is just corporate politics."

Mechanics of Research and Writing

My research notes, some 15,000 pages in all, consisted of six databases: (1) verbatim extracts from the diaries, about 7,000 single-spaced pages; (2) transcripts of the interviews that Bob Wright and I conducted; (3) extracts of the 200-plus volumes of scrapbooks; (4) extracts from over 2,000 pages of David O. McKay's sermons and other discourses; (5) extracts from published sources including books, magazines, and pamphlets; and (6) notes from archives, particularly the LDS Archives, the Marriott Library of the University of Utah, and the L. Tom Perry Library Special Collections division of the Harold B. Lee Library at Brigham Young University.

Once I had all of the sources in my laptop computer, I began the long and arduous task of creating subject files. This involved a line-by-line cut-and-paste job on the computer, sorting each bit of information by subject and building over 100 subject files. Some were quite small, only a few pages, but others were hundreds of pages. It took over a year to build the files. Once they were completed, I took a step back and evaluated them on the basis of importance. Sixteen files made the cut, and those were the basis of the book's sixteen chapters.

Although my approach to research was exhaustive and exhausting on the front end, by the time I had completed the subject files, the heavy lifting was essentially finished. With all of my sources in the laptop, I could write wherever I happened to be. Much of the writing was crowded into the same brief increments of time that I had used for the research and writing of my prior book. Having an autistic son meant that I did not have the luxury of sequestering myself for lengthy periods, and I simply had to learn to use whatever time I could find. Occasionally, I did find an extended block of time, generally on a business trip. On a return trip from Belgium of about eight hours, I wrote an entire chapter.

The Publisher

After eight years of research and two years of writing—I did not begin the writing process until the research phase was completed—I was ready to look for a publisher. Although I had published one book, *Power from on High*, that had been well received in scholarly circles, it was far from a best-seller: the first (and only) printing of 2,000 copies took over twenty years to sell out. So, I had essentially no reputation to precede the biography. The first publisher I approached was Oxford University Press, which has since created a significant franchise of books on Mormonism. The section editor quickly took a pass. (Twelve years later, the same editor took another pass on my fourth book, *Gay Rights and the Mormon Church: Intended Actions, Unintended Consequences.*)

On a trip to Salt Lake City, I dropped in to talk to Greg Thompson, director of special collections in the Marriott Library. When I told him Oxford had rejected the manuscript, he said, "How about our press?" I answered that it was well known that the University of Utah Press had not published any books relating to Mormonism in a decade. "Come with me," he replied.

We walked across the campus to the offices of the press, and he introduced me to the press's director, Jeff Grathwohl. We spoke for over an hour and I left a couple of chapters with Jeff. By the time I returned to Maryland, a contract awaited me.

Neither Bob Wright nor I cared about royalties from the book, and so I made a proposal that the press quickly accepted: We would forego all royalties in return for a higher-quality book than their standard, and at a price under $30.00. Joan Nay, who had worked for decades for Sam Weller Books, had told me that the audience I wanted to reach had a psychological barrier for books costing over $30.00, and so the eventual list price was set at $29.95.

Part of the deal was that there would be two interior signatures of photographs, one of which would be in full color. The main reason I wanted color was to be able to display the marvelous portraits of Arnold Friberg. (Arnold was invested enough in the project that he visited the press to ensure that the color balance was correct.) But there were several other photographs that, I believed, called for color.

The images came from a variety of sources. The majority came from the LDS Church History Library and the Museum of Church History and Art. (The level of cooperation I received from the church in obtaining the images set me up for major disappointment a decade later, when I asked for images to illustrate a biography of Leonard Arrington I had completed. Something had changed, for in return for access to images, they insisted on editorial control over the text. The press and I rejected the terms, and we were able to illustrate the biography by using other sources.) Others providing multiple images included Friberg Fine Art, Inc., the Marriott Library of the University of Utah, Bob Wright (to whom Clare Middlemiss gave not only her papers, but also dozens of photographs), and the Utah State Historical Society.

Sam Weller produced a photograph of David O. McKay visiting a group of elders in the German Mission, one of them being his father, Gustav, the founder of Zion Book Store. The John Birch Society, as mentioned earlier, provided a photograph of their founder, Robert Welch, posing with Ezra Taft Benson. The Tanner Humanities Center of the University of Utah gave us the image of Sterling McMurrin, a major figure in chapter 3, "Free Agency and Tolerance." The Catholic Diocese of Salt Lake City gave us the image of Bishop Duane Hunt, who figured prominently in chapter 5, "Ecumenical Outreach."

In addition to existing images, I commissioned the creation of one. In the first year of his presidency, McKay was visited on his birthday by Arthur Moulton, the Episcopalian Bishop of Salt Lake City. McKay's diary entry of the visit encompassed several pages, ending with a description of Moulton placing his hands on McKay's shoulders and giving him a blessing. Such a gesture of ecumenical camaraderie would have been unimaginable among many of McKay's peers, and the fact that he committed it to his diary in substantial detail indicated that it registered with him as being particularly significant.

I reached out to Rose Dall, an LDS artist who lives in Virginia, a short distance from my home, and asked if she would accept a commission to paint the scene. She had done cover art for LDS Church magazines and her work is excellent and highly respected. She agreed, and proceeded to do research, using the diary extracts and photographs of the two men from the early 1950s, the episode having occurred in September 1951. She even sculpted half-sized heads of the two men in colored clay, complete with combed hair, so as to allow her to get the lighting right. The finished work, which she titled *Blessing the Prophet*, occupies a prominent place in the color signature. The original graces my library.

After the first printing, Rick Grunder, an antiquarian book dealer in upstate New York and friend of many decades, sent me a packet that included a marvelous, sepia-toned, formal photograph of David O. McKay and his three brothers, William, Thomas and Morgan, taken in about 1920. Rick had obtained it at an estate auction, presumably of one of the brother's heirs. His note said, "You need to have this." It is a photograph that I had not seen in any other collection, and I knew it had to be in the next printing. The press cooperated fully, and so the second and all subsequent printings have the portrait of the McKay brothers replacing a photograph of McKay and a grandchild.

The Process of Publishing

University presses operate differently than trade presses. The University of Utah Press does not move quickly, but what it produces is of great quality—particularly given the flexibility that our no-royalty agreement gave them. One adjustment that nobody seemed to notice was to enlarge the size of the book from their standard

6" x 9" to 7" x 10". This allowed us to package the nearly 500 pages inside a book whose thickness would not intimidate the reader.

Peter DeLafosse was my primary contact at the press, and his attentiveness to the entire editorial process made it seamless, even pleasant. While the process was not rapid, it was speeded up a bit by the news that the LDS Priesthood and Relief Society study manual for 2005 was to be *Teachings of David O. McKay*. I had no idea until 2004 that that was to be the case. My book arrived at bookstores in March 2005. (I later learned from Mary Jane Woodger, a professor at BYU, that unnamed church officials had contacted her well prior to 2005 and asked that she write a biography of McKay that could be published prior to mine, with the intent of undercutting its influence. Her book, *David O. McKay: Beloved Prophet,* was published in 2004.)

Aftermath

Just days after the release of the book, I spoke at the Marriott Library. At the end of my remarks, Ed McKay, who was sitting in the front row, spontaneously stood, turned to face the audience, and said, "I just want you all to know how pleased the McKay family is with this biography." All of Bob's and my time was repaid by that single sentence.

Two months later, at the Mormon History Association's annual meeting, held in Vermont to celebrate the bicentennial of Joseph Smith's birth, Richard Bushman came up to me in the book room and said, "I admire your courage." "Stamina" would have seemed a more fitting compliment, but "courage," particularly coming from Richard, was just fine.

Another memorable compliment came from an unlikely source: the Ernest Wilkinson family. Wilkinson was the central figure in chapter 8, "The Education System," and I did not attempt to gloss over his rough edges or to underplay his notable achievements. In August 2005, I spoke about the biography at the Sunstone Symposium in Salt Lake City. Afterwards, a distinguished-looking woman approached the podium and introduced herself to me. "I'm Alice Wilkinson Anderson," she said—a daughter of Ernest. "I read your entire book, but the first chapter I read was on the Education System. Thank you, for you were fair to my father, whereas most other writers have not been." To have achieved sufficient balance to elicit that kind of compliment was as treasured an endorsement as I can imagine.

The book went on to win four awards: the Evans Handcart Award for Western American History, the Mormon History Association's Best Biography of the Year, the John Whitmer Historical Association's Best Biography of the Year, and the Utah State Historical Society's Best Utah History Book.

But the book did not achieve universal acclaim. Two confidants in the church bureaucracy later informed me that on two occasions it was on the agenda of the Strengthening Church Members Committee, whose surveillance of church members and their activities gained notoriety when BYU English professor Gene England "exposed" its existence during a 1990s talk at the Sunstone Symposium. One of them chuckled when he told me the story, because of how it ended. A member of the committee approached him and said that he had taken time to read the book. "It's a good book," he said.

ON WRITING MORMON HISTORY, 1972–95

FROM THE DIARIES AND MEMOIRS OF D. MICHAEL QUINN

EDITED BY JOSEPH W. GEISNER

9

Note: At the end of January 1972, Leonard J. Arrington invited twenty-seven-year-old D. Michael Quinn, a graduate student at the University of Utah, to join the newly forming staff of the official historian of the LDS Church. Forty-eight years later, D. Michael Quinn is the author of some one hundred publications—articles, essays, reviews, etc.—eight books, and three Internet-based monographs. Because Quinn examined little-known and/or controversial aspects of Mormonism, even admirers have sometimes described his work as "polarizing." At my urging, Quinn consented to the publication of a chronology of his attitudes about his works. What follows are excerpts from Quinn's daily diaries (to 1980) and from his memoirs written periodically from 1988 to 2009 that track somewhat his development as an LDS historian and some of his publications. Where necessary for comprehension, I have added brief bracketed and footnoted annotations.

1972

April 14

The Lord has, I believe, blessed me greatly in having access to important documents relating to post-1890 polygamy. ... I have found important MSS [manuscripts] which show the role of [LDS First Presidency counselor] George Q. Cannon in advocating post-1890 polygamy, which show the manipulations and strategies involved in the [Reed] Smoot Case and resultant resignations of [LDS Apostles Matthias F.] Cowley and [John W.] Taylor, and which have highlighted other aspects of post-1890 polygamy. During 1971, I verified that [LDS Apostles] Heber J. Grant and Francis M. Lyman (traditionally considered as implacable foes of post-1890 polygamy) had each performed a few plural marriages after 1890, and that Heber J. Grant unsuccessfully tried to marry a plural wife after 1890. I also found other tid-bits of importance to this subject during 1971.

After I became a member of the HDC [Historical Department of the LDS Church] a few weeks ago, my ability to pick up information increased. Being a staff member[,] I could wander through the stacks of MSS [manuscripts] without supervision. This gave me the opportunity to find what I could by snooping around. In this way[,] I located the sealing records of Patriarch Alexander F. Macdonald of Juarez [Mexico] Stake (1900–1093); the record of some plural marriages performed by Apostle Marriner W. Merrill between 1894–1903, and a record called Temple Book B, which recorded over 300 sealings [i.e., marriages] performed outside the temple from 1891–1903 (at least 9 of which were polygamous marriages—including that of [Apostle] George Teasdale performed [in 1897] by Apostle Anthon H. Lund). ...

... I feel [that] the Lord has allowed me to find as much information as He has for a purpose. I believe that this purpose is for me to write a detailed and comprehensive history of this era [of post-1890 Manifesto polygamy]—why I do not know. But I will never attempt to write such a history unless I have researched those additional sources I regard as absolutely essential to understanding the full story of this period of quiet and secret continuation of polygamy.

May 16

Today he [LDS Church Historian Leonard J. Arrington] also asked me to write two 1,000 word histories for the Ogden and Provo [Utah] Temple brochures. The Church Information Service wants them by Friday. It is the first time CHO [Church Historian's Office] (or HDC) personnel have been asked to write for the historical portions of Church pamphlets. Dr. Arrington hopes that this will set a trend so that we can one day be called upon to rewrite the historical portions of some publications which need it.

He said [that] I was the best encyclopedia article writer on the staff and gave me the job. I am happy that he is pleased with my work.

June 21

At HDC. Still working on [i.e., taking typed notes from] the minutes of the First Council of Seventy. I plan to go only to 1940, and hope to finish tomorrow. Then I think I will try for the minutes of the Council of the Twelve Apostles which are sketchy for most of the nineteenth century[,] but [are] apparently complete for the period 1887 to 1914. These last are, of course, of particular interest to me. If the Lord wants me to have the access, I know He will provide the way[—]even though it might otherwise be impossible.

June 29

At HDC. I spent the entire day, 8_{00} to 5_{00} working on the minutes of the Quorum of the Twelve Apostles.

July 12

At HDC. I called in to Dr. Arrington's office to tell him about the MSS I found in the basement [of the Church Office Building] yesterday. They are unprocessed materials which are stacked in a back area of the basement.

July 28

Dr. Arrington asked if I could give him a ride home, which I was glad to do. ...

Just as I stopped the car in front of his house, Dr. Arrington said an interesting thing. "The only way I could boost your salary appreciably [as a full-time employee] would be if you became an Assistant Church Historian." ...

This last bit of our conversation was really a surpri[s]e to me. It dumbfounded me that he even suggested the possibility of my becoming an Assistant Church Historian.

August 1

At HDC. During the day[,] I suggested to Dr. Arrington that some apparent 1st Presidency Office journals I had found among the MSS in the basement were actually some of the missing diaries of L. John Nuttall, secretary to [LDS Church] Pres. John Taylor. ...

Dr. Arrington was quite interested in seeing these journals, so he and I went to the basement archives. Over a week ago or more, I was snooping around and found a cache of hundreds or perhaps thousands of MSS which were unknown to Dr. Arrington and [LDS Church Librarian] Earl Olsen. Since informing Dr. Arrington of this discovery and [of] my 4 hour survey of the types of MSS in it, he has had HDC staff people doing preliminary processing of the materials ... They have filled over 80 large boxes with the materials.

... Dr. Arrington told me that next to his own call as Church Historian and the establishment of his history-writing staff, the discovery of these MSS is the most important development for the history of the Church in a century.

August 30

[At HDC] Dean Jessee [a member of Arrington's staff] observed that the Ensign [the LDS Church's monthly periodical for adults] apparently prefers the "pablum approach" to history.

… As long as the self-assured guardians of the Church's image refuse to present our history as it is, our people will continue to become disenchanted and disappointed to learn that our history has been full of false starts, doctrinal evolution, and human leaders. I wish that we took the Hebraic approach to our history, as can be found in the Old Testament, New Testament, and to a lesser degree in the Book of Mormon. The great prophets and spiritual leaders were shown as being human with human foibles and who made mistakes. The Hebrews could identify with such heroes and thus have hope that they, too, might overcome their weaknesses to become valiant servants of God. It is difficult for us [as Latter-day Saints] to identify with the demi-gods we have made out of [LDS Church founder] Joseph Smith and [LDS President] David O. McKay and most of our other leaders. They, too, were men capable of sin and who did sin[—]as every man does. Thank God for leaders like [LDS Church authorities] Brigham Young, Heber C. Kimball and J. Golden Kimball whose rough humanity is hard to ignore or gloss over.

November 21

He [Leonard J. Arrington] said [that] my writing is sometimes tendentious. Some of my undergraduate professors sometimes said about the same thing of my research papers. I tend to drive home my arguments and use my evidence too strongly.

December 7

Dr. Arrington said [that] he had something to discuss with me about my article on Young University. [LDS Church Commissioner of Education] Neal Maxwell had returned the MS and had closed his letter with a statement something like this: "I have nothing to suggest about the article on Young University. Concerning the treatment of the conflict between [Church] Presidents

[John] Taylor and [Brigham] Young, I assume that you and your department are the best judges of how to handle such a subject."

Dr. Arrington said, "I think I am being warned about that passage in the article on the personal conflicts between [LDS general authorities] John Taylor and Brigham Young. To protect you and to protect me and the department, I think we had better go over this section again to make sure it says nothing beyond what we want it to say. I am in a position now to give these kinds of warnings more heed than I perhaps have in past years."

We went over the passages in question, and I agonized silently for a while that he would ask me to eliminate all references to a possible conflict between Brigham Young and John Taylor. I feel that the issue of their disagreements was a crucial part of explaining the history of Young University, and I explained how careful I had been not to say that they had opposed each other in their official activities (which in fact they had done), but to say it was in items of personal projects.

Finally, he made some word additions which softened the passage and made the discussion of the conflict more tentative. I was relieved that he did not ask me to change it substantively.

… This experience causes me to wonder how much difficulty I will have [in] saying what I feel needs to be said in my prosopographical study of the Mormon Hierarchy, 1833–1933 [proposed MA thesis at the University of Utah].

[Quinn's article "The Brief Career of Young University at Salt Lake City" appeared in the winter 1973 issue of the Utah Historical Quarterly, pp. 69–89.]

December 14

Perhaps my attitudes toward the conduct and writing of LDS history are not according to His [God's] will. Perhaps the Church does need to be protected from its own history, but it will be a difficult process for me to accept such a position if it is required. Still, I know the Lord has opened the way for me to be where I am now.

For over a decade[,] I have researched out areas—problem areas—in LDS Church history, so that I might understand them thoroughly and be able to explain them with honesty and love. The

Lord has sustained me in this effort, and I feel that He will open the way for me[—]if my desires are right before Him.

1973

April 3

On the article about the Flag of the Kingdom [of God], Dr. Arrington asked me to eliminate thing[s] he thought were too strong. He said [that] the John Birchers and other ultra-political conservatives take great offense at the idea Joseph Smith was ordained a King. He suggested I eliminate my introductory reference to this issue of the article. He also asked me to eliminate most of the references to the Council of Fifty [founded in Nauvoo, Illinois, as the political kingdom of God] for the same reason. The changes are okay with me. The implications of the Flag of the Kingdom are clear enough, without the references I originally made.

[Quinn's article "The Flag of the Kingdom of God" appeared in the autumn 1973 issue of BYU Studies, *pp. 105–14.]*

June 2

Yesterday I met Lester Bush who has written an 80 page analysis of the historical development of our position on the Negro [until 1978 prohibited from receiving the LDS priesthood and temple blessings]. I directed him to one statement in which B[righam]. Young indicated that if no other prophet had ever restricted the Priesthood[,] then <u>he</u> was doing it. Bush was real excited about it. His article will appear in the next issue of <u>Dialogue</u> which will be a special issue on the Negro.

[Bush's article "Mormonism's Negro Doctrine: An Historical Overview" appeared in the spring 1973 issue of Dialogue: A Journal of Mormon Thought, *pp. 11–68.]*

June 8

He [Leonard Arrington] said that nobody has ever attempted what I am in the process of doing regarding the Mormon hierarchy [i.e., Quinn's MA thesis]. He said that the material I present, especially in the 3rd chapter, is like a barrage of unrelenting gunfire or like the constant dripping of the Chinese water torture. Without some kind of change, he said, the effect was devastating. ...

He indirectly suggested that I not submit my work on the hierarchy as a Master's Thesis, but instead print portions of it in larger studies.

As Leonard spoke, I sat leaning on my typewriter[,] listening and saying nothing. When he had finished, I reminded him that I had worked two years on the thesis and I had every intention of graduating with my M.A. I said I "had" to finish my M.A. ... [and] that I would have to do [its thesis as] my prosopographical study on the hierarchy.

July 6

At HDC. In the afternoon[,] I went to Leonard's office to discuss my plans for writing the [MA] thesis. ...

He had me meet with him and Davis [Bitton, Assistant LDS Church Historian and University of Utah history professor] ... I became increasingly concerned that he was regarding my thesis as a product of HDC rather than a graduate thesis. I said I did not feel I should be penalized in my use of sources merely because of my position with HDC.

I resented the possibility that I might not be allowed to use sources [in writing] which even non-members have had access to. I also spoke about my concern that my thesis might be emasculated. Davis agreed with me[,] but I could tell [that] Leonard was becoming irritated.

He was so agitated that[,] instead of addressing me, he directed remarks for my benefit to Davis. Thus, Leonard said to Davis[,] "Now, if this was me, I would appreciate someone watching out for my interests" and later he exclaimed: "Doesn't he trust us to review his thesis without acting as censors?" I tried to mollify the situation, and felt very bad that I had angered Leonard. However, I felt it necessary to express some of my concerns.

———

[From Quinn's 1988 memoir:] I left the Historical Department this day with a profound awareness that my commitment to full disclosure in writing the history of the LDS Church was more

extreme than the kind of "openness" he advocated. The "New Mormon History" meant something different to me than it did to Leonard Arrington, its chief architect.

1974

August 12

In the afternoon[,] I talked with [LDS Church Archivist] Don Schmidt about the materials in the [Church Historical Department] vault (after I had devoted much silent prayer in the day asking the Lord to guide my words, and open the way for my access). ... I asked Don if there was any way I could find out exactly what is in the subject files of the vault, so I wouldn't have to fish around in the dark for what is there.

He readily took me into Earl Olsen's office, picked up the catalogue cards to the vault's contents, and read off the subject titles so that I could indicate which, if any, were of interest to my [PhD dissertation at Yale University] research on the General Authorities. Among the cards he read was the marriage record of 1898–1903, which I said I would like to see in addition to two other items of far less interest to me. He nonchalantly said: "Okay, that's three items. Make up cards requesting them, and give them to me tomorrow." ...

August 13

When I got the marriage record, I immediately recognized it as containing post-1890 plural marriages performed by [Apostle] Matthias F. Cowley. I typed extensive notes from the marriage record[,] which contained the record of plural marriages performed for 50 men by [Apostle] Cowley, and a scrap of paper with 2 post-1890 plural marriages performed in 1903 by Apostle Rudger Clawson. I know that Cowley performed more plural marriages than these, so it seems possible that this was an incomplete collation he made ...

When I had finished with this record, I turned somewhat indifferently to the second item from the vault, catalogued in Earl Olsen's list as [Apostle] George F. Richards' appointment book. I had asked for it primarily to act as a filler, so that the marriage record would not be the only item I was seeking.

To my surpri[s]e I found that this record book contained a rather detailed summary of the [Quorum of Twelve's] meetings held in connection with the resignations J[ohn]. W. Taylor and M[atthias]. F. Cowley [from the Quorum of the Twelve Apostles] submitted in [October] 1905. In none of the available diaries of the Apostles or presidency has more than oblique reference been made to these meetings. Therefore I was profoundly happy and grateful to have stumbled upon this document.

I offered several silent, but heartfelt, prayers to God, thanking Him for giving me access at last to all of the documents apparently in HDC about post-1890 polygamy.

October 5

Today I received a letter from Leonard with an enclosure of the reader's comments on the [1844 presidential] succession article I sent to <u>BYU Studies</u>. The comments are a blistering attack on my scholarship, conclusions, and testimony. ... I am depressed not only at the tunnel vision displayed in the critique, but (more importantly) in the inherent rejection of what I believe to be an essential philosophy of candid historical analysis within a faithful perspective.

[Quinn's article "The Mormon Succession Crisis of 1844" appeared in the winter 1976 issue of BYU Studies, pp. 187–233.]

1975

January 4

I feel, however, that my attitudes and approach toward [LDS] Church history are out of step with the assumptions and intentions of the General Authorities. ... Despite these feelings, I have dreams of researching and writing on many areas of importance to the history of the Church—areas that have been neglected or concealed, but which need to be examined forthrightly and brought to the knowledge of the Saints; or at least to those interested. If my desires are right, the Lord will enable me to accomplish them[—]despite my own misgivings and despite the opposition and hostility by even of some of His anointed servants.

1976

February 14

When [my wife] Jan picked me up in the evening, she brought the new issue of BYU Studies with my 47 page [LDS presidential] succession article in it. I literally have prayed that article into print, and feel such relief in seeing it.

1977

October 13 [At the conclusion of Quinn's session at the Western History Association's annual meeting:]

I plead[ed] guilty to "overproving" (as he [Larry Foster] criticized), but said that I was reacting to the simplistic generalizations and support that have characterized Mormon historiography in the main.

I also acknowledged that I spoke first to a Mormon audience[,] because I felt that it was important for Mormons to see their history as process rather than as a series of discrete "deus ex machina" experiences. But I said that I also felt an obligation and desire to speak to the audience of non-Mormon scholars about a movement that I feel has had profound social-historical influence.

October 21

After getting home from the [wedding] reception, I went to the home of [LDS Presiding] Patriarch Eldred G. Smith at the invitation of his son Gary. Gary invited me there so that I could begin a study of the Presiding Patriarch from the perspective of the patriarch. I stayed with these two men in one of the most absorbing and fascinating meetings I have ever been in. It lasted from 10 p.m. Friday until 1 a.m. Saturday morning.

Patriarch Smith showed me his "relics" of Hyrum Smith [Joseph Smith's older brother, also killed in Carthage Jail, Illinois, in mid-1844]: an 1835 diary; an account book from the 1840s ...

Also they showed me the missionary journals of John Smith (b. 1832) and several notebooks and diaries of Hyrum G. Smith, another Presiding Patriarch.

During the hours of our meeting, Eldred G. Smith disclosed

many fascinating and disturbing things concerning his depriva-
tion of the patriarchal office from the death of his father [Hyrum
G. Smith] in 1932 until his appointment in 1947. After nearly 10
years without a Presiding Patriarch of the Smith line, when the
Quorum of 12 and [LDS President] Heber J. Grant had been at
an impasse over whom to appoint (the Quorum wanting Eldred
G. Smith & Heber J. Grant wanting a descendant of Joseph F.
Smith), Heber J. Grant called Eldred into his office. He told him
that Joseph F. Smith, the grandson of his namesake, was going
to be appointed Presiding Patriarch at this conference [in 1942].
Eldred was of course deeply disappointed ... President Grant responded: "Because I want you to know why I will never appoint a
descendant of John Smith as Patriarch. I <u>hate</u> the man who would
brazenly disobey the Word of Wisdom!" When Eldred asked
Pres. Grant if it was necessary to punish him for the actions of his
great-grandfather John Smith who had died when Eldred was too
young to really know him, President Grant replied: "Yes. No descendant of John Smith will be appointed Patriarch to the Church
as long as I live." ...

Eldred also commented on the extent to which his activities
have been curtailed in respect to the activities of his father as Presiding Patriarch. ...

... As I left at 1 a.m., Patriarch Smith put his arm around my
shoulder and then shook my hand. He said that I should come to
his office or home to obtain the other information I wanted for
the project his son had asked me to begin. His last words that I
remember were: "I am glad that you could spend this time with
us, so that you could see that our bark is worse than our bite." I
left the home, carrying with me xerox copies of the Hyrum Smith
holographs, the John Smith journals, and the Hyrum G. Smith
notebooks. It was certainly the most extraordinary meeting I have
ever had with a General Authority of the LDS Church.

[From Quinn's 1988 memoir:] The Patriarch [also] showed me
what he described as a "cabalistic" document that had been "passed
down" from Joseph Sr. to Hyrum, and from Hyrum's widow to
each eldest son in turn. Eldred Smith asked what I thought of it.

Staring at this gold-colored parchment, inscribed with numerous symbols and words in various languages, I said it was "certainly unusual." I didn't have a clue what any of it meant, and no idea why Joseph Smith Sr. had possessed something so strange in the early nineteenth century.

I wasn't ignorant of Cabala as a medieval Jewish system of occult knowledge. I remembered a brief discussion of it in James A. Michener's historical novel, The Source, but had long-since forgotten what the Encyclopaedia Britannica said about it. Still, I had absolutely no interest in such an arcane topic, and quickly asked Patriarch Smith to show me the journal of his ancestor Hyrum. THAT was evidence I could understand and interpret immediately.

I was so tunnel-visioned at this time that I didn't even think of the talk that LDS Institute director Reed C. Durham Jr. had given three years earlier [at the 1974 annual conference of the Mormon History Association]. I'd carefully read a typescript of his emphasis on Joseph Smith's connection to the occult through a "Jupiter Talisman."

There were dots to connect, but I didn't see them while looking at the golden parchment or remembering it vaguely for years after tonight. Some non-Mormon scholars would have recognized the Joseph Smith Family's artifact as a "lamen" of ritual magic. However, I was unaware of ANY context for the strange item that Eldred Smith had shown to me tonight, and my daily journal didn't even mention something that seemed so unimportant. ...

In eight years, I would no longer be indifferent to the artifact Eldred Smith showed me tonight. Its existence and inscriptions became keys for my understanding the participation of Joseph Sr. and Jr. in the occult activity of the treasure-quest during the early 1820s.

November 4

He [Leonard Arrington] said that at the weekly meeting of G. Homer Durham [recently appointed Managing Director of the HDC] with the division heads in HDC, that Bro. Durham brought up my research on the [J. Reuben] Clark [biography] project and ... asked what documents at HDC might be of use to me, and reference was made to the David O. McKay papers, Quorum of Twelve minutes and 1st Presidency minutes in custody of

HDC, to which Earl Olsen repeatedly prompted Bro. Durham, "Oh, you know he can't see those!" When Leonard said that Dallin Oaks [president] of BYU had requested the 1st Presidency to consider giving me access to those kinds of documents, Earl became silent.

[Quinn's commissioned biography, J. Reuben Clark: The Church Years, *was published by BYU Press in 1983 and later, in revised form, as* Elder Statesman: A Biography of J. Reuben Clark, *by Signature Books in 2002.]*

November 8

I met with G. Homer Durham at 11. ...

When he got to the list of documents I requested, he surpri[s]ed me by saying emphatically: "You will have to see these documents, the minutes of the 1st Presidency, and the others, but I do not want you to get lost in them." ...

December 27 [During a Christmas party at the Arrington residence with History Division staff and spouses:]

We got on the subject of telling the truth of our history and why the authorities resist it. I was doing most of the talking at this point, and said that men like [LDS Apostle] Boyd Packer dislike our approach because they feel we will only cause people to ask more questions, and they are afraid of the Saints asking questions. They feel they are protecting the saints, whereas we feel they are making them vulnerable to attacks by people like the Tanners [i.e., Jerald and Sandra Tanner, evangelical critics of the LDS Church] or by deceptive schismatics [i.e., LDS Church breakaway off-shoots]. I said [that] they could not seem to understand that we were trying to expose the average saint to the broad perspectives of truth and history in order to protect them from being overwhelmed by a barrage of truth or half-truth of our history by a polemicist.

Up to this point[,] Leonard had been generally quiet, but he interjected at this point that we were seeking to "immunize" the Saints by presenting the broad perspective of our history. That was a tremendous idea that I have often described without realizing it.

1978

April 22

As I compare my work as a historian with the work of others, mine does not hold up very well. I have consistently been more concerned with the content of historical data and support than with style and readability. I have the ability to write quickly and reasonably well, and therefore I have been satisfied to turn in first drafts or second drafts at best for publication.

I am not even sure that I am capable of writing beautiful prose, as other historians have done[,] who are as skillful as the best novelist or essayist. I look at my brief article on the rebaptisms of Nauvoo [Illinois] in the Winter 1978 issue of <u>BYU Studies</u> and find that one of the final sentences has 83 words in it. If I wrote as well as [British historian Arnold] Toynbee[,] that would not be bad, but in my work[,] an 83 word sentence is merely another evidence of sloppy writing.

[Quinn's article "The Practice of Rebaptism at Nauvoo" appeared in the winter 1978 issue of BYU Studies, pp. 226–32.]

May 31

Spent the day researching First Presidency files.

1979

February 3 [During Quinn's first visit to LDS Church President Spencer W. Kimball's residence on Laird Drive in Salt Lake City:]

President Kimball showed me the binders in which his journals from 1940 to the present are kept in his study, and he set me up in the livingroom with a cardtable, chair, and old typewriter. For the next five hours[,] I read more than four binders of his journals and took typewritten notes on [them], while President Kimball worked in his study where I could hear him dictating at length concerning the Logan [Utah] Temple. ... As I left, I said that I would contact President Kimball after his return from Hawaii to see when it would be convenient for me to come again to research more of his journals, and President Kimball said that would be fine.

March 20

Sister [Evaline Belle Peterson] Butterfield [secretary to Marion G. Romney, Second Counselor in the LDS First Presidency] said that President Romney had decided that rather than have me read through the journals, that she should read through them and extract anything relating to President J. Reuben Clark, Jr. ...

I asked her to include references President Romney might make to the other members of the Presidency and about the operation of the presidency itself. Sister Butterfield said that President Romney's diaries were not really very descriptive, but she would see what she could do about also including the kinds of indirect references to the operation of the presidency as well as specific references to Clark. *[She eventually gave Quinn eighty pages of typed excerpts].* ...

... After the [Emigration Stake's high council] meeting, Brent Goates [son-in-law of recently deceased LDS President Harold B. Lee] gave me excerpts from Harold B. Lee's 1943 diaries concerning J. Reuben Clark, with the comment that there were some very sensitive things in the excerpts[—]but that he was giving me everything that related to Clark. I asked President Goates if he would also give me excerpts from Lee's diaries of Lee's comments and observations [as an apostle since 1941] concerning the other members of the Presidency and of the operation of the presidency that related to the environment in which President Clark had to work.

April 30

Today, after much thought and prayer, I decided that I must take the only chance I seem to have left to me to seek for access to the materials of the First Presidency's vaults. ... I wrote to President Spencer W. Kimball a three[-]page, double-spaced letter (in the hope that the double spacing will encourage President Kimball to read it rather than simply passing if off to his secretaries). I addressed and mailed the letter to the home of President Kimball, hoping that thereby the letter might reach his attention rather than simply being shelved by his secretary Arthur Haycock.

In the letter, I pointed out why I feel the documents in the First Presidency's vaults are important to understanding the history and developments of the Church, why I feel that understanding is necessary for the strength of the Latter-day Saints, and why I feel that at least one Mormon historian, rather than an administratively burdened secretary, ought to be given full-time assignment to research the documents of the First Presidency vaults. I gave as an example of the vulnerability of the Saints to deception because of their ignorance of Church developments[—]the question of polygamy after 1890.

September 16

As I sat on the stand [of an LDS ward building] prior to the beginning of [sacrament] services, I was surprised to see Apostle Gordon B. Hinckley enter the chapel. ... I introduced myself as one of the visiting high councilmen ... [and] Brother Hinckley remarked, "You teach at Brigham Young University, don't you?" Immediately recognized that when I introduced myself as Michael Quinn, Brother Hinckley had identified me as the Michael Quinn of the prayer circle article [in *BYU Studies*]. ...

... I gave to the Arlington Heights Ward the talk on the burdens of life which I had given previously to most of the other wards in the stake. I felt a good spirit with me as I spoke and testified, and I felt that my remarks reached the hearts of the people in the audience. As I sat down next to Brother Hinckley at the end of my talk, he reached over and patted my thigh in an approving manner.

[Quinn's article "Latter-day Saint Prayer Circles" appeared in the fall 1978 issue of BYU Studies, *pp. 79–105.]*

October 1

After a day of work [in HDC], I was exiting to my bus stop via the Church underground parking area, when I met Jeff Holland, Church Commissioner of Education [and future LDS Apostle]. Jeff asked how things were going on the [J. Reuben] Clark [biography] Project, and I said that I was close to writing. Jeff asked if I had ever been able to obtain the sources from the [First] Presidency that I had been seeking some time ago, and I said that I had not. I expressed to Jeff the difficulty and frustration of trying to write a biography of a counselor to the President of the Church without access to the minutes of the Presidency. Jeff immediately saw the problem, and said: "For the President you can rely on the public record of decisions, but for the role of the counselor you must have the record of the behind-the-scenes discussions. It is regrettable that you have not been given that access for your project." I said that I would do the best I could without it, but that it would not be the kind of study that I will be pleased with as a biography of Clark. I said that I hope that the Presidency would like it, to which Jeff responded as he walked off, "If that is all they will let you write, then they will be pleased with what they have allowed you to do."

October 31

... took time to do more arranging of note cards about the [1890 Wilford Woodruff] manifesto and the practice of polygamy after 1890. The explosive significance of many things I have had in my notes for years was not apparent to me until I saw the things in juxtaposition. I am now sure that if I write the kind of article that I feel must be written and publish it in <u>Dialogue[: A Journal of Mormon Thought]</u> as I plan to do in 1980, that there is no power on earth that will spare me from excommunication if [LDS Apostle] Mark E. Petersen is alive. In fact, as I see the article in my mind's eye, I doubt that my employment at BYU or my membership in the Church will survive under any circumstances if I publish this article ... I am approaching the point where I would prefer to have my collision with the authorities over this matter, and then take whatever consequences may follow.

[Quinn's article "LDS Church Authority and New Plural Marriages, 1890–1904" appeared in the spring 1985 issue of Dialogue: A Journal of Mormon Thought, *pp. 9–105.]*

1980

May 2 [Quinn's paraphrasing, then quoting from his journal:]

... at the Mormon History Association's meeting at Canandaigua, New York, I gave the first overview about the full extent of my research on the LDS hierarchy. Titled, "From Sacred Grove To

Sacral Power Structure," it announced that I would examine "a series of interrelated and crucial transitions" of Mormonism in those 150 years. They were "individualism to corporate dynasticism, authoritarian democracy to authoritarian oligarchy, theocracy to bureaucracy, communitarianism to capitalism, and neocracy to gerontocracy." Richard L. Bushman introduced me as speaker.

One young man in the audience seemed to share the acute personal shock and discomfort at my paper as had the [LDS] commentator from Harvard Business School. The fellow in the audience asked, "How are we to interpret your paper regarding the President of the Church?" I answered, "I can't answer that question for you. It depends on how you define the prophet: whether you regard him in the Catholic sense as infallible, not in his personal conduct, but in his doctrinal pronouncements, or whether you regard prophets as men who remain men despite their divine callings, and therefore one can see the man in the prophet and the prophet in the man." Obviously I directed that answer to those who have faith that the LDS President is a prophet.

[Quinn's presentation "From Sacred Grove to Sacral Power Structure" appeared in the summer 1984 issue of Dialogue: A Journal of Mormon Thought, *pp. 9–34.]*

June 13

Also worked on the [J. Reuben] Clark manuscript. ... I am starting to work on the [David O.] McKay period, and it is not easy to present in the best possible, non-sensational light the irreconcilable differences between DOM and JRC. But there is no way I am going to write a biography of JRC's Church service without dealing with all the controversies involved in his twenty-eight years of service.

1981

March 30 [From Quinn's 1988 memoir:]

Both <u>Newsweek</u> and <u>Time</u> magazines quoted me in their articles about the significance of a document purporting to be the Mormon founder's blessing on [his son] Joseph Smith III to be his successor as Church President. It was "discovered" by Mormon documents-collector Mark Hofmann.

Charlie Gibbs, a senior member of the Public Affairs Department at LDS headquarters, told me privately that its staff was very grateful I had published the 1976 article about the "Mormon Succession Crisis of 1844." He said that this allowed them and the General Authorities to tell the media that <u>BYU Studies</u> and unnamed LDS historians had acknowledged "for years" that there had been such a blessing. Thus, the PR-Machine said: "This newly discovered document is no big deal" for the claims of the Church as led to Utah by Brigham Young and currently led by Spencer W. Kimball.

Instead of provoking a crisis of faith that the secular media headlined, this publicity resulted in a <u>WELL-INFORMED</u> shrug of faith. Under the present circumstances, my article's perspective was even helpful to those who preferred only Utah's method of succession from Mormonism's founder.

This fulfilled what I had hoped to achieve for strengthening the faith of rank-and-file Mormons since I first began my "controversial" research at age seventeen. Exactly twenty years had passed since then.

[Hofmann was later found to have been a forger of historical documents and murderer after he planted two bombs that killed two people. A third bomb exploded prematurely and injured Hofmann himself.]

August 28 [From Quinn's 1988 memoir:]

During <u>Sunstone</u> magazine's Theological Symposium at the University of Utah, I was a respondent on the paper Linda King Newell gave for a session titled, "Washing, Anointing, and Blessing the Sick Among Mormon Women." In view of my own research, I said that she was too tentative about the basis on which early Mormon women performed ordinances of healing from the mid-1840s until LDS headquarters prohibited them from continuing to do so a century later.

Quoting from various sources, including patriarchal blessings given by Joseph Smith's "Uncle John [Smith]" in 1844–45, I said that the Mormon founder's closest associates affirmed that each woman possessed the Melchizedek Priesthood after she received the temple ceremony of Priesthood endowment. I emphasized that this did <u>NOT</u> involve ordination to specific offices of that

Priesthood, but instead each woman received a conferral of Priesthood by receiving the keys of the endowment.

*[For Quinn's views on women and the LDS priesthood, see his
"Mormon Women Have Had the Priesthood Since 1843," in Maxine
Hanks's compilation* Women and Authority: Re-emerging Mor-
mon Feminism, *published by Signature Books in 1992.]*

Early September *[From Quinn's 1988 memoir:]*

A week after I resumed teaching at BYU [following the summer vacation], a graduate student in the History Department
told me of his recent meeting with Apostle [Boyd K.] Packer in
the Church Administration Building (47 East South Temple).
Apostle Packer said that my unpublished biography [of J. Reuben
Clark] "dirties" the public memory of J. Reuben Clark.

In June of this year, I had given my completed manuscript
to BYU's administrators and Clark's children. Somehow Elder
Packer learned of its contents.

"As sure as I am sitting in this chair," he told Harvard Heath,
"Mike Quinn's book on President Clark will never see the light of
day." Apostle Packer obviously expected him to report this back to
me, since he commenced the conversation by asking if this student
knew me personally.

This was disheartening. My concern grew as weeks and months
went by without any word from BYU's administrators or from
Gordon Burt Affleck [a trustee of the J. Reuben Clark Papers]
about the reaction of Clark's family to my book-length draft of
the biography. Nonetheless, I decided not to ask about this silence.

November 4 *[From Quinn's 1988 memoir:]*

Publicly challenging Apostolic views.

For his talk to all the CES [LDS Church Education System]
teachers and BYU religion professors on 22 August 1981, Boyd
K. Packer had given a methodical attack on Mormon historians.
It was titled "The Mantle Is Far, Far Greater Than the Intellect."
This referred to "the mantle of Priesthood authority" held by LDS
leaders. (Packer, That All May Be Edified, 240). ...

... an officer in the [BYU] history student organization of Phi Alpha Theta, asked me to help history majors understand how they could continue their interest in the Mormon past after Elder Packer's talk against the writing of candid Mormon history. Scott was a student of mine, and I couldn't turn down his very reasonable request to give such a talk to BYU students. ...

I felt the Spirit with me and prepared a talk which responded to the criticisms of Mormon historians by Apostles Ezra Taft Benson and Boyd K. Packer. I gave a copy of the prepared text to my Bishop a few days before the Phi Alpha Theta meeting. Its most controversial sentence was probably my assertion that "a Mormon history of benignly angelic church leaders apparently advocated by Elders Benson and Packer would border on idolatry." ...

On November 18th, <u>Seventh East Press</u>, then BYU's unofficial student newspaper, published a front-page story about the talk. Within days, this publicity resulted in some anxious consultations.

November 22 [From Quinn's 1988 memoir:]

Although we had spoken casually three years earlier, [LDS First Presidency] Counselor Gordon B. Hinckley didn't want to directly ask me for a meeting. Instead, he gave his unlisted telephone number to historian Ron Walker, a mutual friend, with instructions to phone "immediately" if I'd like to talk.

Thus, on Sunday, November 22nd, I spent about an hour talking with President Hinckley in the study-library of his home on the hill above Utah's Capitol Building. He said that he had already obtained and read ("several times") the text of my "On Being a Mormon Historian." This was obviously the purpose for the copy that Dean [Martin B.] Hickman [of BYU's College of Family, Home, and Social Sciences] had requested.

President Hinckley said: "I sympathize with many of the things you say, but I am gravely concerned that you have publicly criticized living members of the Quorum of the Twelve." I explained that I didn't intend this as personal criticism of these Apostles. I felt that I had the right as a historian to evaluate their public views about how Church history should be written.

"Of course, you have that right, Brother Quinn," he said, "but when you do it publicly, that can sow seeds of dissension among Church members." I said that wasn't my intent. President Hinckley was completely non-confrontational during our discussion at his home.

He referred to my talk's discussion of half-truths and distortions in traditional Church history, and he asked for an example. I said that contrary to officially published accounts, there were hundreds of authorized plural marriages performed after the 1890 Manifesto. President Hinckley asked for specifics.

For several minutes, I gave him a list (from memory) of the names of the new polygamists with the most prominent Church positions, the dates and places of their post-Manifesto polygamous marriages, and the officiators. President Hinckley was visibly stunned, for as a child and young man he had personally known many of these Mission Presidents, Stake Presidents, general board members, and Bishops. Until today, he had not realized that they married plural wives after the Manifesto.

Gordon B. Hinckley was very candid throughout our meeting. He said that the whole situation was difficult. He acknowledged that there was much about Church history that he didn't know and that he doubted "ANY" General Authority knew. ...

1982

May 14 [From Quinn's 1988 memoir:]

Meeting three anti-historian Apostles at once.

I went to the Church Administration Building (47 East South Temple) with the new Second Counselor in my Stake Presidency [Richard Horne] (whom I had served as counselor when he was [an LDS ward] Bishop) to meet with [Apostle] Mark E. Petersen. It was by this Apostle's phoned request to [the Ensign Stake's] President [Hugh S.] West.

When we learned that this mid-morning meeting would include Apostles [Ezra Taft] Benson and [Boyd K.] Packer, beads of perspiration appeared on Rick Horne's forehead. We both knew that this was the day following the regular "council meeting" of the First Presidency and Quorum of the Twelve Apostles in the Salt Lake Temple. ...

It could have been an inquisition, but they were very careful not to ask me a single direct question. In order of seniority (Apostle Benson first and me last), we each just expressed our own views of the <u>Newsweek</u> article ["Apostles Vs. Historians" three months earlier], the "problems" of writing Mormon history, and the effects of all this on the faith of LDS members. I regarded the 35–40 minute meeting as congenial and supportive, even though the Apostles were frank about the strained circumstances they felt my talk had created. I didn't express my rejoinder that Elders Benson and Packer had created an environment of intimidation by publicly attacking Mormon historians. ...

Confrontation and criticism had never been goals in my work as a Mormon historian, but they had become results of publishing. Nevertheless, sanitizing the past was something I felt that God did NOT require of me or anyone else. I could not agree to tailor the Mormon past to conform to the historical knowledge of current General Authorities. Nor could I accommodate their preferences for public relations.

Late May 1982 [From Quinn's 1988 memoir:]

The assigned intervention of two Apostles.

I had told no one about Apostle [Boyd K.] Packer's vow last year to stop the publication of my biography of J. Reuben Clark, but he apparently made similar statements at Church headquarters. Now the First Presidency appointed two of his Apostolic superiors ([Elders] Howard W. Hunter and Thomas S. Monson) to give the book-manuscript a final review. This virtually guaranteed its publication by making Apostle Packer's opposition irrelevant. Having two Apostles as a reading committee also ended G. Homer Durham's expectation since 1979 that he would have a role in approving my biography.

The exact chronology of that decision by the First Presidency is crucial, but unknown to me. I didn't learn about it until several days after my meeting with Apostles [Ezra Taft] Benson, [Mark E.] Petersen, and Packer.

Upon informing me of that decision, BYU's former Academic Vice-President Robert K. Thomas emphasized that, because of the

<u>Newsweek</u> article, "there was some discussion of removing you as President Clark's biographer." He was now called "University Professor," but his office was still on the presidential level of the [Abraham O.] Smoot Administration Building.

Bob Thomas credited Gordon Affleck with persuading the First Presidency "not to take the biography away from Brother Quinn." In view of the currently disabled condition of its [the First Presidency's] senior three members [Spencer W. Kimball, N. Eldon Tanner, and Marion G. Romney], that decision must have been by Special Counselor Gordon B. Hinckley. He had to be "the unseen hand" behind the assignment of the two Apostles to review and approve my biography.

The Clark Family approved its preliminary manuscript generally, as did First Presidency counselor Marion G. Romney. Because of near-blindness, he listened to it last year as read to him by Affleck. That's what Affleck told me.

Now Apostles Howard W. Hunter and Thomas S. Monson read the manuscript and made recommendations for revisions before its publication. Through go-between Bob Thomas in his office at BYU, I was asked to consider recommendations for changing sensational quotes into paraphrases and for limiting the examples of conflict and controversy in the First Presidency's office.

On the other hand, Apostles Hunter and Monson let the basic conflicts and controversies remain in my official biography of J. Reuben Clark. I've always admired them for that.

May 26 [From Quinn's 1988 memoir:]

Personal intervention of Gordon B. Hinckley.

On 17 January 1979, I had written the Managing Director of the LDS Historical Department [G. Homer Durham] a 12-page, single-spaced summary of authorized plural marriages after the Church announced their official end in the 1890 Manifesto. I also wrote the First Presidency on 30 April 1979 and 20 May 1980 about my knowledge of the topic, the need I felt for publishing a detailed study, and my request for access to the materials of the First Presidency's vault pertaining to post-1890 plural marriage.

Receiving no answer, I renewed the request in letters of 2

December 1981, 17 February 1982, and 15 April 1982 to Presidency counselor Gordon B. Hinckley, with whom I had once discussed post-Manifesto polygamy at his home. I just assumed that his secretaries intercepted these letters and blocked me, as Arthur Haycock [secretary to the LDS Church president] had done. So I kept knocking.

President Hinckley finally spoke with me by telephone on 26 May 1982. He said that he was sympathetic with my request and had inquired unsuccessfully about my getting access to those documents in the First Presidency vault. Since I now knew all I ever would about post-Manifesto polygamy, I told him that I would go ahead and publish the most detailed, supportive study I could of the problem.

President Hinckley replied: "That's YOUR decision to make, Brother Quinn." He then repeated his statement that he had done what he could to help me get access to historical documents in the Presidency's vault regarding post-Manifesto polygamy. Significantly, I thought, he did NOT advise me against publishing what I already knew about it from my research at HDC, research that I had previously outlined to him in his home and again in the correspondence.

1984

Mid-May [From Quinn's 1988 memoir:]

BYU dean is "instructed" about MY publishing.

At the annual meeting of the Mormon History Association held at BYU on the 12th, I gave a paper on business activities of the Mormon hierarchy from the 1830s to the present. This included a summary of current General Authorities who were serving as directors and officers of various corporations. Jan [Quinn's wife] attended my talk, and was with me at the banquet where my biography of J. Reuben Clark received MHA's award for 1983's best book.

In a few days, the Dean of my College [Martin B. Hickman] telephoned me at home and (with great discomfort) told me that he had been instructed "by higher authority" to ask me not to publish the paper I gave at MHA. I pointed out that the information on corporate directorships came from publicly available sources.

Martin Hickman replied: "I know, but Church leaders still don't want you to publish it." I said that he knew I would publish something like it one day in my book about the Mormon hierarchy. Dean Hickman said that wasn't included in his instructions, and he personally looked forward to the book, but that he had to ask me again not to publish my paper as an article. I agreed not to publish it separately.

I wouldn't tell others about this incident until my resignation from BYU four years afterward.

[Quinn's analysis of LDS businesses was published as The Mormon Hierarchy: Wealth and Corporate Power *by Signature Books in 2017.]*

1985

January 10 *[From Quinn's 1988 memoir:]*

Death of unusual ally.

I had felt at odds with G. Homer Durham after his appointment as Managing Director of HDC in 1977, but ironically benefitted from the inconsistencies in his decision-making ... Even though he restricted research by others, he paradoxically continued authorizing my access to sensitive materials.

This might have had something to do with the congenial personal relationship that I had with LDS President Spencer W. Kimball and with his Special Counselor Gordon B. Hinckley. Elder Durham had been the latter's missionary companion, and they remained very good friends.

After my 12-page memo to Elder Durham in February 1979, he knew of my extensive research about post-Manifesto polygamy, yet he continued for six years to give me access to restricted documents regarding plural marriage. This went far beyond the extraordinary access I had been given for researching the authorized biography of J. Reuben Clark from late 1977 until I finished its draft in mid-1981.

Throughout the next three-and-a-half years (when not in Chicago

263

or Europe), I continued getting Elder Durham's approval for my examining heavily restricted documents at HDC. Just days before his death in 1985, he again gave me access to First Presidency files and correspondence, which my request had specified were necessary to finalize my upcoming article on post-Manifesto polygamy. And I specifically stated that it would appear in Dialogue.

"Mike Quinn has helped us explain other historical problems," Elder Durham told newly appointed archivist Glenn N. Rowe: "I hope he can help us here—because this is a tough one." Glenn repeated those words to me in the Research Room of HDC as he handed me the approval slips that Elder Durham had just initialed.

Late April [From Quinn's 1988 memoir:]

Apostle Boyd K. Packer's public condemnations.

Following the April publication in Dialogue of my article on "LDS Church Authority and New Plural Marriages, 1890–1904," I learned from several sources that Apostle Packer condemned me in public meetings as diverse at a stake conference in Denver [Colorado] and a special solemn assembly in the Salt Lake Temple for Priesthood leaders in the Salt Lake Valley. Even though he didn't identify me by name, Elder Packer referred to me in these meetings as "a BYU historian who is writing about polygamy to embarrass the Church."

Sons of the Apostles reported back that Packer told a meeting of the Quorum of Twelve: "What Mike Quinn wrote about plural marriage may be true, but no faithful Latter-day Saint would publish what he did."

Late May [From Quinn's 1988 memoir:]

By order of three members of the Quorum of the Twelve Apostles (communicated by Seventy's President and Area President James M. Paramore), the Stake President of the Salt Lake Emigration Stake reluctantly withdraws my temple recommend.

The General Authorities charged me with unworthiness of a temple recommend for "speaking evil of the Lord's anointed," in my Dialogue article about the First Presidency's approval of post-Manifesto polygamy. The three Apostles also instructed Stake

President Hugh S. West to "take further action" if withdrawing my temple recommend didn't "remedy the situation" of my speaking and writing about Mormon history in a way as to "offend the Brethren" (their phrase). The General Authority message to the Stake President was to pretend this was a decision that originated with him, which he refused to do throughout their two-hour meeting. Paramore was stunned to encounter such resistance.

Stake President West and his Second Counselor (my former Bishop Richard Horne) told me that they both had read the polygamy article, and that they never considered that it could be the basis for taking any kind of Church action against me. They told me individually that the Stake President's First Counselor Richard Hinckley (son of First Presidency counselor Gordon B. Hinckley) agreed with them.

I told the Stake President that I would not be intimidated by anyone and that I would continue my research and writing efforts to sympathetically explain problems in Mormon history. "I'm an insurance executive," Hugh West said, "and I won't tell you how to be a historian. But please try to find some way to be conscientious in Mormon history and still avoid these confrontations with the Brethren." I said that I would try, but didn't see how I could do both at the same time.

The Stake President said that he regarded his instructions from Church headquarters as a back-door effort to have me fired at BYU. Despite the Apostolic order to deprive me of a temple recommend, President West instructed me to protect my employment by telling BYU administrators (if they asked) that I had a current temple recommend: "Don't volunteer that it's in my desk-drawer." He said that he would continually renew my recommend and keep it in his desk, to prevent employment difficulties at BYU.

Since he had been so candid with me about the details of his two-hour meeting and dispute with Paramore, I asked my Stake President to identify the three Apostles who had given these instructions to this General Authority who was our area president. President West said that he didn't feel at liberty to name them.

"If I was a guessing man," I said, "I'd guess that the senior of the three was Boyd K. Packer and that he enlisted the support of two of his subordinates who have reputations as academics and liberals. Therefore, my guess is that the three Apostles were Elder Packer, Neal A. Maxwell, and Dallin H. Oaks." My Stake President smiled: "That's a pretty good guess."

I promised him that I would not tell colleagues or friends about this situation. I didn't want to be the center of more publicity.

And, despite my brave words to President West, I felt sick at heart. This was the death of my Mormon dreams, but (typical for the stages of grieving), I remained in denial about it.

This was hope-against-hope. My lifelong pattern.

August 16 [From Quinn's 2009 memoir:]

Another Apostle joins the anti-historian chorus.

My article on post-Manifesto polygamy was the subtext of remarks that Dallin H. Oaks made during the Sperry Symposium sponsored by BYU's College of Religious Instruction. This was three months after his angry letter to me about its publication in Dialogue. His letter of May 1985 had accused me of underhandedly obtaining restricted documents at LDS Archives and of preparing to publish the article without notifying my "file leaders" or the custodians of those documents.

In response, I immediately mailed to Elder Oaks a summary of my conversations about this research into post-Manifesto polygamy—with HDC's Managing Director G. Homer Durham and with First Presidency Counselor Gordon B. Hinckley—and explained to Oaks that I had specifically informed each of them YEARS IN ADVANCE of my hopes to publish a detailed article about it. With this letter, I included photocopies of my numerous letters about this research to Durham, to President Spencer W. Kimball, to the First Presidency as a whole, and to Counselor Hinckley directly. From 1979 to 1982, those letters had gone to the highest-ranking custodian of HDC's manuscripts and to my highest "file leaders" in the Church. But in 1985 Apostle Oaks seemed angry that I hadn't told HIM during 1977–80, while he was BYU's president (as a non-General Authority) and when was promoting me for J. Reuben Clark's biography. But he had NEVER asked me for reports about ANY details of my research back then. Nor did anyone else, yet I had volunteered those details to the General Authorities who had a right to know—a NEED to know about my knowledge of post-Manifesto polygamy.

After a month without a reply to the May 1985 letter, I phoned his secretary in the LDS Church Office Building to inquire whether Oaks had received it. She confirmed in June that my letter arrived with its attached documents, that he had looked at them all, and that he would undoubtedly contact me again when he returned from a trip. He didn't.

Instead, despite the information and documentation I provided him in May 1985, Apostle Oaks told numerous people during the next two decades that I had allegedly "misused" my research-access at HDC, that I had allegedly done "unauthorized" research about post-Manifesto polygamy there, and that I had allegedly "deceived" manuscript-custodians and Church leaders about my plan to publish that research. Several of his listeners would report this to me.

This August, his talk warned against those who "criticize or deprecate a person for the performance of an office to which he or she has been called of God. It does not matter that the criticism is true." Words to gag on.

August 23 [From Quinn's 1988 and 2009 memoirs:]

Continuing work on Mormon controversies.

During the Sunstone Symposium, I gave a talk at the Hotel Utah about connections between the occult and early Mormonism. Learning that I planned to make a round-trip to BYU to print-out its reading-text, my friend Gordon A. Madsen very kindly invited me to use a computer in his home to prepare the talk. The Salt Lake Tribune featured it on the front page of its local section, along with a photo of one of the Joseph Smith Family's magic parchments (lamens).

I would speak publicly on the same topic four times in 1986, coast-to-coast, and once in Cedar City, Utah, in May 1987. Then I would publish a book about it in August 1987. Nonetheless, Stake President [Hugh S.] West refused to follow the Apostolic instructions to "take further action" (disfellowshipping or excommunication) against me for my continuing to promote controversial history. ...

More than once in 1985, I left Stake President West's office knowing that the temple was not the only part of Mormonism I must learn to live without. Yet I still could not face the reality of total loss.

1986

November [From Quinn's 1988 memoir:]

Former mentor says I've gone too far.

Signature Books asked Davis Bitton to review the first draft of my book on early Mormonism's connections with occult traditions and folk magic [published as *Early Mormonism and the Magic World View*]. He made some helpful criticisms, but most of his review was a plea to me and the publisher to abandon this project. He said that my study was an assault on the faith of average Latter-day Saints. If I insisted on publishing this book, Davis instructed me not to mention in the acknowledgements that he had read the manuscript.

His letter stunned me and I was in deep depression for weeks, while I reconsidered what to do. After telling Signature to put the book on hold, I decided to do an extensive revision to respond to the questions and criticisms by Davis, by Lavina Fielding Anderson, and by Allen D. Roberts. None of them particularly liked the study. This revision and new research took me another seven months.

My second book, and now it's defenders of the New Mormon History who want me not to publish! I guess I AM a radical, even though I've never felt like one.

I had already resigned from Signature's board of directors, because I felt that it would be a conflict-of-interest for me to vote on financial matters at the same time I was submitting a manuscript for purchase and publication. I had served on its board for four years.

When I wrote the preliminary manuscript's introduction during this Summer, I referred to the so-called "Salamander Letter" as a possible forgery. Aside from passing references to it, my first draft excluded this "1830 Martin Harris Letter" because of serious questions then raised about its authenticity. Thus, I needed to revise only a few sentences and a paragraph for the upcoming <u>Magic World View</u> that would be published [in August 1987] after the police released their evidence of Mark Hofmann's forgeries.

[Quinn's Early Mormonism and the Magic World View *was published by Signature Books in 1987; a revised and expanded version appeared in 1998.]*

1988

January 20 [From Quinn's 1988 memoir:]

I resigned from BYU as a full professor and director of its graduate program in history. This was just days after receiving confirmation that I was awarded full-time research grants at the [Henry E.] Huntington Library in Southern California [in San Marino, next to Pasadena]. The resignation was to be effective at the conclusion of Spring term.

May 6 [From Quinn's 1988 memoir:]

As soon as I dropped off the termination form at BYU's personnel office, I drove from Provo to Logan [Utah], to attend MHA's annual banquet. Arrived late. Just in time to hear my name read as winner of the award for best book of the year. [*Early Mormonism and The Magic World View*]

For a moment, I thought of stepping to the microphone to say something in appreciation, in farewell, in summation. Decided that anything I said would be either too much or too little, so I just gave them a big grin and "Thank-you," as I accepted the award.

Davis Bitton warmly congratulated me on winning this award for the book he had advised me not to publish. He urged me, as he often did, to complete my decade-delayed book on the Mormon hierarchy. I assured him that I would work on this full-time during my year-and-a-half fellowship at the Huntington Library.

Many kind words, best wishes, and gentle hugs tonight from members of the Mormon History Association. They regarded me as a fellow-traveler in the often-conflicted quest to write religious history in a rigorous, balanced, sympathetic, and faithful way. Yet I traveled in a solitary manner, even when in their company, as I sought to reconcile conflicts within myself, within Mormon history, within BYU, and within the LDS Church itself. I felt tonight that I was leaving all that behind, as well as BYU and Utah culture.

I was beginning a "separate peace." With myself, with my sense of mission, with God.

1993

February 7 [From Quinn's 1995 memoir:]

Six months after I moved back to Utah [from New Orleans, Louisana], LDS headquarters discovered my address. The president of the Salt Lake Stake, Paul A. Hanks, appeared with his counselors at my door this Sunday morning—holding a written accusation that my recent historical publications constituted apostasy. I had not received any kind of LDS "fellowshipping visit" from anyone else in the ward or stake.

At the top of his typewritten list was my essay "Mormon Women Have Had the Priesthood Since 1843," published last year in a feminist book, Women and Authority, edited by Maxine Hanks, my former associate at BYU. I didn't bother to point out to the Stake President that this article was merely a longer analysis of what I had published in the Fall of 1981 as a professor at BYU. What was merely "controversial" back then was "apostate" in 1993.

I explained that I was on my way to Los Angeles for research at the Huntington Library, where Martin Ridge had given me a three-month fellowship. My Stake President said that disciplinary action would occur immediately after my return.

That evening I typed a letter to Paul Hanks, outlining my previous experience with a Stake President who had been given instructions by LDS headquarters to discipline me and to claim it was a local decision. I explained my post-1988 vow that "I would never again participate in a process which was designed to punish me for being the messenger of unwanted historical evidence and to intimidate me from further work in Mormon history." I refused to meet with him. ...

September 26 [From Quinn's 1995 memoir, after Quinn declined to attend three LDS Church disciplinary councils:]

The Salt Lake Stake's letter stated that I was excommunicated for my refusal to cooperate with the Stake President's inquiry into my alleged apostasy. ...

I was puzzled that the notice of excommunication didn't use the word "apostasy," which the Stake President had repeatedly applied to me since February. Nor did it mention my publications, which had started his inquisition.

1995

Spring 1995 [From Quinn's 1995 memoir:]

I also responded publicly to a member of the John Birch Society who submitted a long criticism of my article about President [Ezra Taft] Benson's controversial years as an Apostle. My response in <u>Dialogue</u> concluded: "Whole sections of the Benson-Birch article surprised me during my dragnet approach to research. However, I did my best to be fair to all concerned in narrating that experience. Other authors may feel it necessary to identify who they think wore the White-hat and who wore the Black-hat in controversial events. Or at least to inform the reader who the author regards as 'right' and who was 'wrong.'

"Instead, I think it's usually better for historians to leave value-judgments to the reader, even though authors may have strong opinions of their own. I've never tried to ignore evidence I disliked or to skew its presentation to force the reader to a pre-determined conclusion. That kind of 'objectivity' was the goal in my biography of the controversial J. Reuben Clark, and I was pleased to learn that both his supporters and detractors felt my book had vindicated their views of Counselor Clark. In twenty years of writing about the Mormon hierarchy, I've felt that I was describing White-hats who were sometimes caught in the dust-storms and stampedes of mortal life."

[See Quinn, "Reply," in the spring 1995 issue of Dialogue: A Journal of Mormon Thought, pp. 173–78.]

Note: Since 1995, Quinn has been a speaker at such diverse venues as the Chicago Humanities Festival, Claremont Graduate University, Affirmation for Gay and Lesbian Mormons, Utah ACLU, Washington State Historical Society, Yale University Graduate School, Western

Literature Association, Casper College, Autry Museum of the West, Wabash College, and Yale Divinity School. He has continued to publish in academic journals such as Sunstone, *the* John Whitmer Historical Association Journal, *and the* Journal of Mormon History, *and has written chapters for historical anthologies, including* American National Biography *(1999). In 1996, he published what some historians have called his most academic and rigorous work with the University of Illinois Press,* Same-Sex Dynamics Among Nineteenth-Century Americans, *which won the Herbert Feis Award from the American Historical Association and was named one of the best religion books of the year by* Publishers Weekly. *Quinn completed his massive three-volume work—*The Mormon Hierarchy: Origins of Power, The Mormon Hierarchy: Extensions of Power, *and* The Mormon Hierarchy: Wealth and Corporate Power—*in 2017. He is highly sought after to comment on Mormon related news articles. Currently, he is working on a history of post–Manifesto plural marriage. He has done extensive interviews for* Slate, Wall Street Journal, *and* Mormon Stories *podcasts, among other venues. In 2016, he received the Leonard J. Arrington Award from the Mormon History Association for "truly outstanding for distinguished service to Mormon history." On August 27, 2018, Brigham Young University President Kevin Worthen publicly quoted from Quinn's biography of J. Reuben Clark. At the Mormon History Association conference on June 8 2019, Gerrit van Dyk, a librarian at BYU's Harold B. Lee Library, reported that Quinn is one of the most frequently cited authors in academic works nationally. At seventy-six, D. Michael Quinn remains one of the most important historians studying Mormonism today.*

THE PUBLICATION HISTORY OF JUANITA BROOKS'S DUDLEY LEAVITT: PIONEER TO SOUTHERN UTAH

CRAIG S. SMITH

10

Juanita Brooks (1898–1989) began her writing career with successes starting in the late 1920s, through the 1930s, and into the early 1940s. During these years, she saw two stories accepted by the national magazine *Harper's*: one, "A Close-up of Polygamy," in 1934 and in 1941, "The Water's In."[1] She also contributed a number of articles including those on St. George, Utah, and Highway 91 to the regional magazine *The Utah*. LDS Church periodicals such as the *Young Women's Journal, Relief Society Magazine,* and *Improvement Era* also published several of her articles.[2] In the early 1940s, she embarked on a biography of southern Utah colonizer Jacob Hamblin, even applying for an Alfred A. Knopf fellowship to write the biography. She failed to receive the fellowship, and the project was never completed, though a book on Hamblin based on a movie script she had produced in 1952 was published in 1980.[3]

In 1942, at the insistence of her father, Brooks wrote and produced her first book, a biography on her grandfather Dudley Leavitt.[4] Levi Peterson, Brooks's biographer, refers to this book as "one of Juanita's finest works" and goes on to say: "Like her two *Harper's*

---

1. Juanita Brooks, "A Close-Up of Polygamy," *Harper's* 168 (Feb. 1934): 299–307, and Juanita Brooks, "The Water's In!" *Harper's* 182 (May 1941): 608–13.

2. See the bibliography of her works in Levi Peterson, *Juanita Brooks, Mormon Woman Historian* (Salt Lake City: University of Utah Press, 1988), 479–87.

3. Juanita Brooks, *Jacob Hamblin: Mormon Apostle to the Indians* (Salt Lake City: Westwater Press, 1980).

4. Juanita Brooks, *Dudley Leavitt: Pioneer to Southern Utah* (St. George, Utah: N.p., 1942).

articles, it is written in a simple, concrete style. Utterly devoid of footnotes and other scholarly apparatus, it convinces through detail. The zeal which characterized Dudley Leavitt and the pioneering adventures which tested that zeal emerge in the pages of this book as palpable, immediate, and real. He was a credible giant, a believable doer of unbelievable deeds."[5] Though agreeing with Peterson's literary judgement, Gary Topping in his book evaluating Utah historians criticizes Brooks's efforts by claiming, "One has more trouble, though, with her invented dialogue, her assured readings of her characters' emotions, and her uncritical acceptance of miraculous manifestations that typically attend pious Mormon narratives."[6]

Despite these criticisms, her "little book," as Brooks referred to it, continues to shine as a window into the life and times of the pioneer era in a remote corner of the Mormon realm. Presenting the "miraculous manifestations" as accepted and believed by the participants adds to the sentiments of the times.

The book was an important learning experience for her. It gave her friend and mentor Dale Morgan, a preeminent historian of the West, an opportunity to give Brooks one of her first lessons on careful historical research. She immediately mailed him a copy when the book was available in mid-June 1942. They were in the midst of the period of their extensive correspondence, often writing at least once a week, that continued through the early 1940s. Upon receiving the unexpected gift, Morgan went directly into his editorial mode and covered an entire single-spaced page with corrections to the historic detail.[7] His comments ranged from fixing names such as Peter Maun to Peter Maughan and B. R. Carrington to A. R. Carrington; adjusting the sequence of events when Brigham Young and Sidney Rigdon made their claims to be president of the LDS Church in Nauvoo following the 1844 murder of Joseph Smith; noting it was not possible for a marriage to occur in Salt Lake City's Endowment House prior to 1855, the date when it was erected; modifying the

---

5. Peterson, *Juanita Brooks*, 127.

6. Gary Topping, *Utah Historians and the Reconstruction of Western History* (Norman: University of Oklahoma Press, 2003), 188.

7. Dale Morgan, Letter to Juanita Brooks (hereafter JB), June 27, 1942, Juanita Brooks Papers, MSS B103, Utah State Historical Society. Unless otherwise noted, all correspondence is from the Brooks Papers.

name of the commander of the Utah Expedition from Johnson to Johnston; and changing the date when the emigrant train containing the Leavitts entered the Salt Lake Valley from the last day of August to August 30, among other observations.

Morgan also lectured her on the importance of copyrighting a work, which she had neglected to do in this case. On a more positive note, he was pleased with the book, especially her discussion of Leavitt's plural marriages. The book included the first account of a marriage to a Native American that he had seen. Morgan continued to offer similar exhaustive comments on her other efforts leading to her first scholarly historical publication in 1944 in the *Utah Historical Quarterly.*[8] Learning from these critiques eventually enabled her to produce her landmark book *The Mountain Meadows Massacre.*[9]

---

8. Juanita Brooks, "Indian Relations on the Mormon Frontier." *Utah Historical Quarterly* 12 (Jan.–Apr. 1944): 1–48.

9. Juanita Brooks, *The Mountain Meadows Massacre* (Stanford: Stanford University Press, 1950).

Brooks's Dudley Leavitt biography also opened doors for her at the Huntington Library in San Marino, California. In 1944, she innocently sent a letter addressed to the director of the Huntington Library requesting information and possibly photostats of the testimonies given at the John D. Lee trials in Beaver, Utah (Lee was one of the principal instigators of the Mountain Meadows massacre). Librarian Leslie E. Bliss responded to her appeal by encouraging her to come to the library. They had acquired a copy of her Dudley Leavitt volume, which impressed them to consider offering her an opportunity to collect pioneer diaries for the library.[10] Bliss in his letter praised the work noting "that you made very good use of the material in hand in the biography. You made out such a good case for your subject that I very much wish I could have had the opportunity of knowing and talking with him." This introduction led to a long relationship with the Huntington Library, resulting in Brooks's collecting early Mormon pioneer diaries and reminiscences for photostating, receiving a Rockefeller Foundation grant to write her Mountain Meadows massacre book, and collaborating with Robert G. Cleland, library research associate, to produce a two-volume edition of a selection of the John D. Lee diaries. All in all, the little volume was a notable stepping stone to her career and fame as an historian.

The book went through four variant printings between 1942 and 1970. Each printing regardless of year printed exhibits the same 1942 date creating confusion as to when each variant was actually printed and which was the real first edition. The lack of a notation of publisher and place of publication adds to the misidentification of the variants. The following details the history and physical characteristics of each variant as gleamed mostly from Brooks's correspondence.

First Printing

Dark blue cloth binding measuring 9¼ x 6 inches, 115 pages. The title and author are in gold on the front cover and the spine is blank. The foreword begins on a separate page after the title page. The verso of the title page is blank. Photographs are on slick paper.

---

10. Leslie E. Bliss, Letter to JB, Feb. 18, 1944.

The first printing of the Leavitt biography was ready for distribution by mid-June 1942. Brooks first had 250 of the 500 printed copies bound. She wrote to Morgan in September 1942 saying that she had the second 250 copies bound and that she had sold all of the first lot.[11] She declared that she was a poor salesman and that they sold because of the strong interest among family members.

In a letter to Ettie Lee, in May 1949, Brooks remembered that she had 500 copies printed and had offered them to family for $1.50 a copy.[12] She claimed that at first, she was disappointed in the sales, but after a few years she raised the price to $2.00 and they were soon gone. She had not advertised the book or attempted to sell it. She also mentioned that she was still getting many requests for the book and was considering producing another edition. She had seen a list offering the book at $7.50.

Second Printing

Lighter sky-blue cloth binding measuring 9¼ x 6 inches, 115 pages. The title and author are in gold on the front cover and the spine is blank. The foreword begins on the verso of the title page. Photographs reproduced on the same paper as the text. Thinner volume with lighter paper than the first printing, but with same typography.

Levi Peterson in his biography of Brooks writes, "She contracted with a Salt Lake firm for a precise reproduction by offset press of the original work. Thereafter she sold copies at a price about five times greater than her cost."[13] However, the letter Peterson references for this information is actually only a quote from the Sugarhouse Press in Salt Lake City for 1,500 copies at $891.95, 5,000 copies at $1,523.11, and 10,000 copies at $2,506.09.[14] The letter ends by mentioning: "Delivery will depend upon receipt of all copy at Sugarhouse Press 1123 E. Twenty-first So., and upon the number of books required." No other correspondence is present in Brooks's papers indicating the number she ordered and when. A letter Brooks wrote to a relative dated December 29,

11. JB, Letter to Dale Morgan, Sept. 23, 1942.
12. JB, Letter to Ettie Lee, May 2, 1949.
13. Peterson, *Juanita Brooks*, 239.
14. Sugar House Press, Letter to JB, Sept. 6, 1955.

1955, provides at least the latest date when the second printing was available.[15] The letter states, "I am mailing a copy of my little <u>Dudley Leavitt</u> book. Because of increased cost of reproduction, I am having to charge $2.50 each for these that I had made up recently. The first edition has been gone for many years, and this is an exact reproduction, done by off-set press." Though the number printed is not given, it was probably no more than 500 copies, the same number as the first printing. Both appear to have a similar scarcity on the current rare book market.

Third Printing

Turquoise cloth binding measuring 8½ x 5½ inches, 115 pages. The title and author appear in gold on the front cover and spine. The verso of the title page is blank. The Leavitt coat-of-arms follows on the next page. The verso of the coat-of-arms is blank. The foreword begins on the next page. The same typography as previous printings, but at a reduced size. Photographs reproduced on the same paper as the text are not as clear as the previous printings. "Hiller Bookbinding Company Salt Lake City" sticker occurs on inside back cover. This third printing was of an inferior quality compared to the first two printings.

Peterson records, "Juanita decided during this summer [1969] to republish her grandfather's biography, *Dudley Leavitt: Pioneer to Southern Utah,* which had been out of print for some time. In July she let the job to Ogden Kraut, who operated a Mormon fundamentalist press in remote Dugway [Utah]. ... Made bold by expressions of family interest, Juanita ordered a printing of 1000 copies, of which 500 were to be immediately bound."[16]

Much confusion exists concerning this printing. Brooks fueled the muddling of events surrounding the printing by making incorrect and misleading assertions in the Author's Statement to her completely revised biography of her grandfather, *On the Ragged Edge: The Life and Times of Dudley Leavitt,* published in 1973.[17] She claimed: "After some twenty years had passed and the *Dudley*

---

15. JB, Letter to Lillian B. Corry, Dec. 29, 1955.

16. Peterson, *Juanita Brooks,* 341–42.

17. Juanita Brooks, *On the Ragged Edge: The Life and Times of Dudley Leavitt* (Salt Lake City: Utah State Historical Society, 1973).

Leavitt books were all sold, a printer asked if I would object to his republishing it. I now believe that he had it all done before he approached me on the subject. I supposed, of course, that he would reproduce it as it was. How sadly was I disappointed. In order to make more profit, he had printed it on cheaper paper in smaller type, making the whole volume smaller. It was not only difficult to read, but the pictures were ruined."[18] Some unsubstantiated rumors also claimed that Lyman Hafen at *The Spectrum,* a newspaper in St. George, was behind the alleged unauthorized printing in 1969. However, no evidence exists for an edition printed in St. George.

To clear up this misinformation, excerpts from the letters between Brooks and Ogden Kraut, owner and operator of Pioneer Press, concerning the arrangements of this printing are discussed and quoted below. Apparently, Brooks did order the printing from Kraut, but left the size of the pages to Kraut's judgment. Kraut printed it in his standard size and format used for most of his publications in an attempt to make the printing job as inexpensive as possible for Brooks.

Brooks and Kraut began their extant correspondence in the fall of 1966 with Kraut sharing with her some of his publications including *B. H. Roberts Defense Before Congress* and *Jesus Was Married.*[19] In March 1969, Brooks wrote Kraut thanking him for a copy of his *Jesus Was Married* and then inquired: "I begin to wonder if you are operating a commercial press. My little book, DUDLEY LEAVITT, published in 1941 has long been out of print. Since it is a family book and a whole generation has grown up and married, I am getting more and more requests for copies. ... IF you do this type of thing commercially, I should like to talk to you about possibilities. The book is now 120 pages."[20]

Kraut responded on March 14, 1969, first mentioning he was working on a *Gift of Tongues* book, and asking Brooks if she had any information on the subject.[21] He then answered Brooks's

---

18. Ibid., ix–x.

19. *B. H. Roberts Defense Before Congress* (Dugway, Utah: Pioneer Press, n.d.); and Ogden Kraut, *Jesus was Married* (Dugway, Utah: Pioneer Press, 1969).

20. JB, Letter to Ogden Kraut, Mar. 5, 1969.

21. The book was published as Ogden Kraut, *The Gift of Tongues* (Dugway, Utah: Pioneer Press, 1970).

request: "As for the printing work which you requested—I would be happy to do whatever you would like to have made up. As for cost, I will try to do it for half of what you have been paying."[22] This response suggests that Kraut was under the impression that Brooks wanted the job completed as cheaply as possible and that he thought of himself as a low-budget printer.

Following this letter, Brooks and Kraut probably spoke on the telephone as the next letter in the files is from Kraut dated May 20, 1969, when he informed her that he had started the printing. He stated: "I have started your book. I called some printers and got estimates and will make my bid as far below any others that I can. Also I am printing it about a ½ smaller—this will save about 30%–40% or more on paper costs—which is your biggest item. ... I am going to be into it about $150.00 which may be enough to get it to the binders. There will be labor to add later and you can pay that when you begin to see the book if you wish."[23]

Brooks immediately replied with a check for the $150.00. She was concerned over the size of the print, but left it to Kraut's judgment:

> Thank you for the word that work on the book is under way. You didn't say anything about the number to be printed at this time, but I think it should be not more than five hundred (500.) I can take care of that many, I think. The general reaction here in the immediate family is that they would have preferred the larger print, since so many are older and find small print hard to read. Or is the cut only on margins? I didn't get that clear. Anyway, I'm trusting to your judgment in this. I enclose a check for one-hundred-and-fifty dollars ($150.00) as a beginning.[24]

After about a month and a half, Brooks wrote to Kraut again noting that she had been busy over the past two months with company and a family reunion, but now wanted to get some things done. She indicated: "Already orders for the Dudley Leavitt book are coming in, and it would be a great help if I could answer with an approximate time as to when they will be ready. It looks now

---

22. Kraut, Letter to JB, Mar. 14, 1969.
23. Kraut, Letter to JB, May 20, 1969.
24. JB, Letter to Kraut, May 21, 1969.

like I will not have any trouble in disposing of 500 books rather soon. Would it be good business to print up 1000 while we are at it and bind up 500 at first? I know that this will pose a problem of storage, so I will depend on your judgment."[25] She was anxious to hear on the progress of the project and was willing to send more money and travel to meet with him if necessary.

Kraut wrote the same day that he had been off work for a month: "Just a note to tell you that I have been off work for a month after an operation ... but I'm back to normal now and expect to be into production again right away. I will send you some pages of the book. I am printing them 90% of the original size so I don't think it will be too small."[26]

After receiving Brooks's letter of July 10, he included another note with the above letter:

> I was just getting ready to mail this note to you and your letter came. I will proceed with the printing of 1000 copies. I know that 500 will not last long—and most of the expense is in the first 500—the last batch will not be very expensive. If there are no delays I should have them finished in the next couple of weeks. There will be some labor on putting them together for the binder but that will not be too long either. So within the next 30 days the Binder should have them about ready for the market.[27]

On July 14, Brooks responded concerned that she was receiving orders for the book and wanted to determine a price she could charge for the book:

> Re: <u>Dudley Leavitt</u>, I am concerned to have everything right and legal and all, and since orders are already coming in, I should know the approximate cost so that I can make some statement on the price. I hope to find members of the family in Salt Lake City, Las Vegas, and Mesquite who will handle some in lots of a hundred at a time, for which they will receive a small commission. ... For all that have been put out to date, I've never had a dollar of profit, but just the fun and satisfaction of having done the book. Now I think you should

---

25. JB, Letter to Kraut, July 10, 1969.
26. Kraut, Letter to JB, July 10, 1969.
27. Kraut, Letter to JB, no date.

get a fair remuneration for your time and work and equipment, and I should also make a little. Would $3.50 retail seem fair to you?[28]

Kraut replied providing an approximate cost per hardback book and a recommended price for which she could sell them:

> At present I estimate the supplies, printing, and collating the book at about $1.00 a copy. The hardback binding—like on my *Jesus Was Married* will be about 50c each. I will find out the cost of binding 500 and 1000 copies and let you know on the quotations. You perhaps could sell the book at $2.95 if you wished and still make a fair profit at wholesale or retail. I will do some further checking to see if I can cut a little more on the printing expense. I am masking the film and making plates now so will be into the final printing very shortly. Hope this all meets with your approval. It should sell very well.[29]

On August 5, Kraut sent a page sample requesting her approval: "Just a note to show you about what the book size will be and also what the printing will show up to be. I hope that this is satisfactory with you. It is the most inexpensive size and yet readable enough that it should meet all of the requirements of your project."[30] After sending the proof sheet, Kraut probably started the printing process using the format provided in the sample to Brooks.

Almost two weeks later, Brooks finally answered saying she had been quite busy the past month and that "all my relatives have been on wheels going from or coming to distant points and stopping here." She continued: "Had three of my sisters all here at once this week. When I showed them the sample sheet of Dudley Leavitt, without exception they protested, saying they'd rather pay a couple-a dollars more for a larger book."[31] She then mentioned that she was told a relative was taking apart one of her books and photocopying copies for other family members causing her to request a printing of only 500 books. She concluded by saying she would call him to discuss. These concerns were probably expressed too late as Kraut had most likely already started the printing process of 1,000 copies.

---

28. JB, Letter to Kraut, July 14, 1969.
29. Kraut, Letter to JB, July 29, 1969.
30. Kraut, Letter to JB, Aug. 5, 1969.
31. JB, Letter to Kraut, Aug. 26, 1969.

The telephone call appears to have occurred sometime before September 2. Brooks was probably informed that Kraut was well into the printing process using the reduced format. They must have agreed on a print run of 1,000 copies, with 500 copies being bound at that time. The second 500 copies would be bound when needed. On September 2, Brooks sent Kraut a check for $200 and a note: "It was good to talk with you a while. I am enclosing my check for $200.00, which will help some, I hope. I feel sure that we have not made a mistake, for we both want to do the best thing for us all. Thank you for everything."[32]

In late October, Kraut apparently delivered some of the completed books (probably 100 copies), and they met for the first time. In a follow up letter, Brooks apologized for her "general dis-array" and that she did not even offer him a drink of water. She continued: "As to the books: I feel sure that I can dispose of all these at the annual gathering at Mesquite on the week-end, and perhaps take orders for more. I'll let you know how I fare. ... If the binders will step it up and get them to us by Thanksgiving or before, we can take advantage of Christmas sales. So many would like them for gifts. — So much for that. We shall see what comes."[33]

Two days later Brooks wrote again to transmit her story on the Three Nephites for a book that Kraut was preparing.[34] At the end of this letter, she mentioned the books and recommended "that the simplest way will be to ship them by Milne Truck Line COD."[35] Anne Wilde, Kraut's plural wife and assistant, writing for Kraut five days later, informed Brooks on how the first 500 copies of the book were distributed: "Just a note to let you know that I gave 30 copies of Dudley Leavitt to Mrs. Selena Leavitt. She will pay you $3 each for them after they are sold. I have the rest of the books— about 120, completing the first 500 that have been bound. Guess

---

32. JB, Letter to Kraut, Sept. 2, 1969.

33. JB, Letter to Kraut, Oct. 20, 1969.

34. Her story appeared as, Juanita Brooks, "Uncle Hube and the Nephite," *The Three Nephites*, ed. Ogden Kraut (Dugway, Utah: Pioneer Press, 1969), 158. The Three Nephites were three disciples of Jesus Christ in the Book of Mormon who were blessed never to taste death so that they could minister unto the people. Stories about modern encounters with one or more of them abound in Mormon folklore.

35. JB, Letter to Kraut, Oct. 22, 1969.

I'll hold them here until I get word as to what to do with them. Hope you got the 250 we sent down with Gary Watson."[36]

Kraut inquired in a letter of November 5 on how the sales of the book were progressing and if she wanted him to deliver some of the books to Zions Book Store in Salt Lake City.[37] He also asked her to inform him when she wanted the other 500 copies bound. Brooks responded to Wilde, also on November 5, mentioning that only 199 of the expected 250 books were delivered. She concluded the letter: "Well, we'll do the best we can. Whether or not I net anything from them, I'm still glad that they have been done."[38] These were the final extant letters between the two for 1969. As of November 30, Brooks had sent Kraut $650 for the printing of the books.[39]

The above sequence of letters clearly demonstrates that Brooks requested, authorized, and paid for the printing of her Dudley Leavitt biography in 1969 by Ogden Kraut and his Pioneer Press. She left most of the decisions on size and format of the book to be printed to Kraut's judgment, though she did express to him at least a couple times that she thought the size of the book was too small. She did not respond immediately after receiving the page sample and probably conveyed her concerns after Kraut was far into the printing. Kraut was under the impression that Brooks wanted to do the printing as cheaply as possible, so he chose the size in which he typically printed his books.

Fourth Printing

White and turquoise paper binding measuring 8¼ x 5¼ inches, 115 pages. The title and author appear in black on the cover front and spine. Same pagination, typography, and print size as the cloth binding edition (third printing). The title on the cover is printed in black.

This printing consists of the second 500 copies of the 1,000 printed in 1969 by Pioneer Press. Kraut wrote to Brooks on Pioneer

---

36. Anne Wilde, Letter to JB, Oct. 27, 1969. Selena Hafen Leavitt (1885–1983) was Brooks's mother's sister.

37. Kraut, Letter to JB, Nov. 5, 1969.

38. JB, Letter to Wilde, Nov. 5, 1969.

39. Tabulation of money spent, Nov. 30, 1969.

Press letterhead in February 1970 forwarding her a copy of his book on the Three Nephites that included a story of hers. He mentioned: "We are collating the last half (500 copies) of the DUDLEY LEAVITT edition. It will take three or four weeks to have them bound. If you would like to have them in about a month, I will be glad to bring them down."[40]

Brooks sent a letter to Kraut on March 3 apparently before she received his letter, as she said she would like to see a copy of the Three Nephites book, which he had forwarded to her with his last letter. She frantically appealed: "I feel that you should have had some of these Dudley Leavitt books that are here. I have 250+ here at home, besides some out to Porter Leavitt, Aunt Selena Leavitt, Mrs. Parley Leavitt of Mesquite, and my sister, Mrs. Vernon C. Rowley, in Las Vegas. Of course, they will go in time, but it looks like it will be some time."[41]

Therefore, as Kraut was notifying her that he was preparing the second 500 copies to be bound, she was overwhelmed with the number she had left from the first 500. This correspondence was the last between the two existing in the files. It is unclear exactly when in 1970 the second 500 copies were bound, who initiated the binding process, and how they were finally distributed. Brooks's level of involvement in the binding and distribution of the second 500 copies is unknown. She probably authorized Kraut to handle the entire process as her focus went elsewhere.

By the end of March 1970, Brooks's life completely changed with the passing of her husband, Will Brooks, on March 28. In August 1970, she moved to Salt Lake City from St. George. Brooks's association with this final printing probably became even more removed as her thoughts turned to writing a completely new version of her biography of her grandfather in 1972. She worked on this revision in the later part of 1972 and well into 1973.[42]

40. Kraut, Letter to JB, Feb. 28, 1970.
41. JB, Letter to Kraut, Mar. 3, 1970. Porter Rockwell Leavitt (1916–95) was a grandson of Dudley Leavitt; Mrs. Parley Leavitt was Martha Lorena Hafen (1890–1989), who was married to Parley Leavitt, a grandson of Dudley Leavitt; and Mrs. Vernon C. Rowley was Charity Leavitt (1899–1999), Brooks's younger sister.
42. Peterson, *Juanita Brooks*, 379.

The biography, *On the Ragged Edge: The Life and Times of Dudley Leavitt,* became available in February 1974.[43]

Brooks's incorrect and misleading comment in the "Author's Statement" of the revised edition of her Dudley Leavitt biography is surprising. She spent a career fighting for truth and honesty in the writing of Mormon history, at times going up against the powerful in the LDS Church. Her enduring legacy is partly the inspiration she provides to those laboring with producing objective history of Utah and the Mormons. This uncharacteristic slip of the truth was probably the result of her failing mental capabilities, which began a downward trend about the time she wrote the "Author's Statement" in 1973. Her mental deterioration eventually resulted in her children moving her back to St. George and ultimately into a nursing home, where she spent the remainder of her days. At the time of her misstatement, she often became agitated and confused as her memory began to fail. Perhaps she mistook Kraut's discussion of binding the second 500 copies as a request for a new printing, forgetting that she had previously authorized the printing. Her dissatisfaction with the print size and quality probably also contributed to her lapse of memory concerning the events leading to the printing.[44] Whatever the reason, Brooks's "Author's Statement" should be understood as an aberration in her lifelong commitment to the truth.

---

43. Brooks, *On the Ragged Edge.*
44. Ibid., ix.

PURSUING FOUR FORGOTTEN CHAPTERS OF MORMON FRONTIER EXPERIENCE

GEORGE D. SMITH

11

Over the thirty-five years between 1985 and 2020, I wrote three books and helped to bring to press a fourth about the Mormon frontier community as it arose in the westward-growing American nation. These books deal with Mormon church founder Joseph Smith's introduction of plural marriage in Nauvoo, Illinois: *Nauvoo Polygamy: "... But We Called It Celestial Marriage"* (2008, 2011); a contemporary view of Smith's life recorded by one of his secretaries, William Clayton, *An Intimate Chronicle: The Journals of William Clayton* (1991, 1995); Smith successor Brigham Young's record of settling the western United States, *Brigham Young, Colonizer of the American West: Diaries and Journals, 1832–1871* (2020); and the reflections of "Defender of the Faith" Brigham H. Roberts who, while acting as spokesperson for Smith's Latter-day Saints church, fielded questions about the historicity of the church's founding scripture, the Book of Mormon, *Studies of the Book of Mormon: [by] B. H. Roberts*, edited by noted Western historian Brigham D. Madsen (1985, 1992). This last book grew out of my public presentations and journal articles on epistemological issues raised by Roberts. These inquiries into Nauvoo polygamy, Clayton's journal record, Young's pioneering across North America to the Rocky Mountains and Pacific Ocean, and Roberts's examination of Book of Mormon "Difficulties" are my attempts to reconstruct institutionally forgotten chapters of Mormon frontier history.

Below, I will introduce each of these books and discuss why I found these issues compelling, looking at the primary characteristic of a community rooted in plural marriage: foreshadowed in the Book of Mormon and practiced in Nauvoo, recorded by Clayton, and taken west by Young. I also review Roberts's examination of Book of Mormon origins in light of antecedent American writings with similar themes. Finally, I briefly describe what drew me to look into these facets of westward American experience.

Beginnings

One spring afternoon in April 1841, a young woman reportedly disguised in a man's hat and coat accompanied two men to a secluded tree near a bend in the Mississippi River. No one in the nearby town of Nauvoo was alerted to the ceremony that was about to take place. Twenty-six-year-old Louisa Beaman was about to become the first documented plural wife of Joseph Smith (1805–44), the thirty-five-year-old founder of the 1830 restored Church of Christ.

Standing by Smith's side, the farmer's daughter, Louisa, listened compliantly as the charismatic prophet told her brother-in-law, Joseph Bates Noble (married six years to Louisa's sister, Mary)[1] what to say as he conducted her wedding ceremony with this already-married man. What was she thinking as she left town accompanied only by her brother-in-law and the married prophet whom she would quietly wed? Did she accept the marriage as a religious calling to which she felt obligated to consent? We don't have any record of what preceded this unusual ceremony. Had Joseph been courting Louisa for some time, in this sub rosa manner?

Notably absent from this private riverside wedding were Smith's legal wife, thirty-six-year-old Emma Hale Smith, and their children: Joseph III, eight; Frederick, four; Alexander, two; as well as their nine-year-old adopted daughter, Julia Murdock—not to mention Smith's own siblings or the parents of the bride and groom (their fathers were deceased, but their mothers lived in Nauvoo).

The practice of polygamy, or plural marriage, specifically forbidden in Smith's decade-old "translation," the Book of Mormon,

---

1. Joseph B. Noble, Affidavit, June 26, 1869, "Forty Affidavits on Celestial Marriage," 1869, History Library, Church of Jesus Christ of Latter-day Saints, Salt Lake City, Utah; hereafter LDS History Library.

"until commanded by deity,"[2] appears to have been launched in Nauvoo on April 5, 1841, before any official communications to legitimize the practice. Smith had introduced the idea of plural marriage to early followers when he published the Book of Mormon in March 1830 at the Grandin Press of Palmyra, New York. Dictated from a reportedly ancient record on metallic plates Smith said he found at a hillside near his home in Manchester, New York, Smith vocally translated the Book of Mormon almost entirely to his schoolteacher cousin, Oliver Cowdery. While presenting a story of ancient Hebrew migrants sailing to America, Smith introduced the idea of plural marriage for his followers. Although initially not a tenet of Smith's Church of Christ, formed on April 6, 1830, polygamy was from the beginning an implicit possibility for the Latter-day Saints—"if commanded" (Jacob 2:30).

---

2. Joseph Smith, Junior, Proprietor, *The Book of Mormon* (Palmyra, New York: Grandin Press, 1830), Jacob 2: 27, 30.

Smith did dictate such a "revelation" in 1843 to his close followers; but even then, polygamy was not publicly announced for
another decade and was not canonized in LDS scripture until 1876.

My reconstruction of the Smith/Beaman plural marriage is
based on the following ten accounts:

1. According to Andrew Jenson, later LDS Assistant Church Historian, Beaman's marriage to Smith was "the first plural marriage
   consummated [consecrated?]."[3]

2. John C. Bennett, the first to publicly announce Smith's marriage
   to Beaman, designated "Elder Joseph Bates Noble" as performing
   the ceremony with "Miss L***** B*****."[4]

3. In 1869 Noble swore out an affidavit to LDS Apostle Joseph F.
   Smith that "on the fifth day of April A.D. 1841, at the city of Nauvoo … he married or sealed Louisa Beaman to Joseph Smith …"[5]

4. On January 22, 1869, Apostle Wilford Woodruff heard Noble talk
   about the marriage.[6]

5. Apostle Franklin D. Richards recorded in his journal that Noble
   specifically had "related that he performed the first sealing ceremony in this dispensation in which he united Sister Louisa Beaman
   to the Prophet Joseph … during the evening under an Elm tree in
   Nauvoo. The bride disguised in a [man's] coat and hat."[7]

6. Apostle George A. Smith wrote on October 9, 1869, to Joseph
   Smith III: "On the fifth day of April, 1841, Louisa Beaman was
   married to your father, Joseph Smith, for time and all eternity, by
   Joseph B. Noble."[8]

7. William Clayton, Smith's personal secretary, included Beaman
   among his list of Smith's lawful wives.[9]

---

3. Andrew Jenson, Plural Marriage, *Historical Record* 6 (May 1887): 232–33, 239.

4. John C. Bennett, *Sangamo Journal*, July 15, 1842.

5. Noble, Affidavit, June 26, 1869, in "Forty Affidavits on Celestial Marriage."

6. Scott Kenney, ed., *Wilford Woodruff's Journal*, 9 vols. (Midvale, Utah: Signature
Books, 1983), 6:452.

7. Franklin D. Richards Journal, Jan. 22, 1869, LDS History Library.

8. Joseph Smith III Papers, Library–Archives of the Community of Christ, Independence, Missouri; Journal History of the Church of Jesus Christ of Latter-day
Saints, Oct. 9, 1869, LDS History Library.

9. William Clayton Affidavit, Feb. 16, 1874, Salt Lake City, "Affidavits [on Celestial Marriage], 1869–1915," LDS History Library.

8. Ann Eliza Webb Young, once a plural wife of Brigham Young, learned from her father, Smith's English teacher, Chauncy G. Webb, of Noble's role in Smith's first plural marriage.[10]

9. Apostle Erastus Snow, who had married Beaman's sister, Artemisia, noted that his sister-in-law, Louisa, was "the first woman that entered Plural Marriage in this last dispensation, Br Nobles officiating in a grove near Main Street in the city of Nauvoo, the Prophet di[c]tating the ceremony and Br. Nobles repeating it after him."[11]

10. Almera Johnson, another of Smith's plural wives, spoke of "many conversations with Eliza [Louisa] Beaman who was also a wife of Joseph Smith, and who was present when I was sealed to him ..."[12]

According to later reports, Smith taught celestial marriage to Noble in the fall of 1840 to prepare him to marry Smith to Beaman.[13] Although neither Smith nor Beaman left an account of their marriage, Noble testified in 1892 that he "performed the marriage ceremony giving him [Smith] my wife's sister, ... Louisa Beaman[,] to the Prophet," at a rented house in Nauvoo. Noble said he knew there was a honeymoon "for I saw him in bed with her, ... right straight across the [Mississippi] river [from Iowa] at my house they slept together."[14] No other family member or Nauvoo villager witnessed the ceremony, although those who became aware of this landmark Mormon marital event recorded what they had learned in their own words, and it is those accounts that comprise the above-noted narratives.

The unusual character of Smith's marriage celebrations without

10. Ann Eliza Young, *Wife No. 19, or the Story of a Life in Bondage* (Hartford, Connecticut: Dustin, Gilman & Co., 1875), 72, written after Ann Eliza divorced Brigham.

11. A. Karl Larson and Katharine Miles Larson, eds., *Diary of Charles Lowell Walker*, 2 vols. (Logan: Utah State University, 1980), 610.

12. Almera W. Johnson Smith Barton, Affidavit, Aug. 1, 1883, in Joseph Fielding Smith, *Blood Atonement and the Origin of Plural Marriage: A Discussion* (Salt Lake City: Deseret News Press, 1905), 70–71.

13. Noble, Affidavit, June 26, 1869. "Celestial marriage" seems to have been the preferred term for plural marriage in Nauvoo.

14. Joseph B. Noble, *Temple Lot Deposition, Reorganized Church of Jesus Christ of Latter Day Saints v. Church of Christ of Independence, Missouri, et al.* 60 F. 937 (W. D. Mo. 1894), deposition testimony, electronic copy prepared by Richard D. Ouellette, Temple Lot Case, part 3, 396–7, 427, questions 45, 46, 53, 683; cited in George D. Smith, *Nauvoo Polygamy: "... But We Called It Celestial Marriage"* (Salt Lake City: Signature Books, 2011), 62.

families or wedding parties was eloquently depicted by Smith's twentieth plural wife, Emily Partridge (1824–99), who recorded in her
journal that she also met Smith out of town to marry him in 1843.
She recalled that, after the ceremony, Smith and she walked back
to their own Nauvoo homes alone, each taking separate paths—"A
strange way of getting married, wasn't it?" Partridge later commented,
"but we called it celestial marriage."[15] Over his lifetime, Smith married thirty-eight known women, beginning with Emma.

Soon after the November 6, 1832, birth of Joseph and Emma's
son, Joseph Smith III, rumors arose concerning Fanny Alger, the
teenage daughter of a carpenter near Kirtland, Ohio, who had been
hired to help Emma care for young Joseph III. Some scholars identify Fanny as among Joseph's plural wives. However, I can find no
reliable evidence of a ceremony, and so do not count her as a wife.

Two of Joseph's scribes, Warren Parrish and Oliver Cowdery,
reported that Joseph and Fanny had been "found" in a hay mow
together "as wife" (per Parrish), in a "dirty, nasty, filthy scrape [af-
fair]" (per Cowdery). Parrish later left Joseph's restored church;
Cowdery was expelled.[16] Apostle William McLellin told Joseph
III that Emma had discovered her husband's intimacy with Fanny.
McLellin visited Emma in 1847 (three years after Joseph died)
and related stories he had heard from Kirtland printer Frederick G. Williams with whose Ohio family Emma had stayed.
According to McLellin, one evening Emma had "missed Joseph
and Fanny Alger. She went [out] to the barn and saw him and
Fanny in the barn together alone. She looked through a crack and
saw the transaction!!! She told me this story too was verily true."[17]

---

15. The subtitle to *Nauvoo Polygamy* came from Emily Partridge's March 19
Temple Lot deposition, in which she described how Smith "taught me this principle
of plural marriage that is called polygamy now, but we called it celestial marriage"
(*Reorganized Church v. Church of Christ*, question 18).

16. Donald Q. Cannon, Lyndon W. Cook, eds., *Far West Record: Minutes of the
Church of Jesus Christ of Latter-day Saints, 1830–1844* (Salt Lake City: Deseret Book,
1983), 162–63; Joseph Smith et al., *History of the Church of Jesus Christ of Latter-day
Saints* (Salt Lake City: Deseret Book, 1963), 3:16.

17. William E. McLellin in a July, 1872 letter to the Smith's eldest son, Joseph
III, Community of Christ Archives. A typescript of the entire letter is found in Stan
Larson and Samuel J. Passey, eds., *The William E. McLellin Papers, 1854–1880* (Salt
Lake City: Signature Books, 2007), 488–89.

Benjamin Johnson, one of Joseph Smith's confidants, said that Alger was with Smith for three years [i.e., ca. 1833–35] but that they broke up as Kirtland headed into apostasy in 1837–38. Fanny married Solomon Custer of Dublin City, Indiana, on November 16, 1836, where they raised nine children.[18] Fanny died in 1889 at age seventy-three.[19]

At the time the first reliably documented plural marriage took place, in Nauvoo in 1841, most of Smith's apostles were away on proselytizing missions to England. Shortly after Smith's marriage to Beaman on April 5, 1841, his apostles began to return from their missions. Smith then invited them to join an "inner circle" of polygamists by marrying plural wives of their own. Brigham Young and Heber C. Kimball were among the first to receive such invitations. The "inner circle" ultimately comprised some thirty-two Nauvoo husbands who embraced their prophet's teachings on polygamy during his lifetime. After Smith's 1844 death, as the LDS community prepared to move west in 1846, some 200 polygamous Nauvoo families brought the practice with them.[20]

Nauvoo Polygamy describes how plural marriage first developed during the westward migration of LDS communities; *An Intimate Chronicle* contains an eyewitness account of how Smith initiated the practice while maintaining a household with his first wife and children; and *Brigham Young, Colonizer of the American West* details how he took polygamy westward from the Mississippi River to the Pacific Coast and planted it in the expanding American empire.

Although plural marriage began in secrecy, rumors of the practice brought schism to the Mormons and a revolt in the larger community, which led to Smith's death on June 27, 1844, and the Saints' subsequent expulsion from Illinois. Despite the inner circle's early awareness of the practice, the Saints publicly denied polygamy for nearly a decade after Joseph's death, then boldly announced it to the world in 1852, only to abandon the practice in 1890 under demands by the United States, which the Saints had long sought to join. As polygamy became an embarrassment after

18. Richard Van Wagoner, *Mormon Polygamy*, 15n14.
19. Smith, *Nauvoo Polygamy*, Table 3.2, 224.
20. Smith, *Nauvoo Polygamy*, Appendix B: "Nauvoo Polygamous Families," 573–656.

federal raids and jailings before and during statehood, the LDS Church sought to erase its institutional memory of the controversial social experiment—until 2014 when the church formally acknowledged it. After a quarter century of unofficial published scholarship, the church posted online the essay "Plural Marriage in Kirtland and Nauvoo," thereby officially "acknowledging emerging evidence of a long-denied practice."[21]

The writings of Brigham H. Roberts deal with various questions about LDS history and doctrine, tying together several of the issues raised in the works on polygamy, William Clayton, and Brigham Young. From the vantage point of the early twentieth century, Roberts was a skilled analyst of Mormon history whom LDS Church leaders relied upon for help in fielding questions that baffled even the leaders themselves. Eventually, Roberts collected the most difficult of these inquiries (such as parallels between the Book of Mormon text and earlier stories of American Indians descending from Hebrew migrations) which he used to craft his own inquiry into early Mormonism, and which he referred back to the church leaders for ultimate resolution.

To consider the significance of Nauvoo polygamy, Clayton, Young, and Roberts, let us first examine in more detail Nauvoo polygamy, the practice which once defined—and for many observers still does—the community of Saints.

Nauvoo Polygamy

To see a homily such as "Honesty Is the Best Policy" posted on an LDS chapel bulletin board, one might assume that church headquarters is forthright in telling its story. Hearing contemporary accounts of the "secret" plural marriages that reverberated throughout Nauvoo, in contrast to the public denials that such marriages were happening, understandably raised the curiosity, not only of Nauvoo's citizens during the 1840s, but of later observers who asked how this unusual "marriage practice" took root in Joseph Smith's riverfront town of 10,000–15,000 inhabitants. From the vantage point of the late twentieth century, accounts of

21. Peggy Fletcher Stack, "New Mormon Essay: Joseph Smith Married Teens, Other Men's Wives," *Salt Lake Tribune*, Nov. 14, 2014, 1.

plural marriage had been nearly excised from official LDS history and came to seem more like hostile rumors than an actual historical occurrence.

Indeed, on July 12, 1843, on the third floor of Smith's Red Brick Store in Nauvoo, the Mormon prophet dictated a revelation of what he said were God's words permitting men to marry plural wives without the guilt of adultery:

> Verily thus saith the Lord, unto his servant Joseph ... prepare thy heart to receive and obey the instructions which I am about to give unto you ... I [give] unto thee my servant Joseph, an appointment, and restore al[l] things ... if any man espouse a virgin, and desire to espouse another, ... and they are virgins, and have vowed to no other man, then he is justified; he cannot commit adultery, ... for they are given unto him to multiply and replenish the earth.[22]

This revelation spoken for William Clayton to write was not published for the general membership to read until years later, after Smith's death and after the Latter-day Saints had migrated from Illinois to the Great Salt Lake Valley. Then, the 1843 revelation was printed in the Salt Lake *Deseret News* on September 14, 1852, a month after polygamy was publicly broadcast from the Tabernacle in Salt Lake City, six years after the Saints had escaped an increasingly hostile Nauvoo. Polygamy became an official doctrine of the LDS Church in 1876 when it was published as Section 132 of the church's compilation of founding revelations, the Doctrine and Covenants.

As noted, Smith first took a plural wife in 1841. When Brigham Young returned from the British mission in mid-year, he had hoped to reunite with his family and to father a "homecoming child." Instead, he was met by Smith's request to join him in practicing plural marriage, which entailed courting a second wife. One of the families Young had met in England, the Brothertons, had a daughter, Martha, whom Young sought as his first plural wife. Not only did Brotherton refuse Young's courtship, she recorded her unpleasant experience in an affidavit published in the July 22,

---

22. Smith, *Nauvoo Polygamy*, Appendix A: The 1843 Revelation (excerpts), 567–73.

1842, *Sangamo Journal* in Springfield, Illinois.[23] Undeterred, Young persuaded Lucy Ann Decker Seeley, a twenty-year-old mother of two children who had recently separated from but not divorced a prior husband, to marry Young on June 14, 1842. At the time, Young's civil wife, Mary Ann Angell, was pregnant with their third child. Young's colleague Heber Kimball brought his own plural wife, Sarah Peak (Noon), into his family sometime in that same year (the precise date is not known) and may have even fathered a child (born and died in 1843).

Ironically, just after Young and Kimball joined Smith in the practice of plural marriage, the unusual marital activity was becoming an embarrassment to Smith. Rumors of polygamy gained momentum in 1842 when John C. Bennett, Smith's confidant-turned-critic, published documentation of Nauvoo polygamy in his exposé *History of the Saints.*[24] That fall, Young and Kimball, even as they themselves had just acquired plural wives, were sent on "a preaching mission" in southern Illinois to support Smith's presidential candidacy and reassure citizens that plural marriages were not really happening.[25]

Not all of Smith's congregation of Illinois citizens went along with the practice of plural marriage, and those who did not practice were embarrassed by the publicity. Although the 1843 revelation had not been presented to the Saints as a body, whisperings affirmed that such marriages had indeed been taking place. Smith's inner circle of Nauvoo polygamists had grown to sixteen by that July and would continue expanding until it reached thirty-two members.[26]

With more rumors following the revelation, hearsay only increased. Such rumors became even more embarrassing as Smith sought the nomination to run for US president. To confront the rumors, Smith stood up in a church meeting in May 1844 and issued

---

23. "Miss Brotherton's Statement," July 13, 1842, St. Louis, Missouri.

24. See John C. Bennett, *History of the Saints; or, an Exposé of Joe Smith and Mormonism* (Boston: Leland & Whiting, 1842).

25. Leonard J. Arrington, *Brigham Young: American Moses* (New York: Knopf, 1985), 110.

26. Smith, *Nauvoo Polygamy*, Table 3.4, Joseph Smith's Inner Circle of Nauvoo Polygamists, 240.

a public denial of accusations that he had plural wives, pointing to Emma as his only wife. On that Sunday morning, Smith asserted:

> I had not been married scarcely five minutes, and made one procla-mation of the Gospel, before it was reported that I had seven wives ...

> This spiritual wifeism! Why, a man dares not speak or wink, for fear of being accused of this.

> A man asked me whether the commandment was given that a man may have seven wives; and now the new prophet [William Law, pre-viously Smith's counselor] has charged me with adultery. I never had any fuss with these men until that Female Relief Society brought out the paper [*The Voice of Innocence* from Nauvoo] against adulterers and adulteresses. ...

> What a thing it is for a man to be accused of committing adultery, and having seven wives, when I can only find one. [27]

The *Nauvoo Expositor*, a newspaper published by Smith's critics on June 7, 1844, two weeks after Smith's denial, made public the views of those opposed to Smith's plural marriages. In the *Ex-positor*, William Law, who had previously served as a member of Smith's First Presidency, wrote an editorial announcing "many items of doctrine, as now taught, some of which, however, are taught secretly, and denied openly." Smith responded by calling for the city council, over which he presided as mayor, to destroy the press "without delay." Law recorded on June 10 that, upon returning to Nauvoo, he found "our press had actually [been] de-molished." That same day, Smith was arrested on a complaint that he and seventeen others had "committed a riot" when they "broke into the office of the *Nauvoo Expositor*" and "destroyed the print-ing press." Although the Nauvoo court released him, Smith was arrested again a few days later on June 24, and taken to the jail in nearby Carthage where on June 27 he, joined by his older brother Hyrum, died in a gunfight, while their associate, future church president John Taylor, was wounded and a fourth LDS leader, Willard Richards, escaped unscathed.

---

27. Sunday address reported by Smith's scribe, Thomas Bullock, and recorded on May 26, 1844 (Smith, *History of the Church*, 6:408–11).

An Intimate Chronicle

William Clayton (1814–79) migrated from Britain's Industrial Revolution to become Smith's personal secretary in Nauvoo. Clayton's literate personal journals provide a detailed portrait of Smith and his new church. After serving as a trained record-keeper in English factory towns exporting woven cloth to world markets, Clayton was a trained eyewitness of his prophet's exploits. Clayton not only documented two major migrations from Britain to America and from Illinois to the Salt Lake Valley, he recorded an intimate picture of Nauvoo and the beginnings of plural marriage. In fact, Clayton's record is a contemporary eyewitness account of the new doctrine, including his own practice of polygamy. Smith told Clayton explicitly: "I want you to take care of the records and the papers; and from this time ... when revelations are to be transcribed, you shall write them."[28]

On April 12, 1843, Clayton joined the inner circle of polygamists when he married, with Smith's encouragement, Margaret Moon, his legal wife's sister. Six months later, Margaret became pregnant. So as not to appear to condone an out-of-wedlock pregnancy, Smith responded with a facetious reprimand and told Clayton to "just keep her at home and brook [endure] it and if they raise trouble about it and bring you before me I will give you an awful scourging and probably cut you off from the church and then I will baptize you and set you ahead as good as ever."[29] Three months later, Smith dictated his plural marriage revelation, which Clayton dutifully recorded.[30]

After polygamy rose to public awareness in Utah, Clayton proudly wrote, "I have six wives whom I support in comfort and happiness and am not afraid of another one. I have three children born to me during the year and I don't fear a dozen more."[31]

---

28. George D. Smith, *An Intimate Chronicle: The Journals of William Clayton* (Salt Lake City: Signature Books/Smith Research Associates, 1995), 535–36. A revised and expanded edition is forthcoming as George D. Smith, ed., *William Clayton's Nauvoo Writings*. In addition, the LDS Church has announced plans to publish Clayton's complete Nauvoo journals in the future.

29. Smith, *An Intimate Chronicle*, 122 (Oct. 19, 1843).

30. Smith, *An Intimate Chronicle*, 557–59.

31. Clayton Letterbooks, Nov. 7, 1869 (Smith, *An Intimate Chronicle*, xxvii–xx1x).

Through his lifetime, Clayton married ten women and fathered forty-seven children.[32]

Colonizer of the American West

When Brigham Young (1801–77) and his vanguard arrived in the Great Basin in mid-1847, the year after Sam Brannan reached California by ship, the Latter-day Saints were spread across the country from the Mississippi/Missouri Rivers to the Pacific, as well as, in the succinct words of Bernard DeVoto, "eastward across" much of "America and halfway across Europe." DeVoto concluded that "a history of the Mormons in the West would be … a history of a mad prophet's visions turned by an American genius into the seed of life."[33] Smith and Young, though different in many respects, shared significant common goals. One was a relentless westward orientation, which Smith initiated and Young fulfilled.

Young descended from families of Brighams[34] and Youngs, which had each resided in a once-Catholic England, swept up in Protestant Reformation. The Brighams and Youngs migrated to the New England colonies, where they joined in resistance to the excesses of King George III. (Brigham Young's father volunteered in the Continental Army of the American Revolution.)

The union of these two migrant families was celebrated by naming one of their sons Brigham Young. Born in Vermont soon after the colonies separated from Great Britain as the new American nation formed, Brigham Young stood at the edge of a nascent westward migration. Soon after Young was born, Lewis and Clark (in 1805–1807) explored the rivers and valleys of the western lands acquired in the Louisiana Purchase. Young was born facing westward toward lands to be colonized under a national assertion of "Manifest Destiny."[35]

Joseph Smith initiated his own westward vision, as he was expelled from various settlements and took his acolytes from New

32. Smith, *An Intimate Chronicle*, lxix.

33. Bernard DeVoto, *The Year of Decision: 1846* (Boston: Houghton Mifflin, 1942), 92–101, 469: quoted in Smith, *Nauvoo Polygamy*, 281–82.

34. The surname Brigham referred to a "hamlet by a bridge."

35. The American Constitution was ratified in 1792, Young was born that same decade in 1801.

York and Ohio to Illinois. With eyes on Oregon, California, and Texas, Smith was stopped in his tracks at Nauvoo when the non-LDS citizenry rebelled against plural marriage and other excesses. There, violence against *The Nauvoo Expositor*—coupled with Smith's apparent threatening of neighboring towns by parading an armed cavalry—led to his incarceration and assassination.

Following Illinois Governor Thomas Ford's advice after Smith's death, Young formed an extensive wagon train which he led beyond the Mississippi River, across the Rocky Mountains, and into the Great Salt Lake Valley. On their date of departure, Young had commissioned New York newspaperman Sam Brannan to take the ship *Brooklyn* with 238 passengers south from New York City, then circle around South America, to a stop at the Sandwich Islands (Hawaii), and into the San Francisco Bay, which they reached in mid-1846, a year before Young's wagons arrived in the Great Salt Lake Valley.

To help raise funds for the move west, Young also supplied a Mormon Battalion to join the US army forces and help secure the border with Mexico along the Rio Grande. Young's battalion marched from Council Bluffs through New Mexico and Arizona to San Diego, extending Mormon influence along a large portion of the Pacific Coast, and into Texas. When retired from military duties, Young's army volunteers headed north from San Diego, through the newly-settled Mexican pueblo de la Reina de Los Angeles, and into the Sierra Foothills east of San Francisco, to be present at Sutter's Mill in the Sacramento Valley when gold was discovered in January 1848. Brannan's newspaper, *The California Star*, carried news of the discovery first by Pony Express to New York City and then to Washington, DC, where Brannan's copy was quoted in the State of the Union Address on December 5, 1848, by President James K. Polk. The dissemination of Brannan's article to the nation led to the California Gold Rush in the "Days of '49." Young may never have visited the West Coast, but he built an empire in the Rocky Mountains, its influence extending to the Pacific.

Young's older sister, Fanny, joined in a double wedding with her brother Brigham on November 2, 1843, as Fanny became Joseph Smith's thirty-eighth wife in his last-known plural marriage before his death the following spring. In the same ceremony, Brigham married Harriet Elizabeth Cook and Augusta Adams, his fourth and fifth wives. Young would eventually participate in twenty-seven known marriages that produced fifty-seven children. In addition, he engaged in thirty-one afterlife marriage "sealings" (not forming households, but designated as celestial spouses). Joining his twenty-seven marriages with the thirty-one afterlife sealings, he accumulated a total of fifty-eight wives as his eternal "possessions" in the next world. Young, along with Heber Kimball, also wed most of Smith's polygamous widows, including Smith's first plural wife—Louisa Beaman (on September 19, 1844).

Brigham Young provided a singular rationale that for years defined Mormons to the rest of the world: polygamy as a means of accelerating "the Lord's work," of bringing spirit children from a pre-existent world onto the earth to inhabit "tabernacles" (human bodies) and thus facilitate the plan of eternal life begun with Adam and Eve in the Garden of Eden (Gen. 2:4–3:24). Young also justified polygamy as a civil improvement over prostitution. Plural marriage was not only a moral practice but a way to distinguish Mormons from their (less moral) "gentile" Christian neighbors.

Another of Young's visible legacies was his design of Salt Lake City along horizontal and vertical quadrants across the Great Salt Lake Valley. Wide streets were named as numbers of blocks emanating from the temple in north, south, east, and west directions. An address might be "200 North 400 West," a grid wherein any address could be immediately located. Other Utah towns would be laid out in similar directional grids.

Within the new world that Young pioneered, he established a structure of religious groupings called stakes and wards (like dioceses and parishes) to form an ecclesiastical and social organization within those communities. Social life was encouraged and dances were regularly held in various wards. Theaters and libraries were built to enhance the culture. The Mormon profile that Young sought to establish would have religious, political, and social dimensions, sometimes with unintended consequences. In his diaries and journals, Young mentioned the problems he occasionally encountered with local congregation leaders who might stay out too late at

Saturday night dances, and then find it difficult to attend to their early Sunday morning ecclesiastical responsibilities.

The expression of social life, as well as patterns of eating and drinking, introduces another of Young's unique characteristics: he seemed to have less rigid views of restricting alcohol and tobacco than might be interpreted from Joseph Smith's renowned "Word of Wisdom," the health code Smith included in his published revelations, but which was not a required abstinence until the twentieth century.

While leading wagons across the country, Young sometimes stopped with his men to have coffee. Traveling to "the Warm Spring," they arrived at a local member's residence "where ... [the owner] invited us all to partake of tea or coffee which was very refreshing." A decade later in 1857, Young's journals record traveling with Apostle (and future LDS president) Lorenzo Snow, and having a breakfast of "beef roast & boil tea, coffee, pies &c. All good & plenty of them ..."[36] And although he apparently did not smoke, Young did chew tobacco to alleviate dental discomfort.

The reality of the Word of Wisdom is that it was, for a long time, treated as advice rather than commandment. It was not until US Prohibition in 1919 that Mormons joined that movement in forbidding alcohol in their communities, tying abstinence to Smith's Word of Wisdom. Ironically, LDS leaders included coffee as a forbidden "drink ... not good for the body," a curious restriction for those involved in national Prohibition who had substituted coffee for alcohol. When Prohibition ended by constitutional amendment in 1933, the nation returned to its legal enjoyment of alcoholic beverages. (However, coffee, never banned by prohibitionists, continued to be forbidden for Mormons, first as a "hot drink," then for its caffeine. Eventually, other caffeine drinks such as colas were frowned upon. In fact, until recently, even Coca Cola and other cola drinks had been restricted from the campus of LDS-owned Brigham Young University.[37])

---

36. Brigham Young Journals, Sept. 4, 1849, May 25, 1857, Brigham Young Papers, LDS History Library.

37. See George D. Smith, "Catch-up Wisdom on Coca-Cola as a Hot Drink," *Sunstone*, Spring 2018, 62.

Studies of the Book of Mormon

Brigham Henry Roberts, born in Lancashire, England, in 1857, one of six children of Mormon converts, grew up during Brigham Young's presidency. Later, he was called to become a member of the LDS Church's First Council of the Seventy and in 1922 was appointed president of the church's Eastern States Mission. Prior to that, he was sent to Liverpool, England, to edit the church's *Millennial Star* magazine. In 1887–88, as his studies focused on the origins of the Book of Mormon, Roberts's reputation grew as an articulate "Defender of the Faith." Asked to record and edit the history of Joseph Smith, he published the seven-volume *History of the Church of Jesus Christ of Latter-day Saints* which presented faithful church history as "related by the persons who witnessed them." Questions of doctrinal coherence directed to church apostles were routinely passed on to Roberts to answer. Eventually he focused on commentary about Indian origins that may have influenced the production of the Book of Mormon.

Two of these pre-Book of Mormon works were Ethan Smith's *View of the Hebrews* (1823, 1825) and James Adair's *History of the American Indians* (1775). To defend the Bible as scripture for people in both the eastern and western hemispheres, these authors asserted that the American Indians could have descended from Hebrew tribes that migrated from Jerusalem prior to Babylonian captivity. This view circulated widely and also happened to represent the Book of Mormon's essential thesis.

To defend the ancient historicity of the Book of Mormon, the resourceful Roberts was assigned to deal with critics. However, in 1922, after discovering arguments that he could not fully answer, he compiled a manuscript he entitled "Book of Mormon Difficulties," followed by two others: "A Book of Mormon Study" and "A Parallel," which compared the Book of Mormon to Ethan Smith's *View of the Hebrews*. On December 29, 1921, Roberts wrote to LDS Church President Heber J. Grant and his apostles, advising the men to become familiar with these Book of Mormon "problems." Not quite six years later, on October 24, 1927, Roberts sent to another church official a "parallel between some main outlining facts in the Book of Mormon in a matter published in Ethan Smith's *View of the Hebrews*." Roberts's concerns about Book of Mormon authenticity outlined in this "parallel," an abbreviated version of his longer "A Book of Mormon Study," fascinated Mormon scholars in the 1920s and 1930s.

Roberts's son, Ben E. Roberts, subsequently shared some of his father's findings in "Book of Mormon Study" with attendees at a dinner address in Salt Lake City in 1946. In January 1956, Mervin B. Hogan of the University of Utah faculty drew from Roberts's work to compile eighteen similarities between the Book of Mormon and Ethan Smith's *View of the Hebrews* and recorded them in an article "'A Parallel': A Matter of Chance vs. Coincidence," which appeared in the *Rocky Mountain Mason*, January 1956. Roberts's personal papers, including his Book of Mormon studies, were later acquired by the University of Utah and now reside in the Special Collections Department of the J. Willard Marriott Library.

In 1980, during the first annual Sunstone Symposium, in Salt Lake City, Madison U. Sowell and I discussed some of the questions Roberts raised (see *Sunstone*, May–June 1981; at the time, Sowell taught Italian at Brigham Young University). Soon after, I further addressed Roberts's inquiries in an article: "'Is There No Way to Escape These Difficulties?' The Book of Mormon Studies of B. H. Roberts," which appeared in *Dialogue: A Journal of Mormon Thought* (Summer 1984). Consulting with noted University of Utah philosopher Sterling McMurrin to bring Roberts's writings to publication, I contacted several academic historians to compose an introduction to Roberts's work. Some in the LDS community expressed concern that Roberts's questions could "threaten believers' testimonies" and should not be published. McMurrin suggested inviting a University of Utah colleague, noted Western American historian Brigham D. Madsen, to edit the manuscripts. Madsen agreed, and the University of Illinois Press published the work as *Studies of the Book of Mormon*. Signature Books (est. 1981) released a second edition in what would become an ongoing emphasis on historical publication.

One year after my own exposition of Roberts appeared in *Dialogue*, I was glad to see Roberts's full analysis finally published in book form. In a sense Roberts had given me a voice, as if I had become a co-editor in presenting his concerns for examination.

Roberts brought the inquiry about Joseph Smith's church and its practices into historical analysis. What Smith initiated, Clayton recorded, and Young conveyed to pioneer communities, Roberts redacted into a list of questions and concerns that centered on the Book of Mormon. Roberts brought some of the issues raised by polygamy, Clayton, and Young into focus.

Each of these four chapters of Western American history contributes to the articulation of historical perspective as formulated and remembered.

A Personal Note

Perhaps our interests are conditioned by our roots—our parents, initially, then our community. My mother was a Utah native, delivered into the world by physician and polygamous wife Martha Hughes Cannon (1857–1932) in the decade following the 1890 Manifesto,[38] which ostensibly ended the official practice. Thereafter, many Latter-day Saints were left to wonder about their own history, as institutional forgetting obscured the memory of plural marriage for over a century.

In the decade after the practice was outlawed, my mother's family (which had migrated west from New York in 1869 with the new transcontinental railroad) left Utah for California around the turn of the century, as did many friends in Martha Cannon's family. From Pacific Grove, my mother went to southern California, where she attended Pasadena High School and once rode on a float in the Rose Parade. She and her widowed mother then moved to a boardinghouse in south-central Los Angeles where they met my father's family, who had just arrived from a Nebraska farm community—a land of corn, wheat, and soybeans. Dad's folks were Congregationalist, from England and Scotland—whose

---

38. In 1887 the Edmunds–Tucker Act became law permitting confiscation of LDS Church property in response to bigamy violations. After an 1890 Manifesto, the church rescinded polygamy and President Grover Cleveland signed the Utah statehood bill on January 4, 1896, the year after my mother was born.

Breed ancestors saw the Revolutionary War battles at the Bunker/ Breed hills on the north side of Boston.

This young LDS-Congregationalist couple eloped to Riverside, California, and set up household in Los Angeles. Dad pursued night classes and employment, and then, during the Great Depression, both migrated to New York City, where I was born in 1938. On Sunday mornings, my mother took me to her birth church, as my skeptical father read and worked at home. My view of religion became diversified at the outset.

Along the way, I became an Eagle Scout in an LDS troop, attended early morning LDS seminary classes before high school, ended up a political science major at Stanford, and became interested in the political thought of western civilization. For me, the westward Mormon migration of the LDS Church, though looming large in its own community, appeared as just one interlocking component of western civilization.

As I sought to reason out what struck me as miraculous Mormon origin stories, the "missing gold plates" presented an initial conundrum. Such seemingly incredible LDS accounts were difficult to explain. Parenthetically, we now know that archeology and DNA evidence are not particularly helpful to the church, and, in fact, both tend to contravene the thesis that American Indians are descendants of original Hebrews. By now, the Community of Christ, the branch of Latter-day Saints formed by Joseph Smith's residual family headquartered in Independence, Missouri (as opposed to the Saints Brigham Young took to Utah), considers the book that Smith published to be contemporary nineteenth-century record.[39]

So when I needed to make decisions on future directions— to decide whether that included law, business, family, the army, or perhaps postpone all of these impending alternatives with a two-year LDS proselytizing mission (encouraged by my committed home congregation bishop, who happened to be a direct male descendant of Parley P. Pratt—one of Joseph Smith's inner circle

---

39. What Smith published in March 1830 as "author and proprietor" contains a number of contemporary KJV translation errors, and is not a correct rendition of early biblical texts as was later asserted.

of Nauvoo polygamists)—such decisions were heavily influenced by contemporary events.

A liberal-conservative debate beginning in the late 1950s engulfed the country. In college I took the same "political theory" course twice, first, from one Mulford Sibley, a liberal visiting professor from the University of Minnesota, and, second, from a conservative *National Review* editor, Willmoore Kendall, who gave me a rare A+ and directed me toward a PhD program at the University of Chicago.[40] Such discussions of national politics broadened my focus beyond the accuracy of any particular faith-text.

With Vietnam calling, along with a possible LDS mission, I dealt with both issues by signing up for six months of active duty in the Army Security Agency (communications intelligence), followed by a five-and-a-half-year reserve obligation. My well-connected bishop then pressed for a mission call and made appointments for me to discuss any concerns I might have with two members of the Quorum of Twelve Apostles in Salt Lake City.

One apostle, Richard L. Evans, stressed that I might be seeking "the truth" too seriously—that there may be "more than one road to Rome." He noted that he didn't try to convert his associates at CBS, which for years had broadcast Evans's popular *Music and the Spoken Word* program with the Mormon Tabernacle Choir (now the Tabernacle Choir on Temple Square) each Sunday morning. His message was essentially to focus and go about life.

The second appointment went quite differently. Apostle Gordon B. Hinckley (later church president) dealt with my questions in another way. He suggested that I should not even be asking them. I should return home, study the scriptures, and recognize the vital importance of a lifetime calling to serve the "true" church. (Later, in 1998, then President Hinckley would dissemble on CNN the extent to which Mormons had ever taught or practiced polygamy.[41]) In response to the character of these interviews, my questions about religious presuppositions were affirmed, and

---

40. A Sibley–Kendall debate became a campus political event, like MSNBC vs. Fox News.

41. Larry King interviewed Gordon B. Hinckley on CNN, September 9, 1998; "Hinckley Attacks Polygamy on National TV," *Salt Lake Tribune*, Sept. 9, 1998, A-1.

I grew more curious about the historiography of the Mormon account of its own history, let alone its otherworld mythology.

These contradictory responses from two Mormon leaders prompted me to visit a former college roommate at his proselytizing mission in upstate New York, just south of the "Burned-Over District" where Joseph Smith had reported finding the buried plates of the Book of Mormon in 1827. In 1961, after a graduate semester at UCLA, I showed up that late spring at the official mission residence in Binghamton. My friend's missionary companion's absence allowed me to tract for a day in his place, knocking on doors as we introduced people to a church with uniquely local origins. An encouraging slogan posted at the mission headquarters declared, "It will be done in '61!" After this brief tracting mission, I found the other decisions I faced to be more compelling, and I returned to graduate school, military reserves, and employment. My questions about doctrinal credibility focused on the adaptation of a transient people under stress.

Later on I continued to explore the issues about my mother's faith through participation in journals like *Sunstone*, *Dialogue*, and *Free Inquiry* (a non-LDS secular-humanist journal), attending conferences, submitting papers, and in 1981 helped to co-found Signature Books, which focused on western American history. A major issue facing the LDS Church during the 1970s was its policy of excluding black women and men of African descent from full participation in LDS membership. I wrote and joined in discussions about this issue, including one Sunday evening address in suburban New York City attempting to frame the problem. The presentation was well received by most in attendance, excepting one of the church's professional educators who warned me away from speaking about such controversial subjects, especially at a "Sacrament Meeting."[42]

A few years later, my wife's uncle, LDS Church President Spencer W. Kimball, ended the embarrassing racial exclusion policy with a carefully written statement in 1978 that ignored

---

42. The LDS First Presidency declared officially in 1969: "Negroes [are] not yet to receive the priesthood, for reasons which we believe are known to God, but which He has not made fully known to man."

its nineteenth-century origins but proclaimed the acceptance of "every worthy male member" to full church membership.[43] I remember visiting Kimball in his Salt Lake City home to hear his concerns that colleagues might not accept the proposed change, as past inclusive efforts had been resisted by senior church councils.

One of the other subjects that raised questions for me grew out of collectively dismissing the historicity of Joseph Smith's practice of plural marriage. Clearly a part of LDS history—Smith's wives in Nauvoo were well documented—however, it seemed that almost no one in the twentieth century knew of such events that the church membership had been encouraged to forget.[44] I sought to confirm what began to be published as part of the "rediscovery" of plural marriage, and to locate the names of the participants. When I asked one LDS scholar how many plural wives Smith had, his vague answer suggested a scant "fewer than twenty." The LDS Church had spent nearly a century forgetting what had become a political and social embarrassment and had discouraged inquiry into this aspect of its history.[45]

I launched into a foray through church historical and genealogical libraries, looking up case-by-case the plural families of the most likely subjects: Joseph Smith, Brigham Young, Heber Kimball, Orson Pratt, et al., listing birth, death, and marriage dates, as well as children of each of these families. Those patient librarians who helped me were solicitous but also curious that I must have had so many ancestors among notable past-Mormon leaders. I was surprised eventually to find some 200 polygamous families in Nauvoo who would launch the trek west. Here, I tried to

---

43. At the present time, LDS women of the Ordain Women movement are petitioning for admission to male-attended conferences and leadership offices as held by women in the Community of Christ, headquartered in Independence, Missouri. LDS women have, at least, begun a conversation.

44. A list of Joseph Smith's then-known thirty to forty wives was published by Fawn McKay Brodie, *No Man Knows My History: The Life of Joseph Smith* (New York: Alfred Knopf, 1945; 1971), reviewed by Bernard DeVoto in *The New York Times* as "the first honest and intelligent biography of Joseph Smith." Brodie's uncle, David O. McKay, was LDS Church president, 1951–70.

45. See B. Carmon Hardy, *Solemn Covenant: The Mormon Polygamous Passage* (Urbana: University of Illinois Press, 1992).

answer questions concerning the "forgotten" practice of polygamy and gain a more accurate view of this redacted history.

In like manner, each of the above books I worked on addressed unresolved questions. I sought by these efforts to facilitate a more accurate, nuanced view of forgotten chapters of Mormon frontier experience.

TO HELL IN A HANDBASKET
MY JOURNEY TO FIND THE TRUTH ABOUT THE ANGEL AND THE BRASS PLATES
VICKIE CLEVERLEY SPEEK

12

I was buying materials at a craft store in Burlington, Wisconsin, in the fall of 1992. My last child had entered school full time, and I finally had time during the day to do something fun. I decided to take lessons in basket weaving. It was a trendy thing to do in the 1990s. I loved it, but the materials I needed for one particular basket were hard to find. It was called a handbasket because it had a nice braided handle. I lived in northern Illinois, and the nearest store that sold the material was in Burlington, Wisconsin, about forty-five minutes away. I could leave as soon as my son got on the school bus and still be home before he got there in the afternoon. How could I have known that a side-trip down a country road that day would affect the rest of my life? I just wanted to make a pretty basket.

I carefully followed the road atlas to Burlington. The store was on State Street (Highway 31), at the corner of—Wait! That can't be! Mormon Road? There were no Mormons in Wisconsin—at least none that I knew of—and I figured I ought to know. I am fifth-and-sixth-generation Latter-day Saint on both sides of my family. Some of my ancestors were stubborn Scots and Danes who were disowned by their families when they joined the Church of Jesus Christ of Latter-day Saints. They ventured across the Atlantic Ocean in rickety ships and walked alongside covered wagons across the American plains. Brigham Young called my great-grandfather, Jesse Cleverley, to help settle a Mormon colony in southeast Idaho. Charles Cleverley, my grandfather, and his brothers and cousins helped build the LDS Church's Idaho

Falls temple. I was born in nearby Shelley, Idaho, attended schools in Idaho Falls where the student body was probably 80 percent Mormon, and graduated from high school with four years of released-time seminary. I even attended a year at Ricks College in Rexburg (now BYU-Idaho) on two small church scholarships. Granted, I did marry a non-Mormon when I was nineteen, but I insisted he take missionary lessons. Bob Speek was baptized two weeks after our wedding. I was Mormon, through and through! I even had a convert to prove it.

My new husband was in the US Navy, and we were soon transferred to Groton, Connecticut, where he was stationed on a fast-attack nuclear submarine. New England was nearly 3,000 miles away from Idaho Falls, and Bob was gone to sea almost all the time. I was so homesick. Long distance phone calls were very expensive back in those days. We couldn't afford for me to call my mom and dad more than once a month. So, the Groton Ward of the LDS Church became my substitute family.

The ward was full of young married women my age who also had husbands in the navy. Those women became my sisters. Their little children became my nieces and nephews, cousins to my own two babies. The older ladies in Relief Society became my mother. My home teachers became my dad. These people taught me the life skills I had not yet learned, like how to bake a turkey for Thanksgiving, how to take care of two babies with chicken pox, and how to drive over the big scary bridge on the Thames River that joined together Groton and New London. Along the way, I learned even more about my religion, and developed a deep faith that the church was true.

After five years in Connecticut, Bob and I moved to Monroe, Michigan, where he started work at a civilian nuclear power plant. We had two more children before moving to Gurnee, Illinois. In 1993, at the age of thirty-nine, I was called to be the ward relief society president with stewardship over more than a hundred women. Bob was assistant to the bishop. This was our physical and religious status when my faith in my religion started going to hell in a handbasket.

———

Mormon Road. Mormon Road. Why do they call it Mormon Road? I was compelled to drive down that quiet country road. Giant oak trees provided shade on either side, contented cows munched grass, and an abandoned graveyard lay in a pasture with no headstones. A monument stood beside a giant evergreen tree that announced this meadow was the old Voree cemetery where a few followers of James Jesse Strang had been buried from 1844 to 1850. Later, I discovered Strang himself had been buried there. A farmer built his barn over the site, so he could walk over James Strang's grave every time he milked his cows. I guess he didn't like Strang very much. Now, Strang is buried in a cemetery across town. Strangers paid for his reburial and headstone.

The monument at Voree cemetery mentioned a sacred place nearby called the Hill of Promise. That's where James Strang reportedly was anointed by an angel and dug up a set of brass plates buried under a tree. The plates were written in an unknown language that recorded the last battle of an ancient people who fought at that site and died to the last man. Strang supposedly translated those brass plates. Holy Shades of Joseph Smith! I had never heard of such a thing in my life.

A little farther down the road stood an old Mormon house, an old church, and the little stone house where a sign said Strang died on July 9, 1856. The White River where the Strangites conducted baptisms for the dead ran parallel to Mormon Road. I was dumb-founded but intrigued. Who was James Jesse Strang and who were these people who lived in Voree more than a hundred years ago? Why didn't they go to Utah with Brigham Young? And why hadn't I heard about them before?

I did what I always did when I needed answers. I went to the public library. (Nowadays, I go to my computer and look on the Internet, but there was no Internet for regular people in 1992, and I didn't have a computer. I certainly didn't know how to use one.) There were lots of books at the Burlington Library about James Strang, including hardbound copies of the newspapers the Strangites printed from 1846 to 1856. I went home and checked out a biography of Strang from my local library. It was published in 1897 by Henry Legler. Then I checked out a 1930 Strang biography by Milo Quaife. I stopped making baskets and started spending as many hours as I could each week reading the old newspapers and pamphlets in the Burlington Library. Then I would go home and research some more.

I soon learned about the succession crisis that occurred after the death of Joseph Smith in 1844, and how up to 3,000 Mormons traveled to Voree (Burlington), Wisconsin, to be with Strang, instead of moving with Brigham Young to Salt Lake City. Why? I thought it must be because the people were weak in their faith. It would have been far easier for them to move 300 miles north to Wisconsin, than to traipse 1,200 miles over the Great Plains and Rocky Mountains.

After six years in Voree, most of the Strangites moved to Beaver Island, a remote island in the middle of northern Lake Michigan, inhabited seasonally by a few fishermen. It was there on July 8, 1850, that Strang was crowned King of Beaver Island, the only king ever to be (publicly) crowned in the United States.

The Strangites struggled to make their homes on the island, but they were not the only people who wanted it. Beaver Island was in the center of the lucrative fishing industry. It was also heavily timbered. Steamships running the Great Lakes burned vast amounts of wood in their journeys from Buffalo, Cleveland, and Detroit to Green Bay, Milwaukee, and Chicago. Beaver Island also had a protected, deep-water harbor.

Certain people were willing to do anything to keep those natural resources away from the Mormons. They succeeded. Six years of conflict between the Strangites and the so-called gentiles (anyone who was not a Mormon) ended in the murder of James Strang and the forced exile of over a thousand men, women, and children. Those people were loaded like cattle on to ships bound for differing destinations and unloaded, friendless and penniless, onto wooden wharfs with no place to go.

I read about the Strangites and wanted to know more of their stories. Especially the women. The history of women is usually told through their husbands and fathers. But what if their husbands and fathers were dead? I have always been interested in genealogy (part of my Mormon upbringing, I suppose), and I knew about PERSI, the Periodical Source Index System that lists articles in genealogical and historical journals from all over the United States. The nearest PERSI repository was at the Wisconsin State Historical Society Library in Madison, a couple of hours away. It was a huge library. They also had the articles listed in PERSI. Within a month, Bob and I were in Madison feeding books to the copy machine. Ten cents a page. Fifty dollars and a stack of photocopies later, we were on our way home, and I had become an official James Strang junkie. Seduced by a would-be prophet whom, I was convinced, was a total charlatan.

It sounds so absurd now, and I'm quite ashamed to admit this, but I had a plan in mind. I wanted to get the youth in my LDS stake to make a trip to the temple. I would compile the names and data of the Strangites, and the kids could do the baptisms for the dead. After all, I was sure the Strangites wanted to be members of the true church—they just got confused along the way. God in his wisdom must have sent me down Mormon Road so I could set things straight.

For the next ten years I researched in as many places as I could—Madison; Beaver Island; the Michigan State Library in Lansing; Central Michigan University in Mount Pleasant; the Jackson County Historical Society in Wisconsin; the Chicago Historical Library; Brigham Young University; the LDS Church Archives; the Community of Christ Church Archives—all the while accumulating as much data as I could. I even purchased a microfilm from Beinecke Library at Yale University. It contains images of more than 600 letters written to and from James Strang. I used the microfilm reader and printer at my local library to make paper copies. Ten cents a copy at every library, and I made thousands of copies. I also immersed myself into the early history of Joseph Smith and the Mormons in New York, Ohio, Missouri, and Illinois as background for the Strangites.

On one of my research trips to Black River Falls, Wisconsin, I was thinking about Strang's five wives and what happened to them after Strang died. Four of those women were pregnant when he was murdered. I was fascinated with Strang's first plural wife, nineteen-year-old Elvira Field who ran away from home, cut her hair, put on a man's suit, and traveled with Strang as his sixteen-year-old nephew Charles Douglass. Then there was the old maid, Betsy McNutt, who bragged that the only man she would ever marry was the prophet himself, and the teenaged cousins Sarah and Phoebe Wright. What about Strang's first wife? How did she feel about the church her husband had started? How did she feel about him taking additional wives—all of them much younger than she? What happened to those women and their children after they were forced off Beaver Island? Where did they go? How did they survive? Did any of their descendants stay in the church?

I had been asked to write an article about Strang's five wives for the Beaver Island Historical Society, and I was mulling over my approach. Suddenly, right there, on Interstate 90 near Tomah, I had an epiphany. The wives didn't join the Strangites on their own. Every one of them joined the Strangite Mormons with their parents, their brothers and sisters, their aunts and uncles, and cousins. The article I wanted to write wasn't about just the wives, it was the story of the Strangites themselves. It should be a book and each wife needed her own chapter. The book would have two parts. Part one would tell the story about James Strang and the Strangites up to their forced removal from Beaver Island. Part two would tell their story from the exile to the modern day church in Burlington. Nobody had ever told that part before.

The University of Illinois, in my home state, had recently published a number of respected books about Mormon history. I sent a book query and manuscript, but they already had a book about Strang. I sent my proposal to Signature Books in Salt Lake City and waited.

In 2003, I presented a paper about Elvira Field at the John Whitmer Historical Association Conference (which tends to focus on topics of interest to the Community of Christ, previously the Reorganized Church of Jesus Christ of Latter Day Saints) in Missouri. That was such an amazing conference! So many experts in Mormon history were there—Mike Quinn, Jan Shipps, Will Bagley, Todd Compton and his girlfriend (now wife) Laura Hansen, Mike Marquart, Bill Shepard, and my new friend John Hamer. I was surrounded by excellence. It is a cliché, but I felt I had died and gone to heaven!

Historian Newell Bringhurst sat in the front row during my presentation. Afterward, he asked me if I had plans to write a book. "Yes," I said, "I submitted a query to Signature Books, but they haven't responded to me." "I have some friends over there. I'll call them as soon as I get home," he said. Three days later, Gary Bergera from Signature Books called me. "Newell Bringhurst says we need to publish your book," he said. Signature turned out to be a perfect venue for my book. I had thought of them earlier but didn't think my manuscript was of good enough quality for them. I was thrilled!

Now that I had a publisher, I had to get down to business and make sure the book was finished. The previous year I had met Strangite Bill Shepard at a John Whitmer Historical Association conference in Nauvoo, Illinois. He invited me to go to lunch with him and his friends. Eight of us sat around a table in a little sandwich shop in downtown Nauvoo. Four Strangites, two LDS, an RLDS (Community of Christ) member, and an Episcopalian (former LDS). It was one of the most interesting lunch hours I had ever spent. We sat around discussing Mormon history and what we were all researching. No arguments, no jealousy. Just friendship and respect.

Bill invited me to come to his home in Burlington to look over his files. I was there bright and early the following Saturday. That was when Bill became my mentor. He helped me copy the files I wanted, and, more importantly, he taught me how to use civility and kindness when dealing with Mormon historians. "I always share my materials," he said. "Then, other people share with me. We have a good dialogue. It's none of this, 'I won't share with you because I want to be first.' We talk it out together. If I have a question, I'll ask them. And if they have a question, they'll ask me."

Bill and his wife, Diana, have hosted scores of people over the years, from researchers searching for information about James Strang, William Smith (Joseph Smith's younger, more erratic brother), or Nauvoo, to seekers looking for answers to their questions about the Strangite religion. All are welcome at Bill's house and he usually throws in a tour of Voree. As he did with me.

We drove down Mormon Road to the pasture, through the gate, past the cows, and across the grass to the edge of the quarry where the Strangites obtained the stone in the late 1840s for their Tower of Strength. The tower was never completed, and the quarry is now filled with water. Then, Bill parked the car, and we walked up a hill to the Strangite version of the Sacred Grove. On this gentle, shady Hill of Promise, on the evening of June 27, 1844, Strang said an angel anointed him to be a prophet. A few feet away, I saw the dugout remains of a crude home that had been built in Voree's heyday. And there was the spot where Strang found a clay case containing the metal records of an ancient people.

It was a sacred space, an area for reflection. I picked up a couple of feathers lost from some wild turkeys that flock in that place and considered that small clay box. That box and those little records were a big deal to me. I had spent so many hours reading about the Hill of Promise, how Strang received a revelation to go to that spot in the woods to find ancient metal plates. An angel showed him in a vision where to dig and gave Strang a urim and thummim to translate them.

Strang asked four of the most honest and respected men in the community to go with him and bring their shovels. He disclosed his vision and told the men they would find a case of rude earthenware buried under an oak tree at a depth of about three feet. The tree had a diameter of about one foot and was surrounded with deeply rooted grass. The men carefully dug up the tree, then dug down through the undisturbed grass and inter-twined tree roots to find a flat rock about one foot wide and three inches thick. Under that rock lay a rough clay box. Inside were three small plates of brass scratched on all six sides with strange writing and drawings. They measured about 2½ inches long by 1½ inches wide and were the thickness of tin. Strang took the plates home and translated them with the aid of his urim and thummim. The four men signed a document attesting to what had happened. A week later, Strang displayed the plates and gave a translation. People from all over the area held the plates in their own hands and examined them.

For years I could not understand how so many people could have been duped by such a false prophet as James Strang. I felt my own testimony of the LDS Church had been enhanced by my re-search, but the story of the angel and the brass plates confounded me. How did Strang fake the plates and plant them under the tree? I spent hours thinking about it, trying to figure it out, but, in the end, I scoffed. Joseph Smith had been a teenager when he first saw the Angel Moroni and the golden plates on the Hill Cumorah. He was an uneducated boy who translated the plates into the Book of Mormon and started the one and only true church, the Church of Jesus Christ of Latter-day Saints. James Strang was a brilliant lawyer. If Strang was trying to copy Joseph Smith, which he most certainly was, I thought, he definitely could have done better than the little bitty brass plates of what Strang dubbed *The Record of the Raja Manchou of Vorito*. Oh, I was so arrogant!

Before our trip to the Hill of Promise, Bill Shepard had taken me to visit the Strangite church near his home. He opened the front door, and there, on the foyer wall, hung two large portraits. One was of Joseph Smith; the other was of James J. Strang. The portraits shocked me. Holy Smoke! These people really believe this stuff! They really think Strang was a prophet! Suddenly, James Strang became a real person to me, not a character in a history book. His followers, both past and present, unexpectedly became real, too. Those people who left Nauvoo and went to Voree weren't weak in their faith. They truly thought Strang was a prophet of God, just like the members who attended this church. I didn't know what to think.

As I stood on the Hill of Promise, I silently pondered for the hundredth time. Were the brass plates real? Ordinary people saw them with mortal eyes, not their spiritual ones. They held those plates in their hands. The signed witness statements said the men had to dig up the tree and dig the soil out around the intertwined tree roots. The ground under the box was so hard it had to be chopped out with a pick ax. How did the brass plates get there? Either the brass plates were real and Strang was a prophet, or the plates were a fake and Strang was a fraud. It was one or the other. But which one was it?

Strang was thirty-one years old in January 1844 when he traveled to Nauvoo to meet Joseph Smith. Some of Strang's relatives were Mormon, and he wanted to know more about the religion. James Strang discussed the church with Joseph Smith. At least once, they conversed while eating dinner at Emma's table. Smith baptized Strang in the basement of the uncompleted Nauvoo temple on February 25. On March 3, Hyrum Smith ordained Strang to be an elder in the priesthood.

Strang was an astute, observant, intelligent man. He saw the power Smith held. He knew people were secretly married in polygamy. He personally saw the increasing tensions between the differing cliques of people in the town. He would have been aware of the secretive Council of Fifty (or political Kingdom of God), because Joseph Smith asked Strang to scout for a place in Wisconsin where the Saints could eventually gather if the decision was made to vacate Nauvoo.

Strang returned to his home in Spring Prairie, outside of Burlington, and took stock of the available land. He owned a large amount of property there with his wife, Mary Perce. He wrote to Joseph Smith in May telling him that Wisconsin would be a favorable place for an immigration of Saints and asked for further instructions. Then he waited for an answer.

On June 27, 1844, Joseph Smith and his brother Hyrum, awaiting trial in Carthage Jail, were killed by a mob. According to Strang, the news of the deaths reached Burlington on July 9, the same day he received a letter in the mail from Joseph Smith, apparently in answer to his letter about the property in Wisconsin. Postmarked at Nauvoo on June 19, the so-named Letter of Appointment instructed Strang that if anything happened to him (Smith), he (Strang) was to be the new leader of the church. Strang could not have been surprised by the letter, of course, because at 5:30 p.m. on June 27, the exact time of Smith's death, an angel appeared to Strang on the Hill of Promise. The angel put his hands on Strang's head and anointed him with oil to be Smith's successor.

Over the next six years, hundreds, if not thousands, of Mormons joined Strang in Wisconsin. Four years later, most of the Strangites moved to Beaver Island. The church Strang organized, which still exists today, is called the Church of Jesus Christ of Latter Day Saints (capital D in Day, no hyphen).

Personally, I believe Strang set up his claim to the succession by imitating Joseph Smith in nearly every way possible. In addition to his visit from the angel, Strang sent out missionaries, prepared to build a temple, performed baptisms for the dead, and set up a communal organization called the Order of Enoch. He called Smith's former supporters to be his leaders—John E. Page as apostle, William Smith as church patriarch, William Marks as bishop of Voree, and others. In 1850, he had himself crowned as King of Beaver Island in preparation for the second coming of Jesus Christ, just as Smith was named king by the Council of Fifty in March 1844.

And there were those darned metal records! The first set was dug from the Hill of Promise, and a second later set, called the Brass Plates of Laban, was translated into a book of sacred scripture called the *Book of the Law of the Lord*. How did Strang make, plant, and translate those darn brass plates?

In the summer of 2005, I drove out west to see my family and to finish up a few items of research. I was excited to talk about my upcoming book with my uncle Dave. Only about ten years older, Dave and I were more friends than relatives. He was the person I wanted to be—successful in all three aspects of his life: family, career, and religion. His wife was in the stake relief society presidency, his kids were all married in the temple, and his son had served a proselytizing mission in South America. A former member of his stake high council, Uncle Dave had a tremendous knowledge of the church and its inner workings. He and I shared an intense love of Mormon history and often exchanged books and articles.

Uncle Dave asked the same question he always did when I came to visit or talked to him on the telephone. "So, Vickie, do you still think the church is true?" I usually responded, "Of course, I do! Why do you ask?" "Just checking," he always answered.

During this visit we talked about James Strang and Joseph Smith. I told him about my idea of having a group of youth from my stake do baptisms for the dead for the Strangites, so they could become members of the Utah-based Church of Jesus Christ of Latter-day Saints (hyphen, small d). After all, they were seeking for the true church. I thought they would have wanted it that way.

I asked Uncle Dave what he thought of my idea. Instead of supporting me, he listened thoughtfully and replied, "Did you ever read that book I told you about—*An Insider's View of Mormon Origins*, by Grant Palmer?" I promised to read it. "Give me a call when you're done," he said. "Then we'll talk."

Before I left Idaho, I stopped at the Deseret Book store and asked for a copy of Palmer's book. They didn't have it. The clerk said they wouldn't be getting any in. "The brethren have banned it," she said without explanation. When I got back to Illinois, I immediately ordered it from Amazon and waited impatiently to see what the controversy was all about. The label "banned" has always made me want something, even when I didn't want it in the first place.

The introduction to the book was intriguing. Palmer wrote, "I, along with colleagues, and drawing from years of research, find the evidence employed to support many traditional claims about the church to be either nonexistent or problematic. In other words, it didn't all happen the way we've been told."

At first, I didn't see what the big fuss was about. Palmer presented evidence that Joseph Smith was a treasure hunter and that he translated the Book of Mormon from a seer stone placed at the bottom of his hat. That was nothing new. I figured everybody knew that. The Book of Abraham was an ordinary Egyptian funeral document—nothing new about that either. The same was true for the other sections of Palmer's book: multiple accounts of the First Vision; different testimonies from Book of Mormon witnesses than we use in church today; different accounts of the restoration of the priesthood; comparisons of the Book of Mormon to evangelical camp meetings and early-nineteenth century literature; and segments from the King James version of the Bible (with known errors in translation) repeated in the Book of Mormon.

Palmer didn't write anything new, he simply compiled controversial topics together in one volume. But, for some reason, seeing the material grouped together really shook me up. It was like I had been looking all these years at individual puzzle pieces, and then I finally fit them together. The finished picture looked like nothing I recognized. I was uncomfortable with what I saw. I started questioning my beliefs.

At the same time, I was finishing the research on my book manuscript. I made a second visit to the Community of Christ archives in Independence, Missouri, where I found a file I had previously skipped. Inside was a letter from a former Strangite to the RLDS newspaper *The Saints' Herald* stating that Strang made the brass plates of Vorito from Uncle Ben's old brass kettle and that he used an auger to bury them inside the hill. I recalled that Strang and his wife, Mary, had lived for a time in Spring Prairie with her uncle, Benjamin Perce. I'm sure Uncle Ben had an old brass kettle.

I found a corroborating manuscript about one of the apostles on Beaver Island who was doing repair work to Strang's house and found, hidden in the attic, the brass remains of the plates of Laban. Samuel Bacon then gathered up his family and possessions and left the island. One of Strang's rules was if you left the church, you had to leave your possessions behind, so Bacon left as rapidly and discreetly as he could. Another letter spoke of a Strangite, Samuel Graham, who helped Strang make the plates on Beaver Island.

I felt I finally knew the secret of the angel and the brass plates—the answer to the questions that had plagued me for so long. I also knew the answer to the questions that had bothered me since I had read Palmer's book. Everything that happened to Joseph Smith happened to Strang. Everything Smith did and said, Strang did and said. The evidence was crystal clear. Strang was a charlatan. But was Smith the original fraud? Did both men start their religious quests with deceit, not intending for it to go very far, but quickly became wrapped up in their own narratives, and couldn't stop? Did they start to believe they truly were God's prophets and died as martyrs to their cause? Is that why neither man named a successor before they died? Both churches were left in a succession mess.

I wanted to throw up. I couldn't sleep that night, or the following night, or the next. The differing versions of Mormon history I had previously thought unimportant had now become vital. I went to the library and picked out some of the books I had not yet had time to read. I learned about the lack of Hebrew DNA in the American Indians proving they are not descended from the Lamanites. There was the similarity of the LDS temple ceremony to Masonic ritual, the fragments of papyrus found in a museum that proves the Book of Abraham is an ordinary Egyptian funeral document, and the number of young girls and the married women who participated with Joseph Smith in polygamy. The clincher came when I learned that Smith's "golden plates," as described by witnesses, would have weighed 400 pounds if truly made of gold. That's far too heavy for anyone to carry. But plates made from tin would have weighed forty pounds, the exact weight witnesses described.

Just like that, as suddenly as I had experienced the epiphany on the road about writing a book, my faith was gone. I was always taught the Book of Mormon was the keystone of the church. Without it, there was nothing. It now appeared to me that Joseph wrote the Book of Mormon, which meant there was no keystone. The structure of my world collapsed, and there was no bottom. I prayed. I cried inconsolably. Then I prayed again.

I called Uncle Dave. "So, Vickie, do you still think the church is true?" I answered, "Why didn't you tell me?"

"It's something you had to figure out by yourself," he replied. "I've had my doubts for a long time."

"But I thought you were strong in the church."

"I was. And as far as my friends and ward members know, I still am. This is Idaho, Vickie. You can't live here and not be a Mormon. If people knew I was no longer a believer, they would stop coming to my business. They would ostracize my family. I don't care if they do that to me, but my wife really loves the church."

"So, that's why you always ask people if they still think the church is true," I replied in sudden clarity. "You're speaking in code, trying to find other people who are doubters."

"That's right," he answered. "People in the church are funny. They don't trust you if you don't believe the same way they do."

"You know what bothers me the most?" Uncle Dave added. "Mormons worship Joseph Smith. They care more about him than Jesus Christ. If you don't believe me, go to church next Sunday and count how many times the name of Joseph Smith comes up and how many times the name of Jesus Christ comes up. They don't even realize they're doing it."

Even after talking with Uncle Dave, I still held out a small ray of hope. For weeks I recited a mantra in my head, thinking if I repeated it enough times the words would be self-fulfilling: "The church is true. The church is true. The church is true." Surely the Lord would ease my fears, show me that my suspicions were wrong. "Heavenly Father," I pleaded. "Please tell me the church is true." He didn't answer.

The Sunday after I spoke with Uncle Dave, I went to church. During sacrament meeting, Joseph Smith was named over fifty times, Jesus Christ twenty-three. I was a counselor in the young women's organization. Our lesson that day told the story of Smith's beloved first wife, Emma. It encouraged the young women to be faithful to the prophet, so they could be "elect ladies" like her. There was no mention of Smith's thirty-plus other wives. At the end of the meeting, I went to the young women's president and told her I was really busy, and I needed to be released from my calling immediately. I went out the door of the church and didn't go back.

That night I got so sick, I thought I was dying. I figured I must have appendicitis, cancer, the flu, or some other awful disease. I couldn't function the next day at work. I cried all the time at home. Severe depression, the doctor told me and put me on medication. I constantly had one thought on my mind: "What if I'm wrong? What if I'm wrong?"

"Do you think you're wrong?" my dear husband asked me.

"No," I answered. "But what if I am? You just don't understand. The church is my life. The church is everything to me. The church made me who I am. If I don't believe in this church, I won't get to be with you when we die. We won't have an eternal family!"

I wish I could say I had a dream, a vision that set me straight, but I didn't. A thought gradually took hold in my mind and led me to peace. The Lord did answer my prayer. It was not the reply I expected to hear. God didn't tell me the LDS Church was true, he simply whispered in my ear, "You are my daughter, and I love you just the way you are." That was all.

Leaving the church was by far the hardest thing I have ever done. I loved the church. I believed it totally. I never, ever, thought I would be the one to leave. I was a former relief society president. I accepted every calling I was ever given. I supported my daughter on her mission. I held my family to the church standards. Then one day, my faith was gone. It was shattered into a million pieces. I felt as though I had lost my soul.

My husband and my youngest son accompanied me out of the church. When we left, everyone assumed we had been offended by someone or something. We must have committed a grave sin. The truth is we simply stopped believing. In most ways, we are still the same people we always were. We live the same way we have always lived—we just don't go to church anymore. I don't drink. I don't smoke. I've have developed a taste for coffee, but it's for medicinal reasons, of course.

For a long time, I felt angry towards the church. I felt lied to. I felt betrayed. I lost my social life because I didn't have any friends outside of the church. But to be fair, the members didn't know how to act around me. I was different, changed. They didn't know what to say, because I became antagonistic anytime the church was mentioned. In my own self-inflicted mental turmoil, I wasn't very nice to them.

It took a long time, but the bitterness and anger I felt gradually went away. If I were to walk into my old ward building tomorrow, I know I would be wrapped into the arms of the people who still love me. They would shed tears of joy at my return. Mormons are my people, my tribe, my kin. I dearly love them. I respect their decisions to stay in the church.

On November 5, 2015, the prophet of the LDS Church announced that the children of parents who were gay or lesbian would not be allowed to be blessed, or baptized, or ordained to the priesthood until they were eighteen years old. In addition to being eighteen, they must renounce the parent who was gay or lesbian and not live in the same house with them. I cannot believe God would reveal such a hurtful thing. I decided the time was right for me to have my name removed from the records of the church. I am no longer a member. I have officially gone to hell in a handbasket of my own making. On April 4, 2019, the church reversed this ruling, but the damage had already been done.

I still have a great love of Mormon history. I respect and love my friends and relatives who are still strong in the faith. I admire the Strangites in Voree who have kept their church alive for so many years. Losing your faith is a hard thing to go through, although, at the same time, it has been intensely freeing for me. Religion is a good thing whether the name of the church has a hyphen and a small letter d, or a space and a capital D. Latter Day or Latter-day. If it works for you, stay with it.

I went back to Burlington a few weeks ago to visit my Strangite friend and history mentor Bill Shepard. The building at State Street and Mormon Road is still there, but it no longer sells craft supplies. It's just as well, nobody makes baskets anymore. I haven't made baskets for years, not since the time I drove down Mormon Road and became seduced by the story of James Strang. Would I write that book if I had it to do over again, knowing it would change my life? Yes, I would.

I think about the Mormons in Nauvoo who lost their leader, Joseph Smith. How devastated they must have been. They sought another prophet to follow. Some joined with James Strang, some with Sidney Rigdon, Alpheus Cutler, or Lyman Wight. Many took the path to the west with Brigham Young. Many chose to wait for the son of Joseph Smith to grow up. Joseph Smith III became the leader of the Reorganized Church of Jesus Christ of Latter Day Saints. Still others decided to stay where they were and to follow nobody. All these people sacrificed for their religious beliefs.

Some devout people in the LDS church might say I've shamed my own pioneer ancestors by renouncing the church they sacrificed everything for. Rather, I think I am a pioneer myself, setting a new path for my descendants to follow. I am the weaver of my own destiny. I am a daughter of God, and he loves me just the way I am.

13

AN ACCIDENTAL CHURCH HISTORIAN
ON THE TRAIL OF A BOOK OF JOSEPH
SUSAN STAKER

When I can smell a controversy brewing and put up my guards,
When I can spot a phony Salamander at a hundred yards,
When I am granted access to the archives of the DUP,
Then I'll deserve a pardon and an honorary PhD.
When I learn that I need much more than a scholar's normal bag of tricks,
Especially a healthy grasp of bureaucratic politics,
In matters economical, political, folklorian,
I'll be the very model of a modern Church Historian.[1]

I am an accidental church historian.[2] Growing up, I imagined myself an English teacher, and a mother. After all, I grew up a Mormon girl in southeastern Idaho, Mormon country, during the 1950s and 1960s. Looking back, I understand that my mother and her sister and the female teachers I admired in a tiny Idaho village set me on this path. My mother and her sister were a rare breed in their place and time. Both went away to college right out of high school and worked while their children were small. Those women licensed a path for my life: a Mormon mother could remain a student and a worker, a professional.

---

1. During the annual Sunstone Theological Symposium in 2018 (after the death of her husband Paul), Lavina Fielding Anderson read the words to a song, set to the music of Gilbert and Sullivan's "I Am the Very Model of a Modern Major General," written for past LDS Church Historian Leonard J. Arrington by Jill Mulvay and Paul, as part of a panel celebrating the recent publication of Arrington's diaries.

2. I was thinking of Anne Tyler's 1985 novel, *The Accidental Tourist*, later made into a movie, when I landed on this phrase. I googled "accidental historian" today and found that I am not the first to think of this title.

By my early twenties, I had achieved my childhood goal. I graduated with honors and a teaching degree in English from Brigham Young University. I married as I left my first graduate year and landed a job teaching English at a junior high school near Seattle, where my husband studied at the University of Washington. I lasted four months and knew immediately that I was mistaken about my calling as teacher of English to the young.

My passion, it turns out, was not so much English and teaching as narrative and stories. I was nearing fourteen when I encountered the big novel, and since then the enduring theme of my life with its spooling thread of careers and enthusiasms has been reading novels. I read *Lady Chatterley's Lover* in the tenth grade and vowed no one would ever censor what I read. This is one vow I've kept.

My heathen reading was rather miraculous because by ninth grade I'd also found Mormon religion of a conservative, even fundamentalist, brand through a charismatic seminary teacher, Brother Foster, my mentor well into my years at BYU.[3] In his wake, I framed myself into a rather unforgiving version of Mormonism. But Brother Foster also introduced me to an extravagant and dangerous version of Joseph Smith, very unlike the drab character from my Idaho Mormon Sunday school classes. This charged glimpse of pain and ecstasy remains the lasting gift of my teacher.

I like to think that reading novels saved my life. Certainly novels expanded my view on a world I made straight and narrow. Loving novels and refusing to censor my reading eventually led me to Mormon history and later to graduate school. In my retirement years, I sit at my desk as a reader and interpreter of stories and an "independent scholar" of Joseph Smith's Bible stories, my investigation of the profoundly narrative economy of Joseph's religious imagination I am calling A Book of Joseph.[4] I will now

---

3. I presented a remembrance of Brother Foster at Seattle's Sunstone Symposium in the fall of 2015. Links to this presentation and others I mention in this essay are posted at susanstaker.academia.edu.

4. A Book of Joseph for many reasons. I focus on Joseph Smith's textual history, hence "book." A Book of Joseph of Egypt is read by Lehi to his sons and includes the choice seer prophecy, comparing Joseph, son of Joseph, to Moses. Joseph describes a Book of Joseph with the Book of Abraham amongst the Egyptian artifacts, a book he never translates. Joseph's shadowing seer characters within his textual chronology dramatize scripts for Joseph's life and that of his community, beginning with a Book

indulge in something of a picaresque tale of an accidental historian. I'm hoping the details accumulate into a useful retrospect on my still in-progress book and my notion of how to engage the project of "history."

Finding History

My young husband introduced me to Mormon history, to his eventual chagrin. I decided to apply my "novel" rule to Mormon history. A transforming decision as it turned out. No censorship. Truth wins out. Such reading loosed me from the bands my religion, set early by the mentor I loved and couldn't follow, had become.

In the late 1970s my husband landed a job working for the

---

of Mormon. Always then a Book of Joseph. I generally use first names (Joseph) rather than last names (Smith), the more "scholarly" convention. At least two reasons. The God voice–my term for the revelations' narrator–uses first names in Joseph's early revelations, and the convention is followed in other early documents Joseph dictates. Also the use of first names accentuates the parallel between nineteenth-century characters and biblical characters.

Mormon church within the burgeoning realm of arts and history.[5] This was the time imagined in retrospect as a Camelot—Leonard Arrington, Davis Bitton, a fine historical department opening Mormon texts to full view and consideration. I was now a mother of two, a daughter and a son. Our new friends were historians, archivists. I was still ambitious, we were poor. And I landed a job that set an arc for my life.

I would work part time with Jill Mulvay and Maureen Ursenbach[6] researching Mormon women's history at the church's historical department. I was assigned to research the Primary, the Mormon organization founded in the nineteenth century for children. Jill was to write a history of the primary with Carol Cornwall Madsen. My focus: the first half of the story, from 1877 to 1939 (the tenure of two women, Louie Felt and May Anderson).

What an amazing place. I had liberal access to minute books, diaries, newspapers, photographs. I met friends for a lifetime who were working there. I could browse the stacks, looking for possible openings onto this story of the women and the children. Carefully take the books to my desk. And then back again to the stacks. My research also led me into the broader field of women's studies and American history as I worked to place Primary projects, especially the ambitious Primary Children's Hospital, against the backdrop of early-twentieth-century social welfare movements, immediately before and after World War I.

Soon I had a mass of information and ideas about the project ready for Jill. She told me to begin drafting and then championed my draft to Leonard Arrington. It was because of her efforts that my name rather than hers appeared with Carol Madsen's on *Sisters and Little Saints*, the book eventually published by Deseret Book in 1979.

---

5. I had written this essay when the stricture against Mormon came out from the current Mormon prophet. I don't see myself changing my habits with this very old word.

6. Later, Jill Mulvay Derr and Maureen Ursenbach Beecher. In my early writing while working at the LDS Church Historical Department and occasionally writing for church publications, I signed my name Susan Oman. My mother was annoyed by this. She gave me no middle name, since she was always annoyed by her long married name: Rose Marie Birch Staker. Once married, I would only need deal with three names. But I was only using two: she insisted I add in the Staker so folks would know who I was, hence Susan Staker Oman. I later returned to my simple birth name: Susan Staker.

The manuscript went through readings by certain church general authorities and the primary president before going to press. We smiled at feedback that the book made it seem the women were independent from the male leadership in their work for the children. Of course, in the beginning they were—their own meetings, money, publications, projects such as the hospital. I remember dutifully searching for examples of male leaders attending or commenting on the children's organization that I could add to the manuscript, though such additions could do little to change the story.

My own pride in the book centers on telling of the enduring partnership of two childless women—one a plural wife, one never married—who together led the primary from its beginnings to the eve of World War II. Louie Felt and May Anderson shared their personal lives (living together from 1889 to Louie's death in 1925) as well as their church lives. May then led the organization alone until 1939.[7]

During this period, I also worked with Jill and Maureen on vignettes on Relief Society presidents for the official church publication. This work licensed me to read the Relief Society minute book from Nauvoo. Beginning to think about women in Nauvoo, the structure of those meetings, the women involved, who knew what, the circuit of gossip and secrets in Nauvoo, was deeply troubling and left me with many questions as this job ended. But I had proved to myself, and others, it seems, that I could research and write, that I was some kind of Mormon historian.

My next adventure in accidental history came when I was hired by Hal Cannon at the Utah Arts Council for a year-long stint preparing for a folk arts exhibit with accompanying catalogue. During that year, I traveled around Utah looking for artifacts and artists we might highlight in the exhibit—a physical, intimate kind of history I never knew again.

---

7. Carol Cornwall Madsen and Susan Staker Oman, *Sisters and Little Saints: One Hundred Years of Primary* (Salt Lake City: Deseret Book Co., 1979). See also Susan Staker Oman, "Nurturing LDS Primaries: Louie Felt and May Anderson, 1880–1940," *Utah Historical Quarterly* 49, 3 (Summer 1981): 262–75.

I would drive into town and ask for the woman with the key to the local Daughters of the Utah Pioneers (DUP) museum, a woman who invariably helped me access an ongoing culture, a history in progress. I would mine for contacts, visit the museum and other homes—of women (almost always) with fabrics, hats, carvings, paintings, bowls, sculptures, knives … And stories, stories, stories. Two of the prizes I discovered at DUP museums: a very old and large, multi-part, carved butter mold from Orderville. Used in the communitarian experiment of that town, I was told. And a huge, carved all-seeing eye buried under layers of open storage in the Ogden DUP that had once graced, I was told, the Ogden tabernacle. Very like the one on the old tabernacle in Salt Lake City. At Hal's behest, I looked for beehives (the Mormon symbol of "Deseret") and found them everywhere—carved, painted, on fire hydrants, glass ones, wood ones, fabric ones. We staged a beehive section in the exhibit, and Hal would later stage an entire beehive exhibition.

The next stage of this project was the trickiest—convincing the guardians of these treasures to let us have them for a year, to take them to the Hotel Utah and then to BYU and additional venues around Utah. Anyone donating to the DUP museums had signed a pledge, on penalty of death, as I recall, that the items would never again leave that DUP building. The DUP was overseen by the redoubtable Kate B. Carter, who guarded these covenants without exception. I learned the virtues of a strategy that still serves me well, ask forgiveness, not permission, as I explained the wonders of having these items seen by hundreds and immortalized in the color photographs of a fabulous catalogue. We honored these promises. And both my butter mold and my all-seeing eye eventually found their way into the exhibit.

Writing history with physical artifacts was a whole new world. Creating crates to travel these fragile artifacts around the state. Presenting a story, an organized and contextualized pathway through artifacts. This accidental historian was learning to write a kinetic and physical history.

Our catalogue included photos of the exhibit but was largely comprised of essays on Mormon folk art and material culture. My

334

husband and I wrote one of the essays.[8] I edited the essays, my introduction to the craft.

———

My next part-time job gleaned from our historian friends: secretary and receptionist for *Sunstone* magazine, recently taken over by Peggy Fletcher and Allen Roberts. I had met Peggy while working at the historical department, where she had been working on her great grandfather Heber J. Grant. Peggy, after Brother Foster, was the second charismatic to slam into my life. In Peggy, I found a friend, collaborator, mentor who bent the arc of my life. By then I was a mother of three children, my final daughter as I was soon to learn profoundly, developmentally handicapped (yet another story). This job allowed me to work in the evenings so that our children were mostly in the care of either a father or mother. So many of those evenings spent in intense, hopeful conversation about what might happen in the wake of Sunstone. I was soon more editor than secretary.

Peggy is an ambitious and driven visionary, a golden networker. We will publish the best, she said. Those early years were intense and magical. I was privileged to edit and collaborate with Mormon studies heroes: Thomas Alexander, Michael Quinn, Jim Allen, Davis Bitton, John Sillito, Linda Sillitoe, Phyllis Barber, George Smith, the list goes on and on. For Peggy, gathering existing articles wasn't enough. We would generate thinking and writing, and the Sunstone Symposium was born.

These were painful years for Mormon history. The Mark Hofmann forgeries and murders. Attacks from Mormon leaders such as Boyd Packer. Michael Quinn is a friend of mine from BYU days. I was at BYU as Mike gave the presentation on Mormon history that got him fired. Near its end, he was unable to continue and asked me to finish reading. Many Mormons in pain and bewilderment made their way to Sunstone. We listened and tried to help. I gained confidence as an editor, seeking an author's

———

8. Hal Cannon, ed., *Utah Folk Art: A Catalog of Material Culture* (Provo, Utah: Brigham Young University Press, 1980). See Susan and Richard Oman, "Mormon Iconography," 109–26.

argument and voice in a bit of chaos, collaborating about possibilities. But I longed to wield my own pen, find my own voice.[9]

Life on Two Tracks

When I left Sunstone in the early 1980s, I was looking for my own place. In retrospect, I see it took me decades to settle into what I now experience as my place as reader, writer, critic, and historian of stories—mostly of Joseph's stories.

In one terrifying month in my early thirties, I left my house, my ward, my church, my marriage, my job (at Sunstone). I have remained immersed in Mormon studies but have never returned to the institutional church. I found myself with the same questions I had as a young girl in Idaho. What will I be? Whatever the difficulties as a now single mother, I was going to graduate school.

History? I asked. Certainly my jobs over the previous years had made of me a lover of Mormon history, an accidental historian. But my love of stories, of the novel, of the secret uncensored landscape preserved from my teenage years, won out. I became a graduate student of English literature—with the prospect of becoming a professor, a teacher, but of college students, not youngsters.

I spent near a decade as graduate student at the University of Utah. I completed a master's degree and turned to my doctorate, eventually specializing in nineteenth- and early-twentieth-century British literature with a focus on the novel and on narrative theory. There I found frameworks and language for exploring the novels and stories I love—and, as it turned out, for exploring Joseph.

As a single mother, I needed to support those student years, and again, my friends, the historians, found me a job, this time as editor at Signature Books, working with George Smith, Gary Bergera, and Ron Priddis. I met George while editing at *Sunstone*. He presented an article and, given my "less is more" commitment, I edited his presentation into a shadow if its former self. What relief when he enthused at my editing, and we have been friends ever since. Moving from Sunstone to Signature was a relief, deadlines of months, not days.

---

9. I'm thankful for the opportunities to write while I was at Sunstone, especially on the short-lived *Sunstone Review*. I used articles written at Sunstone as writing samples when I applied for graduate school at the University of Utah.

And so I settled into my lives as Signature editor and graduate student of English literature and narrative theory. These two lives intertwined and informed each other.

———

Editing at Signature spanned a broad spectrum. I might add commas, rework local sentences, suggest a structural reworking, or rewrite research. Whatever the scope, I was engaging in a robust intertextual conversation with the best in Mormon studies.

This work was constant backdrop to my graduate studies. Not only did I edit books but also took on special projects that deepened and broadened my relation to Mormon studies. A book is a deep dive into a subject. I would often spend months studying its argument, its structure, its reference. I have laughed with friends that I helped to edit pretty much all the books for which Mormon scholars were excommunicated in the 1990s.

In addition, I typed (remember this was before scanning technology) and then indexed (with index cards and spreadsheets) several manuscripts for Signature's "Classics in Mormon Thought" series. I recall with fondness work on *The Essential Orson Pratt*. Creating an index engages a deep dive into a structure for reading and interpreting a text, considering its themes and hierarchies of meaning. Indexes also lead into the details and strange eddies of a text. Consider entries for vegetable spirits and so on.

Always needing more money, I rashly agreed to index the nine published volumes of the journals of Wilford Woodruff, which Signature published from 1983 to 1985. I did not fully understand the scope of these journals as I jumped in with my cards and spreadsheets and soon discovered that Wilford rarely spelled even his own name consistently. His journals begin with Joseph in Kirtland, Ohio, and end with the Manifesto and elevators in the Salt Lake temple—the 1830s through the 1890s. Work on that index spanned several years—Wilford's long life informed my busy life as graduate student and single mother.[10]

———

10. My son, Nate, wrote on his Facebook page (Aug. 22, 2018) as the church began posting high-quality photos of the entire Wilford Woodruff diaries online: "My mom (Susan Staker) indexed all of Wilford Woodruff's diaries by hand using 3 x 5 cards when I was growing up. For years, I kind of felt like Wilford was this presence in our

Nearing the end of this crazy project, I realized that I was amongst a handful who had read this massive journal many times and considered the landscape for nineteenth-century Mormonism made by Wilford's pages. Rather than stop while I was ahead, I agreed to create a one-volume version of the journal, with broad accessibility rather than scholarly specialization and annotation as its goal.

I had several goals for the volume. I wanted to include all the "good stuff," the immediacy of a story in the middest (or midmost) with all its strangeness, not yet framed into familiar stories from the stability of an authoritative ending. I wanted the book apparatus to recede and Wilford's personality and words to organize the reader's horizon. That meant minimizing book structures (chapters, contextual explanations, footnotes) and relying wherever possible on Wilford to name and describe persons, places, events. I was convinced I could make such an "abridgment" useful for a scholar but accessible to a Sunday school teacher.

I also wanted to present the breadth, and the oddities, of this man and his monumental journal. A man at the center of Mormon governance from the days of Joseph Smith through his own presidency near the end of the nineteenth century (it is the aspect of governance that Wilford mostly lauds). A plural husband who drafts a document to end plural marriage. Whose New Year's ritual is to gauge the nearness of end times with a list of the year's disasters. A horticulturist. A man who goes to medical "theaters" to watch operations and write detailed descriptions of cancer tumors and other medical events. Who measures a cathedral while on his mission to England. Who loves visiting San Francisco, Joseph Smith's apostate relatives, and the Cliff House Restaurant. (Wilford dies in San Francisco.) A man who writes every day or explains why not. Who writes about an illness until unconsciousness intervenes and then returns with a recap. Whose final entries, usually dutifully recorded by his secretary, detail his final illness—stopped two days before his death. Forever in the middest.

———

home, if only because the Kenney transcripts took up half the shelf space in the living room. Very cool to see this."

During this decade, I had fellowships at the University of Utah, both teaching and research. I also supervised rating sessions for placement essays written by incoming undergraduates and trained raters for these sessions. This meant ensuring secondary English teachers plus doctorate students from both academic and creative writing tracks used the same criteria for rating the essays and the same language for talking about student writing. I learned lessons in thinking about the structure and behavior of texts as valuable as any from a graduate seminar.

Work on my dissertation eventually framed my approach to Joseph Smith. My dissertation began with an interest in "endings." In the twentieth century, it becomes a commonplace to compare nineteenth- and twentieth-century novels by contrasting the "closure" or "openness" of their endings. This contrast proves particularly neat in describing stories about (and by) women. The nineteenth-century novel is characterized by closure, an ending retrospectively patterning what the narrative may mean. With women, such closure means marriage, madness, or death. In contrast, twentieth-century modernist novels write beyond the ending, opening narrative to new possibilities.

In truth, few novels, whether nineteenth or twentieth century, so neatly reside under the sign of a closed or opening ending. Take Thomas Hardy's *Tess of the D'Urbervilles*. At its most obvious level, Tess's story has a rather full end stop with Tess dead on a heathen alter. But the novel's enduring power is little tamed by gathering its details onto a path leading to the ending. More interesting is the way the novel takes up such themes as endings, closures, enclosures, escape, openings, and within its confines can be seen to explore, theorize, investigate such structures by way of its plot, characters, language, narrative behavior. Novels, and other narratives, are often quite canny in making strange, undermining the very themes and commitments, the order, evoked by the stature of an ending, a retrospect.[11]

---

11. For example, see Rachel Blau DuPlessis, *Writing Beyond the Ending: Narrative Strategies of Twentieth-Century Women Writers* (Bloomington: Indiana University Press, 1985). Another important argument is Peter Brooks, *Reading for the Plot: Design and Intention in Narrative* (Oxford, England: Clarendon Press, 1984).

Theorists such Mieke Bal opened for me the analysis of narrative behaviors, or "narrativity," as an epistemological tool of exploration. Bal, who taught at the University of Amsterdam, is exemplary in applying such narrative analysis to texts and artifacts beyond the novel. Along the arc of her early career, Bal authors three books on women in the Old Testament—one on dangerous love (for example, the stories of Tamar and Delilah), another on stories of murder involving women in the book of Judges, and a final on the structures or codes of meaning in varying approaches to reading the story of Sisera. Later in her career, she moved to analysis of painting and sculpture.[12]

My dissertation focused on novelists and theorists from the late nineteenth and early twentieth century—George Eliot, George Meredith, Joseph Conrad, Ivy Compton-Burnett, Sigmund Freud, Georg Lukacs. Following the lead of Bal and others, I examined "novelists" and "theorists" with the same set of narratological tools—looking at the way theory stages narrative and narrative theory, how both investigate life.

———

Finishing Wilford coincided with another ending—or not quite an ending. I had passed my exams but not completed my burgeoning dissertation. I went on a the job market and failed to find a position. Was I to become a permanent adjunct? My alternative was refreshing. I married again and moved to California

---

12. Mieke Bal, *Narratology: Introduction to the Theory of Narrative*, Christine van. Boheemen, trans. (Toronto: University of Toronto Press, 1985); the most recent edition is 2017. See also *Lethal Love: Feminist Literary Readings of Biblical Love Stories* (Bloomington: Indiana University Press, 1987); *Death & Dissymmetry: The Politics of Coherence in the Book of Judges* (Chicago: University of Chicago Press, 1988); and *Murder and Difference Gender, Genre, and Scholarship on Sisera's Death* (Bloomington: Indiana University Press, 1992). I am also indebted to the work of my mentor at the University of Utah. An early book of his is Robert L. Caserio, *Plot, Story, and the Novel: From Dickens and Poe to the Modern Period* (Princeton: Princeton University Press, 1979). His most recent book came off the press this year: Robert Caserio, *The Cambridge Introduction to British Fiction, 1900–1950* (New York: Cambridge University Press, 2019). In my work, I often use the phrase "economy of Joseph's texts." My notion of "economy" is indebted to another of my professors, a notion organizing this exploration: Henry Staten, *Nietzsche's Voice* (Ithaca, New York: Cornell University Press, 1990). Henry's most recent book is *Techne Theory: A New Language for Art* (London, England: Bloomsbury Academic, 2019).

with a dissertation I intended to finish and a final Signature Books project. Then I would decide next steps.

As *Waiting for World's End,* the Wilford volume, came from the press in 1993, I was living in Sacramento, California.[13] I began work on my Signature project, which took me back to my first confrontations with Joseph Smith while working at the LDS historical department in the late 1970s. My final work there led me to the secrets of Nauvoo and the beginnings of the Relief Society captured in those compelling minute books. My final Signature project involved consolidating existing essays on the development of the endowment ritual into chapters for a book and augmenting them with contemporary (as near as possible) reminiscences and records from Ohio and Illinois about the two endowments and temples. I immersed myself in this story and in these early documents. I eventually managed to harness my growing obsession with Joseph Smith's story and finished my final project as editor at Signature.[14]

Adventures in Writing: Secrets, Seers, Mirrors, Shadows

In the wake of the endowment project, I decided to begin a book on Joseph Smith rather than return to my dissertation. So far this essay mostly describes events in my "self" life and how they led me to study Mormon history, literature, and narrative theory. At this point, I shift to events in my reading, thinking, and writing life and how such events inform my writing about Joseph. Ultimately my Joseph project tracks his textual chronology rather than his self life chronology. So humor me, even if the going gets rough, as I follow a mirroring model in describing the arc of my writing life as a reader of Joseph.

Bal's work on the Old Testament led me to consider the profoundly narrative structure of Joseph's imagination and the continuous thread of the King James Bible in his career. I came to believe that Harold Bloom's appreciative reading of Joseph Smith

13. Susan Staker, ed., *Waiting for World's End: The Diaries of Wilford Woodruff* (Salt Lake City: Signature Books, 1993). See also Susan Staker, "Waiting for World's End: Wilford Woodruff and David Koresh," *Sunstone* (1993): 11–16. This essay adapted portions of my introduction to the Woodruff volume.

14. David John Buerger, *The Mysteries of Godliness: A History of Mormon Temple Worship* (San Francisco: Smith Research Associates, 2002).

gets it about right: "He was anything but a great writer, but he was a great reader, or creative misreader, of the Bible. Mormonism is a wonderfully strong misprision, or creative misreading, of the early history of the Jews."[15] What Bloom calls "creative misreading" maps usefully to what Joseph calls "translation." Within this context, think of Joseph's body of work (the Book of Mormon, the New Translation of the Bible, the Book of Abraham, temple rituals, environing revelations and documents) as readings or translations of Bible stories.

Research interests from my graduate school days, narrativity and endings, proved a fortuitous frame for exploring the narrative economy of Joseph's religious imagination, his career as a seer and translator. My first close encounter with Joseph almost twenty years earlier had been the Relief Society minutes from Nauvoo. I decided my beginning would be Joseph's ending, the secrets of Nauvoo.

Already immersed in Nauvoo through the endowment book, I began drafting. My first drafts focus on the culture of secrecy in Nauvoo, on a structure of gossip and lying. Sections from these early drafts will make their way into my final book. But in retrospect, I see rather conventional historical writing: laying out a linear story and providing context. I had not yet discovered an approach deploying my specialized set of narratological skills.[16]

I began finding my way with a Sunstone presentation in the

---

15. Harold Bloom, *The American Religion: The Emergence of the Post-Christian Nation* (New York: Simon and Schuster, 1992), 84. See also his *The Anxiety of Influence: A Theory of Poetry* (London, England: Oxford University Press, 1973). The magnitude of Bloom's compliment is even better gauged by the fact that he comes very close to giving Smith priority over his own habitual heroes, Emerson and Whitman: "I myself can think of not another American, except for Emerson and Whitman, who so moves and alters my own imagination. For someone who is not a Mormon, what matters most about Joseph Smith is how American both the man and his religion have proved to be. So self-created was he that he transcends Emerson and Whitman in my imaginative response, and takes his place with the great figures of our fiction, since at moments he appears far larger than life, in the mode of a Shakespearean character. So rich and varied a personality, so vital a spark of divinity, is almost beyond the limits of the human, as normally we construe these limits" (126–27).

16. My first drafted chapter was titled, "'The Tongue Is an Unruly Member': Nauvoo's Culture of Secrecy," with a tag from Heber C. Kimball in 1857: "You have received your endowments. What is it for? To learn you to hold your tongues." This tag line demonstrates that I had not yet found my focus on Joseph's dictation plot.

early 1990s, focusing on Joseph's 1842 work on the Book of Abraham, which Joseph says he translated from some Egyptian papyri.[17] I still focus on Nauvoo's culture of secrecy. But the essay depends on an extended reading of Joseph's first 1842 paragraphs—Abraham presenting Sarai as his sister (the naming dissymmetry is Joseph's) to prevent the Egyptians from killing him and taking her. This reading suggested how I might bring the parallel tracks of my life—Mormon history and narrative theory—together.

In Joseph's final 1835 Kirtland work on the Book of Abraham, he falls into his New Translation workflow: closely tracking and revising sections from the King James Bible. In Nauvoo, Joseph resumes this workflow for the brief Abraham/Sarai incident and then launches into an astronomy based on Kirtland's Egyptian project and then a revision of the creation stories of Genesis.[18]

In both the King James version and Joseph's translation, the brief incident focuses on transactions involving Abraham's wife. In the King James version, the transaction is between Abraham and Egypt's pharaoh, with Abraham assuming responsibility for the lie that his wife is his sister. In Joseph's 1842 translation, the conversation and transaction are between Abraham and God, the energies of language and motivation within a domain of male desire. God tells Abraham to claim his wife as his sister, because she "is a very fair woman to look upon" (*very* added to the language of King James).

My essay focuses on the intertextual conversation between the Bible incident and Joseph's translation of the incident—the echoes as well as the structural changes. In researching the context for Joseph's textual work in 1842 on the Book of Abraham, I discovered that this reading of Abraham's story is a belated version of many. Joseph tells versions of Abraham's story in the Book of Mormon

---

17. Susan Staker, "'The Lord Said, Thy Wife Is a Very Fair Woman to Look Upon': The Book of Abraham, Secrets, and Lying for the Lord," in Bryan Waterman, ed., *The Prophet Puzzle: Interpretive Essays on Joseph Smith* (Salt Lake City: Signature Books, 1999).

18. Joseph had revised both the creation stories and the Abraham sections of Genesis 11–12 once already during his work on the New Translation of Genesis in early 1831.

and in his early work on a translation of Genesis in 1831.[19] Both of these events in the textual plot focus on the meeting between Abraham and Melchizedek, to different ends.

In 1835, Abraham is central to Joseph's work on the Egyptian project. His initial explorations in the Egyptian Alphabets and bound Egyptian Grammar and Alphabet depart from the King James Bible story about Abraham. His final work in Kirtland in 1835 returns to the territory of the his New Translation, where Joseph made few changes. In 1835, his translation of the Abraham passages of Genesis is different but not extravagant in its changes.

Joseph's 1842 reading of Abraham seems animated by the concerns pressing against him within Nauvoo's culture of secrecy (especially regarding plural marriage). His earlier readings similarly unfold against horizons of contemporary problems and concerns—how to organize a new church, what endowment comes with a high priesthood, how to plot a story of origins for priesthood and sacred language (the pure language of the first fathers, the privileged Egyptian language of the Book of Mormon), how to tell a renewed seer story encompassing a cosmic story of heaven and magic accoutrements.

––––––

Given my graduate school project, I should have known that writing from an ending is a fool's errand. Confronting multiple Abraham stories along Joseph's textual arc from 1829 through 1842 brought into view a complex and accumulating intertextuality. For my investigation of Joseph's reliance on narrative, its complex structure of return and layering, its issue in action and theology, I would need to begin where the intertextual conversation begins.

The chronology for Joseph's texts (with provenance tied to contemporary events) begins with an 1828 "revelation" describing Joseph's loss of the first Book of Mormon pages. In the spring of 1829, Joseph begins dictating where he left off in 1828—with the story of King Benjamin passing a cache of sacred records and

19. These early stories engage the version of the encounter in Hebrews 7 more than the version in Genesis 12. See David P. Wright, "'In Plain Terms That We May Understand': Joseph Smith's Transformation of Hebrews in Alma 12–13," in Brent Lee Metcalfe, ed., *New Approaches to the Book of Mormon: Explorations in Critical Methodology* (Salt Lake City: Signature Books, 1993), 165–230.

artifacts, including interpreters or seer stones, to his son and heir, King Mosiah. These men are called "seers."[20]

That Joseph's textual beginning comes in the middle of the story told by the Book of Mormon turns out to be a felicitous accident for the interpreter of Joseph's work. The textual chronology of Joseph's work is out of sync with the story told within the world of the book. The development of themes and structures along the textual chronology is implacable, repeatedly overwhelming chronology within the world of the story.[21]

I call this textual chronology a *dictation plot*. *Plot* underscores the durability of narrative within Joseph's imaginative economy. *Dictation* focuses on Joseph's early structure for making texts—rarely an author writing a holograph, more generally a public event with Joseph speaking the text transcribed by a scribe. (More later on why *dictation plot* proved a happy choice.)

I would begin where Joseph begins, with the father and son seers, and signed up to write an essay for a Signature collection on the Book of Mormon. With this essay, I found a working frame for my Joseph

---

20. My understanding of the dictation order of the Book of Mormon comes from Brent Metcalfe's important essay, "The Priority of Mosiah: A Prelude to Book of Mormon Exegesis," in *New Approaches to the Book of Mormon*, 395–444. Brent's ongoing support has been crucial in helping me sort through often tangled issues to arrive at a textual chronology of Joseph's work. His work on the Book of Mormon was transformative for my thinking about how to approach Joseph. More recently he has helped me through the textual chronology of Joseph's Egyptian papers.

In my original essay I focused almost exclusively on Mosiah as the one first called seer. But I later discovered that King Benjamin is the one first referenced as seer in the 1830 version. This was changed by Joseph to Mosiah in the 1837 version. I have silently changed this here. The ambiguity in these early references is important. Susan Staker, "Secret Things, Hidden Things: The Seer Story in the Imaginative Economy of Joseph Smith," in Brent Metcalfe and Dan Vogel, eds., *American Apocrypha: Essays on the Book of Mormon* (Salt Lake City: Signature Books, 2002), 235–74.

21. Joseph's work on the New Translation and also the Egyptian Project with its Book of Abraham present similar disconnects between the world of the story and the textual chronology, similar felicitous accidents. With the New Translation, Joseph works through a good chunk of Genesis and then turns to the New Testament. After finishing the New Testament, he returns to Genesis and works through to the end of the Old Testament. In preparing the book for possible publication, Joseph reviews both the Old Testament and the New Testament. This work happens between 1830 and 1833.

With the Egyptian project, Joseph first works through the Egyptian Alphabets and the bound Grammar before substantive work on the Book of Abraham in 1835. A gap of seven years occurs before Joseph returns to work on the Book of Abraham, along with facsimiles of portions of the papyrus, for a few weeks in the spring of 1842.

project—the continuity of the seer character and the workings of narrativity along the arc of Joseph's dictation plot. Joseph's authority is established on the narrative foundation of this seer character.

Seer characters prove the single, unbroken line along the arc of the Book of Mormon dictation plot. Other lines are broken, discontinuous: lineage or family, priesthood, structures of governance (kings, judges, and so on). But in each generation a seer passes on the guardianship of sacred records and artifacts to the next seer. These shadowing guardian characters all enact some version of "the seer after the manner of old times": a revelator and prophet who knows past and future, makes secret things manifest, translates (with wondrous devices) and writes records, performs miracles, sees God, and often escapes a traditional death sentence (is "translated"). In Lehi's final words to his son Joseph as Joseph nears completion of his Book of Mormon text, Joseph dictates himself into the text as a "choice seer" described by Joseph of Egypt and compared to Moses. (The piling up of Joseph characters is instructive.)

This seer character continues in Joseph's following translations. At the beginning of the New Translation in 1830, Enoch is also called a "seer." The first fathers (beginning with Adam and his Book of Remembrance) are drawn under this sign of the seer. Joseph as "choice seer" is written into Genesis. John (disciple and revelator in Joseph's work) and Elijah are examples. Abraham along the arc of Joseph's work from 1829 to 1842 easily stands under the sign of this seer character, with his wondrous device the Urim and Thummim, his miracles, his association with writing and encounters with Gods and angels, and his pact of secrets/lies with Father God. As within the Book of Mormon world, stories of priesthood, governance, and lineage often prove discontinuous.

These mirroring stories of seers and records also introduce what I think of as a seer model for how to read: God's sacred secrets come into view through stories or characters that "shadow" one another. Both King Benjamin and Abinadi introduce a new secret into an old world—that the One God will descend into the world as Jesus God. They both speak of the notion of type or shadow for considering how plots and characters in their old world predict or shadow the new—for example, Moses's story predicts Jesus God's.[22] This shadowing of one story with another functions in at least two ways along the arc of Joseph's Book of Mormon dictation plot. One story parallels or rereads another story within the world of the story—the shadowing stories of the seer characters being the exemplar.

A related but different version of such shadowing is enacted by the scene of reading with Kings Benjamin and Mosiah. This scene within the Book of Mormon world enacts an enfolding scene made by a reader taking up Joseph's text in the 1820s—an embedded story which mimes the enfolding historical world. The term *mise en abyme*, often used to describe this phenomenon, comes from heraldry, where a tiny mirror version of the crest is embedded within the larger crest.[23] As Benjamin reads and in-

---

22. I speak of One God to describe the undifferentiated God character introduced at the beginning of the Book of Mormon. Where God characters are differentiated, I speak of Jesus God or Father God. In situations where Joseph's text is not explicit, I generally use the term God. At the beginning of the Book of Mormon dictation plot, the One God is two-part, not three-part as later (with inclusion of Holy Ghost). See Mosiah 3:15 and Mosiah 15–16. I strategically take up the word *shadow* (rather than *type*) in describing the mirroring relation described. *Type* comes with a good deal of baggage from tomes on "typological" criticism in both biblical and Mormon studies. With *shadow*, the words of Joseph's dictation can, I hope, find a less cluttered page. *Shadow* more easily lends itself to a focus on doubling or mirroring characters and stories rather than symbols and abstractions, so important for getting at the imaginative economy in Joseph's readings of Bible stories. Shadow also echoes the language that Paul uses: Moses is the "shadow" that predicts the "image" of Jesus. Paul deploys this trope from the stability of a known ending, coming after both Moses and Jesus.

23. My own thinking about the mirroring structure of narratives is informed in particular by what Mieke Bal calls "mirror-texts." See Bal, *Narratology*, 146. Bal suggests that "when two fabulas can be paraphrased in such a way that the summaries have one or more striking elements in common," then "an embedded text … may be taken as a sign of the primary fabula." Tzvetan Todorov describes the same phenomenon of mirroring in these terms: "the construction represented in the text is isomorphic to the one that takes the text as its point of departure." According to Todorov, such a mirror-text (what he calls "isomorphic construction") demonstrates that such "a text always contains within itself directions for its own consumption." Considered within this context, the narrative about Mosiah translating golden records can be taken as a "sign" of Joseph's work translating gold records, a key, an implicit set of directions, for consuming (to use Todorov's term) or reading and interpreting Joseph's story. For the most part, Bal and Todorov are speaking of stories embedded within a single text. But I submit that the same notion is useful within the somewhat different context I am suggesting. See Todorov, "Reading as Construction," in *Essentials of the Theory of Fiction*, eds. Michael Hoffman and Patrick Murphy (Durham, North Carolina: Duke University Press, 1988), 403–18.

terprets sacred records, he is modeling a script for the reader of Joseph's sacred book and for a latter-day seer, guardian of God's secret, hidden things.

Many Book of Mormon incidents involving seers can be seen as mirror stories, a seer story within world of the story shadowing a story in the enfolding historical world. Mosiah with his interpreters and gold records, mining for God's secrets, modeling authority for Joseph and his community. Alma going into the waters of baptism with Helam modeling a baptism ritual for Joseph and Oliver Cowdery. Seers within the world of the story provide scripts for Joseph and his followers.

The revelations environing Joseph's work on the Book of Mormon take mirroring/shadowing stories one step further, explicitly commenting on and extending these mirror stories. For example, a June 1829 revelation dictated by Joseph stages a scene of reading very like the one with Kings Benjamin and Mosiah at the beginning of the Book of Mormon dictation plot. Joseph, Oliver Cowdery, and David Whitmer are dramatized as looking at the Book of Mormon records Joseph has dictated—writing that is the voice of God.[24] Soon the intertextual conversation staging these mirror stories is so porous it ignores boundaries between the world within the translated story and the historical world. Joseph as choice seer dictated into Lehi's final scene is a prime example.[25] This structure of shadow and mirrors, of complex intertextual conversations strategically staged, would continue within the economy of Joseph's texts.

I now had a working methodology for my book: trace Joseph's texts with reasonable contemporary provenance (translation, revelations, letters, self writing) along the chronology of their creation; follow shadowing seer characters within Joseph's translations of King James Bible stories, whether direct readings or interpolations; track mirror scenes miming the enfolding world and their strategic use; and consider how such narrativity issues in theological

---

24. Susan Staker, "Reading and Writing Shadow Seers: Life Narrative and Joseph's Bible Stories," presentation at Sunstone Symposium, 2015.

25. The story of Joseph as an unlearned man, a version of the Anthon incident with Martin Harris is another example.

explorations, propped onto this intertextual layering of Bible stories and plots along the arc of Joseph's textual economy.

Interruption and Return

But I could not wander indefinitely in the world of Joseph's Bible stories. I needed a job. And hence a grand interruption in this accidental church historian's career: fifteen years within the centralized content group at Adobe, a software company probably best known for Photoshop and Acrobat. In my interview with the woman who became my mentor and boss during those fifteen years at Adobe, I told her that a good editor can cut 20 percent, to the better, once a writer finishes. (She was my third encounter with a charismatic.) On my first day at Adobe, she gave me the Photoshop manual, asked for the 20 percent, and left on her sabbatical.

For her return, I identified a set of edits, and so began my career at Adobe. This multifarious experience extended my skills analyzing large bodies of content, finding patterns and structures, considering how language can be manipulated and organized in pursuit of strategic goals, exploring how such structures might be described.[26]

During my first years at Adobe, I struggled to continue my Joseph project.[27] But with intense and unforgiving deadlines, I ultimately abandoned ongoing work on Joseph. Still Joseph pressed my imagination. Finally I decided to return full time to my Book of Joseph. I engineered a felicitous exit, a retirement, from this grand interlude and nearly five years ago returned full time to my book (and to a garden and dog on Whidbey Island near Seattle).[28]

---

26. In my final five years, I worked closely with a new content group In India (New Delhi and Bangalore). I traveled to India multiple times and consider this experience the best of my Adobe career. I also worked with content groups in Switzerland, Canada, multiple U.S. sites, Japan. In my role as "editorial director" for centralized content creation, I was pulled into many a tricky situation. I also helped to define editorial requirements for tool implementation: two publishing systems, Google custom search, translation memory, editing software, data mining, database publishing for support content.

27. For example, I spent my first Adobe sabbatical in 2002 working on the book. As punctuation to my initial work, I presented "'The Purifying Touch': An Economy of Reading and Revision in Kirtland's Sacred Texts" at a Mormon History Association meeting in 1997. In this essay, I first described the structure of retrospect demonstrated by Joseph's work on the 1835 edition of the Doctrine and Covenants.

28. For the bio I have come to use for presentations about my project, see the description in the contributors section to the present book.

The day after leaving Adobe, I sat down at my computer and began an archaeological dig. The fifteen-year gap proved fortuitous, enabling a critical distance on hundreds of pages. Often my drafting seemed written by someone else. I was sometimes excited as I read—and sometimes confused and bored.

I also began reading fifteen years of work on Joseph Smith. Against the backdrop of a maturing scholarship, could I still contribute? I was struck by the lucky mirroring of my focus on narrative behaviors or narrativity as tools of investigation and Joseph's own mode of seeking—his translations of Bible characters and his use of narrative.

A key change is the robust presence of the Joseph Smith Papers Project by the LDS Church Historical Department. I had worried at the reliability of the Joseph texts I layered along my dictation plot. Many came from the so-called Mormon underground—documents copied or transcribed, often without scholarly attention to provenance. Like a child at Christmas, I was thrilled to find Joseph's texts published and annotated in printed volumes and available and searchable online, a robust textual platform laid out along a timeline, complete with provenance, textual description, and scholarly annotation. As I returned, the JSP project had published volumes through Kirtland.

Such availability confirmed the feasibility of a responsible textual chronology—revelations, translations, letters, journals and personal writings, minutes, and other documents. The criteria for documents included in the JSP project substantively maps to my own—texts whose making is closely tied to Joseph and whose provenance ties them into Joseph's contemporary textual workflow. From this larger chronology, I select texts tied to the Bible with versions of the seer character, and the angels and God(s) of heaven.

Given all this change, I returned once again to the beginning of Joseph's dictation plot, with a reliable chronology for a widening array of texts and with a narrower focus on how to address them. I have now worked my way to Nauvoo, where I began my journey towards Joseph. This means I am again reviewing my Book of Joseph—considering the reworking and substantial cuts necessary for a final draft. Writing this essay on writing Mormon history provides an opportunity for considering the series of happy accidents that led me here. And allows me to consider the substance of my project.

Dictation Plot

The notion of "dictation plot" remains a happy invention, distilling organizing principles in my project. It proves useful both for its failures and its successes. *Dictation* succeeds in focusing how the texts associated with Joseph are made but increasingly fails to accommodate the transforming structures of such making in the final years of Joseph's career. *Plot* succeeds in focusing on narrativity along the arc of Joseph's textual life.

A focus on *dictation* distances Joseph's making of texts from any conventional notion of the "author." A solitary maker with a pen. Very few texts survive in Joseph's handwriting—so rare are holographs that the JSP project transcribes Joseph's handwriting in bold. Joseph's texts are almost always written down by a scribe—at first, in something like "real time" by a scribe as Joseph dictates. The early revelations and his translations (the Book of Mormon, New Translation, Book of Abraham) are created this way.[29] Along the arc of his career, this real-time creation process is more and more attenuated. Scribes construct minutes from notes or from memory. Eventually Joseph's journals and histories are made by others and reconstructed in the same way, though they continue to appear in the I-voice of Joseph. His self history continues to be written in this I-voice for decades after his death. The I-voice of Joseph then increasingly becomes the construction of a character, often written by others.

Joseph's texts then are almost always made in a social context that depends on collaboration with others. At least a scribe. His early revelations are almost always addressed to one or more persons in response to questions. Often Joseph receives a revelation in front of a group, the making of texts as performance. Events of

---

29. Within my book, I explore the Egyptian Alphabets and the bound Egyptian Grammar and Alphabet. These are very close to dictated documents. Certainly Joseph is intimately involved with scribes in their making.

making as well as the fact of the texts made are foundational for Joseph's authority.

By Nauvoo, surviving texts are rarely accommodated by the notion of dictation plot—Joseph speaking a text directly. Increasingly, I focus on textual chronology or economy of texts instead. In Nauvoo, Joseph often speaks in outdoor venues in front of thousands.[30] But the textual traces of speeches survive largely by happy accident, recorded in personal journals, often by Joseph's close associates but sometimes by someone in the crowd.

In truth, Joseph is reluctant to have his words preserved. His speeches tell increasingly dangerous stories about seers, angels, gods. Men becoming gods. Gods once men. His most radical utterances, about the endowment or plural marriage, occur in secret, rarely written down, and then with commands to burn the text. Telling a secret in Nauvoo makes one a liar and an apostate, lost to God and heaven. The endowment ceremony itself revolves around swearing on pain of punishment to keep secrets.

The genre Joseph adopts for the secret endowment in Nauvoo (layered upon his encounter with Masonry) is increasingly that of drama—not just a story told as an implied script for life but an actual script made to be enacted with costumes, scenery, props. This ritual enactment on earth literally binds heaven. This same ritual drama will be replayed at the gates of heaven. Increasingly then, Joseph's stories of the former day not only shadow stories for a latter day but increasingly plot a "real" cosmos where gods and men live in the same story, not mirroring stories.

A focus on *dictation* then, the how of making, ultimately layers in another kind of plot within Joseph's story—how the form or genre of Joseph's texts transforms over time. Such a consideration is a necessary foundation for thinking about what the content of form might be, as well as the content of content.[31]

---

30. It might seem that Joseph is taking up the mode of presentation adopted by King Benjamin at the beginning of the Book of Mormon dictation plot. King Benjamin speaks to a large crowd in an outdoor venue, but Benjamin causes his speeches to be written and circulated to his community (closer to the real time documents of Joseph's early career). In Nauvoo Joseph rejects King Benjamin's example.

31. The exemplary work of the JSP project again provides textual work necessary for any deep dive into a consideration of the content of form. See for example, Mark

A focus on *plot*, a timeline within narrative, brings into view useful boundary crossings. A textual chronology cares little whether a text is a revelation, a translation, a letter, minutes, journals, and so on; whether boundaries between constructed or textual worlds and real or historical worlds are transgressed; that the textual chronology often ignores chronologies within the constructed world, or even the historical world. Thus the dictation plot provides an opportunity to imagine Joseph's story against a different horizon.

Single-mindedly tracking the textual plot, next and then next and then next, brings into view a story always "in the middest,"[32] a plot whose ending is accidental, made only by Joseph's murder. Readers are comforted by stories easily read from an ending that retrospectively patterns details into meaning. Structures of commitment, faith, ideology, each with an end game, write comfortable stories. Throwing such comfort into relief, making it strange or unfamiliar, is a win for interpretation, revealing the structures of its making, the ways of its authority.

I certainly consider Joseph's retrospects, placed within the arc of his unfolding textual chronology, and those of participants if written at the time. Retrospects "in the middest." Mormon history mightily depends on retrospect. Participants writing after Joseph's death, writing from Utah, writing after leaving the church, and so on. Telling the story of Nauvoo, with its secrets and sparse textual record, almost demands such retrospect. That Joseph's "journals" and "histories" are often written in retrospect by someone other than Joseph only complicates the problem.

It is striking how effective are Joseph's unfolding retrospects

---

Ashurst-McGee, Robin Scott Jensen, and Sharalyn D. Howcroft, eds., *Foundational Texts of Mormonism: Examining Major Early Sources* (New York: Oxford University Press, 2018). This volume contains essays by a variety of scholars exploring the textual issues surrounding a variety of genres associated with Joseph Smith, including speeches, journals, and so on.

My thinking on form as content in historical writing was early influenced by Hayden White. See Hayden White, *The Content of the Form: Narrative Discourse and Historical Representation* (Baltimore: Johns Hopkins University Press, 1990); *Metahistory: The Historical Imagination in Nineteenth-Century Europe* (Baltiimore: Johns Hopkins University Press, 2014).

32. Echoes the notion of a story that begins *en media res,* in the middle of the action or story line.

in laying down plots for stories still told. His work on the 1835 Doctrine and Covenants is exemplary in demonstrating his structure of retrospect, filling in the lack—interpolating new stories for familiar and newly important characters, propping authoritative explanation, "theology," onto such stories.[33]

An example of the first strategy can be seen in Joseph's robust additions to a brief August 1830 revelation on acquiring wine for the sacrament ritual. Joseph adds a cast of characters to meet with Jesus God at a grand sacramental celebration at the end of times, characters whose former day backstories prepare for a latter day finale—Moroni, Peter, James, and John, John the Baptist, Abraham.[34]

Such elaborations or transformations of characters and plots trail explanations in their wake. This impulse to belated intertextual summary can be seen in the framing structure Joseph makes for the revelation half of the book. Joseph eschews the chronological ordering of the Book of Commandments, the first attempt to print his revelations in Missouri, and places an explanatory frame, "On

---

33. For example, the unlearned man who could not possibly create the Book of Mormon. The story of Melchizedek and Aaronic priesthoods. Joseph's first encounters with angels and Gods. For an overview of the priesthood backstory, see Susan Staker, "A Book of Joseph: Bible Backstories for a Seer's Life," *John Whitmer Historical Association Journal* 36, 1 (Spring/Summer 2016): 145–59.

I take the phrase "filling in the lack" from the example provided by Joseph's revisions for the minutes of the meeting organizing high councils in February 1834. He brings his revisions to the same group a day after the meeting. The difference between the minutes and Joseph's revisions are substantive. The revisions are approved with little comment and that Joseph can continue to fill in any additional lack he may find. Gerrit J. Dirkmaat, Brent M. Rogers, Grant Underwood, Robert J. Woodford, and William G. Hartley, eds. *The Joseph Smith Papers: Documents, Volume 3: February 1833–March 1834* (Salt Lake City: Church Historian's Press, 2014), 435–43.

34. "Revelation, circa August 1830 [D&C 27]," in Michael Hubbard MacKay, Gerrit J. Dirkmaat, Grant Underwood, Robert J. Woodford, and William G. Hartley, eds., *The Joseph Smith Papers: Documents, Volume 1: July 1828–June 1831* (Salt Lake City: Church Historian's Press, 2013), 164–66. In Nauvoo, this grand end-time meeting transforms into a final meeting at Adam-ondi-Ahman.

Another striking example of interpolation comes in the "On Priesthood" frame revelation, where Joseph describes a grand family council attended by multiple generations of Adam's family at Adam-ondi-Ahman. Again, new micro-biographies are given for key characters. See "Instruction on Priesthood, between circa 1 March and circa 4 May 1835 [D&C 107]," in Matthew C. Godfrey, Brenden W. Rensink, Alex D. Smith, Max H Parkin, and Alexander L. Baugh, eds., *The Joseph Smith Papers: Documents, Volume 4: April 1834–September 1835* (Salt Lake City: Church Historian's Press, 2016), 308–21.

Priesthood," near the beginning. He creates a revelation (with no date, outside of time) that wraps a frame of 1835 story-telling plus explanation around a revelation kernel from November 1831.[35]

Given the mobility and restlessness of Joseph's economy, it is important to trace named seer characters (and gods and angels) along the textual plot and to consider the contours and use of a story at a given point in time. Because theology is belated within this economy, generally an explanation propped on a specific story, any attempt to track Joseph's "theology" or explanation must first be routed through his Bible stories.

Narrating Heaven

Another happy choice, my focus on seer characters, proved reliable along the full arc of Joseph's textual career. Already in 1829, seer stories highlight Joseph's canny sense of narrativity. I have come to see a close alignment between Joseph's narrative impulses and the radical stories he eventually tells in the wake of his shadowing seer characters. The story of Mormon, penultimate Nephite seer, is exemplary in staging an arc towards a certain kind of story and its enduring usefulness for Joseph.

Along the arc of the 1829 dictation plot, it is not immediately clear why Joseph calls his translation a Book of Mormon. But by its end a seer called Mormon, Joseph's most fully explored Nephite character, proves himself equal to the title. Most immediately Mormon solves Joseph's problem of how to replace Lehi's lost story.

At its beginning, the Book of Mormon dictation plot seems told by an *external narrator*, a speaker not tied to a single character but ranging across all characters and plots with the Book of Mormon world, possessing a power often referred to as "omniscience." This mode shadows the King James Bible.[36]

---

35. "Instruction on Priesthood" from early 1835 embeds a November 1831 revelation. This kind of explanatory impulse also can be seen in Joseph's work (with Sidney Rigdon) on the *Lectures on Faith,* printed as the first half of the 1835 Doctrine and Covenants. Explorations of first fathers and their encounters with God become the platform for the story told in Joseph's "On Priesthood" frame revelation.

36. The language Joseph dictates has little resembles the spare prose of the King James Bible—his external narration is more inclined to explain and elaborate (except when quoting the King James Bible). I am again indebted to Mieke Bal for her explorations of focalization and external narration, beginning with *Narratology*, 100–14.

With external narration, it is useful to distinguish between *narration* (who speaks) and *focalization* (who sees). External narration seems spoken from beyond the world of the narrative but often aligns itself with a character's view, or given omniscience, with multiple characters' views. Focalization may narrow or shift. Along the early Book of Mormon dictation plot, this external-type narration generally aligns itself with seer characters and their friends.

After a third of Joseph's book, a substantial I-voice begins intruding, staging himself as a seer character preoccupied with sacred records and writing, and finally naming himself as Mormon. It turns out that the Book of Mormon is being told by a character dramatized as living within the story rather than an external narrator. His interruptions focus on his dilemmas as a seer writer. He has multiple records to choose from for his abridgment (and keeps finding more) and worries over how much of the Nephite story to include. He also anticipates coming to the point in Nephite history when he can write his own self story.

Many pages and some 300 years later, Mormon's I-voice wins out as he tells his own seer story (a book of Mormon within the Book of Mormon). Then his son Moroni and Lehi's family follow in adopting the I-voice convention. A final I-voice book by Mormon (the Words of Mormon) sutures together the I-voice replacement stories from Lehi's descendants with the external narration mode at the beginning of the Book of Mormon dictation plot.[37]

In late spring 1829, while finishing Mormon's abridgment, Joseph dictates a revelation demonstrating the fortuity of Mormon's discovery of new records. The Jesus God voice of the revelation does not credit Mormon but depends on his discoveries. It turns out that Joseph's initial translation was from the plates of Nephi, a source often mentioned by Mormon. And there was also a more particular account on the plates of Nephi (those plates latterly discovered by Mormon). These can be used for Joseph's replacement text.[38] Joseph as "author" also appends a "preface" to the Book of

---

37. Joseph appends a preface to the 1830 print edition that includes a final mention of Mormon: "An account written by the hand of Mormon." This preface is signed: "By Joseph Smith, Junior, Author and Proprietor."

38. "Revelation, Spring 1829 [D&C 10]," in JSP D1:37–43.

Mormon retelling this same story of multiple records and their use in solving his dilemma of the lost pages.

This arc of Mormon's story foregrounds a set of narrative strategies that serve Joseph well. A narrator positioned in time and place, relying on memory (what mine own eyes have seen), and on multiple shadowing stories and texts, telling the story of a self who meditates on his own status as a character, solving Joseph's problems.

This impulse to personalize shadowing seer characters overtakes Joseph's presentation of heaven, of angels and god(s). God is described by King Benjamin at the beginning of the Book of Mormon dictation plot and confirmed with the same words by Samuel the Lamanite on the eve of Jesus God's descent into Nephite history. An impersonal "One" God shadows the omniscient external narrator convention: "Jesus Christ the Son of God, the Father of heaven and of earth, the Creator of all things from the beginning." During the period framed by Benjamin and Samuel, ministering angels appear quoting God, the "voice" of God comes to some prophets—dramatized as a Jesus God voice. This One God coming to a seer's mind as a Jesus God voice also characterizes the environing revelations Joseph dictates while working on the Book of Mormon.[39]

The impulse towards personalized characters, demonstrated by the textual arc of Mormon's story, organizes Joseph's presentation of this One God, ephemerally become two God characters, as Jesus God descends into Nephi history. On the eve of his coming, the Jesus God voice speaks. As the physical being of Jesus descends into the story, a quiet Father God voice is heard for the first time.

Certainly Jesus is dramatized as a God in this story. Jesus God on earth speaks to his Father God while the Nephites kneel before

---

39. Royal Skousen, *The Book of Mormon: The Earliest Text* (New Haven, Connecticut: Yale University Press, 2009), 201 (Mosiah 8:8), 556 (Helaman 14:12). Abinadi's description is similar: "Teach them that redemption cometh through Christ the Lord, which is the very Eternal Father." Skousen points out that in the earliest texts King Benjamin and Samuel the Lamanite use the same words.

For description of the early Mormon notion of God, see Dan Vogel, "The Earliest Mormon Concept of God," in Gary James Bergera, ed., *Line Upon Line: Essays on Mormon Doctrine* (Salt Lake City: Signature Books, 1989), 7–16.

Jesus God and pray to him. But Jesus God is also dramatized as a shadow version of the seers. In a scene of reading, he sits down with Nephi Jr., seer and first disciple, considers the records Nephi is keeping, and notes an error to be corrected. Jesus God then reads from the same brass plates King Benjamin reads at the beginning of the Book of Mormon dictation plot (Isaiah). And then he quotes his Father's version of another record, Malachi.[40]

The beginning of Joseph's dictation plot for his New Translation of the King James Bible (its prelude dictated in June 1830) personalizes Father God as a shadow version of Jesus God among the Nephites. Father God appears to Moses face to face. Father God differentiates himself from his son, and also underscores the parallel between Jesus God and Moses, the prototypical seer. Father God then dictates a personalized, I-voice account of the creation and garden stories from Genesis, taken down by Moses the scribe. Father God is thus presented as a shadow of the seer characters.

This impulse to accumulate shadowing character "effects" for gods and seers (a story, a place to live, a family, and so on) recurs along the textual chronology of Joseph's career. But increasingly he moves to narrate heaven, to accommodate gods and seers, not in shadowing stories but in a single shared story, a move that issues in Joseph's radical explorations in Nauvoo.

A characteristic move by Joseph to accommodate and consolidate various versions of his shadow stories is to expand the timeline or plot, to move back toward beginnings and forward toward endings. Back to Moses, to Joseph of Egypt, to Abraham, to Babel, to Noah, to the first fathers. And forward to the end where Joseph and his community live in the latter days.[41]

---

40. It is striking that only after Jesus God discloses himself as a character somewhat separate from Father God, that characters along the dictation plot see God: Mormon, Moroni, the Brother of Jared. I also argue in my book that along the arc of the Book of Mormon dictation plot, Nephi's vision of the Spirit of the Lord replays Jared's vision of the Spirit of Jesus God. See Susan Staker, "God(s) as Character(s) in Joseph's Bible Stories: March 1830 to September 1830," *John Whitmer Historical Association Journal* 35, 2 (Fall/Winter 2015): 137–49.

41. Joseph's dictation of Father God's dictation to Moses of the creation stories demonstrates this move to origins. Father God accommodates the two versions of creation in Genesis—one becomes a spiritual creation, the other a natural or physical creation. One of the terms in the Egyptian Alphabets, where Joseph begins his

Near the beginning of the Book of Mormon dictation plot, Alma introduces a potent phrase that recurs along the intertextual conversations within Joseph's economy into Nauvoo. In a long speech on "the mysteries of God," Alma speaks of a priesthood order as "being without beginning of days, or end of years," calling up a version of the story in Hebrews rather than Genesis.[42] Here Alma is misquoting Hebrews, where this phrase describes Melchizedek: "without father, without mother, without descent, having neither beginning of days, nor end of life." In Alma's reading, the transformed phrase is aligned with an order associated with Jesus God and a shadowing relation to Melchizedek. Joseph's misreading, "without beginning of days, or end of years," is generative and durable within the economy of his religious imagination.

By Nauvoo, Joseph deploys his creative misreading in search of a story *without* beginning or ending. A radical version of a story without beginning or ending comes in the funeral speech for King Follett little more than a month before Joseph's murder. This speech makes concrete what it might mean for gods and men to live in a shared story without beginning or ending. With such

---

work on the Egyptian project in 1835, is "Zool" (in the Alphabets, become Zaol in the bound Grammar): "From any or some fixed peried of time back to the begining." Other terms circle around firsts, beginnings, creation, origins. A key impulse within the Alphabets and bound Grammar and then in the Book of Abraham is to find a plot from Abraham back to the first fathers and creation. See www.josephsmithpapers.org/intro/introduction-to-egyptian-material.

42. Certain potent phrases from the Bible, what I have come to call "kernels of mystery language," become part of the intertextual conversation unfolding within the economy of Joseph's texts. Such kernels become recurring and generative platforms for exploration within the shadowing stories Joseph tells of seers, angels, men gone to heaven, gods. I am focusing here on one phrase, but Joseph returns to this passage from Hebrews directly or obliquely often within the economy of his texts. The passage contains a trove of mystery language that is generative in multiple contexts for Joseph's explorations over the years. Juxtaposes notion of the office of "priest of the most high God" or "high priest" with evocative references to Melchizedek and Abraham as well as Moses and Aaron (and the term Levitical priesthood), all in relation to Jesus God and a conduit for mystery and power. For a detailed exploration of the dependency of Alma 12–13 on Hebrews, see Wright, "In Plain Terms that We May Understand'." For exploration of "mystery language," see my presentation, "Men Gone to Heaven: From Enoch's City to The Vision," presented at John Whitmer Historical Society, 2016. For discussion of this story of a "holy order" along the arc of Joseph's work, see my "Angels in Nauvoo, Adam and Enoch (1831–1841): Whence and Whither," Joseph Smith Papers Conference, 2019.

scope for the cosmic story, gods and men live through the same story—men gone to heaven as priests, kings, gods. An impulse to narrative become radical theology.

Women Gone to Heaven?

So why do I speak of men gone to heaven? So far, I mention a woman only in discussing the transaction between God and Abraham over Sarai. That first essay focuses a troubling structure of gender dissymmetry (signaled by the naming structure Abraham/Sarai) that is also continuous—a profoundly homosocial economy with seers, angels, and gods all men.[43]

Joseph's textual economy rarely attends to personalized female characters. Within the Book of Mormon, women are members of groups—mothers, daughters, sisters, murderers. Within Joseph's New Translation of the King James Bible between 1830 and 1833, revisions associated with women are rare, and incidental. Joseph's revelations rarely mention women—mostly with children in relation to ordinances of baptism or sacrament. The Vision, Joseph's first view on the kingdoms where the gods live, focuses on the inhabitants as men gone to heaven. Only one of the revelations printed in the Doctrine and Covenants is addressed to a woman, the "elect lady" revelation to Emma Hale, Joseph's own first wife.[44]

Women finally capture Joseph's attention within the 1835 Egyptian project. A woman's story plots a relation between the pure language of Adam and Egyptian, one of the questions pressing Joseph as he worked with the papyrus.[45] "Zip Zi" is one of the terms in Joseph's initial Alphabet document from July 1835: "woman married or unmarried, <or daughter>." Within the bound Egyptian Grammar and Alphabet, this term elaborated along its degrees is associated with "all women" and with "the first woman, who was Eve."

---

43. Joseph comes to gather other men, his friends and the friends of God, under the sign of the seer. Priesthood is the term often, but not always, not continuously, associated with this gathering and alignment.

44. Revelation, July 1830-C [D&C 25], JSP D1:161–64. See my essay "Men Gone to Heaven" for discussion of The Vision.

45. Other pressing questions include: how to plot the story of lineage and adoption (generally evoked as a "priesthood" story) from Adam to Abraham, how to accommodate the story of seers with powerful (magic) devices such as seer stones and powerful words.

"Woman" signals "under or beneath, second in right or in authority or Government." With a focus on the fecundity of women, this term can also be used to note increasing or decreasing degrees of importance and "a fruitful place or fruitful vine." With this term, women are underscored as wives and mothers and second in relation to their men.[46]

Against this horizon, the pure language of Adam and Egyptian hieroglyphics are gathered into a hierarchical relation made by the woman's story. The granddaughter of Noah, descended through Ham, inherits a system of governance and speaks the pure language, but both her gender and her heritage as Ham's daughter breaks a line of priesthood inheritance from the first fathers. Egypt is close but "under" the first fathers by way of a woman—she discovers Egypt under water, she is a wife, this is a not-priesthood story (through Ham her sons are severed from priesthood inheritance). And presumably, Egyptian governance and language are close but "under" that of the first fathers.[47]

In Nauvoo, Joseph's Book of Abraham installment evokes Sarai in a similar relation. The dissymmetry of Abraham and Sarai's naming, a transaction between men (transposed from Abraham and Pharaoh to Abraham and God who commands the lie because of her desirability), an ending before the woman speaks. Against a similar horizon, Joseph's 1842 work on the Book of Abraham ends with the creation of Eve. A transaction between Adam and God (she is created from Adam's rib), ending before the woman gets a chance to speak.

Women remain scarce in the surviving documents from Nauvoo, but always the gender structure is problematic. We have the Relief Society minutes, where I began my quest and my discomfort. In recent months, I have explored Joseph's approach to plural marriage courting as suggested by a handful of Joseph's texts surviving from 1842 and 1843 created for Nancy Rigdon, Sarah Ann Whitney, and Joseph's wife Emma.

Joseph's unsuccessful courtship of Nancy Rigdon in the spring of 1842 happens in close proximity to Joseph's dictation of Sarai's

---

46. See www.josephsmithpapers.org/intro/introduction-to-egyptian-material.
47. The expansive explorations of the Alphabets and bound Grammar only obliquely make their way into Joseph's 1835 Book of Abraham installment.

story, a story, as we have seen, dipped in male desire.[48] A letter
Joseph sends to Nancy by way of Marinda Hyde, his plural wife
as well as wife of an apostle away from Nauvoo on a mission, is
pitched in a related language of "happiness": "Happiness is the object and design of our existence, and will be the end thereof if we
pursue the path that leads to it. ...Whatever God requires is right,
no matter what it is, although we may not see the reason thereof
till long after the events transpire."The results of this courtship are
immediately disastrous—a showcase for John C. Bennett's attack
on Joseph during the summer of 1842.

That same summer Joseph deploys a very different approach to
Sarah Ann Whitney. Joseph, in effect, courts the Whitney family,
one of the first to join Joseph's church in Kirtland in late 1830.
Sarah Ann is six when Joseph and Emma live with the Whitney
family on their arrival in Kirtland. In 1842, Joseph dictates a revelation to his long-time associate Newel that contains the plural
marriage ceremony for Joseph and his daughter, Sarah Ann, barely
seventeen, promising eternal life to the family, to their ancestors
and descendants. Newel standing next to his wife marries Sarah
Ann and Joseph in July 1842. A year later, Joseph sends his young
wife a revelation in his own handwriting with similar promises: "if
She remain in the Everlasting covenant to the end as also all her
Fathers house Shall be Saved in the Same Eternal glory and if any
of them Shall wander from the foald of the Lord they shall not
perish but Shall return Saith the Lord and be Saived."[49]

Near the time Joseph writes this holograph revelation for his
young wife, he dictates a second revelation at his brother Hyrum's

---

48. The provenance of the Nancy Rigdon "happiness" letter is problematic. The
earliest copy survives in John C. Bennett's 1842 exposes, but it was eventually included in the *History of the Church*. For an overview of difficulties, see Gerrit Dirkmaat,
"Searching for "Happiness": Joseph Smith's Alleged Authorship of the 1842 Letter
to Nancy Rigdon," *Journal of Mormon History* 43, 3 (2016): 94–119. For a differing
exploration of these incidents, see Devery S Anderson, "'I Could Love Them All':
Nauvoo Polygamy in the Marriage of Willard and Jennetta Richards," June 7, 2013,
Sunstone magazine, at www.sunstonemagazine.com/i-could-love-them-all-nauvoo-
polygamy-in-the-marriage-of-willard-and-jennetta-richards.

49. "Blessing to Sarah Ann Whitney, 23 March 1843,"p. [1],The Joseph Smith Papers, accessed October 9, 2018, http://www.josephsmithpapers.org/paper-summary/
blessing-to-sarah-ann-whitney-23-march-1843/1.

request—a last-ditch attempt to convince Emma. That spring, Emma had briefly assented to Joseph's plural marriage and attended his marriage to the two Partridge sisters, Emily and Eliza, but then drew back. Emma did not know that Joseph was already married to the sisters. The revelation dictated by Joseph at Hyrum's request never directly addresses Emma. Rather she is a subject of conversation between the God voice and Joseph. This conversation, in effect, replays the conversation between God and Abraham about Sarai. It seems likely that Joseph has already tried the earlier arguments (happiness, save everyone) on Emma. This revelation makes clear that she must comply. Joseph may continue to take plural wives whatever she thinks, and her failure to comply means her damnation. Something more like a post-courtship approach.[50]

I pause over these examples to demonstrate both Joseph's general lack of attention to women—and the problematic structure made when he does attend. Any line of continuity in Nauvoo is still profoundly homosocial—seers, angels, men gone to heaven, gods once men. Still gender, the discontinuous, generally a story "under," is crucial. Remember that priesthood is a discontinuous and incommensurate theme along the arc of Joseph's texts. Who can deny tracking discontinuities associated with priesthood as crucial to Joseph's story. So, too, gender—but a tricky enterprise for a woman, a feminist scholar, writing about Joseph. I like to think that my extended encounter with Wilford Woodruff helped to prepare me for this challenge. A desire to be fair, but not implicated. To remain in the middest, refusing a story that comforts my contemporaries or me.

As I write, I am still, alas, in the middest of my Book of Joseph. Joseph came to champion a story without beginning or ending, because, as he often said in Nauvoo, a story with a beginning must have an ending. For my own Book of Joseph, I can only hope Joseph is right. I have described my beginnings, what led me into my unexpected, even accidental role, as a Mormon historian. With luck, I will have a happy ending.

---

50. "Revelation, 12 July 1843 [D&C 132]," p. 1, The Joseph Smith Papers, accessed October 9, 2018, http://www.josephsmithpapers.org/paper-summary/revelation-12-july-1843-dc-132/1. See my "Many Wives: Joseph Smith's Courting in Nauvoo, 1842–1843," American Academy of Religions (Northwest) and John Whitmer Historical Society, 2019.

RESURRECTING A BURIED LIFE: WRITING WILLIAM BICKERTON: FORGOTTEN LATTER DAY PROPHET

DANIEL P. STONE

14

William Bickerton (1815–1905), the poor English immigrant who started what is now the third largest Latter Day Saint denomination, known as the Church of Jesus Christ, died in frustration. That was something I was not expecting to learn while researching his life. Growing up in Bickerton's church, I learned that he had received a powerful revelation where he stood on a mountain, with God telling him that if he did not preach the gospel, he would be thrown into a chasm. I later learned that was not exactly how he described his life-changing revelation.

Writing the first comprehensive biography of Bickerton changed my life, along with my perspective on how my church has preserved its history. For over a century, the leadership of the Church of Jesus Christ has promoted heritage history (also referred to as faithful history), that is, a history that espouses spiritual faith and often neglects to offer in-depth examinations of the past, passing over complicated or controversial details.[1] To be sure, I love my church and the overall values it has instilled in me, but for years I was curious as to why the church's official histories did not offer more information, especially about Bickerton.

This is where my story begins.

---

1. For in-depth examinations about writing "faithful history," especially within the field of Mormon history, see George D. Smith, ed., *Faithful History: Essays on Writing Mormon History* (Salt Lake City: Signature Books, 1992).

University of Florida

In 2005 I enrolled at the University of Florida to start my undergraduate coursework. My first major was advertising, with a minor in history. My first love was history, but I chose to major in advertising because I thought, "What on earth can I do with a history degree?" It didn't take me long to realize that I needed to change my major to the subject I adored, especially after my cousin and roommate, Tony, who was also an advertising major, bluntly said to me one day, "Daniel, why don't you just change your major? You love history." He was right, and his advice encouraged me to dive more into history courses, as well as into my own personal library, which included the official history books of the Church of Jesus Christ.

There are two volumes of the church's history. Even though they offer important information, they are both heritage histories. Volume one was written by William H. Cadman in 1945, who was the president and historian of the church. He was also the son of William Cadman Sr., who replaced Bickerton as president of the church in 1902. This is likely one of the main reasons why the first volume does not go into detail about Bickerton's life. Cadman Sr. had become a bitter rival of Bickerton, and William H. most likely did not want to address the discord the church had suffered, especially since his father had helped to create it. Volume 2 offers only vignettes of Bickerton's life as well.[2] At first, I was puzzled by these absences. "Wasn't Bickerton the founder of the church?" I wondered. "Wouldn't he have played a major role in establishing and fostering the church?" As of yet, I did not know about the quarreling that occurred between Cadman Sr. and him, a blot on the church's history that would help to convince future writers to relegate Bickerton's memory to the sidelines. All I had learned about were the miracles that occurred in the past, along with the curious accusation that Bickerton had committed adultery. He had left the church, the official history books insinuated, but toward the end of his life, he repented and was restored to

---

2. William H. Cadman, *A History of the Church of Jesus Christ* (Monongahela, Pennsylvania: Church of Jesus Christ, 1945); Robert A. Watson, et al., eds., *A History of the Church of Jesus Christ* (Monongahela, Pennsylvania: Church of Jesus Christ, 2002).

full fellowship. The miracles, along with the lack of information, piqued my interest to learn more.

As a student of history, I like origin stories and biography. Even today, when I learn about new historical subjects, I'm first drawn to the origins of those subjects and the people who initiated them. According to Paula Backscheider, an award-winning scholar of biography, I'm not alone. "The last literary genre to be read by a very wide cross-section of people is biography," she noted. "Publishers can count on steady sales of biographies of film stars, military heroes, bank robbers ..., rock stars, adventurers, writers, sports figures, and murderers, and the readers of these books defy the usual marketing categories based on age, sex, occupation, education, race, and class."[3] After reading the church's history books, I decided to be the first person to write Bickerton's biography. And since most of Bickerton's life revolved around the church,

---

3. Paula R. Backscheider, *Reflections on Biography* (New York: Oxford University Press, 1999), xiii.

I believed that writing a biography would be an engaging way to reevaluate the church's history.

During the winter 2008 semester, I enrolled in a history research seminar entitled, "History of American Religion." I was excited to take this course for a couple reasons. I was interested in American religious history generally, but, more specifically, I wanted to do supervised research on Joseph Smith and the early Mormon movement. The professor of the class, Alan Petigny, specialized in twentieth-century American religious and intellectual history. He not only allowed me to write my first substantial research paper on Joseph Smith, but fostered my love for American religion and Mormon history. He took the time to mentor me during class, his office hours, and even treated me to coffee and lunch a few times. Although my research paper was primarily on Smith, Petigny encouraged me to write a small section of the paper on Bickerton and how he perceived Smith's prophethood. Again, the only information I knew about Bickerton was what the official church literature presented, so my summation was not thorough, but the experience once more stirred my curiosity to learn about Bickerton's life and his early church.

While visiting my parent's house during a school break, an elder at church introduced me to a scholarly article he had stumbled on while doing research on the internet. He told me it was about our church's migration to Kansas during the late nineteenth century. I was intrigued. "A non-member had written an in-depth examination about our church?" I wondered. "Where did he find the information to write the article?" I also knew little about the church's migration into the West, so this news piqued my interest. I found the article on the Kansas Historical Society's website. Written by Gary R. Entz and published in 2002 in the journal *Kansas History*, the article is entitled, "Zion Valley: The Mormon Origins of St. John, Kansas."[4] When I arrived back at school, I read the article while in the library as I waited for a class to start. I was engrossed. The article was fantastic; well written and researched. I was especially interested in the fact that I had never heard most

4. Gary R. Entz, "Zion Valley: The Mormon Origins of St. John, Kansas," *Kansas History* 24, 2 (Summer 2001).

of the information presented in the article. How could this be? How could I have not learned that Bickerton attempted to create a communal society in Kansas, only for the experiment to be hampered by the church members he led? I checked Entz's footnotes. He had found a lot of information in local Kansas newspapers. I never knew that church members in the past had written to the press, or that newspapers were interested in the church. All this information was fascinating. It seemed as though a veil had been lifted from my mind. For the first time, I realized that my church had a real history, a history that was rich and could be told with professional objectivity. Yet for one reason or another, the church itself had not attempted to do this. Most of the information in Entz's article was not in the church's literature. At that moment, Gary Entz changed my life. I was convinced even more that I wanted to be a historian and that I wanted to be the first person to present the details of Bickerton's life.

Florida Atlantic University

Toward the end of the winter 2008 semester, Petigny asked me if I planned on applying to graduate school since I was only one year away from graduation. I planned on it, I told him, but I wanted to get a job first so I could save money to pay for school. He then took me aside and said, "You know, you could go to graduate school for free." "How?" I asked. "You could get funding as a teaching assistant," he replied. I never knew that was possible. "Actually, I have a friend in the history department at the University of Alabama," he said. "He owes me a favor, so if you'd like to get your PhD, I can get you into the program." I was flattered. Although the offer was tempting, I decided to turn it down, only because I missed my family and wanted to move back to South Florida. Petigny then said to me, "Well, you should go to graduate school. I think you're meant to study history. If you want to go to graduate school in South Florida, I'll be happy to write a letter of recommendation." After that conversation, he continued to encourage me to apply to a graduate program. It didn't take long for him to convince me, and after researching a few programs, I settled on enrolling at Florida Atlantic University to earn an MA in history. With

Petigny's help, I was also able to get a teaching assistantship and fellowship from FAU, which paid for my education.[5]

All the history professors at FAU were terrific. They honed my research skills, taught me how to write compelling history, and fostered my interest in the study of religion. With this new education, I serendipitously stumbled on another groundbreaking article about the Bickertonites, once again authored by Gary Entz. Published in 2006 in the *Journal of Mormon History*, the article is entitled, "The Bickertonites: Schism and Reunion in a Restoration Church, 1880–1905."[6] I obtained a copy of the article, and after reading it, I felt excited. The article examined twenty-five years of dramatic history that was not discussed in the Church of Jesus Christ's own literature. The article noted significant historical events about my church that I had not heard before, and for the first time I learned why Bickerton's life was overlooked by the church's publications. Unlike what the church's official literature implied, Bickerton had not apostatized. Rather, he was accused of adultery by a jealous husband, an act of which he was never found guilty. And instead of William Cadman (who was president of the Quorum of Twelve Apostles) rending the leadership of the church from a fallen president, as some of the church literature taught, the church had actually split in two for twenty-two years, one schism following Bickerton, the other Cadman. As Entz explained, the church did reunite before Bickerton's death, yet his memory was largely forgotten after he died. In the church's first official history book, William H. Cadman took his father's side of the story and painted Bickerton as an adulterer and apostate. Entz made a compelling argument that rather than dig up messy details that could possibly engender strife, William H. instead "wrote William Bickerton and the western branch in St. John [Kansas] out of much of the Church's chronicles. The result has been that the memory of Bickerton has become obscured within his own

---

5. Unfortunately, Dr. Alan Petigny passed away in September 2013. I have nothing but the fondest memories of him. See Jeff Schweers, "UF History Professor Found Dead in Apartment," *Gainesville Sun*, Sept. 30, 2013.

6. Gary R. Entz, "The Bickertonites: Schism and Reunion in a Restoration Church," *Journal of Mormon History* 32, 3 (Fall 2006).

church."[7] Entz also revealed that Bickerton had asked for the nineteenth chapter of Job to be read at his funeral, a telling piece of scripture that exposed the prophet's feelings before he died: "My kinsfolk have failed, and my familiar friends have forgotten me" (v. 14). I now understood why the details of Bickerton's life had become elusive. To spare the church of a complex past, William H. chose to simplify the story of the church's schism for its first official history, siding with his father's story and, in turn, subjecting Bickerton to an obscure memory. I now recognized that a study of Bickerton's life would not only fill a gap within Mormon historiography, it would challenge the Church of Jesus Christ's official historiography.

Proposal

In December 2011, I wrote a proposal to the Quorum of Twelve Apostles of the Church of Jesus Christ to ask for access to the church's archive. Without permission, the archive is normally restricted from researchers. I was a new member of the church's historical committee (a non-paid strictly volunteer position), and to give my proposal more clout, I wrote the proposal as a member of that committee. I planned on researching and writing the book independently, but the church's general historian and assistant historian agreed to serve as advisors. In the proposal, I stated that I wanted to write an academic, scholarly history. "The benefits of this biography will be twofold," I wrote. "The Church will have an objective examination of William Bickerton's life, and members of the Church will gain a rare access into the mind of Bickerton, as well as the captivating social and political times in which he lived." I also informed the apostles that while writing the book, I would address sensitive issues, "such as false revelations, public quarrels, and the reorganization of the Church in 1904."[8] Thankfully, after reading the proposal, the apostles granted me access to the archive. As far as I know, only a handful of individuals had ever received this opportunity. I was ecstatic.

---

7. Entz, "The Bickertonites," 44.

8. Daniel P. Stone, "'But to this Man Will I Look': The Life and Times of William Bickerton Proposal," Dec. 22, 2011, in my possession.

After doing some initial research in Kansas and Pennsylvania, I began writing the book in February 2013. I actually didn't begin with writing the introduction or chapter one, but rather chapter two. I had researched enough to write a short overview of early Mormon history, along with Bickerton's time as a member of Sidney Rigdon's Church of Christ in Pittsburgh, Pennsylvania. (Rigdon broke from the main body of the Latter-day Saints after Joseph Smith's death in 1844.) I also learned that it is better to start writing in the middle of one's research, rather than waiting until after the research is done. Books will take much longer to write if authors wait until they have completed their research. Besides, as authors write, they often find that they need to go in another direction than previously anticipated. This was one of the best pieces of advice I ever read (thanks to Richard Bushman's preface in *Joseph Smith: Rough Stone Rolling*),[9] and it proved to be true. By March 2013, I completed a rough draft of chapter two. Of course, I felt excited. I had never written a book before, and after having written one chapter, I realized that it was possible to write others.

For the next two years, I continued to write and conduct research in my spare time. I usually did research on the weekends, sometimes taking research trips with my wife, Laura. I wrote whenever opportunities arose, sometimes late into the evenings after arriving home from my full-time job as a research archivist for a private archive in Detroit. As a research archivist, I not only archive the collections of my boss, but I'm often called on to conduct research for time-sensitive projects using the archive's materials. Over the years, this job has certainly helped hone my research, writing, and time management skills. I completed five chapters of the book by January 2015, and in those two years, I learned more than I ever anticipated, and more than I could put in the book. Two things, however, stood out that changed my perspective on how my church has told its history. First, I had been taught that my church began after Bickerton received a powerful vision where God placed him on a mountain, telling him that if he did not preach the gospel, the Lord would throw him into a chasm. However, after reading

9. Richard Lyman Bushman, *Joseph Smith: Rough Stone Rolling* (New York: Vintage, 2005), xxiii.

Bickerton's accounts of his vision, he actually described it in more pleasant terms. According to Bickerton, God had placed him on the highest mountain on the earth. He was told that if he did not preach the gospel, he would *fall* into a chasm.[10] In the vision, God did not threaten Bickerton. Rather, the Lord encouraged him to stay on the path he was on so that he wouldn't fall into the chasm. Second, as Gary Entz first explored, I learned in greater detail why Bickerton, after enduring a decades long feud with Cadman, asked for the nineteenth chapter of Job to be read at his funeral.[11] As Entz explained, before Bickerton died, he had even written to the *St. John Weekly News* in Kansas, "I feel like Job that the balance of my life I will wait until my change [death and resurrection] comes."[12] It was humbling to grasp that Bickerton compared himself to Job, one of the most persecuted people in the Bible. And after reading the nineteenth chapter of Job in full, I was saddened that Bickerton had asked for these words to be read at his funeral. In the chapter, Job laments that his family and friends have forsaken him, and begs for his story to be told one day. Part of the chapter reads, "Oh that my words were now written! oh that they were printed in a book! That they were graven with an iron pen and lead in the rock for ever!" (Job 19:23–24). Never had I expected to learn that Bickerton, by adopting Job's lamentation, requested from the grave for his story to be told in the future. Bickerton must have presumed that his side of the story would be tucked away by his own church. As one can imagine, this information was jolting, especially because I was attempting to write his story.

After completing five chapters of the book, I decided that it was time to show the apostles my progress and ask whether they

---

10. William Bickerton, Charles Brown, George Barnes, William Cadman, and Joseph Astin, *The Ensign: or a Light to Lighten the Gentiles, in which the Doctrine of The Church of Jesus Christ of Latter-Day Saints, is Set Forth, and Scripture Evidence Adduced to Establish it. Also, a Brief Treatise upon the Most Important Prophecies Recorded in the Old and New Testaments, which relate to the Great Work of God of the Latter Days* (Pittsburgh: Ferguson & Co., 1863), 5, typescript in The Church of Jesus Christ Historical Archive, Greensburg, Pennsylvania; William Bickerton, "Testimony, June 1903," 2, in Church of Jesus Christ Historical Archive, Greensburg, Pennsylvania.

11. "A Pioneer Gone," *St. John Weekly News*, Feb. 24, 1905; Entz, "The Bickertonites," 42.

12. William Bickerton, "Elder Bickerton Writes," *St. John Weekly News*, Jan. 20, 1905.

were interested in potentially having the church publish the completed manuscript. The historian and assistant historian had been offering critiques on the prose and grammar throughout the writing process, and they had offered advice on how to approach the apostles. From the outset of the project, members of the church's historical committee, along with other church members, had advised me to be mindful as I approached the apostles. In the past, church members had attempted to examine the church's history in more detail, but at times they were discouraged to do so. I was also informed that since the church's historical narrative was shaped by William H. Cadman, descendants of the Cadman family, along with those who sympathize with that narrative, can sometimes be sensitive to reexaminations of it. However, I'm not a descendant of Bickerton or of Cadman, which I believe enabled me to look at Bickerton's life and the church's history with greater impartiality.

I sent the apostles the five chapters, along with a cover letter that was not much different from my original proposal. A few months later, I received word from the general historian that the apostles had read my chapters. However, they did not say whether they were interested in having the church publish the manuscript once it was completed. The general historian told me that one apostle informed him privately that what I had written was the best history of the church he had ever read, while others in the quorum were uncomfortable with some of the information that I presented, like the facts that Joseph Smith had practiced polygamy or that Bickerton had believed in the Doctrine and Covenants when a member of Sidney Rigdon's and Brigham Young's churches, along with the fact that he referenced the D&C text as the prophet and leader of his own church. It was suggested that I should consider deleting information like this from the manuscript, but I decided against it. This information was historical fact, and I did not want to overlook it.

After having this conversation with the general historian, I decided to seek an independent publisher. I soon told the general historian my reasons for making this decision, mainly because I felt the apostles wanted to promote heritage history, while I wanted to write scholarly history. The general historian eventually agreed to support me in this endeavor, and he and the assistant historian also agreed to continue to act as advisors for my prose and grammar. I was thankful for their support. I then wrote a letter to the apostles informing them of my decision.

Around this time, I learned from the general historian that the Lamb Foundation for Research and Religious Studies Archive located in Albuquerque, New Mexico, actually held several of the church's original record books. The archive is owned by John E. Mancini, who established the foundation to foster research into Hebrew, Christian, and Mormon religion and history. The news greatly aroused my interest. How the Lamb Foundation received these record books has been the cause of controversy within the church for decades (and, in my opinion, investigating the personal details on how this occurred was not part of my purpose for writing the book), but I knew that in order to continue to write the biography of Bickerton, it was important that I had access to these documents. Normally, the Lamb Foundation Archive is not open to the general public, but after contacting Mancini and explaining why I wanted access to the materials, he granted it. Again, I was thrilled. Now I had access to thousands of pages of church record books, of which Mancini had produced typescripts and high resolution photos of. The path opened even wider for me to continue my research and writing.

Sunstone

In July 2015, I attended the annual conference of the Sunstone Education Foundation in Salt Lake City. I presented a paper entitled, "Woe to the Land Shadowing with Wings: William Bickerton, the Book of Mormon, and the American Civil War." The presentation went well, and I received several great questions from the audience. I also had the opportunity to meet Joe Geisner and the acquisitions editor of Signature Books, John Hatch. Geisner introduced me to Hatch, who gave me his business card. He let me know that he was interested in the book once it was done, and asked if I could send him some sample chapters in the near future. Of course, I was thrilled. I was aware of Signature Books, along with the quality of books it produces. I sent Hatch some sample chapters, and soon after, he informed me that he enjoyed reading them. He also informed me that once the manuscript was completed, it would have to undergo peer review, but reassured me that if I continued to write the book as I had been thus far, he expected the process to go smoothly. All this was exciting news, and I decided to make an effort to finish the book as quickly as possible.

I began making time to write every day, keeping a particular thought in mind. I had once heard from an author that writing a book is like rolling a bulldozer tire. Once a person picks up the tire and gets it rolling, it's fairly easy to keep it going. However, if the person continuously lets the tire fall, they will have to keep picking it up, starting their momentum all over again. I did not want to lose momentum, and I soon realized how much easier it was to stay on task if I just kept writing.

Yet, after a couple months of maintaining this productivity, I began to recognize that the book would take at least another year to finish if I kept up the same pace. This timeline was most likely not going to work for me, especially because Laura was pregnant with our first child, and was going to deliver early the following year. So to finish the book in a more timely manner, I asked my bosses where I worked if I could go into the office only two days a week until I finished writing, with the understanding that I would take a pay cut during this time period. Thankfully, they were understanding and granted my request. This freed up my time, allowing me to write five days a week, about eight hours a day. Keeping this pace, I was able to finish the manuscript by late December 2015. I remember the evening when I emailed the completed manuscript to Hatch. I was sitting at my desk, looking at the computer screen, feeling a sense of relief and accomplishment. I clicked, "Send," smiled, and then gave Laura a kiss and hug.

The Letter

A few days before I finished writing the manuscript, I sent a letter to the apostles to inform them of my progress. Although I was no longer writing for the church, the general historian and I felt it would be courteous to let them know that the book was almost ready to be sent to the publisher for review. I also wanted to assure them that I was not trying to harm the church, but instead write a scholarly biography of Bickerton.[13]

The following month, in January 2016, I received a letter back from the apostles. The apostles asked that I not publish the manuscript until they had time to review it in its entirety and offer critiques and suggestions. Also, they requested that I not examine the twenty-two-year feud that occurred between Bickerton and Cadman. Of course, I understood that the apostles' mission is to promote faith, and I respected that. But I had written the book as a historian and had sent the book to a scholarly publisher to be peer reviewed and considered for publication.[14]

I wrote a letter back to the apostles and tried to explain why I could not follow their request. Maybe I was too bold in my letter, but I believed that it was important to discuss the feud between Bickerton and Cadman, especially because it helped explain why the memory of Bickerton had been obscured for so long:

> The fact that historians and leaders of the Church have ignored this feud, or found it better to tuck it away for over a century, is not only surprising, but has endangered the Church's integrity. Almost all the primary sources that reveal this controversy are located in the public domain. The official Church minutes disclose some details, but the majority of this information is found in newspaper articles, most of which were written by members of the Church. I retrieved all these newspaper articles from the Detre Library & Archives at the Senator John Heinz History Center in Pittsburgh and the Kansas State Historical Society in Topeka. Members like William Cadman, Eli Kendall, J. S. Weeks, and William Bickerton wrote to the newspapers to share their thoughts and concerns. All their letters are open to the public. With a simple Google search, the notations to these newspaper articles can be found. A historian, Gary R. Entz, published two journal articles, one in *Kansas History* and the other in the *Journal of Mormon History*, all of which discuss the controversial aspects of the Church's history in Kansas, and he even shares the information where the newspaper articles can be found. I used Entz's notations as a springboard for my research, which led me

---

13. Daniel P. Stone, "Letter to Q12 about W. Bickerton," Dec. 25, 2015, copy in my possession.

14. Quorum of Twelve Apostles of the Church of Jesus Christ, "Response to Brother Daniel," Jan. 21, 2016, in my possession.

to find even more information. To some, this may be unfortunate, but the fact is that William Bickerton and William Cadman are public figures. They are not owned by the Church of Jesus Christ, and the conflict that ensued between the two men is already public knowledge. A simple Google search allows any person to read the well-researched articles written by Entz, and offers the opportunity to conduct more research. Interestingly enough, about 50% of my entire book was written using primary and secondary sources found within the public domain. Newspaper articles, letters, journals, and books reveal several aspects of Bickerton's life. I did not solely rely on church minutes to write about Bickerton's religious journey, but used all the valid sources I could find, hoping to write a balanced, well-rounded biography.[15]

I did not receive a letter back from the apostles, which I think was a good thing. This meant that I could publish the book independently. And thankfully, after reviewing the manuscript, Signature Books informed me in April 2016 that it had decided to publish my Bickerton biography. Once again, I felt a sense of relief and accomplishment. William Bickerton's story would now be told, placing him more prominently within Mormon and American religious historiography.

Conclusion

Writing the first biography of William Bickerton was a rewarding, yet challenging experience. On top of finding historical documents and writing the book, I had to maneuver through church bureaucracy and politics. I could not include all my experiences in this brief reminiscence, yet in the end, the most important fact is that the book was published, and I consider this one of the most notable successes of my life. The book even served as part of my dissertation to receive a PhD in history from Manchester Metropolitan University in England. Now Bickerton has a more visible place in history, especially within Mormon studies, and I hope that this will enrich the field and encourage other scholars to study the Bickertonites. Thankfully, the overall experience of writing the book has made me stronger, and my faith in God and love of history has only grown more earnest.

---

15. Daniel P. Stone, "Letter to Q12," Jan. 25, 2016, copy in my possession.

WRITING BRIGHAM YOUNG

JOHN G. TURNER

Brigham Young (1801–77) was a religiously curious individual. He investigated several species of evangelicalism before embracing the Reformed Methodists, an almost pentecostal offshoot of American Wesleyanism. He would later visit a Shaker meeting, and he read popular religious literature such as Buck's *Theological Dictionary* and Butterworth's *Concordance*. Presumably, Young bumped into Universalists, Unitarians, and other movements and sects during his relentless missionary travels in the 1830s and early 1840s. When he encountered Mormonism, he figured he could take its measure quickly, as he had sized up Methodism and Freemasonry. "I knew what religion was," he later narrated. Most religions were worthless. He compared such investigations to a trickster who opened up a box to reveal another box, which contained yet another, and so forth, until opening the last tiny box which contained nothing but a useful speck of wood.

Young had found Methodism far more compelling than he suggested in his reminiscence. Along with other members of his family, he was a lay evangelist of sorts for the Reformed Methodists. Nevertheless, it is certainly true that he underestimated the Book of Mormon and the emerging religious movement which had brought it forth. Young explained that when he "searched Mormonism," he found he "could not get hold of neither end of it. It was from eternity. I found it went right beyond time and into eternity again." Young found far more than he expected at first glance.[1]

I can relate. Mormonism proved a much richer and complex subject than I anticipated. After finishing a dissertation and first book on the evangelical Protestant ministry Campus Crusade for Christ, I considered writing a book on Mormonism and conservative politics. Growing up within the subculture of American evangelicalism, I occasionally encountered something about an anti-Christian "cult" called Mormonism. I learned something more about the Church of Jesus Christ of Latter-day Saints in graduate school, in part because I had several very winsome Mormon classmates. And it was 2007. Mitt Romney was running for president for the first time, and many Americans were not sure whether he and his religion were Christian. Part of my interest in writing about Mormonism was simply to satisfy my own curiosity about the Church of Jesus Christ of Latter-day Saints, its doctrines and practices, and its history.

So, like Brigham Young, I investigated. Soon, I no longer wanted to write a book about Mormons and conservative politics. While I think more scholars should train their sights on the more recent history of the church, I found the nineteenth century irresistible and thought I ought to begin at the beginning.

I kept unwrapping boxes. I read Richard Bushman's *Rough Stone Rolling*, Jan Shipps's *Mormonism: A New Religious Tradition*, and Sarah B. Gordon's *The Mormon Question*. And then I read Will Bagley's *Blood of the Prophets*, which blames Brigham Young for the slaughter of nearly 120 men, women, and children at the Mountain Meadows Massacre. I realized that Brigham Young was not only the second president of his church but also a person of enormous significance for mid-nineteenth-century United States history more generally. After reading the existing biographies of Brigham Young, most notably Leonard Arrington's path-breaking *American Moses*, I decided to research and write my own. Only with the benefit of hindsight did I realize the depth of my foolishness.

---

1. Brigham Young, Discourse, Apr. 17, 1853, LaJean Purcell Carruth translation of George D. Watt shorthand, CR 100 912, Church History Library, Church of Jesus Christ of Latter-day Saints, Salt Lake City, Utah (hereafter CHL).

I am certain that Richard Turley perceived my foolishness immediately. In the spring of 2008, I spent a month in Utah, visiting
the LDS Church History Library and other repositories in Utah.
Knowing that gaining access to the Brigham Young Papers in the
Church History Library was of paramount importance, I had written asking for an appointment with Steven Olsen, then managing
director of the Church History Department. He was out of the
country, so Rick—recently appointed Assistant Church Historian— agreed to see me. He was extremely cordial and encouraging.

I felt entirely overwhelmed during my first month at the Church
History Library. The binder with the finding aid for the Brigham
Young Papers was thick. The microfilm room was dark, leading
to drowsiness and dashes for coffee at the nearest McDonald's. I
spent days looking for several drafts of the first sections of Brigham
Young's history ("The Manuscript History of Brigham Young"),
thinking they might shed further light on the story of his early life
and conversion. I finally found those documents a few years later.

I also consulted the Leonard Arrington Papers in the Merrill Library at Utah State University in Logan, which contain many of the Edyth Romney typescripts of the primary sources Arrington used as the basis for his biography: the Brigham Young diaries, the General Minutes Collection, letter books, and the papers of Young's contemporaries. These were an invaluable start, because they allowed me to plunge into primary sources that would have taken me years to decipher on my own.

During that first month in Utah, I attended the Mormon History Association for the first time. This was a revelatory experience. As an academic historian, I was used to attending professional conference which primarily serve as job fairs and opportunities for self-advancement. Early in my career, I always seemed to end up on a Sunday morning panel, in front of three or four people who looked as if they wished they had slept in. I think such experiences are an academic rite of passage. Meetings of the MHA are nothing like those other conferences. At the first MHA I attended, every panel was jammed. Even more remarkably, people listened to the papers. In fact, attendees cared a great deal about what speakers said, in part, because they had some personal stake in the subject matter. Attending MHA made me much more enthusiastic about my research project. If I were lucky, some of those folks would even read what I wrote.

The Mormon History Association also generates a sense of community unusual for an academic conference. The stereotype about Mormons being nice seemed to hold, but it turned out it applied just as much to ex-Mormons and to almost everyone else who turns up at MHA or the Church History Library. Because I came to this project without any prior positive or negative association with the church, perhaps it was easier for me to get along well with people from various factions, and so many of those people were incredibly generous with their time and resources. The very best thing about doing Mormon History is rubbing shoulders with fellow practitioners.

Subsequently, I took my family to Utah for three summers, facilitated by generous research grants from BYU's Charles Redd Center for the Study of Western History. Besides providing blessed

relief from what would have been hellishly hot summers in southern Alabama, these extended stays in Utah allowed me to complete
my research. They also provided me with the opportunity to meet
many fellow scholars and gain some understanding of contemporary Mormonism.

The latter point was very important to me. I share Brigham
Young's curiosity about other religious traditions, and in order to
satiate that curiosity, I needed more than books and historical documents, important as they are. I needed to attend Sunday services,
temple open houses, and Pioneer Day festivities. I needed to visit
Latter-day Saint historical sites. I needed to read Mormon scriptures, though they took me a few years, in part because the Book
of Mormon really is chloroform as an audiobook—at least, for me.
These encounters did not lead me to respond to Mormonism as
did Brigham Young, but they helped me to gain an appreciation
for it as a living and complicated religious tradition, one that I
came to regard as its own distinctive branch of Christianity.

Most important of all, though, was gaining access to the
Brigham Young Papers. Over the past two decades, the church
has gradually made more and more of its nineteenth-century materials available to researchers. I began my project at a good time,
but being able to examine all of the Brigham Young Papers was
still a long process of mostly pleasant negotiation. For the most
part, employees at the Church History Library bent over back-
wards to help. They digitized enormous amounts of material for
me, so that I could continue my research while away from Utah.
Over time, moreover, they gave me access to everything in the
collection, including papers pertaining to marriages, divorces, and
excommunications. In terms of materials in other collections, the
church rejected a few requests, namely the minutes of some prayer
circles over which Young presided in the early 1850s. Since my
book's publication, the church has either published or opened
access to a few additional sources, such as portions of William
Clayton's Nauvoo journals, the Nauvoo Council of Fifty minutes,
and most of the George Q. Cannon journals. These would have
enriched my narrative, but they would not have significantly altered any of my conclusions.

Questions of access directly relate to one of my goals for the book. Leonard Arrington's *American Moses* was the first Young biography that made extensive use of the above-mentioned Brigham Young Papers, building on studies such as Dean Jessee's documentary essays on Brigham Young's family and Ronald Esplin's dissertation on Brigham Young and the Quorum of the Twelve. Arrington's citation and discussion of these documents were enormously useful to me, but I also found that he made insufficient use of many sources, such as the journal of the Church Historian's Office, the General Minutes Collection, and portions of the Brigham Young Papers themselves, such as Young's correspondence with his wives. For a variety of reasons, not least because of the sheer vastness of the archives, Arrington left a number of stones unturned. Moreover, other researchers had in the intervening decades unearthed additional sources, such as the George D. Watt shorthand notes of Brigham Young's sermons that LaJean Purcell Carruth has painstakingly deciphered. A more thorough use of all of the available sources, I realized, could lead to a richer, more fully human portrait of Brigham Young.

I had several other goals for the biography. Brigham Young is primarily known as the practical organizer who followed and tried to carry out Joseph Smith's aspirations. Smith is the dreamer; Young is the builder. There is some truth to these ideas. Young was, at least, among the most influential colonizers in American history, responsible for the settlement of a vast swath of the present-day American West. He helped to facilitate the migration of tens of thousands of Latter-day Saints to the Great Basin, dispersing them to plant towns and start industries. On some occasions, Young dismissed his own prophetic mantle, referring to himself as a "Yankee guesser."[2] As had Leonard Arrington, however, I perceived a complex and evolving spirituality underneath Young's practical exterior and wanted to explore further those aspects of Young's personality and leadership.

It goes without saying that Young was and remains a deeply

---

2. John G. Turner, *Brigham Young: Pioneer Prophet* (Cambridge, Massachusetts: Harvard University Press, 2008), 272. Subsequent references to my book are given parenthetically.

polarizing figure. He was a prolific polygamist and a theocrat within a country that extolled democracy and romantic, companionate monogamy. When I began my research, Will Bagley's *Blood of the Prophets* was still a relatively new title, and Ronald Walker, Glen Leonard, and Richard Turley were about to publish their *Massacre at Mountain Meadows*. My goal was to offer a full and frank discussion of this and other controversial episodes in Young's life, without turning my story into a morality tale of any sort.

Finally, I wanted to write a book people might enjoy reading. One could insert here one of the many jokes about how PhD programs turn decent writers into academics who produce incomprehensible and dull dissertations and books. I wanted to cut against that grain as much as possible. I aimed to limit the book's length to around 400 pages and to avoid both jargon and in-text discussion of prior scholarship.

As I proceeded with my research, I had a number of surprises, many of which reflect my own lack of prior knowledge rather than any original discoveries on my part. I had no idea that early Latter-day Saints not only spoke in tongues, but sang in tongues. Especially because it is such a contrast with the more quiet, reflective public piety of Mormons today, the ecstatic (mid-nineteenth-century Americans would have said "enthusiastic") nature of early Mormon spirituality caught me off guard.

I was even more surprised that the sources existed to document the lives of a large number of Brigham Young's wives. With the exception of Mary Ann Angell, Amelia Folsom, and women who achieved renown in their own right such as Eliza Snow and Zina Huntington, most of Young's wives have remained names on a list. The Brigham Young Papers, though, contains correspondence between Young and many of his wives, as well as other documents that shed light on his relationships with them. I found countless fascinating stories: Augusta Adams, who would have preferred to have married Joseph Smith (or Jesus Christ); Elizabeth Lewis, who told Young that God had revealed that he should marry her; Mary Woodward, who wondered if Young wanted her to have children with her first husband for Young. I would have loved to have done for Brigham Young's wives what Todd Compton accomplished for

Joseph Smith's wives in his *In Sacred Loneliness*. Limitations of space precluded me from a full treatment of Young's family, but I included as much material as I could about his wives and correspondingly less about his children.

I was also surprised to learn—primarily through books such as Kathleen Flake's *The Politics of American Religious Identity* and Sarah Barringer Gordon's *The Mormon Question*—just how central the "Mormon question" was to American politics for a full half-century. Prior to the 1846 exodus from Nauvoo, Mormonism was primarily a local or regional question, with those living near Missouri or Nauvoo often reaching very different conclusions about the Latter-day Saints than Americans who lived far away from Mormon gathering places. For most Americans, Mormons were a strange curiosity rather than a menace. In the years immediately following 1846, the Saints received a measure of sympathy from many Americans because of their persecution. This all changed in the early 1850s, after the church announced and publicly defended polygamy and when Mormon leaders began clashing with federal non-Mormon appointees for the Utah territory. For the ensuing quarter-century, Young defended Mormon autonomy against the US government, its armies, and its officials, standing his ground whenever possible and ceding it when necessary.

Academic historians care as much about their books as other authors. In other words, they—or at least I—check sales rankings relentlessly and cringe at every negative comment. In fact, few things foster narcissism as effectively as the writing of books. Those academic historians with a modicum of experience or wisdom, however, approach a book's publication with realistic expectations. One hopes for positive scholarly reviews and positive feedback from those few family members who feel obliged to read it.

Given such expectations, I am eternally grateful to Willard Mitt Romney for winning the Republican nomination for the US presidency in 2012. I am convinced that the interest in all things Mormon that Romney generated enabled my publisher to secure reviews in outlets such as the *New York Times*, *National Review*, and the *New Yorker*, along with a brief mention in the *Boston Globe*.

Had Romney captured the White House, he probably would have doubled the sales of my next book as well. Oh well.

Also fortunate was the fact that most reviewers recognized the book's many merits and that few commented at length on its shortcomings. See the above note on authorial narcissism. Another thing that feeds such narcissism is the opportunity to respond to book reviews. Only a few comments stung. One was Alex Beam's *New York Times* assessment that "Turner is a good writer in possession of a great story" and his wish that "Turner would make this double-barreled, all-American story sing."[3] As noted above, it's difficult to combine a detailed examination of primary sources with limpid prose, and some of us are more gifted singers than others. Once I got over that comment, I was happy with what was on balance a very positive review.

One of the most negative reviews came from Latter-day Saint historian Gene Sessions, the author of a splendid biography of Jedediah Grant, a counselor in the First Presidency during the mid-1850s. Sessions took issue with the book's allegedly negative tone and alleged lack of balance. "The overall message of this biography," he wrote, "seems to be that Brigham Young in the final analysis was a coarse, deceitful, malevolent, rude, violent, profane, and arrogant man who just happened to have some remarkable leadership ability." More on that point below. What I did not like about the review was Sessions's suggestion that the book's shortcomings related to my own religious affiliation. "It is perhaps understandable," he opined, "that a devout Protestant who won the Alan M. Jackson Preaching Award while earning his master's of divinity at Louisville Presbyterian Theological Seminary would have little sympathy for Mormon doctrines and theology." I'm not as devout as I think I should be, and I did not deserve that preaching award. Furthermore, I reject Sessions's assertion that my book "expends much ink" pursuing an appraisal of contemporary Mormonism or its doctrines. For the record, I have entirely forgiven Joseph Smith or Jesus Christ for the takeaway message of the First Vision that "Presbyterianism is not true." As to any antipathy

---

3. *New York Times*, Oct. 21, 2008, BR16.

toward Mormonism as a religious system, I refer Gene Sessions and everyone else to my 2016 *The Mormon Jesus*.

Still, Sessions's concern about the book's balance and tone raise an important question. "Turner's persistent desire to help the reader see clearly the nastier sides of this complex human being," he wrote, "makes one wonder why anyone would follow this guy across the street let alone across the country." One might even ask why some fifty-five women married this warthog! In all seriousness, Sessions's point is important, so important that I repeatedly answered it in *Pioneer Prophet*. [4]

I highlight Young's spiritual and apostolic leadership on many occasions. For instance, I note that many English emigrants to Nauvoo and Utah "possessed memories of his [Young's] spiritual leadership in England" and quote Young's colleague Ezra T. Benson that many in England "say that it was Brother Brigham's voice that they first heard proclaiming the glad tidings of the gospel" (78). Along the same lines, I explain that in the wake of Joseph Smith's murder, "Young provided the church with other forms of sorely needed spiritual leadership" and "the sort of priestly leadership he had exercised after his return from London" (117). He prayed with the sick and anointed them for healing. Under his oversight, the Saints finished the Nauvoo temple, and Young led thousands of church members through its sacred ordinances. He danced and spoke in tongues in the Nauvoo temple, and he danced with the Saints on the trail west. I point out that while "Young stood above the people as their ecclesiastical hierarch ... he also danced with them late into the night and slept on sofas and pallets" (132). On several occasions, I reiterate that to "most church members, Brigham Young was the church's earthly savior following Smith's death, an indispensable protector and benefactor" (413). I did my best to accentuate Young's sense of humor, his persistence, and his capacity for self-examination and change.

I'm almost starting to like the man, but let's not get carried away. There is a good bit of grim and unsavory material in *Pioneer Prophet*, especially in the post-Nauvoo chapters. It was difficult to

---

4. *Mormon Historical Studies* 14, 1 (Spring 2013): 185–87.

write the Utah War and Mountain Meadows Massacre chapter. How could Mormon settlers in present-day southwestern Utah butcher nearly 120 non-Mormon emigrants bound for California? More to the point, is it conceivable that they would have done so without an express order from Brigham Young? When writing this chapter, I benefited tremendously from both Will Bagley's *Blood of the Prophets* and the tri-authored *Massacre at Mountain Meadows*. Bagley contends that Young sent Apostle George A. Smith to southern Utah in August 1857 to set the attack in motion. Walker, Leonard, and Turley place the massacre in the context of gentile-Mormon animosity for which many individuals bore responsibility and conclude that it was the work of southern Utah leaders. Bagley further alleges that Young sheltered those responsible for justice, later sacrificing John D. Lee as a scapegoat in order to protect his own hide. Walker, Leonard, and Turley do not discuss the massacre's aftermath at length in their book, though they note that Young occasionally addressed the massacre, "condemning it and offering help to government officials in prosecuting the perpetrators."[5]

In *Pioneer Prophet*, I conclude that "there is no satisfactory evidence that Young ordered the massacre." In the end, Young's letter instructing Isaac Haight to "not meddle with them [the emigrants]" is exculpatory. At the same time, legal guilt and moral responsibility are two very different matters. Young's decision to encourage Indian attacks on non-Mormon wagon trains was reckless, and Young "fomented the hatred and anxiety that made it conceivable for Mormons in southern Utah to slaughter men, women, and children" (280). Moreover, Young showed a distinct lack of interest in bringing those responsible to either civil or ecclesiastical justice, certainly in part because he feared that a full investigation would redound to the harm of himself and his church.

According to Wilford Woodruff's journal, Young interpreted the Mountain Meadows Massacre as God's judgment. In a number of other instances, Young condoned violence against Indians, gentiles, and dissenters. There is no debate among historians about whether

---

5. Ronald W. Walker, Richard E. Turley Jr., and Glen M. Leonard, *Massacre at Mountain Meadows* (New York: Oxford University Press, 2008), 229.

or not Young ordered violent reprisals against the Utah Valley Utes in February 1850. The operation included the execution of disarmed male prisoners. Despite this macabre beginning, Young at other times expressed remarkable empathy for native peoples displaced by Mormon settlement. "This is their home," Young rebuked settlers at Springville during the Black Hawk War of the mid-1860s. The Saints had a responsibility to feed the Indians, he continued, because "we are living on their possessions and in their homes" (347).

Perhaps most perplexing and disturbing is the often violent rhetoric Young employed when discussing his own people. During the "reformation" of 1856–57, Young spoke of "transgressors, who, if they knew themselves, would beg of their brethren to shed their blood, that the smoke thereof might ascend to God as an offering to appease the wrath that is kindled against them" (258). At the height of the reformation, a Welsh immigrant named Thomas Lewis in Manti was castrated on orders from Bishop Warren Snow. "I will tell you," Young insisted when hearing objections to Snow's course of action, "that when a man is trying to do right & do[es] some thing that is not exactly in order I feel to sustain him" (259). Scattered in different portions of the Brigham Young papers are letters between Young and Thomas Lewis's mother, who eventually married the church president. While the Thomas Lewis incident is a particular grisly episode in early Utah history, any responsible historian would integrate such sources into Young's biography.

For me, it was important to sort out the details of such cases as much as possible, while recognizing that the historical record sometimes left more questions than answers. In terms of the biography, though, a more important question for me was *why* Brigham Young adopted such a harsh stance toward dissenters and non-Mormon officials. I do not attribute this to any cruelty inherent within Young's soul or personality, nor do I dismiss it as standard fare for the mid-nineteenth-century United States. Rather, I hypothesize that Young was deeply traumatized by Joseph Smith's murder and the collapse of Mormon Nauvoo and determined not to permit those dark chapters of the church's history repeat themselves. In Nauvoo, Young slept in the temple and used bodyguards because he feared anti-Mormons would make him their next target. When other church leaders, including members of the Quorum of the Twelve, resisted his leadership, he feared that factionalism might cause the same problems that it had in the 1830s and early 1840s. When American officials appeared in Utah, and when Young heard that US forces were marching west in the summer of 1857, he feared the worst. Thus, Young humbled men like Orson Pratt and John Taylor, and he threatened miscreants among the Saints with beheading. Young bragged—correctly—that the church did not suffer 10 percent the amount of dissent under his leadership as it had under Joseph Smith's. Young had no intention of becoming a second martyr.

Other instances of violence also sparked my curiosity, in part because they bore little connection to questions of ecclesiastical or political authority. In February 1851, Madison Hambleton shot a physician named John Vaughn. The philandering Dr. Vaughn began an affair with Chelnecha Hambleton while her husband was away. According to Manti settler Phineas Wolcott Cook, Vaughn came to the Hambleton home to set a broken leg and in the process became infatuated with Chelnecha. According to one report, Chelnecha Hambleton darkened her home at night in order to enjoy Vaughn's company with as much privacy as possible. Vaughn had been arrested in Salt Lake City the previous year for adultery, so it is hardly surprising that his attentions to Chelnecha Hambleton attracted notice. After Madison Hambleton returned, he shot Vaughn at point-blank range after a Sunday meeting. "Whether he was guilty of adultary or not at that time I do not know," stated Cook, "but he had sedused a mans wife before." Cook might not have known, but church leaders concluded that Chelnecha and Vaughn had consummated their affair. Brigham Young spoke on Hambleton's behalf at a court hearing. Given that Young himself threatened death for anyone who dared seduce his daughters, it is not surprising that he discouraged Hambleton's conviction. Attorney for the state Hosea Stout recorded that Hambleton was "acquitted by the Court and also by the Voice of the people present."[6]

---

6. *Journal of Phineas Wolcott Cook*, ed. Newell Cook McMillan (N.p.: Phineas Wolcott Cook Family Organization, 1980), at http://cookfamily.org/journal/lifeand-historyPWC.pdf, accessed June 28, 2018; Mar. 17, 1851, Juanita Brooks, ed., *On the*

Perhaps with Vaughn's fate in mind, James Monroe wrote Young a letter asking him for counsel in the wake of an affair with Howard Egan's wife. When Egan returned to Salt Lake City in September 1651 after guiding a party of miners to California, he learned of his wife's unfaithfulness and that she had given birth to a son conceived with Monroe. "I have been informed that Mr. Egan will be advised to shoot me," the desperate Monroe wrote from Fort Bridger, asking the church president whether it would be safe to return home. "I am aware that he will never do it, unless he thinks you will sanction it," Monroe added. There is no record of Young's response. Monroe should have followed his cautious instincts, as Egan hunted him down and shot him two weeks later. [7]

Although some Utahns had qualms about extralegal punishment, most probably agreed with Apostle George A. Smith when he argued in connection with the Egan case that "mountain common law" gave husbands the moral right to kill men who slept with their wives.[8] The Utah territorial legislature codified such justifiable homicides in 1852 when it provided immunity for husbands to kill "in a sudden heat of passion caused by the attempt of any such offender to commit a rape upon his wife, daughter, sister, mother, or other female relation or dependent ... or when the defilement has actually been committed."[9] This went somewhat beyond the main current of American law. In Texas, for instance, a cuckolded husband could kill his wife's "ravisher ... at any time before he has escaped from the presence of his victim."[10] Across the country, though, juries in a series of high-profile murder cases

---

Mormon Frontier: The Diary of Hosea Stout, 1844–1889 (Salt Lake City: University of Utah Press, 2009 reprint of 1964 edition), 396. See also Mar. 17, 1851, Historian's Office Journal, CR 100 1, CHL.

7. James M. Monroe, Letter to BY, Sept. 16, 1851, Box 69, Folder 4, Brigham Young Papers, CR 1234 1, CHL. See Edward Hogan, "The Curious Case of James Madison Monroe," https://www.sunstonemagazine.com/the-curious-case-of-james-madison-monroe, accessed July 2, 2019.

8. *Deseret News*, Nov. 15, 1851. See Kenneth L. Cannon, "'Mountain Common Law': The Extralegal Punishment of Seducers in Early Utah," *Utah Historical Quarterly* 51 (Fall 1983): 312.

9. *Acts, Resolutions, and Memorials, Passed at the Several Annual Sessions of the Legislative Assembly of the Territory of Utah* (Salt Lake City: Joseph Cain, 1855), 204.

10. *The Penal Code of the State of Texas* (Galveston, Texas, 1857), 111.

in the 1850s and 1860s used an "unwritten law" to extend that privilege to include premeditation.[11]

Other historians, namely Kenneth Cannon, have used the Hambleton and Egan cases to discuss the role of extra-legal violence in early Utah. Kathryn Daynes trace the ways that the instances of adultery affected the marriages of both Madison Hambleton and Howard Egan.[12] As was often the case, the voluminous Brigham Young Papers revealed that there was more to the story. To the best of my knowledge, prior scholars either did not have access to Monroe's letter to Young or had not made use of it. Moreover, there was a fascinating and perplexing coda to the Hambleton case.

Sometime after his courtroom intervention for Hambleton, Young changed his mind about the case. The church president concluded that Hambleton was guilty of murder, and Hambleton lost his church membership. When Hambleton discussed the case with Young, the church president told him "to take a loaded Pistol and go to the wife of John M. Vaughn and the Father and tell them I was the man that Killed the Said Vaughn to take that pistol and blow out my Brains or put a ball through my heart or imprisen me or torture me." In response, Hambleton pronounced himself pleased that he could atone for his sin. He put his affairs in order and prepared to leave Utah to find Vaughn's family in the East. He stopped in Salt Lake City to ask Young for the privilege of rebaptism before his anticipated death. Young, consulting with Heber Kimball and Daniel Wells, decided that Hambleton "need not go any farther and said they would forgive me" and that God would also forgive him.[13]

What were Young's intentions with Hambleton? Was it an Abraham-like test of the anxious Hambleton's obedience and repentance? Was it a cruel joke? And why did Young defend Hambleton shortly after Vaughn's death but turn on him several

11. Hendrik Hartog, "Lawyering, Husbands' Rights, and 'the Unwritten Law' in Nineteenth-Century America," *Journal of American History* 84 (June 1997): 67–96.

12. Daynes, *More Wives Than One: Transformation of the Mormon Marriage System, 1840–1910* (Urbana: University of Illinois Press, 2001), 200–201, 278–79n69.

13. Hambleton, Letter to "the Presidency of the sixteenth Quorum Seventies," Jan. 30, 1855, Box 69, Folder 4, Brigham Young Papers.

years later? Cook, whose letter corroborates Hambleton's own account of Young's request, provides an explanation. The church had swiftly excommunicated Chelnecha Hambleton after Vaughn's death exposed her adultery,[14] but presumably she regained her standing at some point. Young was upset because he had counseled the cuckolded Masdison to cast off Chelnecha and "set her down by herself and provide for her and get him[self] another wife." Contrary to this counsel, Madison and Chelnecha continued to live together. Young then informed Madison Hambleton that he had "taken the sins of Doctor Vaughan upon [himself] by living with that woman." By so doing, he had made himself "guilty of his blood" and "must atone for it." Cook interpreted Young's counsel to his friend as a test akin to that of Abraham, though with Hambleton himself as the sacrifice. "I always told him," Cook recounted, "I could not help thinking that thare would be a ram yet found in some thicket."

Young not only spared Hambleton's life but restored him to good standing within the church. He and Chelnecha continued to live together, though Madison married several plural wives as well. In 1856, Hambleton wrote Young for permission to marry Lucy Lacsie, a fifteen-year-old emigrant from England then living with the Hambletons.[15] "It strikes me that this one is rather young," the church president responded, "still if you think not, and all is agreeable, bring her along, and I will, if I think it wisdom, seal her to you."[16] Whether because of Young's subsequent disapproval or for other reasons, Hambleton was not sealed to the young woman in question.

The case of Madison Hambleton was one of many episodes that I researched and included in early drafts of *Pioneer Prophet* but left out of the finished book. Undoubtedly, a future scholar could learn more about the case with a thorough examination not only of the Brigham Young correspondence but also of the Manti and Nephi, Utah, records. I once floated the idea of a two-volume biography

---

14. Isaac Morley, Letter to BY, Feb. 25, 1851, Box 22, Folder 9, Brigham Young Papers.

15. Hambleton, Letter to BY, Feb. 24, 1856, Box 64, Folder 3, Brigham Young Papers.

16. BY, Letter to Hambleton, Feb. 28, 1856, Letterpress Copybook, vol. 2, p. 596, Box 2, Brigham Young Papers.

to my editor, who promptly and intelligently dismissed the idea. So I had to set aside many worthwhile episodes and sources.

For that and out of simple common sense, I make no claims that *Pioneer Prophet* is a "definitive" biography. There could never be a definitive biography of Brigham Young, or of Joseph Smith for that matter. Young is far too complex and at times too enigmatic, a leader with obvious strengths and very human shortcomings. As Young said of Mormonism itself, he is a hard man to grasp with a firm grip, a man with more intellectual and theological depth than his critics have recognized. The good news is that the archival record remains a field ripe unto scholarly harvest.

CONTRIBUTORS

Polly Aird is an independent historian in Seattle, Washington. She is the author of *Mormon Convert, Mormon Defector: A Scottish Immigrant in the American West, 1848–1861* (University of Oklahoma Press, 2009), which received the best biography award from the Mormon History Association in 2010. She is also co-editor, with historians Will Bagley and Jeff Nichols, of *Playing with Shadows: Voices of Dissent in the Mormon West* (University of Oklahoma Press, 2011), which received the best documentary book award from the Utah State Historical Society in 2012. She has written articles for a number of historical journals.

Will Bagley is the author or editor of more than twenty books, including *Blood of the Prophets: Brigham Young and the Massacre at Mountain Meadows; So Rugged and Mountainous: Blazing the Trails to Oregon and California, 1812-1848; With Golden Visions Bright Before Them: Trails to the Mining West, 1849-1852*; and *South Pass: Gateway to a Continent.* His essay-length studies have appeared in *Western Historical Quarterly, Utah Historical Quarterly, Overland Journal, Journal of Mormon History*, and *Montana: The Magazine of Western History.* For twenty-three years, he edited the sixteen-volume series Kingdom in the West: The Mormons and the American Frontier. He is the recipient of twenty-five writing-related awards. In 2014 he was named a Fellow of the Utah State Historical Society. In 2019 he received the Owen Wister Award from the Western Writers of America for lifetime contributions to western literature. Also in 2019 he published the memoir *River Fever: Adventures on the Mississippi, 1969-1972.*

Todd Compton is the author of *In Sacred Loneliness: The Plural Wives of Joseph Smith*, which won best book awards from the Mormon History Association and John Whitmer Historical Association. His *A Frontier Life: Jacob Hamblin, Explorer, and Indian Missionary* received the Juanita Brooks Prize in Mormon Studies, the Evans Biography Award, and the Best Book Award from the Utah State Historical Society. He lives in the San Francisco Bay area, California, with his wife and two boys.

Joseph W. Geisner is an independent Mormon researcher who collects rare books, writes book reviews, and speaks at history conferences. He has published in the *Journal of Mormon History*, *Sunstone* magazine, the *Journal of the John Whitmer Historical*, *Irreantum*, and at various LDS-oriented web sites. With Lavina Fielding Anderson, he created the chronology for *Confessions of a Mormon Historian: The Diaries of Leonard J. Arrington, 1971–1999*, edited by Gary J. Bergera. He is currently on the board of directors for the John Whitmer Historical Association. He and his wife of more than thirty years live in northern California, where they provide residential services for people with developmental disabilities. They have three children.

Brian C. Hales is the author or co-author of seven books dealing with plural marriage including the three-volume *Joseph Smith's Polygamy: History and Theology* (Greg Kofford Books, 2013). He works as an anesthesiologist and has served as president of the Utah Medical Association and the John Whitmer Historical Association. His other publications include articles for the *Journal of Mormon History*, *Journal of the John Whitmer Historical Association*, *Dialogue: A Journal of Mormon Thought*, *BYU Studies Quarterly*, and *Interpreter*. He is currently studying the origin of the Book of Mormon and is working on a couple of book-length manuscripts.

Melvin C. Johnson, a resident of Salt Lake City, Utah, has published books and articles on the intersection of Mormonism in the nineteenth-century American West for many years. He is a writer, columnist, and speaker. His book *Polygamy on the Pedernales: Lyman Wight's Mormon Villages in Antebellum Texas, 1845 to 1858*, won the Smith–Pettit Best Book Award from the John Whitmer Historical Association in 2006.

William P. MacKinnon, an independent historian residing in Montecito, California, has written extensively about territorial Utah. He is a Fellow and Honorary Life Member of the Utah

State Historical Society and has been presiding officer of such diverse organizations as the Mormon History Association, Santa Barbara Corral of the Westerners, Yale Library Associates, and Children's Hospital of Michigan. In his parallel business career, MacKinnon has been a vice-president of General Motors Corporation and is president of MacKinnon Associates, a management consulting firm. He is an alumnus or veteran of Yale College (Magna Cum Laude, Phi Beta Kappa), Harvard Business School, and USAF.

Linda King Newell is co-author, with Valeen Tippetts Avery, of *Mormon Enigma: Emma Hale Smith, Prophet's Wife, "Elect Lady," Polygamy's Foe* (New York: Doubleday, 1984) and past co-editor, with her husband, L. Jackson Newell, of *Dialogue: A Journal* of *Mormon Thought.* She served as president of both the John Whitmer Historical Association (1988–89) and the Mormon History Association (1996–97).

Gregory A. Prince has spent nearly a half-century in biomedical research, with Mormon history being an avocation for the past three decades. After receiving degrees at Dixie College and UCLA, he and his wife, JaLynn, moved to Maryland in 1975, where they continue to reside. His fourth and final book, published in 2019, is *Gay Rights and the Mormon Church: Intended Actions, Unintended Consequences.*

D. Michael Quinn holds a PhD in history from Yale University (1976). From 1972 to 1973, he worked for the History Division of the Historical Department of the Church of Jesus Christ of Latter-day Saints, and from 1976 to 1988 was a professor of history at Brigham Young University. Since 1988, he has been an independent scholar, with fellowships and other honoraria from the National Endowment for the Humanities, the Mormon History Trust Fund, Indiana University–Purdue University, the Henry E. Huntington Library, among others. His award-winning books include *Early Mormonism and the Magic World View*, the three-volume *Mormon Hierarchy* series (*Origins of Power, Extensions of Power*, and *Wealth and Corporate Power*), *Same-Sex Dynamics Among*

Nineteenth-Century Americans: A Mormon Example, and *J. Reuben Clark: The Church Years,* later expanded as *Elder Statesman: A Biography of J. Reuben Clark.* In 2016, he received the Leonard J. Arrington Award from the Mormon History Association for a lifetime of distinguished service.

Craig S. Smith is a retired archaeologist living in the Salt Lake Valley. His interests include archaeology and the history of the West. In addition to many archaeological publications, Smith has contributed historical articles to the *Utah Historical Quarterly, BYU Studies, Overland Journal,* and the *Journal of Mormon History.* He edited *The Selected Letters of Juanita Brooks* (University of Utah Press).

A New Yorker by birth, **George D. Smith** met his future wife, Camilla Miner, in Central Park, and has helped to raise a family of five children and twelve grandchildren (so far). A graduate of Stanford and New York University, he helped in 1981 to co-found Signature Books, which since has published over 600 works in Western American history, religion, and literature. He has written and edited a variety of papers, articles, and prize-winning books. In 2016, the University of Utah awarded him an honorary doctorate in humanities. His most recent publication is a two-volume annotated edition of Brigham Young's diaries and office journals.

Vickie Cleverley Speek is a former newspaper and radio reporter, feature writer, and columnist in Illinois and Michigan; recipient of four first-place awards from the Illinois Press Association; and recipient of the Red Ribbon Media Award from the state of Illinois. In 2001 she received the Award of Excellence from the Illinois Historical Society for her research and writing on the Civil War. She is a past director of the LDS Family History Center in Morris, Illinois. In 2006 she published *God Has Made Us a Kingdom: James Strang and the Midwest Mormons* (Signature Books), and in 2013 *The Amazing Jimmi Mayes: Sideman to the Stars* (University Press of Mississippi). Currently she is a freelance writer and editor living in the Chicago suburbs where she enjoys gardening and collects books that she will probably never get around to reading.

Susan Staker lives on Whidbey Island in Washington state, where she reads, writes, gardens, rides the ferry, and walks her dog. In past lives, she did editorial work for Adobe Systems, Signature Books, and *Sunstone* magazine, and studied narrative theory at the University of Utah.

Daniel P. Stone holds a PhD in American religious history from Manchester Metropolitan University in England. He is the author of *William Bickerton: Forgotten Latter Day Prophet* (2018), which won best biography awards from both the Mormon History Association and the John Whitmer Historical Association. He has taught history courses at the University of Detroit Mercy and Florida Atlantic University. Currently, he works as a research archivist for a private library/archive in Detroit, Michigan.

John G. Turner teaches in the Department of Religious Studies at George Mason University. His most recent book is *They Knew They Were Pilgrims: Plymouth Colony and the Contest for American Liberty*, published in 2020 by Yale University Press. He is also the author of *The Mormon Jesus* (2016) and *Brigham Young: Pioneer Prophet* (2012).